SIXTIES BRITISH CINEMA RECONSIDERED

SIXTIES BRITISH CINEMA RECONSIDERED

Edited by Duncan Petrie, Melanie Williams
and Laura Mayne

EDINBURGH
University Press

Edinburgh University Press is one of the leading university presses in the UK. We publish academic books and journals in our selected subject areas across the humanities and social sciences, combining cutting-edge scholarship with high editorial and production values to produce academic works of lasting importance. For more information visit our website: edinburghuniversitypress.com

© editorial matter and organisation Duncan Petrie, Melanie Williams and Laura Mayne, 2020, 2021
© the chapters their several authors, 2020, 2021

Edinburgh University Press Ltd
The Tun – Holyrood Road
12(2f) Jackson's Entry
Edinburgh EH8 8PJ

First published in hardback by Edinburgh University Press 2020

Typeset in 10/12.5 pt Sabon
by IDSUK (DataConnection) Ltd

A CIP record for this book is available from the British Library

ISBN 978 1 4744 4388 3 (hardback)
ISBN 978 1 4744 4389 0 (paperback)
ISBN 978 1 4744 4390 6 (webready PDF)
ISBN 978 1 4744 4391 3 (epub)

The right of Duncan Petrie, Melanie Williams and Laura Mayne to be identified as the editors of this work has been asserted in accordance with the Copyright, Designs and Patents Act 1988, and the Copyright and Related Rights Regulations 2003 (SI No. 2498).

CONTENTS

List of Figures and Tables — vii
Notes on the Contributors — ix

    Introduction — 1
    Duncan Petrie and Melanie Williams

PART ONE   STARS AND STARDOM

1. Male Stardom in 1960s British Cinema — 11
   Andrew Spicer

2. 'Rebel Rebel'?: Oliver Reed in the 1960s — 29
   Caroline Langhorst

3. Carol White: The Bardot of Battersea — 47
   Margherita Sprio

4. 'The Old Wave at Work': The Transatlantic Stardom of the British Character Actress in the 1960s — 63
   Claire Mortimer

PART TWO   CREATIVE COLLABORATIONS

5. Woodery-pokery: Charles Wood's Sixties Screenwriting — 81
   David Cairns

6. 'Beyond Naturalism': Jocelyn Herbert, *If . . .* (1968) and Design
   for Performance in 1960s British Cinema 99
   Vicky Lowe

7. *Kes*: From Page to Screen 115
   David Forrest and Sue Vice

8. 'I'd like to remember you as you are – as just a grumpy old man':
   Joseph Losey and the Making of *Figures in a Landscape* (1970) 131
   Llewella Chapman

PART THREE STYLE AND GENRE

9. 'Wholesome rough stuff': Hammer Films and the 'A' and 'U'
   Certificate, 1959–65 151
   Paul Frith

10. Widescreen Pyrotechnics: Shot Composition and Staging in the
    Cold War Films of Joseph Losey and Sidney J. Furie 165
    Steven Roberts

11. The Rise and Fall of the Colourful Corporate Fantasy in 1960s
    British Cinema 179
    Carolyn Rickards

12. Witchfinders and Sorcerers: Sorcery and Counterculture in
    the Work of Michael Reeves 193
    Virginie Sélavy

PART FOUR CULTURAL TRANSFORMATIONS

13. 'An Impulse of Anger, Instantly Regretted': Rebellion and
    Reaction in the Early-1960s Naval Film 209
    Mark Fryers

14. Narratives of Race and Identity in Sixties British Cinema 223
    Phillip Drummond

15. Panic at the Disco: Brainwashing, Alienation and the Discotheque
    in Swinging London Films 239
    Sophia Satchell-Baeza

Index 255

FIGURES AND TABLES

Figures

1.1	A new kind of working-class hero: Albert Finney as Arthur Seaton in *Saturday Night and Sunday Morning* (1960)	17
1.2	The quintessential 'young man on the make': Michael Caine as the eponymous *Alfie* (1966)	20
2.1	Hammer's new horror heart throb: Oliver Reed in *The Curse of the Werewolf* (1961)	33
2.2	The hunter has been captured: the (alienated) Byronic Reedian gaze in *The System* (1964)	37
3.1	Crafting a working-class star persona: Carol White as Joy in *Poor Cow* (1967)	50
3.2	Modifying the persona: White dressed in Biba on a Cambridge punt in *I'll Never Forget What's'isname* (1967)	55
4.1	The quintessential English eccentric: Margaret Rutherford in *The V.I.P.s* (1963)	69
4.2	The formidable Dame Edith Evans in her Oscar-nominated role in *Tom Jones* (1963)	72
5.1	Opening out the source material: the cast of *The Knack . . . and How to Get It* (1965) roaming the London streets	84
5.2	Charles Wood's absurdism: John Lennon and Michael Crawford in *How I Won the War* (1967)	90
6.1	Jocelyn Herbert's sketch for the shower set in *If . . .* (1968). JH436 Jocelyn Herbert Collection, National Theatre Archive	110

6.2	The shower scene in *If...* as realised with Malcolm McDowell	110
7.1	The 'smokers' union' scene in *Kes* (1969)	122
7.2	Failed by the education system: Billy Casper (David Bradley) in *Kes*	125
8.1	The helicopter as it appears in the final cut of *Figures in a Landscape* (1970)	139
8.2	End credits for *Figures in a Landscape*: the 'Sir' was removed from William Pigott-Brown's credit at Losey's request	143
9.1	Confirming the Hammer brand: 'X' rated horror in *The Mummy* (1959)	156
9.2	Cultivating a family audience: Christopher Lee in *The Pirates of Blood River* (1962)	160
10.1	Staging working-class unrest in widescreen: Joseph Losey's *The Damned* (1963)	171
10.2	Major Dalby (Nigel Green) marginalised by Sidney J. Furie's expressionistic *mise en scène* in *The Ipcress File* (1965)	175
11.1	Ruthless ambition: Alan Bates as Jimmy Brewster in *Nothing but the Best* (1964)	183
11.2	Losing a grip on reality: Roger Moore as Harold Pelham in *The Man Who Haunted Himself* (1970)	187
12.1	Tourists in Transylvania: Veronica (Barbara Steele) and Philip (Ian Ogilvy) in *The Revenge of the Blood Beast* (1966)	195
12.2	'A soldier with a talent for killing': Richard Marshall (Ian Ogilvy) in *Witchfinder General* (1968)	201
13.1	The destruction of innocence: the crew's reaction to the execution of *Billy Budd* (1962)	214
13.2	The death of Horatio Nelson, Carry On style: *Carry On Jack* (1964)	219
14.1	Early in *Two Gentlemen Sharing* (1969), Andrew (Hal Frederick) visits Roddy's (Robin Philips) flat as a potential co-tenant	232
14.2	At the final party, Marcus (Ram John Holder) enters Roddy's bedroom with a different understanding of the phrase 'two gentlemen sharing'	234
15.1	Psychedelic brainwashing in *The Sorcerers* (1967)	243
15.2	The 'entranced and immoveable group of young people' watching The Yardbirds perform in *Blow-Up* (1966)	249

Tables

1.1	Eight key male stars of the 1960s: their backgrounds and careers	13
8.1	Budgets and estimated final production costs for Joseph Losey's films guaranteed by Film Finances prior to *Figures in a Landscape*	135

NOTES ON THE CONTRIBUTORS

David Cairns is an award-winning filmmaker, critic, and teaching fellow at the Edinburgh College of Art. He runs the blog Shadowplay (https://dcairns.wordpress.com/).

Llewella Chapman is a visiting scholar at the University of East Anglia. She has recently passed her PhD titled 'Representing Henry's Royal Palace: The Relationship between Film, Television and Hampton Court Palace', and is under contract with Bloomsbury to write a monograph titled *Fashioning James Bond: Costume, Gender and Identity in the World of 007*. Her research interests include film history, British cinema and the films of Joseph Losey.

Phillip Drummond is an independent scholar based in London. The exhibitor of a wide range of independent/avant-garde film material as an Oxford undergraduate, he become one of the pioneers of UK film and media studies in the 1970s. He funded the university of London's first MA degree in film and TV at the Institute of Education in 1980, and later the country's first MA in media education. His most recent publications include the eight volumes of conference e-readers published by the London Symposium, 2013–17. He is the new Fast Editor, with Sébastien Lefait, of *Film Journal* published by SERCIA (Société d'études et de recherches sur le cinéma anglophone).

David Forrest is Senior Lecturer in Film Studies at the University of Sheffield. His most recent publications include the co-edited volume *Social Class and*

Television Drama in Contemporary Britain (2016) with Beth Johnson, and the co-authored study *Barry Hines: 'Kes', 'Threads' and Beyond*, with Sue Vice (2017). He is currently working on a monograph on contemporary British realism.

Paul Frith is an Associate Tutor at the University of East Anglia. His research specialism is in British Cinema with on emphasis on colour, censorship and horror. It is work on these subjects has appeared in a member of Journals including the *Historical Journal of Film, Radio and Telivision* and the *Journal of British Cinema and Television* and he is also the co-author of *Colour Films in Britain: The Eastmancolor Revolution*, to be published by Bloomsbury in 2021.

Mark Fryers completed his PhD in film, television and cultural history at the University of East Anglia in 2015 ('British National Identity and Maritime Film and Television, 1960–2012'). Since then he has published work in numerous titles including the *Journal of Popular Television* on subjects including gothic TV and on the TV series *Howards' Way* and book chapters including on *The Onedin Line*, global animated film, gender and the costume drama, the audio aesthetics of British horror television and on the filmic spaces of nautical horror. He is currently Associate Tutor in Film, Television and Media at UEA and NYU London.

Caroline Langhorst holds a BA in Film Studies and British Studies and an MA in Film Studies from the University of Mainz, Germany. She is currently working on her PhD thesis on rebellious actors in 1960s British cinema at the Cinema and Television History Research Institute (CATHI), De Montfort University, Leicester. Her main research interests include British and American cinema, television and culture, gender studies, star studies (British stardom, Classical Hollywood and European stardom), acting/performance studies as well as the 'long' 1960s and the counterculture.

Victoria Lowe is a Lecturer in Drama and Screen Studies at the University of Manchester. Her research is in Film History, specialising in British Cinema, Screen Acting, Archives and the relationship between film and theatre. She is currently researching inter-medial performance practices in the 1960s.

Laura Mayne is a Lecturer in Film and Media at the University of Hull. Her research specialism is in post-war British cinema with an emphasis on industrial histories, institutional practices and production cultures, and she has published widely in this area. She is the co-author of *Transformation and Tradition in 1960s British Cinema* (Edinburgh University Press UP, 2019).

NOTES ON THE CONTRIBUTORS

Claire Mortimer completed her PhD at the University of East Anglia in 2017, *Battleaxes, Spinsters and Chars: The Ageing Woman in Post-War British Film Comedy*. She is currently developing this into a monograph to be published by Edinburgh University Press in 2021, as well as working on other publications around the area of age and stardom, including work on Joan Hickson and Beryl Reid. She has published widely, including *Romantic Comedy* (Routledge, 2010), *Doing Film Studies* (2012) and chapters and articles on Margaret Rutherford and Peggy Mount. She teaches Film and Media Studies in FE.

Duncan Petrie is Professor of Film and Television at the University of York. He is the author of *Creativity and Constraint in the British Film Industry* (Macmillan, 1991), *The British Cinematographer* (BFI, 1996), *Screening Scotland* (BFI, 2000), *Contemporary Scottish Fictions: Film, Television and the Novel* (Edinburgh University Press, 2004), *Shot in New Zealand: The Art and Craft of the Kiwi Cinematographer* (Random House, 2007), *A Coming of Age: 30 Years of New Zealand Film* (Random House, 2008) and co-author of *Educating Film-Makers: Past, Present, Future* (Intellect, 2014) and *Transformation and Tradition in 1960s British Cinema* (Edinburgh University Press, 2019). Duncan has also edited or co-edited a further ten volumes and is co-principal editor of the *Journal of British Cinema and Television*.

Carolyn Rickards is a Researcher based at the University of Bristol. She most recently worked on the AHRC project, The Eastmancolor Revolution and British Cinema, 1955–85 and has published in the *Journal of British Cinema and Television*, *Screen* and *Fantasy/Animation: Connections Between Media, Mediums and Genres* (Routledge, 2018). She is currently including a monograph on *British Fantasy Cinema* with Edinburgh University Press.

Steven Roberts is a final year PhD student and part-time teacher in film at the Universities of Bristol and Exeter. His doctoral research project, 'High-Fidelity Widescreen Cinema', examined VistaVision film production and style in Britain and the USA, and was funded by the UK Arts and Humanities Research Council South West and Wales DTP between 2015 and 2019. In spring 2019, he curated 'Widescreen South West', a display of British cinemagoing artefacts, for the Bill Douglas Cinema Museum, University of Exeter.

Sophia Satchell-Baeza lectures at University of the Arts London and is an associate research fellow at the Cinema and Television History Research Institute (De Montfort, Leicester). Her recently completed PhD dissertation in the Film Studies department at King's College London explored the psychedelic moving image in Britain during the long 1960s, and was supported by the Arts and Humanities Research Council. Her writing has appeared in film journals and magazines including *Sight & Sound*, *Mediapolis*, *La Furia Umana*, *NECSUS*, and *Another Gaze*.

Virginie Sélavy is a film scholar, writer and editor. She is the founder of *Electric Sheep* magazine and was co-director of the Miskatonic Institute of Horror Studies – London. She has edited *The End: An Electric Sheep Anthology* and contributed a chapter to *Lost Girls: The Phantasmagorical Cinema of Jean Rollin*. She has also written about *Peeping Tom* and Victorian London on film. Her work has appeared in publications such as *Sight & Sound*, *FilmRage* and *Cineaste* and she regularly gives talks on surrealism, the fantastique and exploitation film. She is currently working on a book on sadomasochism in 1960s–70s cinema.

Andrew Spicer is Professor of Cultural Production at the University of the West of England, Bristol. His principal research interests are in masculinities, stardom, genre and the production cultures of film and television companies. His most recent co-authored/co-edited books include *Get Carter: Michael Klinger, Independent Production and British Cinema, 1960–1980* (2013), *Beyond the Bottom Line: The Producer in Film and Television Studies* (2014), and *Building Successful and Sustainable Film and Television Businesses* (2017), the principal outcome of a three-year European project, 'Success in the Film and Television Industries' (SiFTI, 2013–16). He is currently leading an investigation into the ecology of the film and television industries outside London and working on a monograph: *Sean Connery: Acting, Stardom and National Identity*.

Margherita Sprio is Reader in Film and Visual Culture in the School of Arts at University of Westminster and is a member of the Centre for Research and Education in Arts and Media (CREAM). She has worked at different universities in and around London, UK, and before becoming an academic she worked as an artist. She has written many artists' catalogues, book chapters, essays in journals and is the author of *Migrant Memories – Cultural History, Cinema and the Italian Post-War Diaspora in Britain* (Peter Lang, 2013). She is currently working on her second book, *Women in the Frame: Feminist Intimacies on the British Screen* (Bloomsbury Academic, 2020).

Sue Vice is Professor of English Literature at the University of Sheffield. Her most recent publications include the co-edited volume *Representing Perpetrators in Holocaust Literature and Film* (2013) with Jenni Adams, the monograph *Textual Deceptions: False Memoirs and Literary Hoaxes in the Contemporary Era* (Edinburgh University Press, 2014) and the co-authored study *Barry Hines: 'Kes', 'Threads' and Beyond*, with David Forrest (2017). She is currently working on a study of rescue and resistance in Claude Lanzmann's *Shoah* outtakes.

Melanie Williams is Reader in Film and Television Studies at the University of East Anglia. She is the co-author of *Transformation and Tradition in 1960s British Cinema* (Edinburgh University Press, 2019), and author of *Female Stars of British Cinema: The Women in Question* (Edinburgh University Press, 2017) and *David Lean* (Manchester University Press, 2014), as well as numerous articles on British cinema. She also co-edited *Shane Meadows: Critical Essays* (Edinburgh University Press, 2013), *Ealing Revisited* (BFI, 2012), *Mamma Mia! The Movie: Exploring a Cultural Phenomenon* (I. B. Tauris, 2012) and *British Women's Cinema* (Routledge, 2009), and is co-principal editor of the *Journal of British Cinema and Television*.

INTRODUCTION

Duncan Petrie and Melanie Williams

REVISITING AND RECONSIDERING A 'FAMILIAR' DECADE

From James Bond to the Beatles, madcap comedy to unsettling horror, social realism to psychedelia, the 1960s witnessed a major resurgence in the creative vitality and international appeal of British cinema. An influx of Hollywood finance gave British films unprecedented access to global markets, boosting their visibility and earning power; the United Artists-backed James Bond series, initiated by *Dr No* (1962), provided the most conspicuous example of this new box office phenomenon. British films attained new levels of international critical acclaim, winning the Oscar for Best Film on no less than four occasions during the decade: *Lawrence of Arabia* (1962), *Tom Jones* (1963), *A Man for All Seasons* (1966) and *Oliver!* (1968). Top prizes at the Berlin Film Festival went to *A Kind of Loving* (1962), *Repulsion* (1965) and *Cul-de-Sac* (1966). British productions also triumphed at Cannes, with three Palme d'Or wins during the 1960s for *The Knack . . . and how to get it* (1965), *Blow Up* (1966) and *If . . .* (1968), and *Accident* (1967) sharing the Grand Prix Award, while the previous year *Alfie* (1966) had picked up the Prix du Jury. These productions, running the generic gamut from historical drama to big-budget musical to art film, from the grim north to swinging London, suggest something of the diversity of Britain's film output during the decade. Although the impact of these films was immediate, their longer-term legacy was also significant. Thirty years later, one of the few scholarly overviews of the period's film culture, Robert Murphy's *Sixties British Cinema*, came to the conclusion that 'the 1960s saw a greater number of significant and exciting films made in Britain than at any time before or since'.[1]

Yet despite that level of success and acclaim (or perhaps because of it), there has been surprisingly little academic engagement with 1960s British cinema in its entirety, Murphy aside.[2] Instead, the 1950s and 1970s, both more contentious decades in terms of their achievements and significance, have been the subject of numerous monographs and edited collections.[3] But while this surge in revisionist British film scholarship took place, a variety of new archival sources providing a deeper and more detailed account of British cinema during the 1960s became available, providing new information on financing and production, on film policy, on the interrelations between cinema and other creative industries and on the careers of individual practitioners. At the same time, the continuing debate over the symbolic relevance of the decade in relation to wider understandings of cultural and social history ensured that the 1960s remained a topic of fascination. How revolutionary and transformative was the decade beyond the bubble of 'swinging London'? Did greater individualism signal the birth of the modern liberated citizen or a disastrous shift from class-based solidarity to a more atomised, marketised identity politics? Did Britain continue its decline as a global power or did it find a way to reinvent itself as a vital player in the contemporary world? Questions like these, and specifically how they were reflected through or influenced developments in British cinema, provided the impetus for revisiting the period afresh.

Our major research project, funded by the Arts and Humanities Research Council, *Transformation and Tradition in 1960s British Cinema*, culminated in a book of the same name, co-written by the project team and published in 2019.[4] This project explored the cinema of a decade most often characterised by modernity, novelty and innovation, its focus on youth culture, social mobility and experimentation in lifestyles and aesthetics reflected in the styles, content and youthful new directors and stars of British films. But the period was simultaneously marked by a remarkable degree of cultural continuity, represented in part by the ongoing centrality of veteran British filmmakers such as Launder and Gilliat, the Boulting Brothers, David Lean and Carol Reed. This was coupled with nostalgia for (seemingly) less volatile times, discernible in the music hall humour of the Carry On films, or the residual Victorian morality of Hammer Horror. In our study of British cinema of the 1960s, the twin concepts of transformation and tradition are deployed to help navigate some of the decade's complexities and contradictions. The project and book focuses on three key areas. Firstly, the funding, production and distribution of films during the decade, a sphere in which the established, powerful but ultimately rather conservative film corporations such as Rank, Associated British and British Lion were forced to compete with smaller and newer independent companies that demonstrated greater entrepreneurial flair in the face of a changing society and market. Meanwhile, the expanded activities of the Hollywood majors, with their financial muscle and international influence, made such a notable impact on the scale and style of 'British' films, boosting production values, enhancing the wholesale take-up of colour and creating new stars. Secondly, the contribution of key creative personnel – writers, directors, cinematographers, production and costume designers and editors – demonstrate how filmmaking craft was impacted by new ideas, themes, aesthetic styles, production techniques and technologies. But it also reveals the resilience and the continuity of creative practices and expertise transmitted by practitioners of different generations. Thirdly, the increasingly close interrelation between cinema and other creative fields that were booming during the 1960s, most notably television, advertising and pop music, represented a new moment of 'convergence' between different industries with the circulation of ideas, styles, techniques and, perhaps most significantly, creative personnel providing the essential connectivity.

In line with 'new film history', which has prioritised archival research over theoretical conjecture, our project made extensive use of a range of previously unavailable or under-explored collections. These include the British Film Institute and National Film and Television Archive, the Bill Douglas Cinema Museum at the University of Exeter, the National Archives, completion guarantee company Film Finances, the British Board of Film Classification, the History of Advertising Trust, and the BECTU oral history project, each of which provided fresh sources of knowledge and new insights into the period.[5] We also made extensive use of industry publications, trade union journals, newspaper reviews and commentary, and film magazines ranging from the highbrow to the populist. One of the project's key achievements was the generation of a detailed dataset of British film production throughout the 1960s, enabling us to track fluctuations and developments in individual careers, in studio provenance and in genre across the decade and make original observations about the industry's dominant trends and most prolific personnel.

Yet we were also acutely aware of the limitations inherent in a project encompassing a whole decade's cinematic output but involving just four people with their own prevailing expertise, enthusiasms and blind spots. It was therefore important to open up discussion and bring in other perspectives, voices, and insights to engage fully with the multi-faceted terrain of British cinema in the 1960s. This led to the organisation of several symposia during the life of the project and two summative conferences held in September 2017, one at the University of York and the other at BFI Southbank. Both events invited proposals on a wide variety of relevant topics, and the corresponding papers given at these conferences then formed the basis of the chapters in this edited volume. The project website (https://60sbritishcinema.wordpress.com/) also generated a series of blogs from members of the project team and guest writers addressing a range of relevant topics. Collectively, this activity constitutes a further exploration of the unusually rich territory of the British cinema of the 1960s, providing a wealth of new research and scholarship on the era from the vantage point of half a century's distance.

How this Book Reconsiders the Sixties

The first of the book's four sections focuses on stardom, one of the most visible aspects of British cinema's resurgent status and international profile in the 1960s. Some of the British stars who emerged at that time have been extensively chronicled, but there are other neglected figures who challenge some of the assumptions around stardom and celebrity during the era. Andrew Spicer provides an opening overview of the impact made by eight key male actors from proletarian backgrounds – Alan Bates, Michael Caine, Sean Connery, Tom Courtenay, Albert Finney, Richard Harris, Peter O'Toole and Terence Stamp – who collectively changed the class politics of British cinema. Caroline Langhorst's chapter then provides a detailed examination of another important emergent male star of the period, Oliver Reed, whose Byronic qualities and compelling screen performances later became overshadowed by his off-screen excesses but who in the sixties exemplified some of the era's key contradictions. Reed's co-star in Michael Winner's underrated film *I'll Never Forget What's'isname* (1967) was Carol White, the subject of Margherita Sprio's chapter. Focusing on how White's working-class London background imbued her performances in the BBC dramas *Up the Junction* (1965) and *Cathy Come Home* (1966) and the feature film *Poor Cow* (1967) with a rare authenticity, Sprio explores how restrictions of class and gender prohibited the actress's ability to become a wider international star on a par with male counterparts like Caine or Connery, or more 'polished' middle-class female stars like Julie Christie. In complete contrast to the 'Battersea Bardot' (as White was labelled by the press), the subject of Clare Mortimer's chapter is a cohort of older character actresses with backgrounds in theatre, who nonetheless enjoyed conspicuous levels of transatlantic success during the long sixties: Edith Evans, Wendy Hiller and Margaret Rutherford. This triumvirate of venerable dames provide evidence for the continued presence and significant appeal of older established figures in a cinema more readily associated with youth, suggesting a greater complexity to the celebrity landscape of the 1960s than is sometimes assumed.

The rise of production studies has encouraged a greater emphasis on creative collaboration and the contribution of production personnel beyond the director in film history, and this provides the focus for the book's second section. With its emphasis on innovation and new ways of working, the sixties provide a rich terrain for investigating key creative relationships and for rethinking the ascription of 'authorship'. David Cairns offers an account of the screenwriting career of Charles Wood, whose scripts for directors as diverse as Richard

Lester, Peter Collinson and Tony Richardson, from *The Knack* to *The Charge of the Light Brigade* (1968), suggest the existence of Wood's own distinctive and strong authorial voice. Victoria Lowe's chapter discusses designer Jocelyn Herbert's collaboration with director Lindsay Anderson on the production of *If...* Using documents from Anderson and Herbert's respective personal archives, Lowe tracks the development of design ideas from conception to execution, shedding light on the often neglected role of the production designer (particularly a woman working with a notoriously solipsistic male director) in the process. David Forrest and Sue Vice also challenge prevailing understandings of the creative provenance of another classic British film of the period, this time *Kes* (1969), through their chapter's consideration of the contribution of writer Barry Hines, who adapted his own novel for the screen and whose writing frequently anticipates the film's cinematic realisation. In thinking about collaborative work in film production, it is vital to acknowledge and explore how this always takes place within industrial structures and in the context of business imperatives. The final chapter in this section, by Llewella Chapman, draws on the files of completion guarantor Film Finances to demonstrate how the troubled late-1960s production of Joseph Losey's *Figures in a Landscape* (1970) provides an object lesson in how a promising project can be derailed by various factors, including a breakdown in the working partnership between director and producer.

No consideration of British cinema of the 1960s would be complete without some investigation of generic and stylistic innovation, the theme of the third section of chapters. This was a decade where bending and breaking rules became almost *de rigeur*, fuelled by novel technologies and new audience demands as well as the desire to represent different kinds of experience and sensation. Such innovation always had to take place within the framework of prevailing standards of censorship and regulation, and Paul Frith's chapter investigates not only how Hammer Films negotiated with the BBFC but also how, having established themselves as purveyors of X-certificated horror films shot in garish colour, the company subsequently adapted their product to accommodate more family-friendly adventure fare with box office potential, such as *The Sword of Sherwood Forest* (1960) and *The Pirates of Blood River* (1962). Steven Roberts visits the archetypally sixties generic terrain of the Cold War thriller in his chapter, with an emphasis on the widescreen innovations of North American émigré directors Joseph Losey and Sidney J. Furie in the black and white sci-fi chiller *The Damned* (1963) and the colour spy thriller *The Ipcress File* (1965) respectively. Style is foregrounded in both productions, with the properties of the widescreen frame pushed in ways that merit comparison with the virtuosity of Godard and Leone. Carolyn Rickards's chapter maintains the focus on questions of colour, which became increasingly ubiquitous as the decade progressed, through a consideration of two films that foreground an aspirational male protagonist in pursuit of wealth and status: Clive Donner's black comedy *Nothing but the Best* (1964) and Basil Dearden's supernatural thriller *The Man Who Haunted Himself* (1970). The shifts between the two, both thematic and aesthetic, suggest some of the broader changes in attitudes taking place over the course of the decade, from a cynical but breezy energy to a darker and more self-destructive mindset. The supernatural moves centre stage in Virginie Sélavy's chapter, which considers the brief oeuvre of talented director Michael Reeves, cut short by his tragic death at the age of twenty-five. *Revenge of the Blood Beast* (1966) (aka *The She-Beast*), *The Sorcerers* (1967) and *Witchfinder General* (1968) are all low budget horrors, but Reeves uses the themes and conventions of genre to interrogate the complexities of contemporary society. Linking witchcraft and the supernatural to the 1960s counterculture in a provocative way, these films collectively pose questions of power and conflict in relation to gender, generation and authority.

The fourth and final section of the book investigates British cinema's mediation of cultural transformation and social change, as films both reflected and contributed to the process of renegotiating what it meant to be British, what it meant to be young or old, male or female, black or white. Mark Fryers analyses a diverse group of naval-themed films that appeared during the decade, including *Billy Budd* (1962), *HMS Defiant* (1962) and *Carry On Jack* (1963). Whether dealing with resistance and rebellion, or emphasising tradition and continuity, their varying explorations of the key national institution of the British Navy share a common interest in cultural anxieties surrounding youth culture; at times signposting emergent attitudes towards gender and sexuality (especially homosexuality), and at times (often in the same scene) reinstating the social 'status quo'. Philip Drummond's chapter surveys changing narratives and discourses of race and ethnicity across the entire decade, beginning with the legacy of empire in films made depicting Afro-Caribbean characters, moving onto the first productions written and directed by black filmmakers in Britain and then gauging the impact of Hollywood and American race relations on the British scene. The chapter culminates in a detailed examination of the neglected curio, *Two Gentlemen Sharing* (1969), directed by Canadian Ted Kotcheff, in which a flat share between an English ad-man and a Jamaican solicitor leads to complex negotiations within the multicultural metropolis. The subculture of psychedelia and its infiltration into cinema is the subject of Sophia Satchell-Baeza's chapter, which considers ideas of alienation, brainwashing and the destructive side of the 'cult of sensation' that so exercised Christopher Booker in his apocalyptic study of the era, *The Neophiliacs*. The case studies here include Michael Reeves's *The Sorcerers*, Michelangelo Antonioni's *Blow Up* and Peter Whitehead's *Tonite Let's All Make Love in London* (1967), each of which sheds light on the costs and limitations of so-called Swinging London.

INTRODUCTION

CONCLUDING REMARKS

A film that crops up in two of the chapters, *The Sorcerers*, features an elderly couple (including one of the last screen appearances of British-born horror legend Boris Karloff) who attempt to defy decrepitude by vicariously experiencing transgressive sensations through their control of a brainwashed young man. This suggests a lethal vengeance to be enacted upon the liberated younger generation by the old and envious; the darkest possible interaction between the opposing forces of tradition and transformation. It also inverts the more familiar confrontation between the two: namely, the challenge to the established order posed by disaffected, rebellious or revolutionary youth, as featured in several of the films discussed in this volume from *The Damned* to *If . . . .* However, in other cultural texts, practices and institutions in the 1960s, the balance between the two is more benignly productive, bringing about positive revision and reinvention, ushering British cinema out of what Jeffrey Richards refers to as the 'doldrums era of the 1950s' and towards 'the emergence of a flourishing and diverse film culture' and a moment of 'revitalisation'.[6]

The essays collected here represent the breadth of work and range of scholarly approaches undertaken in relation to numerous aspects of British cinema of the 1960s. They offer fresh engagements with familiar films of the period as well as drawing attention to those that are lesser known but equally worthy of attention. Through their archivally driven investigations, they present new discoveries on film production and the workings of the industry, creative collaboration, stardom, genre, changing aesthetics and the relationship between cinema and social change; all present important ways of rethinking 1960s British cinema. But given the still untapped wealth of the archives consulted here, and in the project monograph, this is only the beginning of a much greater opportunity for British film scholarship to provide a richer, more grounded, precise, and verifiable account of cinema as an artistic form, a cultural practice, a business and a (technologically dependent) creative process. The reconsideration of a particular 'well-known' decade in both this collection and in *Transformation and Tradition in 1960s British Cinema* offers a demonstration of how the increasing availability of information and data not only provides more detailed and empirical insights and understandings of the subject matter, but can equally stimulate new conceptual approaches and research agendas.

NOTES

1. Robert Murphy, *Sixties British Cinema* (London: BFI, 1992), p. 278.
2. Other key book length studies of the decade include Alexander Walker, *Hollywood, England: The British Film Industry in the Sixties* (London: Michael Joseph, 1974); Terrence Kelly, Graham Norton and George Perry, *A Competitive Cinema* (London: Institute of Economic Affairs, 1966); and John Hill, *Sex, Class and Realism: British*

Cinema 1956–1963 (London: BFI, 1986). For a more detailed contextual discussion of the field, see Richard Farmer, Laura Mayne, Duncan Petrie and Melanie Williams, *Transformation and Tradition in 1960s British Cinema* (Edinburgh: Edinburgh University Press, 2019).
3. See, for example, Christine Geraghty, *British Cinema in the Fifties: Gender, Genre and 'the New Look'* (London: Routledge, 2000); Ian McKillop and Neil Sinyard (eds), *British Cinema of the 1950s: A Celebration* (Manchester: Manchester University Press, 2003); Sue Harper and Vincent Porter, *British Cinema of the 1950s: The Decline of Deference* (Oxford: Oxford University Press, 2003); Robert Shail (ed.), *Seventies British Cinema* (London: BFI/Palgrave Macmillan 2008); Paul Newland (ed.), *Don't Look Now: British Cinema in the 1970s* (Bristol: Intellect, 2010); Paul Newland, *British Films of the 1970s* (Manchester: Manchester University Press, 2013); Sue Harper and Justin Smith (eds), *British Film Culture in the 1970s* (Edinburgh: Edinburgh University Press, 2012); Sian Barber, *The British Cinema in the 1970s: Capital, Culture and Creativity* (Basingstoke: Palgrave Macmillan, 2013).
4. Farmer et al., *Transformation and Tradition in 1960s British Cinema*.
5. James Chapman, Mark Glancy and Sue Harper (eds), *The New Film History: Sources, Methods, Approaches* (Basingstoke: Palgrave Macmillan, 2007).
6. Jeffrey Richards, 'New waves and old myths: British cinema in the 1960s', in Bart Moore-Gilbert and John Seed (eds), *Cultural Revolution: The Challenge of the Arts in the 1970s* (London: Routledge, 1992), p. 218.

PART ONE

STARS AND STARDOM

1. MALE STARDOM IN 1960s BRITISH CINEMA

Andrew Spicer

In 1963, Clive Barnes, a London correspondent for the *New York Times*, profiled 'Britain's new actors – rougher, tougher, angrier', identifying a '"new wave" of naturalistic players [who] are anti-heroes – on stage and off' who were undermining the 'old school tie traditions of London's theatrical Establishment'. A 'new type of Englishman', rebellious and anti-authoritarian, had emerged, achieving international prominence.[1] The object of Barnes's attention was a group of working-class male actors – Alan Bates, Michael Caine, Sean Connery, Tom Courtenay, Albert Finney, Richard Harris, Peter O'Toole and Terence Stamp – which, at the time and subsequently, actively promoted themselves as a new, uninhibited and irreverent generation.[2] Harris contended that they embodied 'a fine madness. We weren't afraid to be different. So we were always dangerous; dangerous to meet in the street, in a restaurant, and dangerous to see on stage or in a film', which, characteristically, conflates on- and off-screen image.[3]

Although at root the product of the 1944 Education Act that provided universal secondary education which afforded working-class children the opportunities denied to their parents' generation,[4] these actors were shaped by and helped shape two separate but *interconnected* cultural myths: 'in the 1950s it was the aggressive ambition of the Angry Young Man; in the 1960s it was Swinging London'.[5] In cinematic terms, it was the British New Wave (1959–63) films that depicted the Angry Young Man, extending the reach of that myth into the early 1960s. By contrast, Swinging London (1963–7) was a more diffuse phenomenon that traded on lifestyle rather than particular cinematic representations. Caine, and especially Stamp, became iconic Swinging London figures, featured in David Bailey's *Box of Pin-Ups* (May 1965), which incorporated male actors into a wider grouping of pop stars, fashion designers, models and photographers that formed a new classless meritocracy.[6] Although the New Wave films depicted the north and Swinging London the metropolis, both emphasised changing social structures, new opportunities and the rise of the young working class that was not prepared to accept its allotted place.[7]

This chapter analyses in what ways this generation of male stars – there were pronounced differences as well as commonalities – represented these transformations and how they changed perceptions of screen acting, masculinity and stardom. My approach to stardom follows Paul McDonald's lead by emphasising its industrial context, the importance of attending to business practices and stars' value as capital assets that can be marketed and monetised. As he observes, 'Rather than the source, the individual is the outcome of the production of stardom.'[8] This understanding does not negate stars' cultural significance but acknowledges its mercantile basis, what McDonald calls the 'symbolic commerce' of stardom. That symbolic commerce is positioned within particular business structures and cultural traditions at specific historical moments: in this case 1960s British cinema and the prevailing uneasiness that UK culture has always had with film stardom.[9]

Although these stars have been the subject of numerous biographies, their collective importance as a generational group and their influence on British cinema have not been analysed in depth.[10] Robert Sellers's book-length study of this generation, *Don't Let the Bastards Grind You Down*, although informative, is a collection of anecdotal vignettes loosely stitched together, reducing what this group stood for to cliché: hellraising and obstreperousness. Because of the extensive literature on the cultural phenomena of Angry Young Men and Swinging London, the account offered here focuses on acting as a profession, including the training these stars received and its importance to their identities, dispositions and performances as this aspect has frequently been ignored or marginalised. In explaining what opportunities became available to these actors, how they were able to grasp them and the consequences of becoming a star, the chapter contributes to a revisionist account of 1960s British cinema and the slender literature on British stardom.[11]

The Stars: Social Origins and the Symbolic Power of Place (see Table 1.1 for overview)

Whereas the origins of the previous generation of actors had been subsumed into a polite, middle-class gentrification, newspaper articles or studio publicity

Table 1.1 Eight key male stars of the 1960s: their backgrounds and careers

Name	Date/place of birth	Nationality	Class/social background (father's occupation)	Education/ formal training	Breakthrough + major early roles	Awards/nominations (selected)
Alan Bates	February 1934 Allestree, Derbyshire	English	Lower middle class (insurance broker)	Grammar school; RADA	*A Kind of Loving* (61); *Nothing but the Best* (64); *Georgy Girl* (66); *Far from the Madding Crowd* (67)	BAFTA nominee for *A Kind of Loving*
Michael Caine	March 1933 South London	English	Working class (fish porter)	Grammar school	*Zulu* (64); *The Ipcress File* (65); *Alfie* (66); *Gambit* (66)	BAFTA nominee for *The Ipcress File*; Oscar/BAFTA nominee for *Alfie*
Sean Connery	August 1930 Edinburgh	Scottish	Working class (van driver)	Secondary school	*Dr No* (62); *From Russia with Love* (63); *Goldfinger* (64); *Marnie* (64); *The Hill* (65); *You Only Live Twice* (67)	
Tom Courtenay	February 1937 Hull	English	Working class (boat painter)	Grammar school; (University); RADA	*The Loneliness of the Long Distance Runner* (62); *Billy Liar* (63); *King & Country* (64); *Dr Zhivago* (65)	BAFTA winner (as most promising newcomer) for *Loneliness*; nominee for *Billy Liar*
Albert Finney	May 1936 Salford	English	Working class (bookmaker)	Grammar school; RADA	*Saturday Night and Sunday Morning* (60); *Tom Jones* (63); *Two for the Road* (67)	BAFTA nominee *Saturday Night*; BAFTA/Oscar nominee for *Tom Jones*
Richard Harris	October 1930 Limerick	Irish	Middle class (flourmill owner)	Jesuit Sacred Heart College; LAMDA	*Mutiny on the Bounty* (62); *This Sporting Life* (63); *The Red Desert* (64); *Major Dundee* (65); *The Heroes of Telemark* (65); *Camelot* (67)	Oscar/BAFTA nominations for *This Sporting Life* – won Best Actor Cannes
Peter O'Toole	August 1932 Leeds	Irish	Working class (bookmaker)	Secondary school; RADA	*Lawrence of Arabia* (62); *Becket* (64); *Lord Jim* (65); *The Lion in Winter* (68)	BAFTA winner/Oscar nominee for *Lawrence*; nominee for *Becket*; *The Lion in Winter*
Terence Stamp	July 1938 East End of London	English	Working class (tug boat skipper)	Grammar school; Webber Douglas	*Billy Budd* (62); *The Collector* (65); *Modesty Blaise* (66); *Far from the Madding Crowd* (67); *Theorem* (68)	Oscar/BAFTA nominee for *Billy Budd*, winner Cannes for *The Collector*

consistently stressed this generation's difference and nonconformity. The *London Evening Standard*'s columnist hailed a 'ginger group':

> On a wave of whisky and expletives, these young performers, from Salford, from Ireland, from the East End of London, have risen to power in a revolution that may have been bloodless, but has certainly not been 'bloody'-less. Even such long-established terms of endearments as 'Dahling' and 'Dear Boy' are being superseded by 'mate' and 'cock'.[12]

Six of these eight stars were working class. The two exceptions – Bates and Harris – became strongly associated with the northern provincialism of the New Wave films, with their aura of authenticity and the direct representation of working-class experiences. Caine and Stamp were cockneys, another cultural archetype, signifying working-class streetwise nous that could, in Swinging London, become chic and glamorous. The three Celts: Connery, Harris and O'Toole, embody what Geoffrey Macnab – discussing their avatars, the Welsh 'Valley Boys', Richard Burton and Stanley Baker, who had come to prominence earlier in the mid-1950s – categorises as the myth of the Celtic hero: born with an abundance of natural talent later squandered, rebels and outsiders for whom deracination was a vital part of the myth.[13] Although born in Leeds, O'Toole romanticised his Irish roots, as did Harris, and both played up to the unruly and hard-drinking stereotype.

Connery's insistence on his working-class Scottishness became stronger and more politicised as the decade progressed. However, from the early stages of his acting career, he understood its importance. He listened to himself on a tape recorder to improve his vocal clarity and diction but without eradicating his Edinburgh accent: 'I wanted to keep my own natural voice and remain true to myself . . . I felt I couldn't . . . express any emotion truthfully if I tried to re-invent my speech patterns in an actorish declamatory way . . . I was going against the fashion of the times, since all actors, regardless of their background, delivered their lines in the well-articulated plummy vowels of standard English.'[14] This suspicion about the hegemony of received pronunciation and the desire to retain their regional vocal authenticity was part of this generation's rebellion. Finney and Courtenay kept their northern tones, Caine and Stamp their cockney twang; Harris and O'Toole cultivated an Irish lilt as integral parts of their identity and, like Connery, to create an empathetic connection with the roles they played. The exception was Bates, whose Derbyshire origins were less easily reified.

Training

As Connery indicated, this insistence on retaining a place-specific accent went against the prevailing norms of British acting. However, the social transformations already mentioned, together with interconnected changes in the theatre, television and film industries, combined to create significant opportunities for young working-class actors during this period. In his invaluable social history of acting, *From Irving to Olivier*, Michael Sanderson argues that the net result of these changes was to shift acting as a profession away from the 'well-bred, public school actor, often from a professional family background' that had dominated since the 1890s towards a more inclusive social mix.[15] Only 2 per cent of actors came from the artisan/manual class before 1945; after the war that figure rose to 24.6 per cent.[16] Sanderson also notes that the acting profession became more selective, professionalised and of a higher standard because the cultural transformation 'enormously increased the artistic opportunities and attractiveness of the profession for the better-educated, more dedicated and more serious-minded player'.[17] All eight actors analysed in this chapter fit this category; five had a grammar school education that encouraged aspiration and social mobility.

In Britain, unlike America, all actors had to have theatrical training. As Stamp observed, 'Nobody considered you at all if you hadn't done stage work. You couldn't get a job without an agent. No agent would represent you unless he'd seen you perform in the theatre and you couldn't land roles in the theatre without an Equity ticket.'[18] The film industry entered into an agreement with Equity in 1948 that ensured that casting directors would only interview professional actors or those who had completed drama training before using outsiders.[19] There were two principal routes to obtaining an Equity card: touring or provincial repertory and education at one of the London drama schools.[20] All eight actors had periods in repertory, which provided high quality, skills-based training with a professional code of practice and discipline in the standard British theatrical repertoire. Six attended drama schools: Bates, Finney and O'Toole were in the same class (1953) at the Royal Academy of Dramatic Arts (RADA), Courtenay joined in 1958; Harris attended the London Academy of Music and Dramatic Arts (LAMDA); Stamp the Webber Douglas Academy of Dramatic Art. Whereas these institutions had been bastions of middle-class privilege by charging high fees, in the 1950s they became accessible to working-class talent through the provision of scholarships and more importantly local authority grants.[21] Although these academies were old-fashioned, and backward in comparison with European institutions or the American 'Method' school, they provided well-honed technical training in the craft of acting with an emphasis on voice production.[22] Above all, they were a highly competitive milieu that fuelled ambition and provided significant opportunities to 'get noticed'; agents took a close interest in drama school graduates.[23] Finney's initial success, for instance, was based entirely on the established system. He was noticed by Kenneth Tynan in a modern dress *Troilus and Cressida* at RADA's Vanbrugh Theatre, which enabled him to gain a position at the Birmingham repertory company – renowned for adventurous and varied material and for discovering new actors – before seasons at Stratford and then the West End.

However, if the drama schools' training remained quite traditional, the theatre industry itself was changing through the impact of the publicly subsidised theatre companies: the English Stage Company (ESC) at the Royal Court and the Theatre Workshop at Theatre Royal Stratford East, which became the foci for new ideas and methods, different, often working-class dramas and a willingness to take risks.[24] Bates, Finney, Harris and O'Toole all performed at the Royal Court. Bates, who played Cliff in the ESC's most famous play, John Osborne's *Look Back in Anger* (1956), thought 'the Royal Court's function was to bring a new force, new thinking, new provocation into the theatre'.[25] The Theatre Royal, under Joan Littlewood's formidable direction, provided more extensive training and a bolder approach to experimentation.[26] She was a formative influence on Harris, giving him the confidence and self-belief to extend his range, to be 'dangerous'. The ESC, and especially Theatre Workshop, encouraged actors to engage with the ideas of Stanislavski and thus to find the 'truth of the part' from the inside rather than from a concentration on extraneous factors – 'representationalism' in Littlewood's parlance.[27]

Although several of the most successful ESC and Theatre Royal plays transferred to the West End and thus gained more attention, television offered far greater exposure. Here too, it was not training that was new – neither the BBC nor the ITV companies provided training for actors – but the content of a range of socially committed dramas, dealing with working-class life and its problems and critical of existing institutions, which began to emerge from the mid-1950s, notably in Associated British Corporation's *Armchair Theatre* (1958–74) under the direction of the Canadian Sydney Newman. Television producers and directors thus looked for actors who could convey these lower-class characters credibly, which encouraged working-class recruits into the profession and was, in Sanderson's view, the principal agent of change. Whereas the previous generation of actors such as Dirk Bogarde might reject television as sub-standard and tawdry, the new generation recognised its value.[28] All eight accepted television roles, which, for Caine and Connery, were more important than their theatrical appearances. Caine did not achieve a starring role until 1964, but the 125 television programmes in which he appeared between 1956 and 1963 provided enormous accumulated knowledge and experience. Connery made a considerable impact playing the washed-up boxer Harlan 'Mountain' McClintock in the BBC's *Requiem for a Heavyweight* (1957), but the corporation subsequently offered him period drama: playing Hotspur in *An Age of Kings* (1960) and Count Vronsky in *Anna Karenina* (1961). Conscious of his lack of formal training, Connery attended classes run by the London-based Swedish acting and dance guru Yat Malmgren to finesse his control of movement and gesture and to understand their importance in the creation of meaning.

The British Film Industry: Breakthrough Roles

The changes that were transforming theatre and television were adopted more slowly in the film industry, which was dominated by two cautiously conservative combines: the Rank Organisation and the Associated British Picture Corporation (ABPC). Both kept a roster of contract players assigned particular roles by producers or studio executives to help create a stable image that was carefully managed.[29] Hence the hegemony of well-bred, middle-class gentlemanliness as represented by Kenneth More or Jack Hawkins, whose acting style tended towards the repression of emotion rather than its expression.[30] The new generation rejected this gentility, considering English actors artificial, mannered and inhibited. Caine contended: 'English actors seemed a bit prissy . . . I identified with Americans.'[31] The new generation of young American actors, notably Marlon Brando, possessed the physicality, directness and working-class authenticity to which these emerging British actors aspired. Their opportunities came, at least initially, through emergent film companies which produced the adaptations of working-class regionally set plays and novels that created the British New Wave.[32] The most dynamic and influential was Woodfall, the creation of ex-actor turned writer John Osborne and director Tony Richardson, both of whom worked at the Royal Court. It was the New Wave's black and white gritty regional realism depicting alienated, rebellious northern working-class young men that provided the breakthrough roles for Finney (*Saturday Night and Sunday Morning*, 1960); Courtenay (*The Loneliness*

Figure 1.1   A new kind of working class hero: Albert Finney as Arthur Seaton in *Saturday Night and Sunday Morning* (1960).

of the Long Distance Runner, 1962); Bates (*A Kind of Loving*, 1962); and Harris (*This Sporting Life*, 1963).

The first and most fêted was Finney. Richardson, who had worked with the actor at the Royal Court and cast Finney in a small part in *The Entertainer* (1959), judged him perfect for the role of Arthur Seaton in *Saturday Night and Sunday Morning* and the director, Karel Reisz, built the film round Finney after quickly recognising his potential.[33] Finney's factory experience, Salford origins and accent, and unfettered physicality enabled him to imbue the role with a vernacular authenticity, albeit in a generalised 'northern' register rather than the Nottingham of the original novel. The first half of the film celebrates the physical pleasures of an unrepentant male anti-hero, concentrating on Finney's robust body working, washing, dressing to go out, drinking, fighting and making love and the relish he brings to those activities. The critic Isabel Quigly thought Arthur's masculinity represented 'the bounce, the youthful bumptiousness of a new class that begins (between bouts of despair at the status quo) to stretch and feel its muscles'.[34] The film's promotion also emphasised both the close fit of actor and role and the character's charisma as 'a convention-smashing, working-class Don Juan', whose rebellion, 'comes from living louder and faster than anyone else'.[35]

An insistent, almost overpowering physicality was also the hallmark of Harris's Arthur Machin in *This Sporting Life*, but keyed to a much more tormented, self-destructive register. Its director, Lindsay Anderson, also associated with the Royal Court and who had seen Harris on stage in a production of *The Ginger Man* (1959), judged he was able to depict a more complex and ambivalent working-class masculinity, a character that had 'extraordinary power and aggressiveness, both temperamental and physical, but at the same time . . . great innate sensitiveness and a need for love of which he is at first hardly aware'.[36] Harris's Theatre Royal training meant he was willing to surrender himself to finding the 'truth' of the role, working closely with Anderson and the author David Storey, who adapted his own novel. Harris, who had seemed set to play professional rugby before a bout of tuberculosis, trained with the Richmond Rugby Club to develop the physical authenticity necessary to convey the brutal reality of the sporting scenes. *This Sporting Life* was a critical rather than popular success, but Harris's BAFTA and Oscar nominations and award of Best Actor at Cannes made him a desirable commodity.

Conspicuously different again was Courtenay's Colin Smith in *The Loneliness of the Long Distance Runner*, resentful, suspicious with a sharp intelligence and wariness. In his remarkable performance, creating a thoroughly convincing anti-hero at odds with a society shown as exploitative and unctuous, Courtenay established himself as a very different star from the charismatic Finney: awkward, angular, flat voiced, with plain, pinched, perpetually worried features. Reviewers thought he was unlikely star material but recognised the quality of Courtenay's performance as a combination of vulnerability, anger and controlled aggression. The production company, Bryanston, marketed Courtenay simply as a 'lean, hungry looking Hull lad' and Courtenay subsequently projected a diffident, shy image, uncertain about his right to success and fame.[37]

Bates's Vic Brown in *A Kind of Loving* is a less rebellious figure; a white-collar draughtsman. Producer Joseph Janni and director John Schlesinger knew Bates's work at the ESC and on television but judged he was also a handsome leading man who could project a convincing ordinariness, the boy-next-door, in a drama that focuses more on the situation than the central male character. Despite his accomplished performance and the film's success, the role did not define Bates as sharply as the other seven. His persona was less distinctive and his subsequent roles more varied: the uptight English writer in *Zorba the Greek* (1964); the amoral social climber in *Nothing but the Best* (1964); the feckless ur-hippy in *Georgy Girl* (1966) and the solid farmer in *Far from the Madding Crowd* (1967).

By 1963 the New Wave was exhausted, replaced by a much more loosely connected set of films that could be aligned to Swinging London. The US studios, which had little interest in the New Wave films, were much more enamoured of Swinging London because they considered British culture to be in the vanguard of international cultural change. Hence the rise of what Alexander Walker calls 'Hollywood England' in which the American Majors became the principal funders of British films either directly, or through bankrolling companies such as Eon Films, the creators of the James Bond franchise. Bond was the most popular fantasy figure who incarnated the style, sexual permissiveness and 'liberated' masculine energy that made him iconic of the Swinging Sixties on both sides of the Atlantic. Connery was eventually chosen for the role because the producers, Albert Broccoli and Harry Saltzman, wanted an 'unknown' actor who could be identified with the role, would sign a five-picture deal and was different from the insipid 'arrow-collar' good looks of the previous generation's leading men who, Broccoli commented, 'lacked the degree of masculinity Bond demanded'.[38] In Broccoli's view, Connery not only 'had the balls for the part' but he and Saltzman were struck by the grace with which Connery moved, a legacy of Malmgren's training. Walker comments astutely that Connery had 'the confident physicality of an American star' but also that his Edinburgh burr was authentically British without carrying direct class connotations, which 'distinguishes him from the now multiplying numbers of young newcomers on the British screen'.[39] What was never acknowledged by producers, publicists or reviewers was the intelligence and accomplishment of Connery's performance, animating Fleming's blank slate with irony and droll humour.

Caine had the conventional leading man's height and good looks and was cast against type in his first major role as the aristocratic Lieutenant Bromhead in *Zulu* (1964). His first defining role came as Harry Palmer in the downbeat spy thriller *The Ipcress File* (1965). Producer Harry Saltzman judged the actor's key strength was his truculent ordinariness as a deadpan anti-hero with whom audiences would identify.[40] Caine's extensive acting experience comes through in his beautifully low-key defiance and pitch-perfect intonations. Caine considered he had a 'fine ear for class structure in the voice' that enabled him to play Harry 'in a dead-neutral meritocrat's accent'.[41] Harry's rebelliousness is different from the northern dissenters as he inhabits a changing social order. Reviewers noted the film's contemporaneity, the 'current bachelor neatness' of Palmer's flat, a working-class figure whose 'cockney vowels' did not preclude elegance, taste and sophistication underpinned by a deep and abiding resentment about the privileges conferred by birth, class, public school education and the Old Boy network.[42] Caine enhanced his reputation for insolent charm, cockney independence and self-sufficient masculinity through *Alfie* (1966) – turned down by Stamp – another 'liberated' denizen of an increasingly meritocratic metropolis.

Although Stamp, as noted, became the iconic Swinging Londoner and a darling of the press as 'The New Kind of Englishman',[43] his breakthrough role in *Billy Budd* (1962) was as a young merchant seaman conscripted aboard a British man-of-war in 1797. Stamp had been seen in rep by the director, Peter Ustinov, who wanted a new face of exceptional attractiveness and was strong enough to resist pressure from the financiers, Allied Artists, not to cast an unknown.[44] The film's repeated close-ups and the promotion of its star

Figure 1.2 The quintessential 'young man on the make': Michael Caine as the eponymous *Alfie* (1966).

emphasised Stamp's somewhat androgynous blonde-dyed beauty, but Stamp's performance, as Alexander Walker enthused, managed 'that extraordinarily difficult feat of making goodness attractive and sweetness credible – a performance of immense delicacy'.[45] Stamp's delicate, trusting masculinity is contrasted with the brutality of Claggart (Robert Ryan) and the film explores the homoerotic undertones of their relationship. Billy's goodness is linked to his class and provincial origins – Stamp uses a Bristolian accent in the role – embodying in his voice and gestures the spirit of the revolution from his original ship the *Rights of Man*. Reviewers thought Stamp looks united the classical and contemporary: 'a cross between a Greek god and a rock 'n' roll idol'.[46]

O'Toole's defining role was also as an androgynous figure in *Lawrence of Arabia* (1962), a part Finney had turned down. Lawrence, the 'blond Bedouin', was another figure whose sensitive, introspective masculinity is ambivalent which, coupled with his masochism and identification with Arab culture, made him another nonconformist Sixties hero at odds with the Establishment and the British imperial mission. Although producer Sam Spiegel wanted an American name, Brando or Montgomery Clift, director David Lean, who thought O'Toole 'had a wonderful face and could act', wanted an unknown: 'the character was an enigma, a major star would lack that important quality of mystery'.[47]

With the exception of Bond – and Connery manages to insert a quizzical distancing to his relationship with M – the characters played by these stars in their breakthrough roles were nonconformists, men who do not recognise or do not accept their role in the existing social order. This enabled them to be marketed as rebels, and for reviewers and publicists to play up the generational shift these new actors were thought to embody and to see them as signs of changing times. Unlike established stars, these actors were fresh, different and relatively cheap. As cinematic unknowns, they had no preformed persona that would trigger a set of expectations in audiences and who could thus become strongly identified with their role: 'Michael Caine *is* Alfie, *is* Wicked, *is* Crafty, *is* Irresistible', was one example. Although, as Table 1.1 shows, they received numerous accolades, there was little contemporary comment on their acting. Their often extraordinarily accomplished performances were not simply the result of a close fit between actor and character but also the fruits of their extensive training and acting experience, which enabled them to bring subtlety, shading and nuance to their characterisations. These actors were used to working closely with directors, to think through a role and to search for the 'truth' of a part rather than its surface mannerisms. It was this dual aspect – of being unknown and at the same time highly experienced and thoroughly professional – that explains their impact. However, these were conditions that could not last.

Stardom: Success, Commodification, Creative Control and Independence

Although stardom conferred money and fame, it did not bring either industrial power or creative influence in a system controlled by producers and American studios, though, as noted, they might defer to directors' casting choices. As Alexander Walker notes:

> Whereas the break-up of the Hollywood contract system in the early 1950s gave the leading American stars the power to raise their fees to heights unheralded since the 1920s, while their tax laws gave them the incentive to set up in production with their own companies, the British actor had no high pay, no tax advantages and no power of any kind in the industry.[48]

These actors attempted to forge artistically satisfying careers in a system that favoured long-term contracts, typecasting, repetition, commodification and easy audience recognition as the guarantors of box office success. However, without this studio support, they faced a difficult and demanding struggle.

The differences in the development of their careers stem, in part, from their own divergent attitudes to film stardom. Bates, Courtenay, Finney and O'Toole saw themselves essentially as stage actors and judged that they could forge a more independent and interesting acting career if they alternated films with live theatre. Each resisted signing long-term contracts. Bates turned down a seven-year contract with Rank: 'Even though it meant security, I felt it meant being owned by somebody. I didn't want to be someone else's property and be told what to do.'[49] Bates, and particularly Courtenay, seemed genuinely uninterested in being a star. As noted, Courtenay maintained a diffident public persona and commented in retrospect: 'I never did anything about my stardom. It never meant anything to me.'[50] Courtenay returned to provincial rep in the 1970s. Finney's decision to take a percentage of the profits in his second major success, *Tom Jones* (1963), had made him a dollar millionaire at the age of twenty-seven, and thus he could afford to be exceptionally picky. But even before that, Finney had turned down the lead in *Lawrence of Arabia* because he did not wish to be typecast or commodified as a 'marketable property'. As he commented: 'it's a bit like being a racehorse, the people who own you, they make sure you're sellable and they can confine your acting in order to reproduce what they thought was successful in the first film'.[51] He even took a year's 'rest' on a tropical island after *Tom Jones* before returning to the theatre rather than film. O'Toole had been, like Finney, fêted as the 'new Olivier' and was to have led the Royal Shakespeare Company's move to London before he was hired to play Lawrence. Although clearly more enticed by the glamour of film stardom than Finney, O'Toole claimed that appearing on stage

> was the only way to get back in touch with what I know I am about. It is the only way I can measure . . . how I have grown or changed. It gets me back the freedom I need as an actor.[52]

By contrast, Caine, Connery and Stamp, having had limited stage success, considered the screen their medium and, once established, never returned to the theatre. Stamp was apparently told by Littlewood that he was too pretty to appear in theatre and should go into films.[53] Caine averred: 'I'm a completely committed movie actor . . . and Britain doesn't produce many of them . . . I think the subtlety of film acting is wonderful.'[54] They embraced film stardom as the natural and legitimate aspiration of an ambitious actor, another significant break with tradition. There was a marked difference in tactics, however. Caine accepted the advice of his agent Dennis Selinger that the surest way to achieve stardom was to be in four to five films a year.[55] He took the male lead in *Gambit* (1966) opposite Shirley MacLaine without reading the script simply because it was a big American movie.[56] By contrast Stamp, though he embraced the glamour of the film star's life, was hyper-selective, taking counsel from his mentor, the producer James Woolf, who told him: 'Stars are choosy. They come out at night. There are lots of fine British actors, but not so many stars. Don't be in such a rush.'[57] Stamp, as Caine observed acerbically, became obsessed by working with particular *auteur* directors: Losey, Wyler, Fellini, Pasolini and the one who got away, Antonioni, when Stamp lost out to David Hemmings for *Blow-Up* (1966). Stamp considered that in surrendering to these gifted filmmakers he would come to understand himself as an actor. Connery spent the second half of the decade attempting to break free from 'Bondage', his clashes with Bond producers Saltzman and Broccoli becoming increasingly acrimonious. They contended that the role had made Connery and he could be replaced; Connery that he had made Bond a success and that he should be made a co-producer, share in the films' enormous profits and have a say in the direction of the series that he thought increasingly emphasised gadgetry and special effects over characterisation.

Harris, who had been recognised as a gifted stage actor but had never been offered major theatrical roles, was the most ambivalent about his career and film stardom. He had accepted parts in American productions – *The Wreck of the Mary Deare* (1959) and *Mutiny on the Bounty* (1962) – before *This Sporting Life* but found himself disappointed by the American stars he worked with, including his idol Brando. He was equally disenchanted working with Antonioni on *The Red Desert* (1964) but, unlike Finney and O'Toole, did not return to the theatre. His subsequent film roles were eclectic: action-adventure,

Major Dundee (1965) and *The Heroes of Telemark* (1965); comedy, *Caprice* (1967); and musical, *Camelot* (1967). Only at the end of the decade did he find another role for his formidable talent to project vulnerability and strength: as the Pinkerton detective in *The Molly Maguires* (1970), opposite Connery's rebellious working-class miner.

In an attempt to gain creative control, several of the eight set up their own production companies. O'Toole, who saw himself as the successor to Edmund Kean and the great actor-managers, wanted to create an actors' co-operative in which he had the final say. Following Ingmar Bergman's model, it would make films, television and stage plays using the same company. This enterprise foundered, but O'Toole set up his own company, Keep Films, with his partner the American producer Jules Buck, in an attempt to exercise creative control.[58] Finney founded Memorial Enterprises in 1965 with Michael Medwin, a production company committed to making 'quality' film and theatre productions. It was not a full-blown company but an 'occasional' producer. Its output included *Charlie Bubbles* (1968), starring and directed by Finney and scripted by Shelagh Delaney, a jaundiced rumination on the price of success and an explicit attempt to examine the problems of stardom. In 1970, Harris set up a production company, Limbridge, for his directorial debut *Bloomfield* (1971). Connery made a condition of returning as Bond in *Diamonds Are Forever* (1971) that United Artists financed two films from his company Tantallon Films. Only one was made, *The Offence* (1973), in which Connery plays a deliberately anti-Bond character, a disillusioned, seedy detective sergeant beset by psychological problems. Following the success of *Get Carter* (1971), Caine formed the Three Michaels production company with producer Michael Klinger and director Mike Hodges, but this only made one film, *Pulp* (1972).

These companies, lacking financial muscle or a distribution deal, had very limited success; *Charlie Bubbles* did not even receive a UK circuit release. However, if they did not achieve their dreams of creative control, these stars, as they recognised themselves, were fortunate in coming to prominence at a time when British cinema was relatively buoyant and the London offices of the American studios were given considerable autonomy in commissioning films. And although they were linked by certain generational characteristics, each, as I have tried to show, was distinctively different, ensuring that although they were rivals and often vied for the same roles, the marketplace could accommodate all of them. This situation did not outlast the decade and all eight struggled to find film roles in the more straitened circumstances of the 1970s. Stamp, the actor most closely associated with the swinging sixties, did not attempt to continue, turning to travel and transcendental mysticism. They were no longer the new generation. Arriving on the set of *The Lion in Winter* (1968) to play Henry II, O'Toole realised that the actors cast to play Henry's sons – Timothy

Dalton, Anthony Hopkins and Nigel Terry – considered him part of the previous generation to whom they now looked for advice and guidance.[59]

Conclusion

Although these stars had not been able to alter the fundamental structures of the film industry, their talents and charisma were an important part of the attractiveness of British cinema for Hollywood studios. Their conspicuous success amply demonstrated the talents, intelligence and importance of working-class males – from the regions, Ireland and Scotland as well as London – and thus they acted as standard bearers for the cultural and social changes that were transforming British life. These eight stars helped broaden acting's social base, showing that acting was not a career confined to the middle class, becoming role models to those who followed.[60] They also extended and decisively altered the range of images of masculinity on British screens, projecting rebelliousness, an overt sexuality, a newly confident physicality but also a softer, more androgynous maleness that had absorbed feminine characteristics.

To demonstrate the impact of these changes would take far more room that I have here and would need to consider much further the role played by producers and the production policies of particular companies – including the role of casting directors, the types of contracts and earnings that were able to be negotiated or imposed, as well as the role played by film or theatrical agents. What I hope to have shown is that stars were made rather than born and thus the importance of studying them as social and economic as well as symbolic phenomena, as creative labourers who have to forge careers in circumstances not of their own choosing. In a UK context at least, their careers fail to make sense unless one analyses the three overlapping but competing industries of theatre, television and film rather than simply the cinema, and also the profession of acting itself at a particular historical moment. If we are to understand Sixties British cinema, we need to recognise the importance of male stars.

Notes

1. Clive Barnes, 'Britain's new actors – rougher, tougher, angrier', *New York Times*, 6 October 1963, pp. 43–4, 52–3.
2. The latest version, at time of writing, is Caine's intelligent if nostalgic documentary *My Generation* (2017).
3. Quoted in Robert Sellers, *Don't Let the Bastards Grind You Down: How One Generation of British Actors Changed the World* (London: Cornerstone, 2011), p. 87.
4. That provision does not apply to Harris, who was educated in Ireland.
5. Robert Hewison, *Too Much: Art and Society in the Sixties, 1960–75* (London: Methuen, 1986), p. 76.

6. For an informative contemporary account of London's 'Swingers' see Jonathan Aitken, *The Young Meteors* (London: Secker & Warburg, 1967). For a retrospective analysis see Shawn Levy, *Ready, Steady, Go! Swinging London and the Invention of Cool* (London: Fourth Estate, 2003 [2002]).
7. Both were highly gendered phenomena: there were far more opportunities for young men than young women, including in acting – see Claire Cochrane, *Twentieth-Century British Theatre: Industry, Art and Empire* (Cambridge: Cambridge University Press, 2011), p. 207.
8. Paul McDonald, *Hollywood Stardom* (Chichester, West Sussex: Wiley-Blackwell, 2013), p. 14.
9. See Bruce Babington, 'Introduction: British stars and stardom', in Bruce Babington (ed.), *British Stars and Stardom: From Alma Taylor to Sean Connery* (Manchester: Manchester University Press, 2001), pp. 1–28.
10. The standard account, Robert Murphy's *Sixties British Cinema*, contends that the 1960s 'were unique in producing an array of British actors who became internationally popular', but he 'found little space to comment on their performance'. Robert Murphy, *Sixties British Cinema* (London: BFI Publishing, 1992), pp. 7–8.
11. See Andrew Spicer and Melanie Williams, 'Introduction', *Journal of British Cinema and Television* 12: 1, 2015, pp. 1–5.
12. 16 September 1960, quoted in Geoffrey Macnab, *Searching for Stars: Stardom and Screen Acting in the British Cinema* (London: Cassell, 2000), p. 187.
13. Geoffrey Macnab, 'Valley boys', *Sight & Sound* 4: 3, 1994, pp. 20–3.
14. Sean Connery (with Murray Grigor), *Being a Scot* (London: Weidenfeld and Nicolson, 2008), pp. 31–2. He was also representative of an emerging trend in which the 'poetry voice' was becoming outmoded and greater emphasis given to physical movement; see Hal Burton, 'Preface', in Hal Burton (ed.), *Acting in the Sixties* (London: BBC, 1970), p. 9.
15. Michael Sanderson, *From Irving to Olivier: A Social History of the Acting Profession 1880–1983* (London: Athlone Press, 1984), p. 292.
16. Ibid., Appendix 1, p. 331.
17. Ibid. p. 287.
18. Terence Stamp, *Coming Attractions* (London: Bloomsbury, 1988), p. 51.
19. Sanderson, *From Irving to Olivier*, pp. 284–5.
20. Cochrane, *Twentieth-Century British Theatre*, pp. 78–108. The other route was university drama societies; only Courtenay, who read English at University College London, made use of this route, but he dropped out to pursue RADA training.
21. Sanderson, *From Irving to Olivier*, pp. 293–300; Cochrane, *Twentieth-Century British Theatre*, p. 213. Harris paid for his training at the LAMDA by selling some of his Guinness shares.
22. Michael Billington, *The Modern Actor* (London: Hamish Hamilton, 1973), pp. 7–19. Billington makes the point that none of the drama schools trained actors for either film or television (p. 10). LAMDA had occasional classes in Method acting and incorporated elements of Stanislavsky in its curriculum. David McCallum observed that although British actors were aware of the Method at this time,

'it didn't really cross over into Britain'; quoted in Sellers, *Don't Let the Bastards*, p. 235.
23. Sanderson, *From Irving to Olivier*, p. 309.
24. Stephen Lacey, *British Realist Theatre: The New Wave in its Context, 1956–65*, (London: Routledge, 1995), pp. 43–54.
25. Quoted in Sellers, *Don't Let the Bastards*, p. 65.
26. Robert Leach, *Theatre Royal: Joan Littlewood and the Making of Modern British Theatre* (Exeter: Exeter University Press, 2006), pp. 78–96.
27. Dan Rebellato, *1956 and All That: The Making of Modern British Drama* (London: Routledge, 1999), pp. 38–9.
28. Sanderson, *From Irving to Olivier*, pp. 280, 285.
29. Andrew Spicer, 'Male stars, masculinity and British cinema, 1945–1960', in Robert Murphy (ed.), *The British Cinema Book* (London: British Film Institute, 2001), pp. 93–100, p. 93.
30. See Andrew Spicer, *Typical Men: The Representation of Masculinity in Popular British Cinema* (London: I. B. Tauris, 2001), pp. 33–46.
31. Qouted in Christopher Bray, *Michael Caine: A Class Act* (London: Faber and Faber, 2006), p. 21.
32. John Hill, *Sex, Class and Realism: British Cinema 1956–63* (London: BFI Publishing, 1986), pp. 35–52.
33. Quentin Falk, *Albert Finney in Character* (London: Robson Books, 2002 [1992]), p. 57.
34. *Spectator*, 4 November 1960.
35. *Manchester Guardian*, 29 October 1960.
36. Quoted in Michael Callan, *Richard Harris: The Biography* (Dublin: Pentheum, 2014), p. 133.
37. Robert Shail, 'Constructions of masculinity in 1960s British cinema', unpublished PhD thesis, University of Exeter, 2002, pp. 56, 69.
38. Cubby Broccoli (with Donald Zec), *When the Snow Melts* (London: Boxtree Books, 1998), pp. 165–6.
39. Alexander Walker, *Hollywood England*, p. 190.
40. Philip Judge, *Michael Caine* (Tunbridge Wells: Spellmount, 1985), p. 34.
41. Quoted in Bray, *Michael Caine*, p. 92.
42. Isabel Quigly, *Spectator*, 19 March 1965.
43. Maureen Cleave, *Evening Standard*, 21 January 1963.
44. Terence Stamp, *Double Feature* (London: Bloomsbury, 1989), p. 12.
45. Walker, *Hollywood, England*, p. 161.
46. Donald Zec, 'From Stepney to stardom . . .', *Daily Mirror*, 19 September 1962.
47. Adrian Turner, *The Making of David Lean's 'Lawrence of Arabia'* (London: Dragon's World, 1994), p. 42. O'Toole had had his nose reduced in size so that his looks were more cinematic.
48. Walker, *Hollywood, England*, p. 93.
49. Quoted in Donald Spoto, *Otherwise Engaged: The Life of Alan Bates* (London: Arrow, 2008 [2007]), p. 30.
50. Quoted in *Empire*, November 1995, p. 52.

51. Quoted in Gabriel Hershman, *Strolling Player: The Life and Career of Albert Finney* (Stroud: History Press, 2017), p. 56.
52. Robert Sellers, *Peter O'Toole: The Definitive Biography* (London: Sidgwick & Jackson, 2015), p. 120.
53. Quoted in Sellers, *Don't Let the Bastards*, p. 236.
54. Quoted in *Films and Filming*, January 1985, p. 28.
55. Bray, *Michael Caine*, pp. 87–8, 112.
56. Michael Caine, *What's It All About?* (London: Arrow, 2003 [2002]), p. 241.
57. Stamp, *Double Feature*, p. 102.
58. Nicholas Wapshott, *Peter O'Toole: A Biography* (Sevenoaks: New English Library, 1983), pp. 13, 75–6.
59. Ibid. p. 145.
60. However, the acting profession still struggles with issues of diversity and inclusivity; see the documentary by Deirdre O'Neill and Mike Wayne, *The Acting Class*, Inside Film, 2017.

2. 'REBEL REBEL'?: OLIVER REED IN THE 1960s

Caroline Langhorst

Being tall, dark and handsome, charismatic, rebellious and intense, Oliver Reed belonged to a new generation of British actors of the 1960s known primarily for their youthful physical prowess. As Pam Cook and Claire Hines suggest, around this time, 'British cinema began to feature muscular, virile, working-class rebel heroes, personified by the likes of Albert Finney, Richard Harris and Stanley Baker, whose bodies were put on display for erotic contemplation, and whose hedonistic, amoral attitudes threatened the polite surface of the public-school ruling class.'[1] Their personae were influenced by the growing importance of youth culture, its related consumerism, and the emergence of the so-called 'permissive' society with a more liberal attitude towards sexuality, and this applies equally to Reed, who can also be seen as a 'zeitgeist icon'.[2] Such figures tend to 'restate, often in new and modern forms, old identities and values, as well as calling a society towards newer, and perhaps confused, emergent values and value systems'.[3] From his time at Hammer between 1961 and 1965 as a (Byronic) horror heart throb, Reed's career, star image and performance style evolved significantly through specific collaborations with two directors: Michael Winner and Ken Russell.[4] Through an analysis of his career in the 1960s, this chapter will explore how Reed's individualistic and rebellious disposition both resonated with the era's shifting zeitgeist, from (pre-)swinging London to the counterculture of the later part of the decade. Reed's troubled on-screen performances, his rather reductive reputation as daring hellraiser and charming womaniser, and his own decidedly ambivalent cultivation of his rebel image will be related to the similarly conflicted nature of the decade and its cinema. Reed was a predominantly physical and 'excessive' performer and he both represents and sublimates a particular kind of rebellious 1960s on-screen masculinity. In this regard, how Reed's rebellion is coded both in different roles (characterisation and diegesis) and on a performative level (how his specific 'excessive' performance style manifests) is an important consideration.

Hammer's Moody New Sex Symbol? – The 'Reedian' Byronic

Robert Oliver Reed was born on 13 February 1938. Despite the early separation of his parents, Reed experienced a comfortable upper middle-class upbringing that included nannies and boarding schools. In this regard, it is crucial to note that the Londoner markedly differed from his working-class contemporaries such as the northern Finney, Welshman Richard Burton or Edinburgh-born Sean Connery in terms of both class and educational background. Reed's grandfather was RADA founder Sir Herbert Beerbohm Tree and his uncle the film director (Sir) Carol Reed. Notwithstanding these fortunate family relations, however, Reed was wary of nepotism.[5] He likewise refused to attend a drama school or join a repertory company in order to receive the customary training.[6] Young Oliver Reed, who was particularly impressed with the swashbuckling ways of Errol Flynn, aspired to become a popular movie star, not a thespian.[7] Therefore, he purposely deviated from the classically trained (British) stage tradition and primarily worked as a screen actor.

His candid refusal to undertake professional acting training seems to have been due to his rebellious disposition, especially his dislike of deference, and a certain degree of personal insecurity. As Reed admitted in his memoir *Reed All About Me*, he was not overly sure of his life goals at the time.[8] His irreverent attitude towards authority (institutional, societal and individual) is also evidenced by his repeated expulsion from various boarding schools, and the strained relationship with his father. But Reed also suffered from shyness and dyslexia which contributed to his difficulties. On the other hand, his defiant attitude was further facilitated and enhanced by his privileged class background, wherein a certain 'I wasn't born to follow' class confidence becomes apparent. However, Reed seemed to rebel against the very foundations of the class system and its hierarchical structure, articulating an ambiguous anti-authoritarian rebellious mindset. But Reed's rebellion, like that of the Angry Young Men before him or the later counterculture, ultimately possessed a conservative core (i.e. the conflation of an anti-authoritarian stance and consumerism or in terms of gender roles), highlighting the transitional status quo of a British society facing numerous challenges and transformations.

Reed's later decision against going to Hollywood in the early 1970s when he ranked as Britain's best-paid film star paradigmatically articulated this highly conflicted attitude.[9] Although he objected to playing the Hollywood game, Reed's decision was also partly motivated by a 'vitriolic snobbishness that was markedly at odds with [his] "one of the boys" image' and an exaggerated sense of patriotism.[10] Hence, the actor's personal stance made the construction of an international star persona rather difficult. Unlike other English actors-turned-Hollywood stars such as Bristolian Cary Grant or Huddersfield-born James Mason who succeeded in adjusting their English star persona to a more transatlantic, even cosmopolitan image, Reed's later, post-*Oliver!* (1968) international stardom did not eclipse his popularity in the UK.

Reed's early screen appearances encompassed both cinema and television. After playing Richard of Gloucester in the TV series *The Golden Spur* (1959), Reed played a small role in *The Angry Silence* (1960). He also made brief appearances as a Teddy boy in the Norman Wisdom vehicle *The Bulldog Breed* (1960), as chorus boy in *The League of Gentlemen* (1960), as dancing youth in *Beat Girl* (1960) as well as a bohemian artist in a cafe in *The Rebel* (1961). *Beat Girl* deals with the generational gulf between jazz-loving British post-war youth and their allegedly conservative parents, and Stephen Glynn aptly stresses its combination of young, emerging talent (Adam Faith, Shirley Anne Field) amidst British veteran actors such as David Farrar, Nigel Green and Hammer's rising star, Christopher Lee.[11] Reed's rather small role is visually emphasised in a dance sequence in which he is depicted in a series of close-ups. His character – rather than the Bardot-echoing female protagonist played by Gillian Hills – temporarily becomes the centre of attention. Thus, even in the very early stages of his career, the audience's attention is directed to the specific gaze that became a key element of Reed's acting style.

Reed's charismatic screen presence is already apparent in these early appearances: his individualistic-irreverent personality and his eyes/gaze, physicality and voice that were equally highlighted in his on-screen performances and promotional material became his trademark qualities. These qualities kept him busy and gradually contributed to his evolving star profile which tended towards individualistic rebels in post-Profumo films addressing the permissive society and in swinging London narratives such as Michael Winner's *The System* (1964), *I'll Never Forget What's'isname* (1967) and *The Jokers* (1967), Guy Hamilton's *The Party's Over* (1965) and Jonathan Miller's *Take a Girl Like You* (1970). Subsequent (increasingly baroque) period roles include an embodiment of painter/poet Dante Gabriel Rossetti in Ken Russell's Pre-Raphaelite Brotherhood portrait *Dante's Inferno* (1967), his Lawrentian anti-hero in *Women in Love* (1969), and his defiantly anti-authoritarian rebel priest Urbain Grandier in *The Devils* (1971).

The Reedian star profile first began to emerge in relation to his first leading role in Terence Fisher's gothic horror *The Curse of the Werewolf* (1961), set in eighteenth-century Spain. The actor's nuanced Byronic performance as the tormented, inwardly torn werewolf Leon also established a recurrent character type – a highly conflicted, contradictory man – he repeatedly both returned to and further developed in different variations of the 'Alienated Young Man'.[12] The young actor's increasing appeal may be regarded both as the result of his on-screen performance and related promotional ephemera. Starting with Christopher Lee's seductive vampire Count in *Dracula* (1958), Hammer had embarked upon promoting their male actors as pin-ups and sex symbols that evoked a mixture of attraction and repulsion in the audience through their irresistible though roguishly villainous charisma that was paired with a compelling masculinity.[13] As Reed biographer Cliff Goodwin highlights, Hammer's publicity focused 'on his image as a new "brooding teenage idol"'.[14] Oliver Reed's nuanced rendering of tormented masculinity in *The Curse of the Werewolf* allegedly 'brought him a sackful of fan mail and more than fifty proposals of marriage from girls he had never met'.[15] Yet this rather affirmative audience reaction and emerging female fandom were not necessarily the result of the young actor's portrayal of a werewolf. Despite the foregrounding of Reed's animalistic sexuality on promotional posters that chose to depict a transformed werewolf instead of Reed without costume, his character is only occasionally shown in a monstrous condition. Therefore, whereas the poster design implies a horror plot centred on a monstrous figure, the actual film mainly presents a romanticised, constantly brooding Byronic character portrayed by an attractive young actor. Promotional material covering the early part of Reed's career trajectory likewise places an exaggerated emphasis upon his distinctive physical attributes. A promotional biography for the Hammer production *Captain Clegg* (1962) advertises his appeal in the following way: 'Oliver Reed, at the age of twenty eight is six feet tall, with coal black hair and intense cornflower blue eyes, and smoulders with the sort of banked sexual fires that are guaranteed to cause conflagration in the hearts of female movie fans', endorsing 'his dark, satanic good looks'.[16]

The contrasts established by *The Curse of the Werewolf* between menacing virile masculinity and sensitive vulnerability, rational self-control and basic instinct, as well as between civility and savagery, was likewise echoed throughout Reed's career, both in terms of roles – the animalistic fur trapper in *The Trap* (1966), the brutish Bill Sikes in *Oliver!* (1968), or the vengeful ex-convict on the run in *Sitting Target* (1972) – and his increasingly uncontrollably rebellious star image. What unites all these roles is the recurrent combination of an inner, simmering restlessness and an intense, potentially menacing gaze. In the post-war British cinema context, the fusion of virile toughness, vulnerability and a certain ambivalence has been explored in relation to Stanley Baker by

Figure 2.1 Hammer's new horror heart throb: Oliver Reed in *The Curse of the Werewolf* (1961).

Andrew Spicer, who classifies him as 'modern tough guy' and 'violent man-on-the-edge fusing aggressiveness with sensitive vulnerability' and 'an insecurity about his role in the world'.[17] This could equally apply to Reed's portrayal of alienated young men but also his action-driven roles including *Hannibal Brooks* (1969), *The Hunting Party* (1971), and *Sitting Target*.

But this particular kind of Byronic brooding masculinity may be usefully traced back to 1940s British cinema's recurrent depiction of conflicted, doomed or neurotic masculinity represented by the likes of James Mason, Stewart Granger, David Farrar and Eric Portman.[18] Mason in particular, with his 'tall, dark and handsome' appearance, rose to prominence on account of his portrayal of brutish, sadistic and saturnine men in Gainsborough melodramas such as *The Man in Grey* (1943) and *The Wicked Lady* (1945). Reed's gradually emerging persona in the 1960s may be said to follow in this vein, given its dynamic fusion of conflicted, doomed masculinity, its dangerous sexuality and related alternating evocation of attraction and menace. Hammer's use of this persona stretched beyond the confines of gothic horror into other productions in which Reed was cast as anti-hero/villain (*Paranoiac*, 1963; *The Damned*, 1963; or *The Scarlet Blade*, 1963) or as attractive young man, love interest or rebel leader (*Captain Clegg*; *The Brigand of Kandahar*, 1965), indicating its versatility in both period and contemporary roles.

Reed most significantly adjusts the Masonian Byronic to contemporary British culture via explicit links with post-war youth. In both *Paranoiac* and *The Damned*, he portrays two highly unstable and (potentially) aggressive young men with either a delinquent (*The Damned*) or psychotic (*Paranoiac*) touch, which then further evolved into the repeatedly portrayed 'Alienated Young Men' character type of the films with Michael Winner. Both Mason's and Reed's star images, in turn, were determined by an 'ultimately self-destructive, uneasy ambivalence' and a defiant and individualistic attitude.[19] Roberta E. Pearson, for example, observes how 'Mason's atypicality rendered him inappropriate for roles that required "ordinariness"'.[20] Reed similarly took delight in deviating from the norm and subverting expectations. Furthermore, both his convincing on-screen portrayal of unconventional anti-heroes and his off-screen defiantly nonconformist attitude resonate with the wider social changes that emerged over the course of the 1960s. Geoffrey Macnab notes how by the early 1960s British film actors tended to be considerably more outspoken than before, no longer 'meekly do[ing] the publicists' bidding', ushering in a new 'era of the anti-star'.[21] Oliver Reed embodies and exemplifies this specific category.

From (Winner's) 'Alienated Young Man' to (Russellian) Baroque

Reed's repeated, post-1964/5 collaborations with Michael Winner and Ken Russell (1965) marked a turning point after the Hammer period. Both directors provided the actor with an opportunity to display an altogether wider range, whilst further refining his distinctive performative characteristics (gaze, body, voice, movement/stillness). They also appreciated the actor's compatibility with the curious, experimental and sometimes contrarian 1960s zeitgeist; yet each adapted and moulded him for their own purposes. Winner repeatedly connected him with the myth of swinging London, although its playful permissiveness tends to turn into existential anguish. Reed's anti-authoritarian attitude, his rebellion against the system and animal magnetism were compatible with Russell's neo-romantic excessive aesthetics and general embrace of forms of sexuality, sensuality and corporeality that do not shy away from 'madness, morbidity, monstrosity and violent eroticism'.[22]

Reed starred in Winner's *The System* (1964), his swinging London films *The Jokers* (1967) and *I'll Never Forget What's'isname* (1967), as an audacious thief with the crown jewels as his target and a disaffected advertising executive respectively, and in the Second World War adventure *Hannibal Brooks* (1969) as an escaped prisoner of war who rescues an elephant. As Spicer states, Reed's collaboration with Winner was mainly defined by his recurrent portrayal of the character type of the sensitive 'Alienated Young Man', a variant of the Angry Young Man, central to Winner's early films 'with their disillusioned, obsessive anti-heroes "who dream of an alternative life that they cannot achieve"'.[23] Spicer notes how *The System* and *I'll Never Forget What's'isname* form 'a diptych, based on original screenplays by Peter Draper, in which the central character moves from the provinces to London'.[24] Draper intended 'to describe the frustrations and anxieties young people experienced, "trying to shape their own shaky morality" in an affluent, exploitative society that showed the bankruptcy of official values'.[25] In both films, it is predominantly Reed's alienated young males who act as vehicles for exploration of anxieties pertaining to sociocultural changes and gender roles. *The System* occupies a transitional position between post-Profumo and 'Mods vs Rockers' and pre-swinging London. The 1963 Profumo Affair and the preceding Vassall incident that merged espionage, blackmail and homosexuality had exposed the highly ambiguous morals of the affluent elite and its sex- and corruption-infused power games. Consequently, both contributed to the emergence of more liberated lifestyles and an increasingly irreverent attitude towards figures of authority.[26]

In *The System*, Reed portrays a drifting seaside photographer called 'Tinker' always on the lookout for casual amorous encounters. At the beginning of the film, he and his friends control the 'system' devoted to exploiting the holidaymakers and picking up *naïve* girls. Class barriers also assume a decisive narrative role and are associated with Tinker who, despite his apparent contempt for class privilege, does not make any attempt at challenging the established hierarchical structure. He falls in love with the affluent model Nicola (Jane Merrow), but she eventually leaves him behind. This proves to be crucial in terms of gender roles as the established active/male and passive/female connotations are reversed. Tinker's suppressed emotions and actual vulnerability get the better of him as he realises in one of the film's seminal scenes that he has become the prey. Moreover, Spicer argues, 'he cannot cope with a woman as rootless and selfish as himself who has far greater confidence and self-possession. Unable to return to his male group which is in the process of breaking up, his only recourse is to dream of the opportunities represented by London.'[27]

In *I'll Never Forget What's'isname* Reed plays the seemingly successful yet troubled advertising junior executive Andrew Quint who sets out to rediscover his own identity by leaving his job and his wife. Tinker's alienation in *The System* moves up a gear in intensity with Quint's ongoing personal crisis in *I'll Never Forget What's'isname*. His highly volatile emotional condition is further highlighted by an 'unsettling, staccato rhythm or rather dissonance that mirrors the surges and reversals of Quint's restless, kaleidoscopic life'.[28] In both films, 1960s consumerism and the process of human beings turned into exchangeable commodities are presented critically. In the latter consumerism is explicitly exposed as hollow farce by means of the rigged advertising competition Quint wins.

The 1960s Reedian male characters often seem to rebel, yet it is sometimes not exactly clear what they are rebelling against. For instance, the actor's performance as Moise, the leader of a group of beatniks in *The Party's Over*, is similar to his Teddy boy gang leader King in *The Damned*, albeit more subdued; Moise is decidedly moody, provocative, delivers cocky lines and is even more reminiscent of Marlon Brando's formative performance as directionless rebel Johnny in *The Wild One* (1953). Rebellion in *The Party's Over* is coded as being aimless; in *The System*, it is even less explicitly articulated. *I'll Never Forget What's'isname*, on the other hand, sets in with a determinedly defiant Reed. His character Quint is introduced carrying an axe and displaying a self-assured body language as he strides through the London streets. This is further accentuated via a longer close-up that shows him looking sideways. Once he gets into his office, he uses the axe to destroy his desk. This act seems at first to be a more focused gesture of rebellion than anything that occurs in *The Party's Over*. Quint appears to be attacking petty, superficial bourgeois morality and its shallow values of economic security, achieved through the cultivation of a subservient mindset. Quint informs his boss (Orson Welles) that he has just resigned and wants to start a new life, complaining his work is 'deceitful, superficial and self-indulgent'. His deliberate opting out of society, an apparent rebellion against restrictive societal mores and conventions, is ultimately a failed rebellion because he returns to both his advertising profession and his estranged wife (Wendy Craig) and child after the accidental death of one of his lovers (Carol White).

At first glance, both *The System* and *I'll Never Forget What's'isname* seem to mirror the permissive society's supposedly less restricted as well as playful approach to sexuality. Simultaneously, they at times display a misogynist treatment of the female characters – the whole notion of the 'system' in *The System* falls into this category as does Quint's (compensatory) philandering. This seems to echo the Angry Young Men's conflicted stance towards women and their shifted social roles to a certain degree, thus exposing their own volatile sense of self and uncertainty regarding their own specific position in ever-changing surroundings. The 1960s, as has been repeatedly noted by the likes of Arthur Marwick and Trevor Harris and Monia O'Brien Castro, were marked by a contradictory coexistence of more or less progressive and reactionary tendencies, especially with regard to gender roles.[29] Therefore, swinging London films and the (later) counterculture were likewise problematic, as their embrace of sexually liberated, alternative lifestyles generally did not necessarily break away from what were predominantly heteronormative constructions. Sue Harper, for instance, states in relation to 1960s British cinema's depiction of femininity that 'British films of the 1960s were in fact far more prescriptive towards women than they had been in the 1950s'.[30] In these two films, the shallow nature of 1960s frivolities is brought to the fore by the realisation that Reed's characters' social alienation and frustration with their condition has not been overcome and the inner void has not been filled, either by love or by colourful consumerist products. In *I'll Never*

Forget What's'isname (and *The Party's Over*), for instance, this insight is triggered by the sudden accidental death of a female character, which is highly problematic, given that by means of their death they are reduced to a cathartic epiphany-inducing moment for the male protagonist in crisis. Situations tend to turn serious and ill-fated when the game-playing, womanising yet actually insecure young men develop feelings that transcend a fleeting affair. Ultimately, however, Reed's troubled male characters' insecurities are exposed, thus undermining heteronormative constructions of (hegemonic) masculinity.

Contrary to Reed's later public macho image, the actor repeatedly delivered a considerably nuanced rendering of conflicted masculinity that eventually results in multiple on-screen breakdowns/meltdowns. Peter Hutchings, for example, notes the unusual display of male emotions in relation to *The Curse of the Werewolf*'s beginning which highlighted one of Reed-as-werewolf's teary eyes, uncommon 'both for horror cinema and for British cinema in this period'.[31] Moreover, Reed was permitted to articulate a deeper emotional range throughout the 1960s than the likes of Sean Connery or Michael Caine. As a result, he may be regarded not only as 'the best example of the damaged male' in the 1970s, as Sue Harper and Justin Smith suggest, but also as having established this type since the early 1960s, thus occupying a unique position within the British film industry of the time.[32] Whereas Mason's role pattern and star persona underwent a shift from sadistic Gainsborough brute to anguished,

Figure 2.2 The hunter has been captured: the (alienated) Byronic Reedian gaze in *The System* (1964).

conflicted men, most of Reed's early Byronic Hammer roles (with the exception of Simon in *Paranoiac*) were not as depraved as Mason's characters. The Reedian portrayal of an existential/masculine crisis is predominantly marked by his specific use of (intense) gazes and bodily composure, which alternates between moments of restless motion/activity and absolute stillness/reflection. Accordingly, Spicer highlights that Reed 'projects a sense of barely contained physical energy and anger that can never find its occasion, becoming a powerless Byronic anti-hero, whose distant gaze suggests that nothing really satisfies or truly engages him and who has nowhere to go'.[33]

Reed's emotional reaction is often highlighted via close-ups. The combination of close-ups, the actor's stillness and the resulting particular framing of his face seem further particularly effective because of their affective impact upon the audience. What makes close-ups of Reed stand out from close-ups of other actors then is his inherent (and untutored) raw power and its intensity that still differs from that of trained actors such as Harris or Brando. By this means, Reed's articulation of raw emotions and his penetrating gaze become more exposed and accentuated. His acting style also proves to be in tune with cinema's specific visual modes of expression. As James Naremore stresses with regard to screen acting, the 'analysis of actors' stillness, restraint and posture (e.g., how they stand) takes on especial importance'.[34] Reed does not need to speak (much) to convey his emotions. His silence is interrupted by a few verbal utterances and his pained facial expressions before and after he breaks down are sufficiently effective. The open exposure of his feelings and the recurrent use of the close-up also bring him closer to the audience. He is not a remote, elusive star. Instead, Reed is there right in front of the spectator. Naremore also notes that even seemingly naturalistic actors 'have learned to master both the performing space and every aspect of their physical presence'.[35] In Reed's case, however, mastery of his craft was gradually achieved by trial-and-error self-tutoring during his time as a film extra and his Hammer years. As a result, his performance style retains a hint of (technical) uncontrollability that is further underscored by his irreverent attitude. Michael Winner, for example, also recalled that British filmmaking in the 1960s was at times more spontaneous and less restricted than in the preceding decades.[36] Thus, Reed becomes an expression of that specific 1960s mindset and related work ethos.

Additionally, it is particularly important to consider that in his role(s) and performance(s), there is at least one moment when the Reedian character suddenly snaps/lashes out or breaks, thereby releasing the inner tension he has been building up to that point. From his early on-screen appearances onwards, it further becomes manifest that Oliver Reed's characters somehow do not properly fit in. Moreover, at times, he even seems to attempt to break out of the films' respective diegetic realm with the actor's 'excessive' performance style contained neither by narrative constraints nor by specific role requirements. Despite Reed's lack of professional training, however, he may be said to have the same specific sense of 'present-ness' as Marlon Brando whose animal magnetism is likewise primarily articulated by means of an intense gaze and a distinctive bodily presence.[37] In this regard, Naremore's distinction between 'representational' (performances focused on the character rather than the performer) and 'presentational' performances ('awareness of the performer's performance overshadows any sense of the character') may be applied to Reedian screen performances.[38] Furthermore, Philip Drake stresses that '*all* star performances must to an extent . . . be already encoded ostensive signs'[39] on the grounds that 'individual stars become associated with a repertoire of performative signs'.[40] For Drake, it is 'an imperative of stardom' that the star's 'signifying function exceeds the diegesis'.[41] Moreover, he argues, it is 'by varying the ostensiveness of their performance, as well as external reframing signifiers (such as publicity and reviews) that they can manage this without disrupting the representational mode of the performance as a whole'.[42] This applies to most of Reed's 1960s performances. Yet given his untrained raw power and his collaboration with maverick directors who adopt a more spontaneous creative approach, and the actor's evolving star image, in some cases, such as his performance in *The Devils* that knowingly plays upon his late 1960s reputation for rebellion and public shenanigans, an occasional shift between both representational and presentational mode may be detected.

Similarly, Paul McDonald uses the distinctions between 'star as character' and 'star as star', referring to Barry King's terms 'impersonation' (an actor representing a certain character) and 'personification' (no clear signs of transformation).[43] In Reed's case, the former term is usually applicable, with occasional forays into the latter. His 'excessive' performance, however, is not (yet) (self-)indulgent for most of the 1960s (until Reed's baroque performance as Grandier). It is rather tied to his raw power, personal irreverent attitude and related physical screen presence and – like many stars – highly contradictory star persona.

After Reed's role as the (hyper)masculine French-Canadian trapper La Bête opposite Rita Tushingham's mute girl in *The Trap*, there is an increasingly explicit emphasis upon his heightened animal magnetism and corporeality in his roles and performances. Originating in his formative role and performance as werewolf Leon, this focus on Reed's virile masculinity and body may be regarded as the result of his physical transformation into more ruggedly mature features, which, in turn, is then also reflected in his developing star persona, choice of roles and delivery of performances. Additionally, it was also elevated at the level of performance intensity, which he managed to maintain in light of different role requirements. Christine Geraghty's and

Justine Ashby's observations about Albert Finney's overpowering, visually accentuated 'sexual charisma' and the 'audience's engagement with and contemplation of Finney as a star whose image has so clearly been constructed around sexual presence' are perhaps eventually surpassed by Oliver Reed.[44] This is accentuated in the D. H. Lawrence adaptation *Women in Love* and even more exposed in *The Devils*, the latter displaying a symbiosis of late 1960s countercultural elements and aesthetics and gender representations associated with excess and the transcendence of societal and moral taboos and boundaries.[45] Reed's role and performance succeed in unleashing his full erotic appeal as Grandier's apparently irresistible manhood drives the physically deformed, repressed and erotically obsessed Sister Jeanne (Vanessa Redgrave) to the brink of a hysterical (psycho)sexual frenzy. Both the film's narrative and cinematography are primarily centred on Reed's performance as anti-authoritarian, excessively hedonistic and ultimately self-destructive priest who resides in the country's last remaining free city, Loudun, and continues to defy the monarchy's and church's expanding power alliance. The power struggle embodied in the film further echoes the 1960s struggle between the individual and the system. Grandier's character also exemplifies the counterculture's contradictory disposition: he may be a rogue priest who engages in merry promiscuity and follows his own rules, but he is still a member of the church, who on top of that also displays a consumerist attitude articulated via his opulent robes and jewellery.

The Devils explicitly makes use of, and comments upon, Reed's by then notorious hellraiser image, his apparently overwhelming aura as Grandier, and compelling gaze. This is further underscored by the reaction of the female characters (not only the lovesick Mother Superior), who almost all seem to be affected by his overly virile presence and charisma, thereby cheekily playing at Reed's by then well-known womanising.[46] In accordance with his growing (hyper)virile appearance, the core characteristics of Reed's formative star profile seem to be gradually transformed into the less controllable hellraiser image. His performance as thuggish Bill Sikes in his uncle's musical *Oliver!* enhanced his star status to an international level. Around the same time, the Reedian Byronic star persona began to be linked with a notion of increasing force-of-nature uncontrollability, with the actor even being considered too hedonistic to take on the role of 007.[47] By the time of *The Devils*, the fusion of Reed's seemingly rebellious screen and private personae was established. Thus, the Byronic 'mad, bad and dangerous to know' component that was also prevalent in his off-screen image tended to be presented as spiralling out of control: 'Reed raised hell so consistently, so predictably and so destructively that people started to recoil from him.'[48] Therefore, press coverage of the time still underlined his status as a popular sex symbol, including headlines such as 'Oliver pushes the virile look' (*Evening News*, 18 March

1969) or 'A sex symbol named Oliver' (*Daily Mail*, 7 January 1971), but also underscored his growing hypervirility and hellraising: 'Oliver's Hard Times in the Wild – Not many things frighten Oliver Reed, the actor who goes out of his way to present a rugged, he-man image to the public.'[49] Other press coverage merges Reed's notorious public image/star persona with his roles, thus accentuating the conflation of his public and private personae: 'Oliver's Twist: All hell breaks loose when Mr. Reed plays a priest' (*Sunday Mirror*, 13 September 1970) employs playful tongue-in-cheek references to his role as Bill Sikes in *Oliver!* and his performance as Grandier in *The Devils*. This example demonstrates how established the, albeit reductionist, notion of 'Ollie the Hellraiser' was by then. Moreover, it indicates that marketing strategies had set out to integrate the simplistic press/tabloid rhetoric into their promotional endeavour to further heighten Reed's star image by adjusting it to the era's change in tides, namely late 1960s excess and an increasingly tense socio-political climate.

To complicate the matter, Reed facilitated this clichéd construction of his out-of-control public persona as he was very aware of his rebel image, thereby consciously cultivating and contributing to his own mythification. This Byronic-turned-baroque/hellraiser myth is likewise constructed, embellished and maintained in biographical accounts (particularly by Robert Sellers, 2008 and 2013) as well as partly in Reed's own memoir.[50] This behaviour may be said to echo the excess-ridden (countercultural) late 1960s zeitgeist, which was particularly associated with rock musicians. Therefore, Reed's friendship with Who drummer Keith Moon and his frequent mingling with musicians further intensified his hedonistically unbridled and indulgent public image as an actor who behaves like a rock star.[51] In this regard, the widely acknowledged problem of separating a discussion of Lord Byron's artistic output from his scandalous public persona and the enduring emphasis upon Byron's corporeality may shed further light on the conflation of Reed's various screen personae and his public image as hellraising ladies' man. Byron scholar Ghislaine McDayter examines the poet's seminal role in establishing modern celebrity and his popularity among a female audience/readership in *Byromania and the Birth of Celebrity Culture*.[52] In an earlier essay she assesses a heightened (and objectifying) interest in Byron's corporeality that by far exceeds that in his work as an artist.[53] Moreover, it seems almost impossible to analyse his poetry while completely ignoring the corporeal aspect as his choice of poetic imagery tends to be quite physical in itself.[54] Ultimately, Byron's body is turned into a projection screen for the reader's emotions.[55] In the Reedian 'Byronic' performances, this symbolic function of the Byronic then may be said to further fuse with classical Hollywood's sublimation of the star system as projection screen for the audience's desires and anxieties.

Conclusion

As this discussion has demonstrated, Oliver Reed may be regarded as a 1960s zeitgeist icon whose star image, roles and screen performances resonate with the sociocultural transformation and irreverent mindset of the decade and the notion of the less demure British 'anti-star'. Reed's foregrounded physicality that becomes a recurrent key performative element of his acting style and its associated notion of virile masculinity further correspond to 1960s British cinema's specific focus upon the (exposed) male body, a candid, rebellious attitude and a vigorous, youthful spirit. As has been indicated, Reed sublimates these characteristics, thus surpassing his contemporaries Albert Finney, Richard Harris, Richard Burton – and even Sean Connery – in terms of animal magnetism, raw power and Byronic moodiness.

Furthermore, the examination of Reedian screen performances has shown that his repeated portrayal of (Byronic) alienated, unstable (young) men was decidedly nuanced and that his range was much more varied than his (reductionist) star image would suggest. The recurrent collaboration with directors such as Michael Winner and Ken Russell significantly helped Reed to enhance his role repertoire and performance style. In this regard, it is important to note that the actor's performative trademark characteristics (intense Byronic gaze and physical presence) could be adjusted to different types of films – adventure, drama, romance, horror, thriller, musical, comedy and contemporary or period settings – and role demands. The further evolution of his acting style throughout the 1960s into the early to mid-1970s then was influenced by the repertoire of roles and the directors he worked with. The development of his star image from Byronic heart throb to hellraiser and the evolution of film styles – Reed's penchant for tongue-in-cheek irreverence and camp that culminates in *Tommy* (1975) – was shared by 1970s British cinema.

Reed's performance of masculinity manages to interrogate, and thus destabilise, notions of hegemonic masculinity (as he is presented bursting into tears more than once on screen and more often than his contemporaries), despite its increasing (hyper)masculinity and foregrounded physicality. Yet a distinction needs to be made between different periods in his career. In the early 1960s Reed combines masculine and feminine traits in his performances (his werewolf Leon is vulnerable and emotional) as well as in his still slightly boyish physiognomy at the time. In *The System*, he plays a passive, alienated young man who ultimately has to acknowledge that he cannot maintain a front of feigned predatory, macho masculinity that does not reflect his actual own disposition. Post-1966 Reed, in turn, displays less soft attributes, which coincides with his increasing (hyper)virility. As a result, he performs a version of hypermasculinity that is, however, as conflicted and contradictory as his earlier performances of his male characters' personal (existential) crises. By this means, (heteronormative) hypermasculinity and its macho connotations are likewise exposed as fragile cultural constructions.

Notes

1. Pam Cook and Claire Hines, '"Sean Connery is James Bond": re-fashioning British masculinity in the 1960s', in Rachel Moseley (ed.), *Fashioning Film Stars: Dress, Culture, Identity* (London: BFI, 2005), p. 149.
2. Martin Shingler, *Star Studies: A Critical Guide* (Basingstoke: Palgrave Macmillan/BFI, 2012), p. 151.
3. Shingler cites John Gaffney and Diana Holmes (eds), *Stardom in Postwar France* (New York/London: Berghahn, 2007), p. 1.
4. The Oxford Dictionary definition of a Byronic hero is '(of a man) alluringly dark, mysterious and moody'.
5. Cliff Goodwin, *Evil Spirits: The Life of Oliver Reed* (London: Virgin Books, 2001), p. 60.
6. Ibid. p. 60.
7. Ibid. pp. 64, 60.
8. Oliver Reed, *Reed All About Me* (London: W. H. Allen, 1979), p. 87.
9. Julian Upton, *Fallen Stars: Tragic Lives and Lost Careers* (Manchester: Headpress, 2004), p. 26.
10. Ibid. p. 24.
11. Stephen Glynn, *The British Pop Music Film: The Beatles and Beyond* (Basingstoke: Palgrave Macmillan, 2013), p. 39.
12. Andrew Spicer, *Typical Men: The Representation of Masculinity in Popular British Cinema* (London/New York: I. B. Tauris, 2003), p. 155.
13. Ibid. p. 149.
14. Goodwin, *Evil Spirits*, p. 86.
15. Ibid. p. 86.
16. *Biography II*. Promotional biography for *Captain Clegg* (1962), p. 16 (BFI press cuttings, no detailed source information given).
17. Spicer, *Typical Men*, pp. 72–4.
18. Ibid. p. 145.
19. Peter William Evans, 'James Mason: the man between', in Bruce Babington (ed.), *British Stars and Stardom: From Alma Taylor to Sean Connery* (Manchester: Manchester University Press, 2001), p. 116.
20. Roberta E. Pearson, 'A star performs: Mr March, Mr Mason and Mr Maine', in Alan Lovell and Peter Krämer (eds), *Screen Acting* (London: Routledge, 1999), pp. 59–74.
21. Geoffrey Macnab, *Searching for Stars: Stardom and Screen Acting in British Cinema* (London/New York: Cassell, 2000), p. 204.
22. See Jack Fisher, 'Three masterpieces of sexuality: *Women in Love*, *The Music Lovers*, and *The Devils*', in Thomas R. Atkins (ed.), *Ken Russell* (New York: Monarch Press, 1976), p. 42, and Barry Keith Grant, 'The body politic: Ken Russell in

the 1980s', in Kevin M. Flanagan (ed.), *Ken Russell: Re-Viewing England's Last Mannerist* (Lanham, MD: Scarecrow Press, 2009), pp. 24–39.
23. Spicer, *Typical Men*, p. 155.
24. Ibid. p. 156.
25. Ibid. p. 156.
26. Jon Towlson, *Subversive Horror Cinema: Countercultural Messages of Films from Frankenstein to the Present* (Jefferson, NC: McFarland & Company), 2014, p. 81.
27. Spicer, *Typical Men*, p. 156.
28. Ibid. p. 156.
29. See Arthur Marwick, *The Sixties* (Oxford: Oxford University Press, 1998); Trevor Harris and Monia O'Brien Castro, *Preserving the Sixties: Britain and the 'Decade of Protest'* (Basingstoke: Palgrave Macmillan, 2014).
30. Sue Harper, *Women in British Cinema: Mad, Bad and Dangerous to Know* (London/New York: Continuum, 2000), p. 102.
31. Peter Hutchings, *Terence Fisher* (Manchester: Manchester University Press, 2001), p. 117.
32. Sue Harper and Justin Smith, 'Social space', in Sue Harper and Justin Smith (eds), *British Film Culture in the 1970s: The Boundaries of Pleasure* (Edinburgh: Edinburgh University Press, 2012), p. 187.
33. Spicer, *Typical Men*, p. 157.
34. James Naremore, *Acting in the Cinema* (Berkeley/LA: University of California Press, 1988), p. 49.
35. Ibid. p. 49.
36. Michael Winner, *Winner Takes All: A Life of Sorts* (London: Portico Books, 2005), p. 98.
37. Susan White, 'Marlon Brando: actor, liar, star', in Ruth Barton Palmer (ed.), *Larger than Life: Movie Stars of the 1950s* (New Brunswick: Rutgers University Press, 2010), p. 172.
38. Shingler, *Star Studies*, p. 41.
39. Philip Drake, 'Jim Carrey: the cultural politics of dumbing down', in Andrew Willis (ed.), *Film Stars: Hollywood and Beyond* (Manchester: Manchester University Press, 2004), p. 87.
40. Ibid. p. 87. He refers to this as 'idiolect'.
41. Ibid. p. 93.
42. Ibid. p. 93.
43. Paul McDonald, 'Story and show: the basic contradiction of film star acting', in Aaron Taylor (ed.), *Theorizing Film Acting* (New York: Routledge, 2012), p. 172.
44. Justine Ashby, 'The Angry Young Man is tired: Albert Finney and 1960s British cinema', in Bruce Babington (ed.), *British Stars and Stardom: From Alma Taylor to Sean Connery* (Manchester: Manchester University Press, 2001), p. 180; Christine Geraghty, 'Albert Finney – a working class hero', in Pat Kirkham and Janet Thumim (eds), *Me Jane: Masculinity, Movies and Women* (London: Lawrence and Wishart, 1995), p. 65.
45. The film draws upon the historical account of an ecclesiastical mass hysteria and resulting witch hunt in seventeenth-century France and is loosely based upon

Aldous Huxley's *The Devils of Loudun* (1952) and John Whiting's eponymous play (1961) whilst incorporating several late 1960s references (the Manson family, John Lennon).
46. Throughout the entire film, the male gaze is constantly inverted as – dressed and undressed – Grandier is turned into a fetishised object of female desire, thus echoing Sister Ruth's (Kathleen Byron) obsessive adoration of Mr Dean (David Farrar) in Powell and Pressburger's *Black Narcissus* (1947) that likewise emanates from a secluded convent's enclosed microcosm.
47. See Robert Sellers, *What Fresh Lunacy is This? The Authorised Biography of Oliver Reed* (London: Constable, 2013).
48. Upton, *Fallen Stars*, p. 28. However, it should be stressed that Reed's pre-1980s star image had not yet turned into a cartoonish caricature.
49. *BFI Information Department*, 27 February 1974.
50. Robert Sellers, *Hellraisers: The Life and Inebriated Times of Richard Burton, Peter O'Toole, Richard Harris & Oliver Reed* (London: Cornerstone, 2008); Sellers, *What Fresh Lunacy is This?*; Reed, *Reed All About Me*.
51. This was also facilitated by the fact that ties between music and film industry had become even closer by then, with 1960s singers such as Mick Jagger, Paul Jones and Roger Daltrey starring in films and actors such as Reed, Richard Harris and David Hemmings recording songs. In Reed's case this was 'The Wild One' and 'Lonely for a Girl' (1961), 'Sometimes' and 'Ecstasy' (1962) or 'Baby It's Cold Outside' (a cheeky duet with Joyce Blair) and 'Wild Thing' (1992).
52. Ghislaine McDayter, *Byromania and the Birth of Celebrity Culture* (New York: SUNY Press, 2010).
53. Ghislaine McDayter, 'Byron and twentieth-century popular culture', in Janet Stabler (ed.), *Palgrave Advances in Byron Studies* (Basingstoke: Palgrave Macmillan, 2007), pp. 130–1.
54. Ibid. pp. 130–1.
55. Ibid. pp. 130–1.

3. CAROL WHITE: THE BARDOT OF BATTERSEA

Margherita Sprio

Although her career spanned the 1940s through to the 1980s, Carol White is best remembered for her television and film roles of the 1960s. Hailed at the time as 'the Battersea Bardot' in the British press, White's nickname not only suggested an analogy to the continental sex symbol but also gestured towards the actress's working-class London provenance. These two elements of her star persona sat in uneasy alliance but also exemplified some of the recurrent concerns of 1960s British culture, which in turn made her a very meaningful star of the era.

Born in 1943 and named after film star Carole Lombard (but dropping the 'e'), Carol White came from an aspirational working-class background. Her father, a scrap metal dealer and former boxer, enrolled her at the Corona Stage Academy near to their West London home, and exercised a controlling influence over White's life.[1] She played many minor uncredited roles as a child in a range of successful British films. These include *Kind Hearts and Coronets* (1949), *The Belles of St Tinian's* (1954), *Doctor in the House* (1954), *Moby Dick* (1956) and *The Thirty-Nine Steps* (1959), before the supporting role of Sheila Dale in *Carry on Teacher* (1959) gained White her first public recognition. The following year, she played the lead in the B-movie *Linda* (1960), now a lost film, and was also cast as the girlfriend of Peter Sellers's ruthless gangster in *Never Let Go* (1960). Continuing to build a profile for her work across British television and film in the early 1960s, White was nonetheless back in the territory of uncredited bit parts when she appeared briefly in the Beatles' first film *A Hard Day's Night* (1964).

But it was a series of roles between 1965 and 1967 that saw Carol White catapulted into stardom. This began with the part of Sylvie in *Up the Junction* (1965), one of a trio of young working-class women whose lives were explored in the iconic *Wednesday Play*. This was followed by the central role of the eponymous protagonist in another BBC single drama, *Cathy Come Home* (1966), before a transition to the big screen (albeit with a higher profile than before) as Joy in *Poor Cow* (1967). All three productions were directed by Ken Loach, perhaps the most notable and enduring member of a cohort of writers and filmmakers who had emerged in the 1960s and were dedicated to presenting working-class narratives on screen.

White's performances in these works eloquently presented a new young female working-class voice, often literally enunciated through voice-over narration or interview responses. However, the actress's own voice is rarely heard outside of her performances and although there are some visual records of White doing publicity for various films, her (now out-of-print) autobiography is the only first person account of her life.[2] Written in 1981, ten years before her early death (partly due to drug and alcohol abuse), it chronicles her life as she wished it to be understood. White's voice is that of a woman who could not quite believe her luck in gaining the recognition that her starring roles had granted her, but the lasting legacy of difficulties that she experienced throughout her childhood provides a darker undertow. Many of the colloquialisms she uses are no longer in common use, and help to convey the working-class origins and sensibility of this British film star at a particular moment in post-war history.

White's autobiography also illuminates a period of social mobility, as the career she pursued and the success she experienced was testament to the possibilities open to those born into poverty. White was also part of a larger group of actresses (for example Glenda Jackson) and actors (of which there were many more, including Michael Caine, Terence Stamp, Peter O'Toole and Tom Courtney) who were able to escape the lives that might otherwise have been predetermined for them. However, as will be explored here, White's success proved to be a very British phenomenon that did not translate easily into an American context, and the personal and professional difficulties that she experienced owed much to this culture clash.

Star Studies has highlighted the cultural significance of stardom as a social phenomenon.[3] Although its original primary focus has been Hollywood, more recent work has explored other nationally specific star systems, including in British cinema.[4] Star Studies has also engaged with questions of gender and longevity in the creation and retention of star personae.[5] But Carol White has not been featured or discussed extensively in any of this work. As feminist historian Carolyn Steedman argues, once a story is told it ceases to be a story: it becomes a piece of history, an interpretive device.⁶ It is my intention in this chapter to make sense of White's sixties stardom and to register her significant role in British cinema history, bringing her own voice and experiences back into play.

The Emergence of a New Star

Although she had already been acting for nearly a decade, Carol White experienced 'overnight stardom' after her appearance in the BBC television play *Up the Junction*, first broadcast on 3 November 1965. Adapted by Nell Dunn from her own short story collection, *Up the Junction*'s frank realism and controversial subject matter – including the depiction of an abortion at the time when this was still illegal in Britain – made a major impact. White's spirited performance as Sylvie helped to make her the only serious candidate for Ken Loach's next project, according to producer Tony Garnett.⁷ Consequently, in the following year she was cast in the leading role in *Cathy Come Home*, also made for the *Wednesday Play* drama strand. Written by Nell Dunn's husband Jeremy Sandford, it was broadcast on 16 November 1966 to an audience of 12 million viewers. The impact of the drama, which follows the downward spiral in the life of a young woman and her children, culminating in them becoming homeless, was substantial and contributed to the founding of the homeless charity Crisis the following year.⁸

Following the success of the two television dramas, Loach cast White once again as the central protagonist in his first feature film, *Poor Cow*, that he adapted with Nell Dunn from her novel. The lyrics of the film's opening song, *Be Not Too Hard*, composed by poet Christopher Logue and sung by Donovan, have a particularly haunting quality that make them synonymous with 1960s Britain. Budgeted at £210,000, *Poor Cow* went on to make £1,400,000, and unusually for a British film, it was successful across most of Europe including in Italy.⁹ It speaks to a specific moment in Britain's cultural history that saw shifting attitudes towards women and issues of sexuality in particular. Until this point working-class women tended to be secondary figures in British film, with some notable exceptions like *A Taste of Honey* (1961). By contrast, *Poor Cow* places its heroine at its centre; she is the object of the title's colloquial assertion. Much is made of her name and she is also referred to as Blossom, Sunshine and Blondie as well as Joy by the different men in her life. Although there is a semblance of British irony in this particular choice of name, the character was actually based on a real woman called Joy who Nell Dunn knew. They had met when the writer moved to Battersea in South London in 1959, a dropout from her upper-class milieu drawn to the greater vivacity and authenticity she felt was present in working-class communities. The original novel and subsequent film are based on both Joy's and Nell Dunn's lived experiences.¹⁰

Figure 3.1 Crafting a working-class star persona: Carol White as Joy in *Poor Cow* (1967).

Although Dunn did not come from the working-class community of women that she wrote about, those she portrayed were more than happy to hear about her version of their lives.[11] Having published short stories and a book of interviews, *Talking with Women*, *Poor Cow* was Dunn's first novel. But it continued what the novelist Ali Smith has described as a life project of dialogue in action and became a bestseller that spoke to an era of change in Britain, giving visibility to an alternative version of London and its inhabitants than that associated with the 'Swinging Sixties'.[12] In both *Up the Junction* and *Poor Cow*, Dunn wrote about the matriarchal community that she encountered in the new life that she forged with her working-class friend Joy in the early 1960s.[13] Dunn felt that working-class women were much more able to live the lives that they wanted, unhampered by the middle-class reserve that she had grown up with. As she writes:

> the lawlessness of the women I met was new, invigorating and liberating. There was plenty of work, so if they lost their job in one factory through cheek or pilfering they could get a job in another the next day. It was the same with boyfriends. Women ruled the roost in those days. Sometimes a man had to change his name to the woman's to fit in with the family. Abortion was illegal, but names were passed around and many young women ended up in the local hospital with perforated wombs.[14]

The year *Poor Cow* was released proved a landmark moment in terms of British laws passed and conventions overturned that helped to forge real changes in the lives of both men and women. The year 1967 saw the passing of the Abortion Act, which legalised abortion by registered practitioners, enabling abortions through the National Health Service. In the same year, all women became entitled to the contraceptive pill, extending its availability beyond married women (as it had been since 1961), while the Sexual Offences Act decriminalised homosexual acts in private between two men aged twenty-one or over. Finally, the Matrimonial Homes Act of 1967 was the Act passed to revert the decision by the House of Lords in 1965 and meant that a 'deserted wife' now had the right to stay in the family home. The following year, the 1965 Race Relations Act was extended to include all wider forms of discrimination. Women's role in the world, therefore, was changing and British society was slowly, and often painfully, adapting to these changes.

The difficulties experienced by women during this societal shift are crucial to understanding the strain that someone like Carol White experienced as a young mother and as a working-class actress. Women were gaining recognition via different ways of being in the world and White's formation as an actress was happening both alongside and within these changes. Another example of a woman embroiled in both success and scandal was the singer Sandie Shaw, whose song 'Puppet on a String' was the official Number One selling pop song in the April 1967 UK Music Charts, having previously triumphed at the Eurovision Song Contest in Vienna. But Shaw's success was almost prevented from happening because the BBC had originally wanted to replace her due to her involvement in a high-profile divorce case where she was named as 'the other woman', concerned that her reputation would ruin the UK's chances of winning the competition. Such moral strictures are now hard to imagine, particularly during a decade with a reputation for permissiveness, but they are an important reminder of the social climate in which Carol White and the characters she played have to be understood.

Poor Cow was therefore a film that emerged in a particular political context and, following Dunn's lead, radically put female pleasure at the centre of the narrative. With a loose and episodic plotline, it focuses on Joy, a woman in her early twenties, married to a petty thief and with a baby son, Johnny.[15] In the opening scene, we see Joy giving birth and the film is an early example of how the use of colour extended the range of representational codes already associated with realism.[16] For reviewer Margaret Hinxman there was far too much 'realism' here:

> the birth is an actual one in glorious Eastman Colour. Like all births, except those with which you're personally concerned, it's a messy sight. It isn't dramatic, or informative, or vital to the story and no woman I know, whether she's had children of her own or not, particularly wants to watch the process.[17]

Straight after this sequence we see Joy walking home alone with her baby, as her husband does not come to see her or to pick her up. Joy's unyielding independence thus shapes the narrative right from the start: we enter a journey of her life whereby we come to realise, as she does, that she cannot rely on any of the men that she meets. Throughout the film, we witness the different relationships that she forges with various men that she encounters, and its first-person narration enables Joy to share her journey with the viewers, recording a young woman who enjoys sex and whose candid quest for pleasure drives the narrative in a manner that is still highly unusual and was ground-breaking in the 1960s. *Poor Cow* coincided with the emergence of second wave of feminism and its interconnected sexual revolution that put women and their sexuality at its core is very much reflected in the way that Joy's character develops.

Joy's only family relative is Aunty Emm (Queenie Watts), who we meet as she performs the ritual of feminine dress-up; having washed her body with soap and water, and put on her girdle, she asks Joy to do up the zip on the back of her dress, before looking at herself in the mirror whilst combing her hair and attempting to glue on her false eyelashes. We learn that Aunty Emm sometimes works as a sex worker and that she is going through 'the change'. She confides in Joy that she had had sex with her landlord to make up for the fact that she was two weeks behind in her rent payments. Joy reacts in mock disbelief and then the two women go on to swap stories about the neighbour downstairs who has given Joy's son Johnny sweets whilst at the same time pestering Aunty Emm for sex.

Both women have to survive in a world without dependable men; in Joy's case both her husband and then her new boyfriend Dave (Terence Stamp) are in prison, and she has a young child to support. Aunty Emm tells Joy, 'I don't think men are capable of feeling pain. They make women feel we need them, but we don't.' The older woman goes out to enjoy herself but the younger one is at home alone with her small child. Accompanied by the soundtrack of the pop song 'Daydream' by the Lovin' Spoonful, the drudgery and hard work involved in washing clothes by hand acts as a metaphor for the isolation for the single mother and wife, and yet Joy is rarely seen feeling sorry for herself. This scene also serves well in highlighting what Roberto del Valle Alcala has observed as a central ambivalence in Joy's attitude towards security.[18] She maintains her rebelliousness towards the social constraints placed upon her, while the wide-angle cinematography of the housing estates where she lives shows the colourful washing and children playing noisily. For Sarah Street, the film's 'chromatic sensibility contributed greatly to its verisimilitude, communicating a sensuous experience of the look and feel of the mid-1960s'.[19]

When Joy and Dave first start to see each other, he tells her that it will be up to her to make the first move sexually, 'otherwise we will be here all night'; a challenge she rises to happily. Joy takes pleasure in her body and gains strength from her fleeting power over men.[20] As this scene of seduction is played out, black and white photos of Fulham football players pinned to Dave's bedroom wall overlook them. Men overlook her, but Joy enjoys taking her pleasure where she can. Her playfulness and ability to never take the men in her life too seriously is a key aspect of how she copes as a single parent managing to get by from day to day. But White's own life as a working woman with two young sons suggested less resilience. Of her experiences as a rising star during this era, she noted:

> for all the acclaim and all of the appreciation, there is a price that has to be paid. That price is demanded by the men who mould your personality from the movie screen, and often precipitate the mental problems, which result from living a double reality. This knowledge took a long time coming and only crystallized during the crisis of my second nervous breakdown [. . .] The confusion seemed to be an inherent part of success.[21]

With hindsight, it is striking how much of *Poor Cow* resembles the actual lived experience of its star. Much like Joy the protagonist in the film, White identifies as being content when she is in a relationship with a man and this seems to be especially the case when this man is abusive (whether verbally or physically and often both) as we see in Joy's relationship with her husband. The educational possibilities that were opening up for working-class girls were still nonetheless difficult for young women such as Joy, and *Poor Cow* is a reflection of this. In her autobiography, Carol White continually talks about the two different aspects of her personality: the actress versus the wife/mother; the poor versus the 'toffee nosed'.[22]

In *Poor Cow*, Joy's attempts at being a 'good mother' are filtered through her desire to maintain a normative household for her young son, Johnny, even when this means that she decides to return to her abusive husband. Her limited ability to earn her own living is pitched against the potential earnings that the men in her life can bring her – even if these earning are from illegal means. White's characterisations in all three of her collaboration with Ken Loach serve to highlight the emotional lives of working-class women of this era. White does this against the backdrop of what Steedman, when referring to the ways in which a writer such as Richard Hoggart has discussed working class lives, has called 'the passivity of emotional life in working-class communities', where 'the streets are all the same; nothing changes'.[23]

Poor Cow gave agency to a working-class woman's life, as the upper-class Dunn had understood it, which was re-fashioned by Loach and his particular brand of improvisation. During the course of the filming, he would give both Stamp and White different information so that once the camera was filming much of the 'acting' was completely spontaneous, as he had given them both very different directions.[24] Joy's first person narration in the film echoes the same device in Dunn's original novel, and in both cases it provides a subtle and unobtrusive parody of female romantic expectations.[25] The radicalism of Joy's character remains today and the film is refreshingly free of moral judgement: here is a complicated woman doing what she wants to do and with whom she wants. It is important to note here that 'liberated autonomous femininity was very different from the ideal of even a few years before, when marriage and domestic contentment were generally presented as the dominant goals for young women'.[26]

Difficulties in Sustaining a Career

Aged twenty-three, Carol White was now, in her words, 'a star, but not in the traditional mould'.[27] Her career had reached new heights – 'Every director in every film said it was great to get a sexy young actress who was able to act, but it took *Up the Junction*, *Cathy Come Home* and *Poor Cow* before I was taken as seriously as I thought I deserved' – but her inner life was in turmoil.[28] The conflicting ways in which White was treated and her resentment at how the men in her life made demands on her body and its image paved the way for a difficult emotional time. Her sexualisation in the media was often characterised through the fashions of the era, via short dresses and her signature dyed long blonde hair.

Curiously, some of the press coverage that she received compared her with Julie Christie, although not always in flattering terms. For Penelope Mortimer, White's fleeting resemblance at times to Julie Christie may be her misfortune, whilst in her review of *Poor Cow*, Penelope Houston claims that White looks like Julie Christie and sounds like Clapham Common.[29] Reflecting back on this time in her life, White wrote about how she was 'hailed as the new Julie Christie, but if one bothers to look back to 1962, there was a time when Julie was called the new Carol White'.[30] As Pamela Church Gibson has argued, Christie had an impeccable middle-class background, which the media dissected straightaway, and it is possible to deduce some class snobbery in the way that some film critics wrote about White.[31]

Significantly, Biba, the fashion brand synonymous with the 1960s, provided White's entire wardrobe for her next role in *I'll Never Forget What's'Isname* (1967). In a change to the roles she had become known for, here she plays Georgina Elben, a stylish editorial secretary for a literary magazine who is sexually inexperienced and has to deal with the attentions of a man (Oliver Reed) who already has both a wife (Wendy Craig) and a mistress (Marianne Faithfull). The film's focus is on an advertising executive, Andrew Quint, who grows tired of his working life and tries to escape. The film stars an array of well-known faces (including Orson Welles as the boss of the advertising agency) that crystallised the era, so the casting of White was in keeping with her being one of the faces of the moment.

Figure 3.2 Modifying the persona: White dressed in Biba on a Cambridge punt in *I'll Never Forget What's'isname* (1967).

Although White received some praise for her role, overall the critical reception was uneven. Towards the end of the film, White's character Georgina dies in a car crash having only just openly acknowledged that she knew she was having a relationship with a married man. The actual ending of the film sees the married man, Andrew, returning to his wife and they drive off together to the closing shot of the film. Penelope Gilliatt found the premise of the film to be repetitive and she felt that she had seen a similar picture under different names many times before, every few months. For Gilliatt, White plays another doomed girl whose life is ruined by the central protagonist and sums up the film well when she states that the rotters get their just deserts, and girls suffer no end.[32] The film superficially addressed the way that 'the decade ushered in an affluent society in which traditional attitudes toward gender and sexuality, the feminine body, courtship, the family, maternity, and social class appeared to be crumbling in the wake of the permissive society'.[33]

In the following year, White stared in *The Fixer* (John Frankenheimer, 1968), an MGM film, adapted from the novel of the same name and set in Russia in 1911. This time she is cast as a Jewish peasant, Raisi Bok, a role unlike any other that White had played. Raisi's estranged husband Yakov (Alan Bates) is accused of a rape and then the murder of a child – both of which crimes he is innocent of.[34] White appears with long dark hair and speaks with a Russian accent and she does not appear until eighty-seven minutes into the film when her jailed husband first recalls her in a flashback sequence during their early encounter as they happily dance together wearing traditional peasant clothes. This then cuts to her visiting him in jail as an older woman who comes to ask if he would name himself as the father of the son she has given birth to since their estrangement. She explains that the birth father has left her, and Yakov agrees to be the child's legal father and writes a note for her to take away with her to this effect. Whilst her previous films reflected the 'fundamental effect on society and the environment' wrought by contemporary social changes, *The Fixer*'s literary adaptation gave White her first major role in a period drama.[35]

White's development of a transatlantic career and move to Hollywood marked an exciting time in her professional development, but it proved to be a difficult time for her in her personal life. She relocated to Los Angeles with her two young sons, hoping that the success that she had earned in Britain would translate to America. But her earlier dependency on prescription drugs and alcohol resurfaced, and in Tony Garnett's view, she had followed the false, seductive promise of stardom and 'no longer had Ken's gentle guidance or my caring to protect her'.[36] Writing about this period in her life and the lives of the working-class male stars of this time (including John Lennon and Brian Jones), White noted how

> each in his *own* way was a hero of the sixties, but so, too, were they all its casualties. They shared an element of self-destruction and it is only now that I can see how this trait was a major ingredient in our mutual attraction.[37]

Julian Upton has argued that 'for all the raw investment in her best works, White was never one to turn down the glitzy Cinderella treatment' and arguably 'from the perspective of her career things did start to go wrong in Hollywood almost immediately'.[38]

White was asked by Ken Russell to play opposite Glenda Jackson in *Women in Love* (1969), in which her previous co-star Oliver Reed had already agreed to appear. However, she turned this down as she had been offered a highly lucrative Hollywood three-film contract, initially to star in *Daddy's Gone A Hunting* (1969), something she regarded as the biggest mistake of her whole life.[39] As White wrote: 'After receiving so many awards and so much acclaim for *Poor Cow*, I imagined that success would simply follow success in an endless chain, a fool's paradise that I took with me to San Francisco.'[40] In Mark Robson's thriller she was cast as Cathy Palmer, a young British woman who goes to live in California where she becomes pregnant by her fiancé Kenneth

(Scott Hylands) but decides to have an abortion after she experiences an abusive side to his personality. She goes on to marry another man, Jack (Paul Burke), and gives birth to their daughter, which further disturbs Kenneth who demands that she murder this child as an act of vengeance for the child that she aborted. The film bravely addressed the contested issue of abortion at a time when it was still illegal in many American states (although already legal in California by 1967, it only became fully legal in America in 1973). Contemporary societal anxieties and issues of mental health are embedded in the film's narrative in a way that can make for difficult viewing, as can the way that Cathy is both physically and emotionally abused by the embittered Kenneth. But for Julian Upton 'this was a formula thriller that did not perform to expectations' and although White's performance is impressive the film's lack of critical success negatively marked her career at a time when she needed to win over an American audience.[41] As far as White was concerned, 'the film received little attention and mediocre returns'.[42]

She was also critical of her treatment by a hypocritical industry: 'I was in everyone's bad books because of my affair with Paul Burke because by Hollywood standards he was a happily married man. Talk about double standards.'[43] White claims that it was during her four-year long relationship with the actor that she 'learnt about the seamy side of stardom; the drugs, the booze, the lethal mind-twisting games'.[44] It is possible to understand from this assertion that the seeds of what was to be a ruinous personal life and work experience in America were sown at this point and through this particular relationship.

White made a small succession of films throughout the 1970s, none of which were received with anything like the critical acclaim of her earlier works. These included the drama *Dulcima* (1971), where she played the central protagonist, a young housekeeper who has a relationship with the unhappy older owner (John Mills) of the farm where she is working. In *Made* (1972) she once again plays a young single mother, Valerie Marshall, who has a relationship with a depressed rock star (played by the folk singer Roy Harper) while also having to deal with taking care of a sick mother and the advances of a young priest. The film's conclusion has her deciding to live independently from these men and this role has echoes of the characters she had played in her better known earlier roles. In both *Some Call It Loving* (1973) – where she plays a young widow, Scarlett, in what might best be described as an erotic drama – and the underrated gangster thriller, *The Squeeze* (1977) – where she plays Jill, a wealthy wife and mother who is abducted – White is under-used and marginalised by the male-dominated narratives. Her final film role was as Margaux Lasselle in *The Nutcracker* (1982), where she plays full frontal nude scenes.

White's film work became increasingly sporadic and her depression escalated during the times when she was not working, as did her dependency on alcohol and drugs (some legally prescribed). Recalling this period, she described 'her slip back into the drug scene' as 'written in the stars [. . .] I wasn't crazy, I was lost'.[45] Later attempts to reinstate herself back in Britain, as with her planned appearance in Nell Dunn's 1981 play *Steaming*, collapsed after she was sacked for being unreliable through lateness and missed performances. White retreated to her home in Florida, where she died ten years later in 1991 aged forty-eight.

Conclusion

Tony Garnett has stated that 'Hollywood was downhill all the way for Carol. It is full of functioning psychopaths and they chew people up and spit them out, particularly young women, they get used and then are easily replaced.'[46] Arguably, it was with Ken Loach, with his skill for evoking powerful naturalism, that Carol White gave her best performances. Given that her life was cut short and that she failed to live up to the promise that was envisaged for her, it could also be argued that her class indelibly shaped her destiny.[47]

Carol White serves to remind us of the possibilities that appeared to be opening up for young actresses whose backgrounds had not traditionally been represented on screen. She also serves as the face of an aspirational working-class femininity that was part of an era that transformed ideas of British identity, both in Britain and internationally. As recent research highlights, those avenues that were once open to White did not continue to grow and it is perhaps even harder now for working-class actresses to enter the profession.[48] For example, the actress Maxine Peake spoke in 2018 about the prejudice she regularly experienced from people in the industry and how she had been under pressure to sound more posh.[49]

Garnett suggests that the very qualities that made White such a skilful actress also helped to end her life: her raw, child-like intuitive approach, her lack of self- consciousness and her ability to be the character as opposed to merely drawing on learnt acting techniques.[50] Her lasting legacy is multi-faceted and an act of imagination into the possibilities that might have been open to White had she not died when she did, prompting reflection on the ageing female star. Aged forty in her final film, *The Nutcracker*, White was cast alongside Joan Collins, another British actress in the midst of a career comeback in the late 1970s and early 1980s.[51] Collins was ten years older than White and we see two British film actresses in their fourth and fifth decade who unusually are cast as the middle-aged women that they actually were. Underscoring this was the film's more cynical soft porn qualities, also evident in the British films that had helped to reinvigorate Collins's career, including *The Stud* (1978) and its sequel *The Bitch* (1979), before her huge success in the American television soap opera *Dynasty* (1981–9).

White had begun her career at home in Britain and her attempts to reinsert herself back into this landscape whilst completing *The Nutcracker* and working on *Steaming* were not unrelated choices at this stage in her life. Working with Dunn again brought her back to the familiarity of the city where she was born and where her success had begun. During this time White also had her last ever meeting with Ken Loach and Tony Garnett where she asked them to create a new vehicle for her to star in. Reflecting back on the desperation in her eyes, Garnett remembers her disappointment that they could not give her what she wanted. It was to be the last time that either man saw Carol White.[52]

Notes

1. White started going to the school in 1952, two years after it opened. It supplied young actors for the Royal Shakespeare Company as well as rising stars for the 1963 stage musical *Oliver!* and many notable British actors and entertainers studied there as children, including Mark Lester, Susan George, Dennis Waterman, Ray Winstone and Helen Worth.

   Regarding her father, it is very evident from White's autobiography that her foundational relationship with him was highly influential not only on the course of her professional life but also her personal life: 'Since childhood, I have seen the look of love many times, but if there was ever a man who would have laid his life on the line for me, my father was that man [. . .] in his eyes I saw a special feeling that he saved for me; an anxiety and pride, a love that bordered on passion and was to come between my mother and I in later years [. . .] dad was the centre of everything that was important to me.' Carol White (with Clifford Thurlow), *Carol Comes Home* (London: New English Library Books, 1982), p. 65.

   White's personal life was complicated: she was married three times and had a series of affairs with various men with whom she worked. Her first marriage to Michael King (part of the singing group, the King Brothers), who was the father of her two sons, broke up. Her other husbands were Stuart Lemer, her psychiatrist who she married after a three-month relationship, and Michael Arnold a carpenter who she divorced in 1984 due to his violent outbursts.

2. White (with Thurlow), *Carol Comes Home*.
3. For key studies see Richard Dyer, *Stars* (London: British Film Institute, 1979); Richard Dyer, *Heavenly Bodies: Film Stars and Society* (London: BFI, 1985); Christine Gledhill (ed.), *Stardom: Industry of Desire* (London: Routledge, 1991); Jackie Stacey, *Star Gazing: Hollywood Cinema and Female Spectatorship* (London: Routledge, 1993).
4. See Bruce Babington, *British Stars and Stardom* (Manchester: Manchester University Press, 2002); Geoffrey Macnab, *Searching for Stars: Stardom and Acting in British Cinema* (London: Continuum, 2000); Melanie Williams, *Female Stars of British Cinema: The Women In Question* (Edinburgh: Edinburgh University Press, 2017); Melanie Bell-Williams, *Julie Christie* (London: British Film Institute, 2016).

5. See Diane Negra, *Off White Hollywood: American Culture and Ethnic Female Stardom* (London: Routledge, 2001); Ginette Vincendeau, *Brigitte Bardot* (London: British Film Institute, 2013); Lucy Bolton and Julie Lobalzo Wright, *Lasting Screen Stars: Images That Fade and Personas That Endure* (Basingstoke: Palgrave Macmillan, 2016).
6. Carolyn Steedman, *Landscape for a Good Woman* (London: Virago Press, 1986), p. 143.
7. Tony Garnett, *The Day the Music Died: A Life Lived Behind the Lens* (London: Constable Books, 2016), p. 147.
8. As a direct result of the public response to the television play, the charity Crisis for Christmas, as it was originally known, was founded in 1967 by cross party political support through the work of William Shearman and the MP Iain Macleod who was then the Conservative Shadow Chancellor. The play's broadcast also happened to coincide with the creation of the charity Shelter who benefitted from its raising of the public profile of problems with homelessness in modern Britain.
9. Alexander Walker, *Hollywood, England: The British Film Industry in the Sixties* London: Michael Joseph, 1974, p. 377. White would go on to earn nine different awards for her role in *Poor Cow*.
10. Nell Dunn, 'Preface, Memories of Battersea', in *Poor Cow* (London: Virago Classics, 2013), p. xi.
11. Margaret Drabble, 'Introduction', in *Poor Cow* (London: Virago Classics, 2013), p. xiv.
12. Ali Smith, 'Introduction', in *Talking to Women, Nell Dunn* (London: Silver Press, 2018), p. vii.
13. Dunn, 'Memories of Battersea', p. xi.
14. Ibid. p. xi.
15. John Hill, *Ken Loach: The Politics of Film and Television* (London: British Film Institute/Palgrave Macmillan, 2011), p. 105.
16. Ibid. p. 108. See also Sarah Street, 'The colour of social realism', *Journal of British Cinema and Television* 15: 4, 2018, pp. 469–90, p. 484.
17. Margaret Hinxman, 'Poor Cow review', *Sunday Telegraph*, 7 December 1967.
18. Roberto del Valle Alcala, *British Working-Class Fiction: Narratives of Refusal and Struggle* (London: Bloomsbury, 2017), p. 57.
19. Street, 'The colour of social realism', pp. 484–5.
20. Philip Tew, James Riley and Melanie Seddon, 'Surfing the sixties: critical introduction', in *The 1960s: A Decade of Modern British Fiction* (London: Bloomsbury Press, 2018).
21. White, *Carol Comes Home*, p. 23.
22. This is a reoccurring theme for British working-class women and is apparent in Carolyn Steedman's account of her life, *Landscape for a Good Woman*, as indicated by the invocation of goodness in its title. As Raymond Williams argues in his review of Steedman's book, what becomes apparent, as the diverse accounts (of class) come in, is that even the true generalities of class formation and class transition are crossed by specific circumstances of different kinds: both the specifically personal, as in family situation, family size, the characters of parents, siblings and

neighbours, and the specifically social, in types of settlement, forms of local culture, orientations towards work and education. Raymond Williams, 'Desire', *London Review of Books,* 8: 7, 17 April 1986, pp. 8–9.
23. Richard Hoggart, *The Uses of Literacy* (Livingston NJ: Transaction Publishers, 1957).
24. Sam Adams, 'Interview, Terence Stamp, on accents, first takes and playing a transsexual', *AV Film,* 7 October 2013.
25. Drabble, 'Introduction, Poor Cow', p. xviii.
26. Melanie Williams, 'British new waif: Rita Tushingham and sixties female stardom', in Williams, *Female Stars of British Cinema,* p. 89.
27. Ibid. p. 22.
28. Carol White, *Carol Comes Home,* p. 91.
29. Penelope Mortimer, 'Wanted – an attitude, Poor Cow film review', *Observer,* 10 December 1967. Penelope Houston, 'Up the creek, Poor Cow film review', *The Spectator,* 15 December 1967.
30. White, *Carol Comes Home,* p. 161.
31. Pamela Church Gibson, 'The fashioning of Julie Christie and the mythologizing of "Swinging London"', in Eugenia Paulicelli, Drake Stutesman and Louise Wallenberg (eds), *Changing Images of Sixties Britain in Film, Fashion, and the 1960s* (Bloomington: Indiana University Press, 2017), p. 137.
32. Penelope Gilliatt, 'The current cinema – the spectre of the shrinking brainpan, *I'll Never Forget What's'Isname* review', *New Yorker,* 27 April 1968.
33. Marcia Landy, 'Swinging femininity, 1960s transnational style', in Melanie Bell and Melanie Williams (eds), *British Women's Cinema* (London: Routledge, 2010), p. 111.
34. The film is based on the actual events that occurred to Menahem Mendal Beilis who was finally acquitted after an international outcry about the anti-Semitism that underscored the way that he was treated.
35. Robert Murphy, *Sixties British Cinema* (London: BFI Publishing, 1992), p. 139.
36. Garnett, *The Day the Music Died,* p. 190.
37. White, *Carol Comes Home,* p. 24.
38. Julian Upton, 'Carol White – Hollywood and bust', in *Fallen Stars: Tragic Lives and Lost Careers* (London: Headpress, 2004), pp. 9–11.
39. White, *Carol Comes Home,* p. 53.
40. Ibid. p. 200.
41. Upton, 'Carol White – Hollywood and bust', p. 11.
42. White, *Carol Comes Home,* p. 201.
43. Ibid. p. 201.
44. Ibid. p. 198.
45. Ibid. p. 276.
46. Tony Garnett, personal interview, London, 13 July 2018.
47. Tew, Riley and Seddon, 'Surfing the sixties: critical introduction'.
48. See the project Panic! 2018 – It's An Arts Emergency, that produced the paper *Panic! Social Class, Taste and Inequalities in the Creative Industries* with academics from University of Edinburgh and University of Sheffield.

49. Maxine Peake was in conversation with BFI programmer and curator Danny Leigh at the BFI event, 'Working Class Heroes: a day workshop exploring working class screen talent – past, present and future', 14 April 2018.
50. Tony Garnett, personal interview, 13 July 2018.
51. Like White, Collins had left Britain and gone to Hollywood in her early twenties and appeared in various mainstream films there.
52. Tony Garnett, personal interview, 13 July 2018.

4. 'THE OLD WAVE AT WORK': THE TRANSATLANTIC STARDOM OF THE BRITISH CHARACTER ACTRESS IN THE 1960s

Claire Mortimer

While much has been written about the part played by British stars in the resurgent national cinema of the 1960s, the contribution of character actresses has largely been overlooked.[1] Despite lacking the glamour and pin-up potential of younger stars, actresses such as Edith Evans, Wendy Hiller and Margaret Rutherford were to play a key role in the emergence of a British cinema which appealed to an international audience, at a moment when each appeared to be in the twilight of their film careers. These individuals were cast in roles constructed around iterations of Britishness, specifically Englishness, which played well with American studios and audiences, as well as offering familiarity and continuity for British audiences. Their roles evoked discourses concerning nostalgia, class and national identity, often in counterpoint to the pervasive spirit of rebellion, youth, and sexual liberation more commonly associated with the 1960s.

Melanie Williams likens British character actors to 'brilliant miniaturists', whose work may be exiled to the periphery of the narrative but is 'as vital to the alchemy of the film as its major performances'.[2] As Raymond Durgnat observed at the end of the 1960s, post-war British cinema offered a production context wherein 'roles abound' for the character actress, who offered a 'complete contrast to the equal and opposite Hollywood imbalance, all optimism, glamour and little character'.[3] Nevertheless, despite the opportunities and success enjoyed by the British character actress in the first half of the decade, the mid-1960s marked the beginning of the end of a golden age for female character players.[4]

Evans, Rutherford and Hiller typified this late life career flourish; their talents as supporting actresses were sought after to boost the prestige of film projects and were often key to greenlighting the production and the subsequent promotion of the film. Their value was recognised by the 'old wave' and new directors alike, with Hollywood stalwarts also keen to add the experience and status of these *grandes dames* to their productions. American Studios were keen to embrace their appeal to the American urban arthouse audience. They offered substance and reliability in contrast to the rather less predictable talents of Hollywood A-listers and less seasoned younger stars, on account of their experience and status in the theatrical world.

This chapter will focus on the careers of the older British female actresses whose international status was marked by their success at the Academy Awards during the 'long' 1960s. Evans, Hiller and Rutherford all had long cinematic careers, which waxed and waned due to a range of factors, not least of which the opportunities for roles which suited their expertise and status. All three were enthusiastically deployed by American studios in roles which hinged on their status as icons of Englishness.

A survey of the nominations for Best Supporting Actress at the Academy Awards during the 1960s serves as a blunt measure of the ascendancy of the British character actress, with fourteen nominations between 1960 and 1968. This is compared to just three nominations in the 1950s and 1970s respectively. The majority of these nominees were over fifty years old, with Rutherford being seventy-one when she won the category in 1964 for her role as the Duchess of Brighton in *The V.I.P.s* (1963), making her the oldest ever recipient of the award at that time. Evans was nominated twice in her seventies, before being nominated for best actress at the age of eighty for her role in *The Whisperers* (1967). What is striking about these British nominees for Best Supporting Actress was that they were largely distinguished by personae and roles which defied sixties modernity.[5] They were predominantly a roll call of acting talent celebrating age, experience and a career forged in the theatre rather than film; in short, they embodied tradition and the establishment. In addition to Evans, Rutherford and Hiller, other British nominees included Joyce Redman, Gladys Cooper and Hermione Baddeley, all of whom had sustained careers on the stage before coming to film later in their careers. Their collective status as theatrical royalty tended to be foregrounded, or even perversely subverted, in their cinematic roles. With the British character actress being deployed in films made possible by American funding, such articulations of national identity were inevitably nuanced in particular ways. Whereas younger actresses like Julie Christie and Susannah York were firmly associated with youthful vitality and a newly swinging national identity, imperious older actresses gave performances which often spoke of the waning of British imperial power.

WENDY HILLER: A CAMEL IN HOLLYWOOD

Wendy Hiller's film career during the 1960s typifies the importance of the British *grande dame* to both British and Hollywood cinema with the actress winning an Academy Award in 1959 for her role in *Separate Tables* (1958), and being nominated for two others during the following seven years. Born in 1912, Hiller's film career spanned fifty-five years, but with sizeable gaps, with the majority of her films being made after the age of forty. Following her early triumph as Eliza Doolittle in Anthony Asquith's adaptation of *Pygmalion* (1938), Hiller had prioritised her stage career, appearing in just six films in the two decades before her role in *Separate Tables* (1958). While the Academy Award helped to revive her career, being offered 'roles that were "undull"', the very selective Hiller sought to 'make only films that were "rather special and have stature"'.[6] Such roles were more forthcoming with the influx of American funding into British film production in the 1960s, with Hiller being nominated for awards for her roles in *Sons and Lovers* (1960) and *Toys in the Attic* (1963), before going on to receive the Academy Award for Best Supporting Actress in *A Man for all Seasons* (1966). These were all prestigious productions, possessing literary or theatrical kudos, appealing to a middle-class audience and all made possible by the backing of American studios. Hiller's roles tended to foreground the qualities which had distinguished her performance in *Separate Tables*: that of the long-suffering, lonely and tormented mature woman. *Separate Tables* also established the template of the mid-Atlantic films of the next decade, combining American finance with a British narrative and setting, deploying a cast headed by American stars, bolstered by a panoply of British character actors and supporting stars.[7]

Filmed in Hollywood, directed by Delbert Mann and released by United Artists, *Separate Tables* was adapted by Terence Rattigan from his stage play, with a host of middle-class characters thrown together in a Bournemouth hotel. Hiller was cast as a lonely, middle-aged and respectable hotel manager, Miss Cooper, whose romance with an alcoholic writer resident in her hotel, played by Burt Lancaster, is destroyed by the arrival of his glamorous ex-wife, played by Rita Hayworth. Miss Cooper sacrifices her feelings for John and helps reconcile him to his ex-wife, despite their engagement. The inherent differences between Hollywood and British cinema are embodied by the casting of Hiller and Hayworth as rivals for the affections of Burt Lancaster's inebriate writer. Miss Cooper is the stolid English spinster, embodying restraint, self-sacrifice and silent suffering whilst Hayworth plays a glamorous yet fragile model, overtly emotional and passionate, given to histrionic outbursts. The contrast in terms of stardom, glamour and personae was evident as Hiller remarked that 'Rita was so delicately boned she made me feel like a camel!'.[8] This antithesis worked to Hiller's advantage in throwing her performance into relief, being true to the context of a very British story of repression, which had come to define the work of Rattigan. Hiller's performance was characterised by a physical stillness and understated quality, which powerfully evokes Miss Cooper's mental strength and quiet selflessness. It is the sonorous timbre of Hiller's voice which most powerfully hints at the character's emotions, and was testament to her theatrical training and skills, being able to 'give a performance of breath taking reality and expertise', by approaching 'her acting as a craft'.[9]

Separate Tables received a rapturous critical response in America, with Hiller's Academy Award being matched by David Niven winning the award for Best Actor for the role as Major Pollock. The film received a further seven nominations, which included Best Actress (Deborah Kerr) and Best Screenplay (Terence Rattigan). However when it was released in the UK in February 1959, British critics were largely unimpressed. With the Angry Young Man on the verge of stepping from stage to screen with the release of adaptations of *Look Back in Anger* and *Room at the Top* later in the year, Rattigan's work was judged to be out of touch. The original stage play of *Separate Tables* criticised by Kenneth Tynan as an example of 'the peculiar nullity of our drama's prevalent genre, the Loamshire play' distinguished by a 'country house' setting and the 'playwright's vision of the leisured life'.[10]

Yet Hiller's Oscar winning role owed much to Rattigan's skills in writing more substantial and interesting roles for older actresses. His inspiration for the play was the residential hotel for 'elderly gentlefolk' in Kensington, where his mother lived, in common with the other residents 'mostly living alone in polite, slightly reduced circumstances'.[11] Rattigan excelled in his characterisation of ageing spinsters like Miss Cooper, providing opportunities for mature actresses to demonstrate their craft. These characters were an inflection of Rattigan's evocation of his target audience in the form of 'Aunt Edna', 'the universal type of theatre goer':

> a nice, respectable, middle-class, middle-aged, maiden lady, with time on her hands and the money to help her pass it. She enjoys pictures, books, music and the theatre and though to none of these arts . . . does she bring much knowledge or discernment, at least, as she is apt to tell her cronies, she "does know what she likes".[12]

Aunt Edna was to become an unlikely divisive figure at the heart of the battle between the old guard and the new, commandeered by critics as evidence that Rattigan's work was out of touch, and symptomatic of all that was wrong with British theatre. John Osborne noted that 'The English Theatre isn't merely dying, it's being buried alive to the sound of Aunt Edna's knitting needles', whilst in 1960 the Questors Theatre in Ealing advertised a bill of

Absurdist plays as 'Not for Aunt Edna'.[13] Michael Darlow, in his biography of Rattigan, observed that ultimately, 'Like it or not, she was his most famous character and he was stuck with her', this iteration of middle-class spinsterhood was to thrive on the screen with the aid of American sponsorship of the British cinema.[14] Nevertheless, the influential Tynan was less interested in lonely spinsters than in 'plays about cabmen and demi-gods [. . .] warriors, politicians and grocers'. The critical current may have been turning away from stoical and genteel female characters to dynamic, angry, youthful, masculinities, yet the British character actress was to find a place in the new wave of British cinema and the old wave represented by figures such as Rattigan and Asquith.

Margaret Rutherford and the Prestige Film

It was another Rattigan screenplay which helped Margaret Rutherford to win the Oscar for Best Supporting Actress for her role in *The V.I.P.s* (1963), directed by Anthony Asquith. The film followed the narrative template of *Separate Tables*, both being informed by the portmanteau structure of the Hollywood classic *Grand Hotel* (1932). A group of travellers are thrown together, with intersecting story lines as they navigate their way around personal crises, foremost of which is a torrid love triangle. The cast of *The V.I.P.s* was headed by two British-born Hollywood stars – Richard Burton and Elizabeth Taylor – with their off-screen affair guaranteeing global publicity. As with *Separate Tables* it was the older established British actress in a supporting role who stole the film from the A-listers, with *Time* magazine commenting that 'After Rutherford, Burton and Taylor hardly seem worth watching.'[15] Rutherford's participation was judged to be important enough for Rattigan to work with Asquith and producer Anatole de Grunwald to build up her part after she had initially turned it down on the grounds of its being too insubstantial. Asquith had previously worked with Rutherford on five films, their first, *Quiet Wedding* (1941), featuring the same collaborators as *The V.I.P.s*, de Grunwald and Rattigan. Their work together was distinguished by a nostalgic vision of national identity which was fundamental to Rutherford's performance in *The V.I.P.s*.

The film interweaves the stories of a group of VIP travellers who are marooned at a fog-bound London airport. The Duchess of Brighton (Rutherford) is travelling to America to work in a holiday resort to earn the funds to save her ancestral home – a situation which lends itself as an allegory for the state of the nation, and indeed the British film industry. The Duchess has mixed a heady cocktail of drugs and drink to cope with her fear of flying, resulting in a number of comic scenes of confusion. She is completely out of her depth in the world of international travel, having never flown before, calling the air steward a 'conductress' and repeatedly getting lost in the airport. Her innocence, eccentricity and confusion are evident in her outlandish and dated apparel – as was characteristic of Rutherford's persona – her hat falling over her eyes, festooned in a burgeoning fur coat, and using a capacious tartan bag for comic business, pulling out her wartime ration book instead of her passport. This image of antiquated upper-class English eccentricity is accompanied by a quaint musical motif evoking the Elizabethan era, this mark of heritage compounded by her wistfully quoting Shakespeare. The symbolism of the role is writ large in the title sequence wherein the Duchess is selling a ticket for her stately home to an American tourist. The film finishes with her being saved from having to work in Florida when a movie mogul – played by Orson Welles – leases her stately pile for a vast amount of money. The Duchess describes her home as a 'monster of a house', adding 'it's rather ugly now, they kept adding to it in all the wrong periods . . . but the people who live there, love it'. Her words work as a eulogy for the nation, whose fate appeared to be parallel to that of the Duchess's house, refashioned as a film set for international film production, in hock to international money.

Rutherford's persona was the antithesis of Hollywood glamour, as is teasingly implied in a 1972 obituary in the *Daily Mirror*, which describes her as being the 'most successful British blonde ever to assault the American box-office', adding that 'her vital statistics – three chins and mouth like a ship's funnel – enchanted their way around the globe'.[16] Rutherford had been making films since the 1930s, her capacity for scene-stealing always seeming to result in her parts being built up, having starred in notable British comedies during the 1940s and 1950s, including *Blithe Spirit* (1945), *Miranda* (1948), *Passport to Pimlico* (1949) and *The Happiest Days of Your Life* (1950). As she entered the final decade of her career, after her success as Miss Marple in a series of films, the range of roles she was offered became narrower, chiefly being that of an eccentric aristocrat, past her prime, yet clinging onto the remains of their personal empire. These include Lady Vivian in Paramount's *On The Double* (1961), Grand Duchess Gloriana XIII in *The Mouse On The Moon* (1963) and the Duchess of Brighton in *The V.I.P.s*.[17] Increasingly the roles required her to play characters who were confused, whether under the influence of drugs in the case of the Duchess of Brighton, alcohol in *The Mouse on the Moon* or old age in *A Countess From Hong Kong* (Charles Chaplin, 1967). Such roles targeted a transatlantic audience with Rutherford's characters being an inflection of her British persona for an American audience; an affectionate caricature of a decrepit and failing upper class, and by extension, nation. Her persona was the inverse of the youthful stars of swinging London, who were defined by a disdain for the limitations of class and nationhood, dispensing with the certainties of the past, and transgressing established social codes.

Figure 4.1   The quintessential English eccentric: Margaret Rutherford in *The V.I.P.s* (1963).

Asquith was praised for the 'Englishness' of his films, with Peter Cowie proclaiming that 'no one director has done more to reflect the best of England'.[18] Cowie added that Asquith – son of the former British Prime Minister, Herbert Asquith – was responsible for

> [a] canon of films that reflect like a prism the many facets of English life, the humour, the gossip, the odd character, the maliciousness, the love, and above all the unwritten adherence to a code of behaviour and honour that seems to be vanishing today.

Nevertheless Asquith's transatlantic productions of the 1960s reduced 'Englishness' to little more than a token caricature in the margins of the action. The Duchess of Brighton represents an out of touch and impoverished upper class, ridiculous and irrelevant in a world dominated by international money, glamour and business. Her storyline was the least substantial, providing comic relief in comparison to the other narrative strands, which focused on romance, wealth and glamour.

Although *The V.I.P.s* marked a high point in Rutherford's career, it was judged to be a low point for Asquith, one of his 'increasingly banal prestige productions' at the end of his career according to Robert Murphy.[19] Two years later *Variety* magazine hailed 'the era of the co-production', yet warned of 'a revolution to film production which could well lead to the virtual disappearance of "national" film industries'.[20] Asquith typified the ambivalence of British filmmakers to this reliance on the dollar, welcoming the opportunities, whilst warning that mid-Atlantic productions were no substitute for British film in expressing 'our own attitudes and beliefs'.[21] Despite his reservations,

Asquith was to lead the way in directing the critically maligned 'mid-Atlantic', or 'international films', of the 1960s with *The V.I.P.s* and *The Yellow Rolls-Royce* (1965). MGM Britain played a significant part in this era of the transatlantic film, having long had a base in the UK with its Borehamwood studios, with Mark Glancy commenting on the 'conspicuous Anglophilia' of its commitment to 'British' films.[22] It was judged to be the 'most conservative' of the American majors by Robert Murphy, relying on recycling past successes and commissioning films which largely played safe, rather than embracing the cultural zeitgeist of the 1960s.[23] *The V.I.P.s* typified MGM Britain's ethos in the 1960s, with Rutherford having been the star of the studio's Miss Marple films, which had done well on both sides of the Atlantic, the series inscribed with a deeply nostalgic vision of Englishness. *The V.I.P.s* was also a hit at the box office in the States, being one of the ten highest grossing films of 1963. Despite a mixed critical response, the glamour and scandal surrounding Burton and Taylor made it a financial success.

A tension between the old wave and the new was evident in the British press and publicity, as well as the polarised nature of reviewers' responses. The film prompted heated debates about the direction being taken by British cinema, with de Grunwald proudly boasting that the film had 'the feeling of a good, solid, money-making film, yielding nothing to new waves, kitchen sinks, Lancashire slums', in an interview entitled 'The old wave at work'.[24] Rattigan complained that he was 'getting angry with *Sight & Sound* for the notice on *The VIPs* that they haven't yet written – why should "entertainment" nowadays have become such a dirty word?'[25] He set himself up in conflict with the cinematic new wave, declaring 'You see – whisper it not to *Sight & Sound* – I actually ENJOYED *Grand Hotel*, *Dinner At Eight* and many other such products of Hollywood in its prime.'[26] The *News of the World* praised the film for being in the tradition of 'the escapist, glamour-filled movies we used to get from Hollywood'.[27] Nevertheless it was a British character actress in a supporting role who received the greatest plaudits and recognition for her role in the film, despite the reliance on Hollywood glamour.

Edith Evans: Handbags and Gladrags

Whereas Rutherford and Hiller were associated with the 'old wave', with their careers flourishing in roles written by Rattigan, Edith Evans was an example of a *grande dame* whose film career benefited from her roles in films at the forefront of the 'new wave' of British cinema. She received three nominations for Academy Awards between 1964 and 1968, having been long established as one of the most respected stage actresses in British theatre. Described in an obituary in the *New York Times* as 'A Legend of the English Theater', Evans was born in 1888, her acting career starting in 1912; among her many honours she was made a Dame of the British Empire in 1946.[28] Evans's screen debut had been in the silent era, with a hiatus of thirty years before returning to film, in a leading role in Thorold Dickinson's adaptation of *The Queen of Spades* (1949), as the aged countess who sells her soul to the devil. Such a role was typical of her film career over the following decades, as an imperious aristocratic battleaxe, a persona which informed her ownership of the role of Lady Bracknell both on the stage and in Asquith's 1951 film version of *The Importance of Being Earnest*. The film adaptation brought her performance as the imperious dowager to a broader audience, rendering her an iconic incarnation of the English upper class for a generation.

Evans's subsequent role as a working-class matriarch in Tony Richardson's film adaptation of *Look Back in Anger* (1959) was met with surprise but also praise from critics. Evans responded with impatience: 'The way they go on you'd think I can only play ladies of quality. I know more about the Ma Tanners of this world than I do about the so-called gentry.'[29] Despite her persona, Evans was from relatively humble roots, having worked as a milliner before becoming an actress. The role of Ma Tanner placed her at the forefront of the cinematic new wave, with *Look Back In Anger* being very much the antithesis of *Separate Tables*. The film adaptation was praised for its 'tough, vital style which represents something new in British cinema'.[30] It was made with Warner Brothers backing, based on the international reputation of John Osborne's play and the casting of Richard Burton as Jimmy Porter. Ma Tanner was developed as a character as part of the adaption from stage to screen, her scenes helping to broaden the canvas of the narrative, and develop the substance of Jimmy's character, with a more sensitive, vulnerable side. She is the patron of the original Angry Young Man, being a mother-figure to Jimmy, and lending him money for his stall; her most significant scenes being in a graveyard and her hospital bed, before she dies off-screen later in the film. Sixty years later Peter Bradshaw reflected that Evans's performance was one of the redeeming virtues of the adaptation, noting that it 'humanises Jimmy Porter – and humanises Burton's performance as well'.[31]

Evans's status bridged the divide between the new wave and the old, between the cinema of the 'angry young man' and the international film, with its Hollywood budgets, stars, and international audiences. She was finding herself in demand on both sides of the Atlantic being cast as a mother superior in Warner Bros.'s *The Nun's Story* (1959), an international film with a predominantly European cast, led by Audrey Hepburn and directed by Fred Zinnemann. The role marked her arrival in Hollywood, with Evans professing herself bemused by her 'exalted status'.[32] Her subsequent part in *Tom Jones* (1963), a second outing with Tony Richardson, yoked together these two conflicting directions in her film career, transposing the costume drama to the swinging sixties, and leading to Evans's first Academy Award nomination as the interfering spinster aunt Miss Western.

Figure 4.2   The formidable Dame Edith Evans in her Oscar-nominated role in *Tom Jones* (1963).

Despite its ostensibly masculine focus, *Tom Jones* was a showcase for the British character actress, the only film to have earned three nominations for the Academy Award for Best Supporting Actress in the history of the award. Financed by United Artists, Sarah Street observed that it typified how 'American investment resulted in a variety of British films which looked back to past genres and anticipated new developments', with its template being the 'lavish costume picture in the Korda and Gainsborough mould'.[33] The casting of the film reflected this ambivalence, with Alexander Walker observing that it 'was almost a National Theatre in itself', juxtaposing the youthful energy and looks of stars Susannah York and Albert Finney with established old hands of the British stage, including Evans.[34]

Evans provided solid anchorage to the production with her performance, her persona giving the role of Miss Western substance and veracity, with Bryan Forbes noting that she brought 'her impeccable timing and sense of period to a cast that was largely allowed to indulge in a riot of over-acting'.[35] The ghost of Lady Bracknell informed her performance, being an incarnation of imperious privilege and mannered haughtiness. Evans adopts the same precise enunciation, drawing out her vowels for comic effect, as with her iconic disdainful pronunciation of 'A haaandbag?' in *The Importance of Being Earnest*. This distinctive diction is used to similar effect in *Tom Jones* in the scene when Miss Western discovers that her niece (Susannah York) is in love with

Tom Jones (Albert Finney), with Evans's voice rising to a horrified crescendo to declare 'Mr Jones!' Evans's performance steals all of her scenes, with Richardson ensuring that she is predominantly centre frame, and using close-ups to foreground her. Whereas the other characters rattle off their lines, Evans takes her time to enunciate, peering disdainfully down her nose at her adversaries. She is the personification of upper-class privilege, brooking no opposition, and driving events on by the sheer force of her will, channelled through her imperious delivery of her lines. Her moments in the narrative provide unambiguous comic moments by the virtue of her assured performance style, as with the scene when her carriage is stopped by a highwayman. Miss Western harangues the uncertain felon for his effrontery in waylaying her, pointing her finger at him in admonishment, whilst haughtily reprimanding him 'Don't you point that firearm at me, sir!'

The success of *Tom Jones* at the box office and the Oscars led to a greater influx of American finance for British films, as the Hollywood studios sought to replicate and capitalise on its success. Evans was already in great demand, as is evident in the announcement in American trade magazine *Box Office* of Hollywood producer Ross Hunter's plans for Evans in his adaptation of *The Chalk Garden*. The article describes 'the 76-year-old grand lady of the British theatre who Hunter hopes to make a box-office name in this country'.[36] Hunter cast the film with a clear eye on the international market, declaring that the cast had 'a universal appeal', with Evans appealing to the 'art film devotees'. Evans was cast as Mrs St Maugham, having been pursued by author Edith Bagnold to play the part in the stage version in 1956. Bagnold's description of the character is significant in evoking the essence of Evans's persona: 'an aristocrat, overbearing, wilful, ageless, defiant of age [. . .] but she has something of the 18th Century about her – a Whig pride, a Regency carelessness'.[37] Evans was again nominated for the Academy Award for Best Supporting Actress for her role in the screen adaptation, despite mixed reviews for the film.

Evans's reputation was of such stature that United Artists were happy to bankroll Bryan Forbes's adaptation of *The Whisperers* (1967) with the actress in the leading role as a lonely ageing woman facing destitution. The production climate was such that Forbes was able to convince the studio to allow him the freedom and funds – albeit a modest sum ($400,000) according to Forbes – to give Evans a role suitable for an actress of her status, even at the age of seventy-eight.[38] Evans's performance drew on her role in *Look Back in Anger*, as an evocation of working-class misery in the industrial north of England, and was to lead to numerous awards, including a nomination for the Academy Award for Best Actress. Rather than an eccentric member of the aristocracy she was able to portray a more complex figuration of old age, Alexander Walker evoking Mrs Ross as 'poor but not pitiable', a working-class character with a 'wintry haughtiness from the fantasies lingering on after her days "in service" to the aristocracy'.[39] Unfortunately, the combination of kitchen sink realism and an ageing woman as the central character failed to appeal to audiences at a time of shrinking box office receipts.

In the wake of her success in *The Nun's Story*, Evans's biographer Forbes had opined that she could easily have forged a later life career in Hollywood, as the natural successor to Dame May Whitty, 'claiming every dotty, titled or eccentric old lady' role available.[40] Evans had turned her back on this, but found that Hollywood came to her in Britain, seeing her cast as the eccentric aristocrat in a series of films facilitated by American funding. With the notable exception of *The Whisperers*, the roles she was offered increasingly rendered her as little more than a token cameo in various lightweight comedies typified by her role as Lady Roberta Bates in *Prudence and the Pill* (1968). Described by *New York Magazine* as 'sleazy sort of pap', this topical romp centring on contraceptive mix-ups saw Evans join a distinguished cast of British acting talent, which included a host of ageing Academy Award winners and nominees including Joyce Redman, David Niven and Deborah Kerr.[41] Whereas *Tom Jones* was the film which launched a thousand American chequebooks to bankroll British film talent, *Prudence and the Pill* was symptomatic of the plight of the industry at the tail end of the decade. Robert Murphy described it as one of the 'gimmicky pretentious films' that Fox backed, which appeared to be about 'swinging London', but was ultimately a 'frothily sexless middle class farce' with ageing protagonists.[42]

Although it was clear that Evans was offered roles during the decade on account of her status as a *grande dame*, as well as her skills as one of the foremost stage and screen actresses of the era, there were other, more pragmatic reasons for her late life film career. She found film work less exacting than the stage in her seventies and eighties, with less physical strain, and less of a requirement to commit a whole part to memory.[43] Moreover, Evans was attracted by the money on offer from film companies, fretting about how long she could continue working and provision for future care. The same factors had also been important to Margaret Rutherford continuing her film career in her seventies. Despite her age, Edith Evans continued to find film work into the 1970s, yet the roles did not offer the opportunities for critical recognition and awards that she had enjoyed in the previous decade.

Conclusion

Sarah Street remarks on the contradictory nature of the 1960s, both looking forward and looking back as society came to terms with fundamental shifts in the social and cultural climate.[44] The narrative landscape of the decade may have set out to embrace a youth audience, nonetheless older character actresses played an important role in representing a past which, for better or for worse, was rapidly being left behind. American studios saw the likes of Evans and Rutherford as a way to attracting the arthouse audience to the box office. The casting of these *grandes dames* signified a mark of quality or prestige, a guarantee for, at the very least, critical success, especially given the recognition they received at the Academy Awards. The *grandes dames* were to be a vital component of the international films of the 1960s, cast as archetypal figurations of Englishness, in contrast to the Hollywood A-listers whose glamour and status was commensurate with America's cultural hegemony. But the ageing character actress was not always confined to narrow class stereotypes in her roles, her fame and status sometimes serving to open the doors for roles which were richer, more demanding and drew on their proven expertise as actors. These could be more nuanced in their figuration of the ageing woman, as with Evans's leading role in *The Whisperers* and Rutherford's appearance as Mistress Quickly in Orson Welles's *Chimes at Midnight* (1965). Such performances suggested the potential of the character actress when she was able to break free of the constrictions imposed by having to provide iterations of Englishness in the margins of Hollywood cinema. Nonetheless, the performances of Hiller, Rutherford and Evans would resonate with audiences beyond the extent of merely scene stealing, dominating whole films on occasion and eclipsing the performances of younger female leads in the process.

NOTES

1. See for example, Justine Ashby, '"The angry young man is tired": Albert Finney and 1960s British cinema', in Bruce Babington (ed.), *British Stars and Stardom* (Manchester: Manchester University Press, 2001); Christine Geraghty, 'Women and 60s British cinema: the development of the "Darling" girl', in Robert Murphy (ed.), *The British Cinema Book*, 2nd edn (London: BFI, 2001); Sarah Street, *British National Cinema* (London: Routledge, 1997); Melanie Williams, 'British new waif: Rita Tushingham and sixties female stardom', in *Female Stars of British Cinema* (Edinburgh: Edinburgh University Press, 2017).
2. Melanie Williams, 'Entering the paradise of anomalies: studying female character acting in British cinema', *Screen* 52: 1, Spring 2011, 97–104, pp. 103–4.
3. Raymond Durgnat, *A Mirror for England* (London: BFI, 2011 [1970]), p. 219.
4. Williams, 'Entering the paradise of anomalies', p. 99.
5. More youthful British nominees during the 1960s included Mary Ure (*Sons and Lovers*, 1961), Maggie Smith (*Othello*, 1965) and Susannah York (*They Shoot Horses, Don't They?*, 1969).
6. 'Wendy Hiller, spirited actress, dies at 90', *New York Times*, 17 May 2003. Available at <https://www.nytimes.com/2003/05/17/arts/wendy-hiller-spirited-actress-dies-at-90.html> (last accessed 28 October 2018).
7. Hiller felt it was 'a bizarre idea to transport all that was so English to Hollywood', Brian McFarlane 'Dame Wendy Hiller', *An Autobiography of British Cinema* (London: Methuen, 1997), p. 297.

8. Ibid. p. 297.
9. Sheridan Morley, 'Dame Wendy Hiller', *The Telegraph*, 16 May 2003. Available at <https://www.telegraph.co.uk/news/obituaries/1430166/Dame-Wendy-Hiller.html> (last accessed 28 October 2018).
10. Kenneth Tynan, *The Observer*, October 1954, cited in David Kynaston, *Family Britain 1951–57* (London: Bloomsbury, 2009), pp. 426–7.
11. Ibid. p. 286.
12. Terence Rattigan, cited in 'Terence Rattigan invents "Aunt Edna"', in British Library Collection items. Available at <https://www.bl.uk/collection-items/terence-rattigan-invents-aunt-edna> (last accessed 17 November 2018).
13. Ibid.
14. Michael Darlow, *Terence Rattigan: The Man and His Work* (London: Quartet, 2000), p. 376.
15. 'A Night at the Airport', *Time*, 4 October 1963, BFI Library.
16. Donald Zec, 'Blithe spirit', *Daily Mirror*, 23 May 1972.
17. Rutherford played Jane Marple in *Murder, She Said* (1961), *Murder at the Gallop* (1963), *Murder Most Foul* (1963) and *Murder Ahoy!* (1963).
18. Peter Cowie, 'This England', *Films and Filming*, October 1963, p. 13.
19. Robert Murphy, *Sixties British Cinema* (London: BFI, 1992), p. 91.
20. 'New one world of films', *Variety*, 12 May 1965, p. 55.
21. Tom Ryall, *Anthony Asquith* (Manchester: Manchester University Press, 2013), p. 145.
22. Mark Glancy, *When Hollywood Loved Britain: the Hollywood 'British' film 1939–45* (Manchester: Manchester University Press, 1999), p. 97.
23. Murphy, *Sixties British Cinema*, p. 265.
24. G. Williams, 'The old wave at work', *Scene*, 19 February 1963, BFI Library.
25. Untitled article, *Daily Mail*, undated. Press cuttings file on *The V.I.P.s*, BFI Library.
26. Ibid.
27. 'New films', *News of the World*, 8 September 1963.
28. Obituary, *New York Times*, 15 October 1976, p. 22.
29. Bryan Forbes, *Ned's Girl* (London: Elm Tree Books, 1977), p. 244.
30. Review in *Monthly Film Bulletin*, 26: 305, June 1959, p. 68.
31. Peter Bradshaw, 'Look Back in Anger review – Richard Burton rages in a revealing rerelease', in *The Guardian*, 30 March 2018. Available at <https://www.theguardian.com/film/2018/mar/30/look-back-in-anger-review-john-osbourne-tony-richardson-richard-burton> (last accessed 10 November 2018).
32. Forbes, *Ned's Girl*, p. 244.
33. Sarah Street, *British National Cinema* (London: Routledge, 1997), p. 87.
34. Alexander Walker, *Hollywood England* (London: Orion, 2005 [1974]), p. 144.
35. Forbes, *Ned's Girl*, p. 253.
36. 'Two sides of filmmaking in England viewed by producer Ross Hunter', *Box Office*, 13 May 1963, p. 13.
37. Quoted in Forbes, *Ned's Girl*, p. 236.
38. Ibid. p. 255.
39. Walker, *Hollywood England*, p. 366.

40. Forbes, *Ned's Girl*, p. 244.
41. Judith Crist, 'Recreation and procreation', *New York* Magazine, 27 May 1968, p. 51.
42. Murphy, *Sixties British Cinema*, pp. 268, 141.
43. Forbes, *Ned's Girl*, p. 252.
44. Street, *British National Cinema*, p. 80.

PART TWO

CREATIVE COLLABORATIONS

5. WOODERY-POKERY: CHARLES WOOD'S SIXTIES SCREENWRITING

David Cairns

> Her class was doing the behaving. My lads are made of flesh . . . all that leaping up and down in those . . . that's what I behaviour. That's provocative behaviour. We've all got to make allowances, find our equilibrium . . . at every turn how?

The speaker obviously has something on his mind. The sentences that trail off, the forbidden words 'gym slips' which must not be spoken. Then, far odder, the missing word 'call' in the statement 'That's what I behaviour.' Not a mistake of speech, more like a typo. But I've checked, it appeared in more than one draft of the script. It is like a computer virus is loose in the man's brain, swallowing words and then phrases, until at the end, his speech becomes a series of disconnected fragments, like half a telephone conversation overheard.

This is one brief passage from Charles Wood's screenplay of *The Knack . . . and how to get it* (1965). It gives a small sense of his unusual way with words, his ability to derail grammar, disarticulate sentence structure, isolate and make strange our commonplace phrases and attitudes, sometimes resulting in uncanny renditions of the garbled way real people express themselves, sometimes garbling further into a more stylised, babbling stream of consciousness, incantatory or delirious, with a dreamlike jumbling of the deepest seriousness and the completely trivial. It is this linguistic invention that led John Gielgud, appearing (as a very thinly disguised parody of himself) in the play *Veterans;*

or, Hair in the Gates of the Hellespont at the Royal Court in 1972, to coin the term 'woodery-pokery'.

When the writer David Sherwin addressed the gathering at Lindsay Anderson's memorial in 1994, he sensed a ripple of shock pass through the room: it seemed as if nobody had believed that he, the screenwriter of Anderson's 'Mick Travis trilogy', really existed, so secluded had he been.[1] At the 2019 BAFTA Awards, not one of the winning actors mentioned in their acceptance speeches the writers who had created the roles for which they were winning. And this is the screenwriter's lot, or part of it.[2]

None of the great directors of the British New Wave were auteurs in the sense of being writer-directors, all relied on writers, mostly (apart from Sherwin) drawn from the worlds of theatre and literature, many of them barely known and little appreciated by cinephiles. Harold Pinter's fame was such that his work with Joseph Losey received plenty of attention, but few know of Evan Jones, who likewise scripted four major Losey films: *Eva* (1962), *The Damned* (1962), *King & Country* (1964) and *Modesty Blaise* (1966).

The case of Charles Wood is similar. A celebrated playwright at the Royal Court, he worked in radio and television before adapting Ann Jellicoe's play *The Knack* for Richard Lester. He subsequently forged a partnership with the American émigré filmmaker, resulting in numerous screenplays, five of which reached the screen, with Wood also providing uncredited rewrite work on *Petulia* (1968) and *The Three Musketeers* (1973) and *The Four Musketeers* (1974).

Lester's career has been persistently neglected, despite the colossal influence of *A Hard Day's Night* (1964), *The Knack* and *Help!* (1965).[3] This is probably because that influence was often considered negative: Lester's originals were, at best, just about tolerated by the snootier critics at the *Monthly Film Bulletin*, but the imitations that swarmed onto the screen struck many as unbearable and tainted the response to Lester's later work even as he moved on to different styles and subjects.[4] So it is no surprise that Wood has also been neglected as a cinematic artist, despite his authoring major works for other filmmakers: Tony Richardson's film of *The Charge of the Light Brigade* (1968) in particular being a key work of the New Wave, representing the climax of its ambitions and sounding its death knell. Here I will attempt to illuminate some aspects of Wood's style – in its way as kaleidoscopic as Lester's, as acerbic as Richardson's – concentrating on his sixties works.

THE KNACK AND HOW HE GOT IT

The film of *The Knack* fell into Lester's lap after Lindsay Anderson walked away from the job[5]: Anderson had enough money that he never really needed to work, which partly accounts, along with his irascible temperament, for his making so few films. Anderson was always very down on Lester's film, whose freewheeling, joyous attitude seems to have been anathema to him: as late as 1985 he described it as signalling the end of sixties optimism and the start of the cynical seventies, which is a bit premature for a film released mid-decade.[6] Perhaps there is a small measure of truth in Anderson's assessment, though: while *A Hard Day's Night* celebrated the Beatles wholeheartedly, *The Knack* has a bit of fun at its protagonists' expense, and while making fun of the older generation is a consistent undertone in the movie, it saves some mockery for the callow Colin (Michael Crawford). Nor was Anderson alone: original author Ann Jellicoe was rumoured to dislike the movie, certainly believing it to be a quite different work, in style and meaning, from her play.[7]

The first-time pairing of Wood and Lester accounts for this: though Wood always sought to treat the works he adapted with respect, Lester often set out to explode them, relying on Wood to begin the process of reassembly that would result in a new and cinematic expression. Through a process of multiple rewrites, Lester had Wood throw out the play and then slowly reconstruct it from fragments. By doing so, the essentials of the idea could be discovered: throw everything out and thus discover what you need.

Wood's first draft abandoned the story completely apart from the four main characters, their relationships and the London setting (albeit with a climactic sequence on the Forth Bridge; since one character is always painting, the mental leap to a structure that is always being painted seems almost logical). If the finished film is dreamlike at times, deploying surreal juxtapositions and abrupt, unexplained transitions, the first draft is virtually all dream. Nothing of it made it into the movie, yet somehow it convinced Lester they were on the right track and that Wood was the man for the job.

Though much of what happened to the text could fit the term 'opening out', with multiple scenes played on the streets of London (the Albert Hall looms large), the finished film never feels like one of those conventional, fusty play-films where the characters inexplicably go out so that the same stage-bound scene can be played in a new location. Wood introduces Nancy (the iconic Rita Tushingham) early, in a series of short skits showing her arrive by coach, wander about lost looking for the YWCA, and finally encounter Colin and Tom as they purchase a cast-iron bed from a scrap yard. This leads to the film's happiest and most acclaimed invention, the long sequence of visual gags and aural non-sequiturs as the trio wheel the bed across the capital, gradually abandoning all geographic and spatio-temporal sense, until we see them punting the bed, strapped to oil drums for flotation, down a river.

Jellicoe's dialogue mostly survives, with Wood providing linking material in a similar vein, even pulling in the playwright's character portrait of Tom from the dramatis personae when Colin has to describe him. The joke being that Jellicoe's words try to summarise the man's essence in a way that leaves

Figure 5.1 Opening out the source material: the cast of *The Knack . . . and How to Get It* (1965) roaming the London streets.

casting possibilities open, making it a rather unhelpful list of attributes ('Small, vigorous, balanced, sensitive in his movements') for purposes of identification.

Lester was uncomfortable with the critical thrust of Jellicoe's play, which draws a connection between the womanising male chauvinist Tolen (Ray Brooks in the film) and fascism.[8] Neil Sinyard suggests that the film tends to equate Tolen more with capitalism, consumerism, the world of advertising of which Lester was very much a part in his other job (he treated the making of ads for TV and cinema as a chance to experiment and develop new techniques for his movie work).[9] By considerably softening the film's attack on Tolen (though he's still pretty unlikable), Wood and Lester lighten the film's tone, and this arguably creates or exacerbates an issue that has damaged the film's reputation and made it a more uncomfortable viewing experience than intended in the years since it was made.[10] To turn the tables on the domineering Tolen, in both play and film Nancy makes what I suppose we have to call a false allegation of rape, though it plays out as more abstract than that. By throwing the word 'Rape!' at Tolen, she completely de-fangs him, since his self-image is based on the conceit of no woman being able to resist him. Nancy reduces all three male leads to ineffectual puppets, but she does so in a way that has led to the film being accused of making light of sexual assault.[11]

In a serious feminist farce play likening the all-conquering Lothario to a fascist, use of rape as a metaphor seems, perhaps, acceptable even to the modern sensibility. In the wake of second-wave feminism, and revelations about the criminal justice system's own failure to take rape seriously, the altogether less didactic, more jokey film seems to be straying into territory restricted to more serious approaches. While the repeated use of the word 'rape' in a light comedy *is* uncomfortable, I have never felt the film trivialised sexual violence. Melanie Williams observes:

> But allowing for the context of its time and its generic context as surreal comedy, the film's examination of sexual power dynamics on the cusp of the permissive society is fascinatingly handled. Nancy's provincial innocence becomes the vehicle for her invincibility rather than her victimisation; she does the equivalent of the guileless little boy pointing out the emperor's nakedness in the fairy-tale.[12]

Rita Tushingham thinks the (mis)use of the r-word shows Nancy's naivety and serves as a more acceptable, at the time, substitute for the unsayable f-bomb (*The Knack* got an X certificate in the UK despite containing no violence, swearing or nudity).[13] I think it also introduces interesting complications to how we see all four of the characters.

One of *The Knack*'s innovations is the 'Greek chorus of disapproval', a layer of voices on the soundtrack commenting on the youthful main characters' activities from a disgruntled, middle-aged perspective. Lester covertly filmed passers-by observing the shooting, and had Wood write a sort of commentary track of vox pop interviews, which we associate with the onscreen pedestrians, as if they had been asked to give their thoughts on what had just happened. This meant that Wood was involved in the film all through the edit, writing non-sequiturs and absurdist bluenose grumbling, an unusual workflow, which probably helped cement the collaboration with Lester.

> It's all milk in the schools now isn't it – I blame the national health – I failed milk – they should have more tighter teachers who've seen the world – I've seen many a foreign part – throw out the milk and bring back the belting I advocate . . . that's what I frogle.[14]

These disconnected fragments could either be written in long chains of nonsense, or tossed off as one-liners and dropped into the flow of the film as needed. Both methods were used, with Wood kept on salary through production to produce new lines as needed. Speech became a freeform element of film, capable of being spliced and rearranged without regard for strict sense or relevance. Dialogue becomes more like tiles in a mosaic.

The many drafts of the script held in the Charles Wood Archive, in the Borthwick Institute for Archives at the University of York, contain dizzying reams of this material, sprayed from Wood's overflowing word-hoard. It suggests a potential film-universe in which the existing plot of the movie is only one strand, one walk-through of a swinging London video game where every byway is a possible new collision of action and language (and every draft is written in a new, unconventional format, for some reason). Here's one deleted fragment:

> CANDID FACES OF THE AVERAGE GREENGROCER
> They come here from the North and they expect the earth well they don't get it do they and they deserve all they get.
> I've no sympathy with them.
> I blame their mums and dads – I mean I wouldn't let my child across the street to London with all you read the way they have started this twilight world you read about.
> Two years.
> Flock in they do and of course what do you expect the inevitable takes place of course and then they scream of course and the usual happens and what happens then of course is proverbial and of course who gets the blame the poor bloody slop on the beat of course and how can he be held to ransom for the action of a minority – of course you can't say that.
> Did me a world of good.
> I'd spank their – can I say it – rear parts.[15]

Loose pages in Wood's archive offer scenes that seem to have no connection to the main story, and could conceivably have strayed in from other, unrelated movies. An interview with 'the commanding officer of Her Majesty's Christmas cards' –

> We're glad to have you – no bull like an old bull which we won at Waterloo and we hope that more young people will follow your example and learn to do it the man's way embracing the path of discipline – oh because it's lovely.
> The Americans haven't got it – for all their jazz and ma tazz . . .
> And we all wear lovely hats.[16]

But the Greek chorus of disapproval, originating as just another layer which could run through the film as ironic commentary, turns out to have a narrative purpose when Tolen the seducer, falling from grace as a star of the young, smart crowd, ends up joining a group of bleak onlookers, undercutting the happy ending with their embittered asides. There are always places open for us in this chorus.

Thug Life: *Help!*

The second Beatles film, *Help!* (1965), was a challenging project for all concerned, since *A Hard Day's Night* had been such a success the previous year but nobody wanted to simply remake it. Where the first film had a moderately realist surface, the follow-up was conceived as fantasy and farrago. Lester planned to keep it entertaining with visual fireworks, and wanted a script that did the same with language.

Franco-American pulp writer Marc Behm pitched the plot of Jules Verne's *The Chinese Man from China* without saying where he had stolen it from, but this promising idea was undermined when a rival adaptation went into production. Charles Wood got the job of turning Behm's second proposal into a screenplay. Wood's involvement was a direct result of his collaboration with Lester on *The Knack*, though he later reflected, 'It was just an assignment. I don't think I did a particularly good job.' Wood had been reading *The Deceivers*, John Masters's 1952 novel about the Thuggee cult (he would later write an unfilmed script based on it), which gave him the idea of making an Indian death cult the opposing force to the Fab Four. The unlikely juxtaposition resulted in the Beatles' first encounter with the sitar, an instrument destined to play a key role in their future development.

Help! is a deliberately very silly film in which a Hindu sect pursues the Beatles to get Ringo's sacrificial ring. The stereotyping of Indians arguably can be excused as part of the satire of Imperial fiction from *The Moonstone* to *Fu Manchu*, even down to the casting of white actors in brownface, which was still standard practice even in serious treatments of the same kind of material, such as Hammer films' various colonialist melodramas. The loose plot keeps the action moving between songs, though the result is inevitably somewhat episodic. Though the film is deliberately not about anything, it does include a series of running jokes about Britain's declining place in the world, voiced by villainous mad scientist Victor Spinetti. At its best, this results in light satire, at its worst in dreadful puns: 'It's the brain drain. His brain's draining' does not even seem to *be* a pun, properly speaking. (The annotated script shows that Lester adjusted Wood's earlier attempt at the line: they knew there was a joke to be had, they just couldn't winkle it out.)

Wood's skills come out best in dialogue when it is not trying to deliver jokes, quips or smart remarks, but focusing instead on non sequiturs, slang and garbled clichés and malapropisms. It is remarkable to see the biggest pop band in the world made a film by a Royal Court dramatist whose surreal speeches seem like a mash-up/fold-in of Harold Pinter, Alan Bennett and William S. Burroughs. To find this funny you have to accept that it doesn't make sense. It is not a Marx Bros crosstalk routine because the jokes are nearly all abstract, they are about painting word-pictures you can't quite visualise, or jamming together bits of language that refuse to fit, or importing extraordinary attitudes into everyday life. The Beatles had just discovered marijuana and lost much of their interest in acting, and their skills in this area had never been highly developed, so their throwaway delivery and unconcerned manner allows them to float passively through the melodramatic action, tossing off casual analyses of the ridiculous situations. When Paul is shrunk to the size of an ant, he narrowly avoids being stepped on. 'We thought that was you', says Ringo, pointing at a red spot on the carpet, once Paul regains his full stature. 'No, that's not me', replies Paul, calmly. Likewise, when Ringo is unable to remove the deadly sacrificial ring, he remarks that the fire brigade once got his head out of some railings. 'Did you want them to?' asks John. 'No, I used to leave it there when I wasn't using it for school', Ringo explains serenely. 'You can see a lot of the world from railings.'

Wood at War

For Lester's next film, *A Funny Thing Happened on the Way to the Forum* (1966), the director was forbidden the services of a screenwriter to rework the existing script, so ended up cloistered with cinematographer Nicolas Roeg to cobble together a new draft in secret. He reunited with Wood, however, for his following work, *How I Won the War* (1967), based on a comic novel by Patrick Ryan, a former army officer in the Second World War whose experiences loosely parallel those of his inept hero, Lieutenant Ernest Goodbody (played by Michael Crawford in the film). Once again, Lester was making a film in opposition to its source, but while *The Knack* sought to gently divert the flow of Ann Jellicoe's argument, this film was an all-out attack on entertainments based on war. Again, Wood's own attitude was perhaps more sympathetic to his source, but as the author of several plays on military subjects which used humour and horror in close proximity – *Dingo* (1967), *H, Being Monologues in Front of Burning Cities* (1969), *Jingo* (1975) – he proposed a Brechtian assault on the traditional war movie.

The film fractures the chronology of Ryan's narrative and ruptures its fictive 'reality', at one point jumping back to reveal the characters performing their roles on a cinema screen (in a prophetically deserted auditorium). Lester wanted to demolish the audience's connection to the characters by undercutting realism with surrealism and jokes, and then sabotaging the comfort value of the humour with grisly horror and glimpses of the real war. Wood's stage plays had shown the way to do this with words, some of which he gamely recycled here. 'The thing about fighting a desert war [. . .] is that it is a clean war—without brutality', says the title character of *Dingo*, the same year Goodbody utters the words in Lester's film: 'clean-limbed, without dishonourable action on either side'.[17] Goodbody is a useful Candide-like stooge, a reverse barometer of the film's intentions, since everything he believes, says and does is wrong. From an early draft:

A PLEASANT ENOUGH LIEUTENANT CHAP FOR ALL HIS STUPID. HE WEARS GLASSES, THE TIGHT STEEL RIMMED GLASSES THAT THE ARMY ISSUES FOR SERVICE IN THE FIELD OF HUMAN CONQUEST. HE HAS EYES BEHIND THE GLASSES THAT ARE STUPID EYES BECAUSE YOU CAN SEE THEY BELIEVE ALL THEY SEE AND ARE TOLD.[18]

Goodbody does not wear the glasses in the film – they were passed to John Lennon, who needed them and kept them.

To Wood's absurdist words and imagery, the film would add 'the great toys'[19] of the war movie, but throw every possible obstacle in the audience's path to prevent them being seduced by the usual satisfaction of following characters on a mission, which usually results in our becoming emotionally invested and thus rooting for one side to blow up the other. 'Brechtian alienation is a synonym for audience's backs disappearing down a street', reflected Lester, ruefully. But he still regards the film as one of his most successful, in terms of communicating what he wanted to say.[20]

Wood begins the film on the Rhine, with Goodbody being captured and starting to recount his story. But his men, watching from a distance, are simultaneously in Germany during the war and in an English pub in 1967, discussing the events: though they are young, in uniform and on location, they talk to the camera and sip from pints handed to them with the accompanying sound of a cash register. Then, even more strangely, we are at a cricket match where Goodbody and his men are playing the Germans, with Hitler keeping score. 'Every word of this film is written in pencil in my own handwriting', Goodbody confides to the lens. He and his men are intermittently aware of being in a film, but they do not seem to know what kind of film. Corporal Transom (Lee Montague) assumes it is a typically patronising propaganda piece ('Haven't you insulted us enough without films?'). Goodbody imagines it's his heroic memoir.

Much of the story and dialogue is faithful to the source, even speeches which feel very Wood-ish. The demented Colonel Grapple (Michael Hordern) delivers a monologue about the wily Pathan that's verbatim from the novel, but instead of cosy satire it brings further disorientation, another tonal shift: 'India is a hot, strange country, full of wily Pathans and up to wily things, which is why I always wear spurs, even in hot weather.'

Lester purposely cast the film with actors from the widest possible range of backgrounds – naturalistic, comedic, tragic, Beckettian, Beatle – to help the film fail to cohere. Most war movies were about disparate bodies of men who finally come together into an efficient fighting unit. Lester's film

Figure 5.2 Charles Wood's absurdism: John Lennon and Michael Crawford in *How I Won the War* (1967).

would deliberately do the opposite. By purposely excluding all camaraderie, Wood was excising a big part of the military experience he knew, and which is present in most of his other work on army life. But what remains is still informed by an attention to realistic detail that makes the absurdist elements harder to shrug off. It's a difficult, prickly film that doesn't welcome the viewer. Obscure slang is delivered in thick regional accents against a roar of vehicles and gunfire and explosions; the colour comes and goes, tinted stock footage interrupting (or continuing) the action; the familiar actors are gradually, bloodily eliminated, to be replaced by anonymous 'replacements' whose faces and uniforms are tinted the colour of the battle they died in.

At a time when Vietnam was becoming the issue, and any vaguely anti-war sentiment expressed in a film seemed hip and radical, Charles Wood managed to write three films tackling war head-on which were not widely embraced by young audiences; a perverse badge of honour, in a way. Refusing easy attitudes, Wood drew upon his own military experience (five years with the 17th/21st Lancers) and understanding of fighting men to make *How I Won the War* and the following year's *Charge of the Light Brigade* too savage to be nostalgic, yet too compassionate to be simple anti-war tirades. Both lead their audiences into bleak terrain where simply sympathising feels inadequate and inappropriate.

In *How I Won the War*, a soldier with both feet blown off is comforted by his wife who emerges from nowhere in domestic attire in the middle of the North African desert to deliver a panegyric to us about noble sacrifice. When he interrupts to plead 'It hurts Flo', she blandly replies, 'Run them under the cold tap, love.' (The film's deliberate tone is summarised when Goodbody is asked if he had many amusing incidents during the war. He agrees that he did, but asked for a specific example, in a rare moment of insight, responds, 'They're not funny, really.')

In another chilling scene, Transom predicts that he will be unable to go home after the war, and we know he is right since the characters, not fully anchored in their fictional roles, are similarly unmoored in time, jumping forward to imagined futures (the present of the film's production, 1966/7). 'There's a lad I know, saved a grenade at Dunkirk. Didn't drop it in that sandbag as he came off the ferry boat. Saved it. Took it home. And put it on his stomach holding it tight between belly and thigh and went to bed with it. Pin out. Relaxed and died.' Wood's choice and ordering of words is obviously striking, pyrotechnic. His original and risk-taking approach to story and image are aspects of the screenwriter's trade that can be overlooked when one focuses on this. But his use of *punctuation* – see above – is also extraordinary, and it subtly directs the actors' performances.

In *The Long Day's Dying* (1968), a Second World War drama adapted from Alan White's novel and directed by Peter Collinson, the protagonist narrates another account of a soldier's return home:

> A girl – a wife dead I know of. Which comes to mind. But I never fired a shot in anger – or killed a man I know of. We've all fluttered down in the night and started private armies – us. Behind the lines – behind the lines, read.
>
> This girl was loved by one of our lads who once met Germans and had burns placed with system on his cheeks but survived and came home though, surviving, home to bed and beauty and she kissed him this girl, wife at night asleep with love and he arches and sticks a knife into her without waking – to her heart.
>
> In Broadmoor. This bloke with the knife in his wife.

But in fact the full text is more remarkable, as Wood intersperses this tragedy with a straightforward description of a tactical procedure, so that the words emerge in a distracted, emotionless manner, leaving the audience to find the horror for themselves.

In *The Charge of the Light Brigade*, a wounded man is helped up after the (anti-) climactic massacre. 'You have received a cut across the forehead, which has blinded you', explains the soldier (Norman Rossington), with odd formality. 'Am I in pain?' asks the man. 'I believe you are.' The peculiarity of this exchange rings absolutely true: you feel the author, whoever he is, must have had experience of men hurt and in shock. Although Wood's military background stranded him in a no man's land between the counter-culture attitudes of his artistic friends and collaborators, and the people who knew what soldiering was like from personal experience, it was a very productive piece of ground to occupy. The lines, incidentally, do not appear in the shooting script. Rather, they were created on location by Wood, following his preferred (if unusual) practice of altering the script on set if necessary.

Wood's involvement in *The Charge of the Light Brigade* was a convoluted form of happenstance. The project had initially been offered him as an alternative to *The Knack*. John Osborne had done a lot of work on it before bowing out. Then the producers, Woodfall Films, got slapped with a lawsuit by the actor Laurence Harvey, who owned the rights to *The Reason Why*, a popular account of the same historical events. So Wood was recruited to quickly produce a convincing draft that would demonstrate that the planned film had nothing to do with Cecil Woodham-Smith's book. Writing about the film for *Sight & Sound*, Wood explained:

> I shall never know what was going on but it is possible that had I been a more 'professional' screenwriter, capable of producing a standard comprehensible screenplay I would not have been approached by Tony who I am sure wanted from me a first draft document he could use to bewilder the chaps in wigs: which I duly produced, three hundred pages or so of it, wildly surreal, anachronistic, savage, overwritten, pornographic, crammed with art student polemic, optimistically ironic, bitter about class and privilege; everything I felt about the British Empire, the British Army, England under Queen Victoria and the first of the modern wars [. . .][21]

Richardson reacted enthusiastically to Wood's purposely unfilmable draft — which is now lost to history unless one of the lawyers retained a copy – noting only: 'I think it's too long, and I don't think we can have Queen Victoria fucked by a bear, not even a very funny Russian bear, do you?'[22]

As with *The Knack*, in a way, Wood then had to manoeuvre the successive drafts back to touching distance with the original material, in this case historical events rather than a specific text, though the film's script supervisor, Angela Allen, recalls that everyone knew they were making *The Reason Why*, but weren't allowed to ever admit it.[23]

Wood's interest in history also added authenticity and strangeness to his writing. For *Charge* he developed a style of dialogue partially derived from contemporary journalism and literature, partly his own invention, making it one of the very few period movies that makes the viewer feel like a time-traveller, dropped into another era without a guide. Why does Lord Raglan keep talking about 'cherrybums'? You have to work it out from the context: his red-trousered cavalrymen had a nickname.

> You see them tight, my cherrybums – ten thousand a year of my own money spent on their backs to clothe them, my own pocket. Was a time there was not a private trooper could do more than frig himself in a corner, he looked like a scarecrow, couldn't get a pot to put his mutton in, let alone back stairs a nice clean cookie. Kitchens is full of cherrybums now since I dressed them, can't get 'em paraded for them busy buttering buns . . . good, if they can't fornicate, they can't fight, and if they don't fight I'll flog their backs I tell 'em . . .

Wood never shies away from letting his characters say strange things, because they are often strange people, but they never say them for our benefit. Every sentence has both a feeling of otherness and familiarity. Like the subtle vignette around the edges of the frame (courtesy of David Watkin's cinematography) which creates a barely-perceptible distance from the action, Wood's dialogue always keeps us at a slight remove. He recalled:

> I had invented a language based on dips into Carlyle, Thackeray and contemporary memoirs. Once you find a language for characters to speak fitting the mood and aim of the film the rest seems to follow, though it wasn't all that easy getting actors to speak it properly at first. Tony gave me permission to call 'Cut!' when I heard it going wrong, words dropped, apostrophes creeping in: the dialogue had to be said exactly as written and was for me the framework of the film, set the style, was a determining factor in the way characters wore their costumes, stood, ate their food, danced.[24]

In fact, Wood says he never dared to exercise his right to stop a take, but his mere presence was enough to achieve Richardson's goal and the enforcement of his 'rigid and unfamiliar syntax' acted as a form of verbal corsetry.

Love and Bombs

Prior to *The Charge of the Light Brigade*, Wood had done some uncredited writing on Lester's *Petulia* (1968), another adaptation from a book the author had little love for (*Me and the Arch-Kook Petulia* by John Haase). A research trip to San Francisco had produced notebooks full of overheard dialogue and startling images, many of which found their way into the finished film, dropped into the background action or buried in the sound mix. The 'Greek chorus' of *The Knack* is now slightly more naturalistic, masquerading as real eyewitness commentary rather than a vox pop addition. This would become a favourite device of Lester's ('It worked very well for the "them-and-us" quality of *The Three Musketeers*'), his signature approach always being to undercut anything that threatened to become too simple.

> ARCHIE TOUCHES HER AND IT LOOKS LIKE ONE OF THOSE MOMENTS WE ALL KNOW AND LOATHE THAT ARE HOLLYWOOD SHORTHAND FOR YOU ARE A WONDERFUL HUMAN BEING AND I DEARLY TRULY LOVE YOU ABOUT TO BE SEALED WITH SPITTLE.
> JUST BEFORE WE PUKE SHE SCREAMS AND FAINTS.[25]

From the above script sample, it is easy to see that Wood was working hard to wrench the film away from the twee 'kookiness' of the source novel, which Lester felt was dishonest about the people it portrayed, people from a social class he knew well. The more acerbic tone established by Wood's work is carried into the movie, whose affecting romantic elements just barely survive the bruising transition: as often with Lester (see also *Robin and Marian*, 1976) these appealing aspects are really used as a supportive structure upon which to hang the social observation Lester is primarily interested in.

The film's final draft was by Lawrence B. Marcus: Lester felt the viewpoint of an American resident, and one who had experienced divorce, was needed. But many of Wood's observations remain in the film, and he helped to originate the extreme fragmentation of the timeline which turns the story into a kind of unfolding mystery, whose revelations are not so much about whodunnit but why. The slow revelation from disconnected moments resembles the mental process of reconstructing in one's mind a really disastrous drunken evening the morning after, which suits the film's air of bleary disenchantment.[26]

The script of *The Bed Sitting Room* (1969) is credited to John Antrobus, co-author with Spike Milligan of the original play, with Wood consigned to an ambiguous 'adaptation' credit, but in fact he was a principal collaborator on it, taking over the writing to help concretise the film's world and firm up the storyline. It all transpires in a fantasy of post-apocalyptic London, so the abstraction of the play's settings had to be made concrete: locations were found around Britain that already had the look of atomic wasteland. Milligan defined the point of the play as being that atomic war would change nothing: human beings would go on being the same disastrous imbeciles even if the population were reduced to double figures. When society is blown up, the fragments continue to operate as if the whole still existed, with institutions reduced to individuals. For example, Frank Thornton is a one-man BBC, visiting people's homes wearing the top half of a dinner jacket and crouching behind their hollowed-out TV sets to read them the latest, pre-war news. Meanwhile, Marty Feldman is a predatory NHS, always on the lookout for patients he can kidnap. In a sense, then, the film is more about human inertia than atomic war.

Apart from the danger that the settings' bleak reality might impinge on the comic action, the lack of plot was also a challenge. Wood attempted to beef up the romantic subplot, in which Rita Tushingham and Richard Warwick attempt to find love in the nuclear wilderness, temporarily thwarted by the older generation (parents Arthur Lowe and Mona Washbourne; suitor Michael Hordern), but for the first time Lester and Wood's real interest seems to reside with the older characters. Ralph Richardson is so magnificent as an English lord mutating into the titular bedsit, bringing his Shakespearean gravitas to low comedy and bizarre surrealism, that the youngsters seem just a bit bland by comparison.[27] Antrobus's discomfiting original fade-out gag, in which a Pakistani family disembark from a row-boat onto England's irradiated shoreline,[28] was replaced by Wood with a majestic visualisation of the play's off-screen monarch, Mrs Ethel Shroake, nearest in line to the throne of the score of surviving Brits:

> Sitting on an old horse sits MRS ETHEL SHROAKE in her Guards officer dress with a pinafore looking for all the world like Dandy Nicholls.
> 'God save Mrs Ethel Shroake, Long live Mrs Ethel Shroake etc.'
> She waves and the curtains draw.[29]

The disappointing box office of Lester's last three films of the sixties (*The Bed Sitting Room* barely managed a belated release a year after it was shot), coupled with a downturn in the British film industry's fortunes generally, led to a period of unemployment for Lester during which he worked on commercials. Charles Wood collaborated further with Lester in the coming decades, as well as writing prodigiously for the stage and television. He is now retired, describing himself as 'a recovering writer'.[30] His sixties work is a vital part of British cinema's development from the classical period to the modern: he not only caught the updraft from the explosion of exciting filmmaking in that period, but he added considerably to its fire.

Notes

1. As described in David Sherwin, *Going Mad in Hollywood: And Life with Lindsay Anderson* (London: Andre Deutsch, 1996), p. 295.
2. For more on this, see the introduction to Jill Nelmes, *The Screenwriter in British Cinema* (London: BFI, 2013).

3. See Neil Sinyard, *Richard Lester* (Manchester: Manchester University Press, 2010) and Steven Soderbergh's book-length interview *Getting Away With It: Or—Further Adventures of the Luckiest Bastard You Ever Saw* (London: Faber & Faber, 1999).
4. For example, fun but 'dated' and lightweight movies like *Smashing Time* (1967), more serious but gimmicky fare like *Morgan: A Suitable Case for Treatment* (1966). The far-from-snooty Alan Parker summed these up as 'red London bus movies', in his 1985 Thames TV documentary *A Turnip Head's Guide to the British Film Industry* and Manny Farber expressed limited enthusiasm in his essay *The Day of the Lesteroid* (1966).
5. As described in correspondence, January–February 1964, between Wood and his agent, Peggy Ramsay, preserved in the Charles Wood Archive at York University, CW/2/53/3/2.
6. In his own 1985 Thames TV documentary, *Free Cinema 1956–? An Essay on Film by Lindsay Anderson*.
7. Jellicoe did not go on the record about the film adaptation, though Peggy Ramsay, the agent she shared with Wood, wrote that she would never like any version that wasn't a completely faithful copy of the play. In the foreword to her published play *Shelley, or The Idealist* she wrote 'I begin to feel alienated (temporarily I hope) from a society which has adopted *The Knack* and, it seems to me, subtly degraded it: A New York reviewer was able to write of the film that it was all the better for the elimination of the moral values of the play.'
8. As described in Soderbergh, *Getting Away With It*, p. 38, and in an interview with the author conducted for the Blu-ray of *A Hard Day's Night*, Criterion, 2014.
9. Sinyard, *Richard Lester*, p. 43.
10. Sue Harper, *Women in British Cinema: Mad, Bad and Dangerous to Know* (London: Continuum, 2000), p. 113.
11. Lester described the shifting audience response in a 27 February 2014 interview with the author.
12. Melanie Williams, *Female Stars of British Cinema: The Women in Question* (Edinburgh: Edinburgh University Press, 2017), p. 100.
13. As discussed in an interview with Melanie Williams, included on the Blu-ray *The Knack: And How to Get It*, BFI, 2018.
14. The BFI's Blu-ray disc subtitles give the last word as 'froggle', but really they're doing awfully well to get that close. *The Knack: And How to Get It*, BFI, 2018.
15. *The Knack*, The Charles Wood Archive, The Borthwick Institute for Archives, University of York, Assorted Draft Material CW/2/53/1/2.
16. Ibid.
17. *Plays: 'H', 'Jingo', 'Dingo' v. 2*, by Charles Wood, Oberon Modern Playwrights, 15 March 1999.
18. *How I Won the War*, First Draft, The Charles Wood Archive, The Borthwick Institute for Archives, University of York, CW/2/48/1/1.
19. Sinyard, *Richard Lester*, p. 63.
20. Ibid. p. 63.
21. Charles Wood, 'Into the Valley', *Sight & Sound* 2: 1, 1992, p. 26.
22. Ibid. p. 26.

23. Interview with the author for the Criterion Channel, 11 December 2019.
24. Wood, 'Into the Valley', p. 26.
25. *Petulia*, First Draft, 1967, The Charles Wood Archive, The Borthwick Institute for Archives, University of York, CW2/79/1/1.
26. *Petulia* was invited to the 1968 Cannes Film Festival, along with *The Long Day's Dying*, making it a remarkable year for Wood, even though he had no credit on the former and had tried unsuccessfully to have his name removed from the latter. It would have been even better if the festival had actually taken place.
27. Although they should not: Tushingham calls Warwick 'as stupid as the sun'. The language is as poetically off-kilter as ever, but the conception of the characters in the original play is a bit sentimental (Milligan's love of children projected onto twenty-somethings).
28. *The Bed-Sitting Room* 1st draft screenplay, John Antrobus, 8 March 1968, The Charles Wood Archive, The Borthwick Institute for Archives, University of York, CW2/7/2/1.
29. *The Bed-Sitting Room* 5th draft screenplay, Charles Wood, 9 May 1968, The Charles Wood Archive, The Borthwick Institute for Archives, University of York, CW2/7/2/5.
30. Email to the author, 14 September 2017.

6. 'BEYOND NATURALISM': JOCELYN HERBERT, IF... (1968) AND DESIGN FOR PERFORMANCE IN 1960s BRITISH CINEMA

Vicky Lowe

> The world she (Jocelyn Herbert) comes out of is one of total theatre, where the director, the designer and the writer are working together for a unified concept, and her work isn't born out of conflict but collaboration.[1]

This chapter will examine the artistic collaboration between director Lindsay Anderson and designer Jocelyn Herbert on the production design of the film *If . . .* (1968), offering a historical account that locates this partnership within a broader creative environment encompassing practice across film and theatre. My contention is that the writing of theatre and film histories is often constrained by ad hoc disciplinary boundaries, which preclude a fuller examination of practitioner experience. Whilst intermedial approaches have transformed our understanding of contemporary media forms in recent years, historical accounts of creative practitioners' work remains largely media-specific and therefore not necessarily reflective of their professional and cultural experience or able to encompass the cross-fertilisation of practice that impacted on their work.

Intermediality as a term is used in this chapter to refer to a process within a broader historical framework, where the boundaries between media blur. Mueller's definition is useful in this respect:

> Intermediality would not be a question of content (which I would link to intertextuality) but of form, or more precisely, of interactions between specific media 'structures'/'procedures' which can/could be reconstructed on the basis of the traces which these processes left in the media 'products'.[2]

Anderson and Herbert were only one example of creative practitioners who worked across theatre, film and television. As Geoff Brown has noted, because of the geographical proximity of the production centres for film and theatre in Britain, cross fertilisation between the two industries was already well established.[3] Yet the influence of theatre on the development of cinema in this country has often been understood to be detrimental, tying film to an over-dependence on adaptation and literary material and limiting its cinematic potential as a result.[4] 'The history of cinema', as Susan Sontag has suggested, 'is often treated as the history of its emancipation from theatrical models'.[5]

Whilst I have argued, alongside others, that the relationship between theatre and cinema can be understood in much more productive and positive terms,[6] their shared identity as performance mediums has continued to be underemphasised and visual reciprocities between the two practices have been overlooked. For instance, one of the key influences in the 1960s across theatre and film was the German director and playwright Bertolt Brecht. The effect of Brechtian dramaturgy and practice was important across media in terms of what television historian Billy Smart has described as 'the political and aesthetic direction and value' of drama at that time.[7] Both Lindsay Anderson and Jocelyn Herbert were actively thinking about these questions in relation to their creative practice in theatre and cinema and it is the intention of this chapter to think through how production design ideas in the feature film *If*... can be contextualised with reference to similar experiments for the stage. In this respect, Charles Musser's plea for an 'integrated history of stage and screen' is relevant as research suggests a system of reciprocal borrowing between the different media.[8]

However, this chapter will argue that it was not just in terms of the film's visual aesthetics that exchange of ideas between theatre and cinema can be understood. As Knopf argues, 'We have to look beyond the product – the theatrical performance and the cinematic screening – towards the interweaving of influence and differentiation between the two media.'[9] Notwithstanding the very different producing contexts of film and theatre, I will argue that ways of working involving creative collaboration, established in the theatre, characterised the making of *If*... Asserting the importance of collaboration in film perhaps sits uneasily with analytical protocols which have asserted the overall importance of the director as the governing principle in understanding the film's creative impact. Martin Stollery has argued for the importance of scholars attending to the collaborative nature of film production in understanding key issues such as relative individual control and influence over the shape of the finished film:

> For film historians, research into the power wielded by technicians, as well as the more subtle forms of influence they may bring to bear, can precede analysis and evaluation of their creative contributions, and

provide a solid grounding for the latter. The outcome is likely to be an enhanced understanding of collaboration rather than the identification of purely personal artistic expression.[10]

Anderson himself had very clear ideas on the notion of the auteur and refuted the idea that the director was solely responsible for the creative vision of the art work. As he wrote in the 1980s:

> We certainly had no time for the auteur theory. From the start we knew that the film director was the essential artist of cinema – but we also knew that films have to be written, designed, acted, photographed, edited, and given sound.[11]

This view is further emphasised by research into the creative relationship between Anderson and the co-writer of *If...*, David Sherwin, with Charles Drazin arguing that the refusal to acknowledge the importance of collaboration in the production of the film, in effect occludes an appreciation of Anderson's achievement in recognising and marshalling individual talent towards as shared vision. As Drazin writes:

> This is not to deny Anderson the status of 'author' but rather to assert that in the kind of close collaboration *If...* was, the film was an example of the key creators in effect pooling their authorship through shared values.[12]

Whilst acknowledging, alongside Drazin, that it is almost impossible to dissect a creative relationship in retrospect, I would like to investigate Anderson and Herbert's working relationship to try and comprehend the importance of the look of *If...* and how it worked with the narrative structure. This necessitates going beyond the idea of sole authorship to think about creative collaboration and shared values. The musician Brian Eno has used the concept of 'scenius' as a corrective to 'genius' to describe 'the creative intelligence of a community' with the innovations of individuals dependent on an 'active flourishing cultural scene'.[13] Whilst the Lindsay Anderson who emerges from his diaries and archive materials would probably strongly deny that there was any 'flourishing cultural scene' in Britain at the time, there is a sense that both he and Herbert sought to find like-minded people with whom they could work. Indeed, after his experiences working with filmmakers of the Czech New Wave, Anderson bought over cinematographer Miroslav Ondricek to film *The White Bus* (1967) and then *If...*.[14]

Where possible, I will draw upon Anderson and Herbert's respective archives, alongside oral history collections to track their collaboration and explore the ideas that underpinned their conception of the visual aesthetic of the film. The Lindsay Anderson Archive at the University of Stirling provides a fascinating insight into the director's life and career and consists of a comprehensive collection of his private papers and working files. Records of the production, promotion and reception of all his films and some forty plays are present along with correspondence to colleagues and friends.[15] The Jocelyn Herbert Archive at the University of the Arts in London is an extensive holding of twentieth-century theatre and film design spanning the late 1930s to 2003. The main body of the collection comprises over 5,000 of Herbert's drawings for set and costume design, and includes production photographs, notebooks, sketchbooks, research materials and correspondence with key figures of the period such as Anderson, Tony Richardson and John Osborne.[16] One of the challenges of using these archives together is that they are very different in terms of the type and scope of materials that they hold. Anderson's archive mostly consists of written materials – he was an extensive letter writer and kept diaries for most of his life. They offer a comprehensive account of his understanding of events at the time, although one of the few omissions is the coverage of the production and pre-production of *If* . . . Herbert's archive, in contrast and as you would expect from a designer, is overwhelmingly visual: there is some written material but it is often to be found in her scrapbooks. These combine sketches, scribbled notes, thoughts, phone numbers and shopping lists and perhaps reflect the gendered nature of her professional practice, combining work with domestic and familial obligations (Herbert had four children). Very different to the ordered and information 'rich' offerings of Anderson's archive, they demand different competencies in fully interpreting the materials.

The danger, of course, is that Anderson's more extensive written account can dominate the historical record, a problem that has been identified as of particular relevance for researchers investigating women's place in film history. As Gledhill and Knight argue, 'many women have left few historical traces, their roles in production or film culture obscured by more publicly visible or self-promotional male partners or concealed behind collective or collaborative practices'.[17] Thus whilst the respective archives offer rich sources for understanding the nature of collaborative work, I do not want to underestimate how much patriarchal structures of power might be replicated within them. To try and offset this, I will also be referring to a fascinating series of interviews recorded between Herbert and Cathy Courtney that look back over her career.[18] In addition to literally restoring Herbert's voice to the historical record, they offer a comprehensive account of the designer's challenging relationship with Anderson, one that is difficult to codify but gives an indication of how much their output can be understood in terms of their creative collaboration.

There is also a methodological challenge in researching intermedial performance practice in terms of the disparity between what remains of the finished film compared to the theatrical performance in terms of tracing the currents of influence between the two. Matthew Reason has contended that 'Instead of containing the original thing itself, therefore, the performing arts archive represents the formal collecting, cataloguing, preserving and consecrating of traces of past performances, but crucially not the performances themselves.'[19] Whereas with cinema the finished product remains as an artefact, live performance is essentially ephemeral and although traces might endure in the form of both written and visual material the 'original thing itself' disappears at the moment of its showing. Diana Taylor has explored this question in the *Archive and the Repertoire*, making a clear distinction between the archive 'of supposedly enduring materials (i.e., texts, documents, buildings, bones) and the so-called ephemeral *repertoire* of embodied practice/knowledge (i.e., spoken language, dance, sports, ritual)'. Considering the 'repertoire' then allows historians to consider traditions and influences as more than simply material traces, but also how 'embodied and performed acts generate, record, and transmit knowledge'.[20] My approach therefore will be to combine research into the practitioners' respective archives and oral histories with textual analysis of the film and understandings of relevant theatre productions, with a view to thinking about the reciprocity of practice between theatre and film at the time of making *If . . .*

Background: Herbert and Anderson

Production design is often overlooked in writing on both British cinema and theatre but in films there is a notable downplaying of how agency is invested in the visual setting. For instance, Laurie Ede argues that cinema is often characterised as how light interacts with film but 'it is 'also crucially about the play of light on structures of various kinds'.[21] Therefore, the production designer has to think about how to represent the narrative world; the places in the scripts and how they are inhabited by the actor; whether they are adapted from 'real' locations or whether they are constructed in the studios. Ede argues that British cinema has often invested in a realist aesthetic, and thus the production designer's role is a kind of paradox: to create environments unobtrusively that serve to underpin the realness of the dramatic action.[22] However, Herbert, who was more used to the very different design paradigms of the theatre, had very clear ideas on how the visuals presented on film should operate.

Jocelyn Herbert was still more of an accidental film designer and her work in in the cinema seemed very much to emerge out of her initial collaborations with creatives in the theatre and the working relationships that developed. Described as a 'quiet revolutionary' by director Tony Richardson she studied set design at the London Theatre Studio, established in the 1930s by director Michel Saint-Denis, with the help of Motley, the ground-breaking design trio of Sophie Harris, Percy Harris and Elizabeth Montgomery. In the mid-1950s Herbert found employment as a prop maker at the Royal Court, just as a new wave of writers and directors were developing an anti-establishment body of work, including plays such as John Osborne's *Look Back in Anger* (1956) and Arnold Wesker's *Roots* (1959). She swiftly became the in-house designer and was a champion of the writer-director-designer team system by which the head of the Royal Court, George Devine, set great store. Between 1957 and 1966 she designed an average of three plays a year at the Court.

Herbert first came into contact with Lindsay Anderson at the theatre. The first play they worked onto together was John Arden's *Sergeant's Musgrave's Dance* in 1959. Anderson recalled that Herbert 'terrified him' by 'removing realistic protective walls and furniture' from the set of which he remarked 'there weren't a great deal to start with at the set up'.[23] A measure of the play's challenge to established orthodoxies was that it was not particularly well received at the time, leading to Anderson producing a leaflet asking, 'What kind of theatre do you want?' to be distributed to potential audiences, encouraging them to ignore the critical notices and come and see the production at the Court.[24] Anderson and Herbert went on to collaborate on thirteen film and theatre productions over a period of twenty-four years, including David Storey's *Home* at the Royal Court in 1970, *O Lucky Man* (1973) and *The Whales of August* (1987).

It is clear from the extensive letters in their respective archives that there was a long-standing, mutual respect and closeness between Herbert and Anderson and a sense of them bouncing ideas about projects off each other. The boundaries between friendship and a professional relationship were blurred because even when not directly working with each other on a project, there were shared attempts to articulate artistic philosophies through commenting on their own and other peoples' productions, evidenced through many of the letters to each other in their respective archives. There is a sense that artistic collaboration was important to both of them, however difficult a process it might be. Although, their working relationship was relatively harmonious on the production of *If . . .*, it came to be sorely tested by their collaboration on Anderson's subsequent film, *O Lucky Man* , to the point that Herbert swore she would never do another film with the director again.[25]

Herbert's ideas about the relationship between the director and the designer can be identified by some jottings from her notebooks, indicating how in the theatre, working with other people allowed artistic endeavour to thrive:

> For me the only interesting way to work in the theatre – whatever you do – is to work with a group of people whose ideas and talents you know and respect – only then can theatre as you have it here can [sic] happen.[26]

For Herbert, the designer's relationship with the director was crucial. In the same notebook there is a small scribble on the margins of a page, where she explores what she means by collaboration. She writes that ideas have to 'grow' for a successful design project; that a bad relationship would be when the director has no ideas and lets the designer plan it and then in the course of the production has no idea how to use the sets and the lighting.[27]

In the recordings made with Cathy Courtney about her career, Herbert indicated that she was well aware of how these ideal collaborative conditions could be tested by the very different hierarchies that characterise film production. For instance, she talks about how the relationship between director and designer is often usurped by the director's relationship with the lighting cameraman. This was her experience making *Isadora* (1968), her first film as a production designer, after working as an art director on *Tom Jones* (1963). She describes the director Karel Reisz as being 'absolutely under the thumb of his cameraman and lighting' and how she 'kept saying it should be dressed a certain way and I'd go back the next day and it had all been changed'.[28] She also reveals the many instances where her design ideas were sabotaged by art directors and set dressers who are more interested in things looking 'nice' than having an aesthetic coherence:

> In films very often the set dresser puts in the set what he thinks should go in and the designer doesn't have anything to say, or he doesn't say it as it makes it much less trouble for him [. . .] It's alright if you don't have any feeling about it but if you have been born in the theatre you do have. You regard everything you see as your responsibility.[29]

There are also practical impediments to design ideas being realised on screen, as at the moment of shooting, a cinematographer can often rearrange the props and change the lighting whilst the designer is busy preparing the next set-up. Herbert gives the impression that in the film world she wasn't regarded as 'one of them', and there is a sense of her sticking to the design practices learned from the theatre, often in the face of the very different protocols involved in film production:

> If you do a set drawing, most real film designers, they do it from an angle. I can't do that. I have to say 'this is the kind of room this scene should be taking place in, this is the kind of place these people would live in or whatever.[30]

Production of *If* . . .

It is clear that even before Herbert was officially involved with the filming of *If* . . ., Anderson was sharing his thoughts and concerns with her about how the project was developing. In a letter dated 27 October 1967, whilst

Herbert was on location shooting *Isadora* with Karel Reisz (in which he also indicates his troubled relationship with his former Free Cinema collaborator), Anderson refers directly to the script of the *Crusaders*, the original title of what became *If . . .*

> I hope it is coming out a bit stronger, less bittily charming in a suggestive rather literary way which I feel is the danger with the present version. I still have no absolutely clear image of what the film should look like – not just visually but also in terms of casting. It is going to be a style difficult to hit.[31]

Herbert did not actually become involved with the production until filming had started, as she describes in her contribution to the Anderson *Diaries* covering the making of the film (as it is one of the few productions where no direct entries from the diaries exist, details of the filming are given over to Herbert, Malcolm McDowell and interviews conducted by Anderson at the time). She details how she was brought in to replace the incumbent designer the moment she had finished *Isadora*. From the evidence of this entry, demonstrating Herbert's typical modesty, it would seem as if all she did was 'buy a few things and repaint the Hall' because Anderson was dissatisfied with the original designer's work.[32]

However, Herbert's own archive and the oral history collection suggests she had a much more critical impact on the look of the film. In the tapes, Herbert describes how she had been called up by Anderson to come and re-do the Hall at Cheltenham (actually the interior of St John's Church in Cheltenham) as they were shooting in it the next day for the final scene. Her description of the problems reveals not only her eye for detail but also her conviction that the visuals had to mean something. She describes how she found the Hall painted 'bright orange' with reproductions of random generals all with 'the same white wood big frame'. She notes how the platform had 'little swivel chairs' and awful, tatty little red curtains' and 'was impossible', because the designer hadn't realised that 'the whole humour is that it's conventional'. She relates how they, 'got some old masters' and 'other chairs' and 'some new curtains' and

> set to start painting this bloody great church [. . .] I heard a voice saying, "Oh thank god that's better" [. . .] The boy who was designing it said he didn't mind but then he left. He got paid his full fee and I got whatever was left.[33]

Herbert's archive also offers visual evidence of her particular contribution to the film's production design. Of interest here are an extensive set of coloured pen and ink drawings for each of the key locations. This is a practice that corresponds to her approach to designing theatrical productions, in which she would start with pen/ink drawings before embarking on scale models of the set. Through cross-reference with the oral history, it is clear that these were produced after Herbert visited Cheltenham, when she had been officially appointed as the film's production designer. Although a few scenes were shot on location at Cheltenham, much of the material was filmed elsewhere, including some on sets that had to be specially built. Herbert's drawings therefore give a coherent visual aesthetic to the range of disparate locations and imposed a sense of the visual style that Anderson could not quite understand whilst writing the script. They also give clear indications of how sets, on location or otherwise, should be dressed. Herbert mentions in her interviews with Courtney that Anderson and cinematographer Miroslav Ondricek saw the drawings and gave them their blessing.[34] The speed with which the film was subsequently made, along with the restricted budget (500,000 dollars according to Alexander Walker[35]), meant that the locations and studios had to be made ready extremely quickly with little preparation time. In the press book for the film, Herbert talks about a frequently occurring scenario of Anderson shooting one end of the corridor, whilst the other was being repainted.[36]

Although the designer's drawings provide an imprecise pictorial match with the film itself (with some of the interiors being more impressionistic than exact), it is clear that the colours used were key. Colour is usually only talked about in *If . . .*, in relation to the switches between colour and black and white in the film.[37] What has been overlooked is the use and function of the colour within certain sequences. Here Herbert's drawings give a vital sense of the overall film's colour palette. Steven Peacock argues colour is often overlooked in film as it can appear 'uneasily abstract [. . .] existing only as a property of an object' and thus gets 'subsumed into broader qualities of film style'.[38] The dominant colours in the drawings for *If . . .* are dominated by dark browns, blacks and dark green, colours which communicate the sense of tradition, conformity and claustrophobia that Anderson wanted to impart with his public school setting, but also gesturing at the 'dark heart' of Britain's powerful social system of privilege and power.

Against this overall impression of dark browns and blacks, Herbert occasionally includes a dash of mustard yellow. For example, a picture entitled 'Rifle Room' is accented with a queasy yellow against the drab dark browns.[39] This yellow can be seen almost quite obtrusively at various points throughout the film: in a schoolboy's jumper in the introductory scene of boys arriving at their bedrooms; in the colour of the shelves in the close-up of Travis's (Malcolm McDowell) reflection in the mirror, whilst shaving; the yellow of the prefect's dressing gown and even at the end in the gloves worn by Jonny (David Wood) as he lifts up the crocodile, whilst looking through the objects under the stairs. Significantly, yellow has been used by other film makers (most memorably of course by Fassbinder in *Fear Eats the Soul* [1973]) both in terms of affect to evoke uneasiness and repulsion, but also as a way of drawing attention to the artificiality of the image.

Although the film was shot at Anderson's old school Cheltenham College in addition to another four locations (one of which was Aldenham School in Elstree, Hertfordshire), these had all been dressed and given an overall coherent visual aesthetic by Herbert. This element of what has been termed a 'rendering of real life', shooting on sets (which can be manipulated) combined with real locations had been essential to Anderson's aesthetic from *This Sporting Life* onwards.[40] The design thus had be plausible as a realistic environment while also working on a more symbolic level to show the school as a microcosm of the nation, as 'the school does not teach the getting of wisdom but dullness, obedience and conformity: for Anderson the nation is far from great'.[41] This corresponds with Herbert's insistence that the visuals of a film had to mean something, beyond simply being a plausible environment. Her strategic deployment of colour is therefore essential to the overall purpose and meaning of *If . . .*

Beyond Naturalism – Influence of the Theatre

Charles Drazin has talked about the influence of the French filmmaker Jean Vigo on Anderson and Sherwin. As many critics have noted, the famous ending of *If . . .* can be understood as a tribute to Vigo's *Zero de Conduite* (1933):

> The affinity of approach that Vigo, Sherwin and Anderson share lies in suppressing conventional suspense so that we think more deeply about the relationship between the people and the objects in the frame. They shift the emphasis from a series of steps in a sequence, where the primary drive is the unfolding narrative, to the texture of the sequence itself.[42]

Attention is drawn therefore to the interplay between elements in the frame. The drawings indicate this play of texture(s) within the image and I would argue that Herbert's experience as a production designer in the theatre would have made her aware that this needed to be taken account of in the visual style of the film. Space precludes a detailed discussion of Herbert's design practice in the theatre, but it was clear that in her work at the Royal Court, she was constantly addressing the visual, sonic and kinetic aspects of the stage space. For instance her design for Arnold Wesker's *The Kitchen* (1961) opened up the back wall of the theatre, so the bare brick wall was exposed to the audience. Herbert recalls how they

> used the bare stage for the first time with the back wall and all the pipes showing. It was a real breakthrough and I think it was also the first time we put the lighting rig above the set and allowed everything to seen.[43]

For the first performance of the play, the designer used trestle tables for the stoves and put black material on them. She wanted to show a contrast with the sweets and salad tables so a last minute addition was distinguishing them by covering them with white sheets. The importance of sound to the production was also clear as she recalls that the serving points made from orange boxes were covered in tin so they made the right clashing noises during the frenzied service. Sound was also highlighted by the growing hiss of the ovens as they are turned on at the beginning of the performance and was coordinated with the lights getting brighter one by one. John Dexter recalls how '*The Kitchen* pointed me in the direction – not of minimalism that's the wrong word – but of provoking the audience to think for themselves and to use their imagination.'[44]

The experience of watching film is both material and haptic, in that visual perception is not cut off from sensory experience. Moreover, texture is clearly the designer's province, in terms of the choice of materials and their rendering for the camera. As production designer Richard Sylbert notes, 'even the smallest detail, like the surface of a wall texture, is part of everything'.[45] Lucy Donaldson has considered the importance of texture on film, arguing that the invisibility of the relationship between construction and expressivity that forms texture is one reason why it has not been of sustained interest to writing on film. She quotes Pye and Gibbs in terms of the importance of trying to identify this decision making and its affective significance:

> Much filmmaking seems to encourage us to treat this complex tapestry of decision making as 'transparent', so that we are often unaware of the craft and artifice involved. But all this decision making is material and it has material effects on our experience of the film.[46]

The drawings in the Jocelyn Herbert Archive allow a partial access to the ideas that informed the texture of materials used in certain scenes, for example the sequence in the shower block, where Travis, Knightley and Wallace are forced to take cold showers, given out as punishment for drinking, under the supervision of the sadistic prefect, Denson. Herbert's drawings demonstrate a fascination with particular details of the scene, such as the shape of the shower heads. They seek to convey a sense of the various textures of the scene: the decaying brown tiles and tinny shower heads, which are old and rusting, conveying a haptic sense of alienation and austerity. This works in tandem with performance. McDowell's naked back facing the camera, alive with possibility, flinches against the cold water coming from the shower. Set against those dull brown tiles, it fairly bristles with febrile tension and repressed violence. It is a scene where very little is expressed in dialogue and much in the haptic qualities of location and performance combined.

CREATIVE COLLABORATIONS

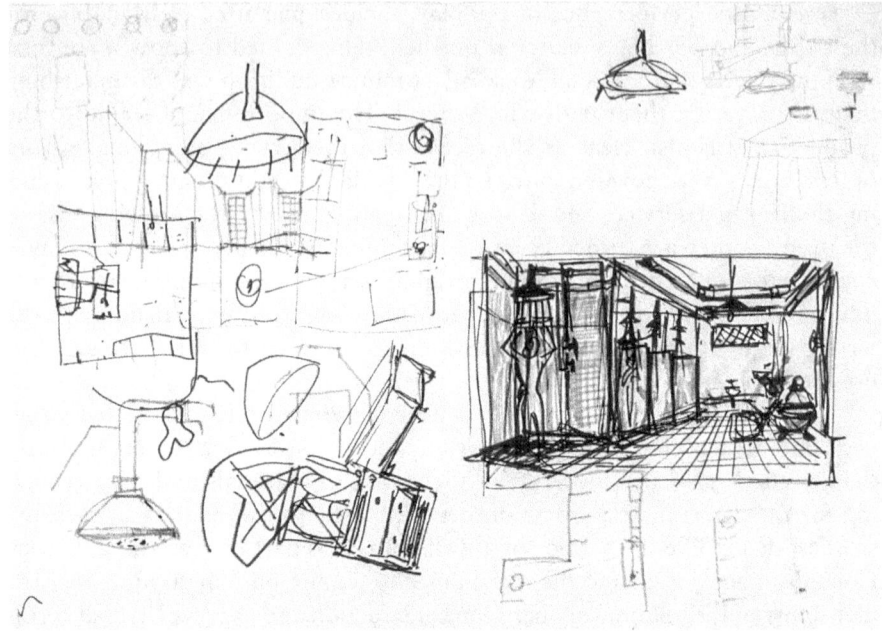

Figure 6.1 Jocelyn Herbert's sketch for the shower set in *If....* (1968). JH436 Jocelyn Herbert Collection, National Theatre Archive.

Figure 6.2 The shower scene in *If....* as realised with Malcolm McDowell.

The only setting in Herbert's sketches to eschew the overall colour and texture aesthetic is the cafe scene, which is coloured in pink, blue and white and gives a sense of space and light that is clearly in contrast to the claustrophobic browns and greens of the school environment. Although the cafe interior as shot is more confined, it is notable that this section is shot in black and white which I would argue underlines the sense of liberation and escape that is inherent in Herbert's design and potentially challenges the notion that the black and white sequences were filmed at random.[47]

Although it is clear that budgetary constraints determined the use of black and white film stock (for example, the chapel scenes were easier to light for monochrome), Anderson, in the preface to the published script to the film, describes them as a way to keep the audiences constantly aware of the film as a construction: 'I also think that in a film dedicated to understanding, the jog to consciousness provided by such colour change may well work a kind of healthy Verfremdungseffekt, an incitement to thought, which was part of our aim.'[48] 'Verfremdungseffekt', or alienation effect, was a key element of Brechtian dramaturgy that sought to create a distancing effect to the world portrayed so that instead of having their responses confirmed, the spectator would be constantly questioning their instinctive reactions to the material. In an article for *The Observer* in December 1968, Anderson writes how a Brechtian approach was taken to the film's aesthetic construction: 'We were after something bigger, something that went beyond naturalism, yet with *realism*, an inner logic that would enable us to progress from an apparently naturalistic start to a violently epic conclusion.'[49]

Various critics have discussed the Brechtian influence on *If...* in terms of Anderson's 'Epic' style, as well as the use of titles, non-linear narratives and switches between colour and black and white.[50] However, it is clear that Herbert and Anderson, developing on from their collaborations in the theatre, where they tested the limits of naturalism, sought to achieve a similar ambition with the visual aesthetic of this film. Sophie Jump has described the poetic realism of Herbert's work at the Royal Court as 'providing a recognisably real but mediated environment that could communicate both the physical and psychological context of the play'.[51] The drawings that indicate the settings in the film give us a sense of a real place (important for Anderson to root his fiction in an observable reality) but also of the 'something that went beyond naturalism', through Herbert's strategic use of colour and texture.

Conclusion

I just wanted to say how glad I am about '*If*', not because of the critics but because it really is good 'a Masterpiece' as you say yourself. Somehow the whole operation – in spite of the agonies, has been a great experience and somewhat revived my flagging faith. You just are different to work with than anyone else – far more demanding – and far more rewarding – the difference I suppose between being a creative artist or not?[52]

This chapter has argued that we should attend to collaborative practice in the cinema, despite the difficulties in piecing together who did what in a collective enterprise from the traces left behind. It also considered how collaborative practice in the 1960s facilitated and was facilitated by the work of practitioners across media, notably film and theatre, through the consideration of the collaboration between Jocelyn Herbert and Lindsay Anderson on the production of *If....* Economic necessity often meant that creatives worked across media during this time, but this in turn created the conditions receptive to a cross-fertilisation of ideas and personnel. To a certain extent, this research indicates that creative units were forged in the theatre, which then transferred across to film and television, but there is little doubt that ideas worked through in film and television made their way back to the theatre too. Archival material can point to some of these practices and relationships but there is still a necessity to connect film production to other cultural forms and determine patterns in cross-media discourse. One of the challenges of this kind of work is balancing the obviously subjective understanding of the environment represented in the archive materials of a practitioner with broader industrial or cultural understanding of the historical moment. Further research is therefore needed into this cultural ecosystem, which did not just involve dramaturgical influences but also provided models of practitioner working relationships. In this way we can begin to understand how theatre and film are, as Christine Gledhill argues, 'cultural spaces open to each other's products and practices'.[53]

Notes

1. Tony Richardson, in Cathy Courtney, *Jocelyn Herbert A Theatre Workbook* (London: Art Books International, 1993), p. 213.
2. Jurgen Mueller in Andrew Shail, 'Intermediality: disciplinary flux or formalist retrenchment?', *Early Popular Visual Culture* 8: 1, 2010, p. 4.
3. Geoff Brown, '"Sister of the Stage" British film and British theatre', in Charles Barr (ed.), *All Our Yesterdays: 90 Years of British Cinema* (London: British Film Institute, 1986), pp. 143–67.
4. See Roy Armes, *A Critical History of the British Cinema* (Oxford: Oxford University Press, 1978); Thomas Elsaesser, 'Between style and ideology', *Monogram* 3, 1972, pp. 2–10.
5. Susan Sontag, 'Film and theatre', *The Tulane Drama Review* 11: 1, 1966, p. 24.
6. See Christine Gledhill, *Reframing British Cinema 1918–1928: Between Restraint and Passion* (London: British Film Institute, 2003); Laurence Napper, *British Cinema and the Middlebrow in the Interwar Years* (Exeter: Exeter University Press, 2009); Vicky

Lowe, '"Escape" from the stage?: from play to screenplay in British Cinema's early sound period', *Journal of Screenwriting* 2: 2, 2011, pp. 215–28.
7. Billy Smart, 'Brechtian television: theatricality and adaptation of the stage play', in André Loiselle and Jeremy Maron (eds), *Stages of Reality: Theatricality in Cinema* (Toronto/Buffalo/London: University of Toronto Press, 2012), p. 30.
8. Charles Musser, 'Towards a history of theatrical culture: imagining an integrated history of stage and screen', in John Fullerton (ed.), *Screen Culture: History and Textuality* (Eastleigh, Hants: John Libbey, 2004), p. 3.
9. Robert Knopf (ed.), *Theater and Film: A Comparative Anthology* (New Haven, CT: Yale University Press, 2004), p. 2.
10. Martin Stollery, 'Technicians of the unknown cinema: British critical discourse and the analysis of collaboration in film production', *Film History: An International Journal* 21: 4, 2009, p. 379.
11. Lindsay Anderson, quoted in John Izod, Karl Magee, Kathryn Hannan and Isabelle Gourdin-Sangouard, *Lindsay Anderson: Cinema Authorship* (Manchester: Manchester University Press, 2012), p. 104.
12. Charles Drazin, 'If . . . before If . . .', *Journal of British Cinema and Television* 5: 2, 2008, p. 333.
13. Available at <https://www.youtube.com/watch?v=d-53tzx69fM> (last accessed 14 January 2019).
14. Paul Sutton, *If . . .* (London: I. B. Tauris, 2005), p. 20.
15. Lindsay Anderson Archive, University of Stirling, <http://libguides.stir.ac.uk/archives/LAnderson/> (last accessed 14 January 2019).
16. Jocelyn Herbert Collection, National Theatre Archive, London, <http://www.jocelynherbert.org/> (last accessed 14 January 2019).
17. Christine Gledhill and Julia Knight, *Doing Women's Film History: Reframing Cinemas, Past and Future* (Urbana-Champaign: University of Illinois Press, 2015), p. 4.
18. Cathy Courtney Oral History Collection, Sound Archive, British Library, <http://cadensa.bl.uk/uhtbin/cgisirsi/?ps=K5Pm65e22u/WORKS-FILE/93540056/9> (last accessed 14 January 2019).
19. Matthew Reason, *Documentation, Disappearance and the Representation of Live Performance* (Basingstoke: Palgrave Macmillan, 2006), p. 37.
20. Diana Taylor, *The Archive and the Repertoire: Performing Cultural Memory in the Americas* (Durham, NC/London: Duke University Press, 2003), pp. 19–20.
21. Laurie Ede, *British Film Design* (London: I. B. Tauris, 2010), p. 2.
22. Ibid. p. 4.
23. Lindsay Anderson, in Paul Ryan (ed.), *Never Apologise: The Collected Writings of Lindsay Anderson* (London: Plexus, 2004), p. 86.
24. Lindsay Anderson, [Pamphlet] 'What kind of theatre do you want?', 1959, LA 3/5/5/1, Lindsay Anderson Archive, University of Stirling.
25. Jocelyn Herbert, Interview, *Times*, 7 August 1983.
26. Jocelyn Herbert, [Notebook] JH 1/6, Jocelyn Herbert, Collection, National Theatre Archive, London, n.d.
27. Ibid.
28. Jocelyn Herbert, C968/100/01-23 (Track 8), 1985, Cathy Courtney Oral History Collection, British Library Sound Archives, London.

29. Ibid.
30. Ibid.
31. Lindsay Anderson, [Letter], 27 October 1967, Jocelyn Herbert Collection, National Theatre Archive, London.
32. Jocelyn Herbert, in Paul Sutton (ed.), *The Diaries: Lindsay Anderson* (London: Methuen, 2005), pp. 246–7.
33. Jocelyn Herbert, 1985.
34. Ibid.
35. Alexander Walker, *Hollywood, England: The British Film Industry in the Sixties* (London: Stein and Day, 1974), p. 402.
36. *If*, Press Book, 1968.
37. See Mark Sinker, *If . . .* (London: British Film Institute, 2004); Paul Sutton, *If . . .*, 2005.
38. Steven Peacock, *Colour* (Manchester: Manchester University Press, 2010), p. 3.
39. Jocelyn Herbert, [Pen and ink drawing] 'Rifle Room', JH 3214, Jocelyn Herbert Archive, University of the Arts, London, n.d.
40. John Izod et al., *Lindsay Anderson: Cinema Authorship*, p. 50.
41. Ibid. p. 56.
42. Charles Drazin, 'If . . . before If . . .', p. 329.
43. Jocelyn Herbert, in Courtney, *Jocelyn Herbert: A Theatre Workbook*, p. 38.
44. John Dexter, in ibid. p. 38.
45. Richard Sylbert, in Vincent LoBrutto (ed.), *By Design: Interviews with Film Production Designers* (London: Praeger, 1992), p. 52.
46. Jon Gibbs and Douglas Pye, in Lucy Donaldson (ed.), *Texture in Film* (Basingstoke: Palgrave Macmillan, 2014), p. 10.
47. For example, Izod et al., *Lyndsay Anderson*, p. 128.
48. Lindsay Anderson, in Lindsay Anderson and David Sherwin, *Modern Film Scripts: If . . .* (New York: Simon and Schuster, 1969), p. 2.
49. Lindsay Anderson (1968), 'School to screen', *The Observer*, 1968, reproduced in Paul Ryan (ed.), *Never Apologise*, pp. 113–14.
50. For example, Sinker, *If . . .*; Sutton, *If . . .* .
51. Sophie Jump, 'The convergence of influences on and evolving praxis of mid-twentieth century British theatre design (1935–1965) through a close study of selected works by Motley and Jocelyn Herbert'. Unpublished PhD thesis, University of the Arts, 2016, p. 147.
52. Jocelyn Herbert, quoted in Izod et al., *Lyndsay Anderson*, p. 119.
53. Christine Gledhill, *Reframing British Cinema 1918–1928*, p. 178.

7. *KES*: FROM PAGE TO SCREEN

David Forrest and Sue Vice

Barry Hines's 1968 novel *A Kestrel for a Knave* follows Billy Casper, a school leaver living on the edge of poverty in an unidentified northern English town. Bullied mercilessly by his brother and his classmates, Billy finds new purpose and hope through his relationship with a kestrel, Kes. In 1999, Penguin chose to re-publish the novel in its Modern Classics series, and yet the image on its front cover is of David Bradley, the star of the 1969 film *Kes* which was adapted for the screen by Hines, along with Ken Loach and Tony Garnett. Bradley's face is indelibly associated in the British national imaginary with a production that was ranked seventh on the BFI's list of the top 100 British films of all time, and which is marked as a foundational work of its much-admired director. While the decision to use an image from the film as the cover image is clearly justifiable for marketing reasons, it irrevocably positions the page as secondary to the screen: *A Kestrel for a Knave*, we are told, is the book of *Kes*. This privileging of film over book is symbolic of a wider failure in both academic scholarship and popular criticism to adequately register the complexities of artistic labour in works like *Kes* that are subject – as many films of the 1960s are – to the mythology of the auteur. This chapter will therefore aim to examine and acknowledge the role of the writer, Barry Hines, in the ecology of *Kes* as a means of inviting a more holistic view of convergent authorial practices in the period.

Given his status and the prolific nature of his output, Ken Loach has understandably attracted a great deal of academic attention. For example, both Jacob Leigh and John Hill have written monographs on the director, and these will be referenced in this chapter, but it is first worth examining briefly the ways in which accounts such as these have examined Hines's roles in *Kes*. While Hill acknowledges that the 'novel's themes, dialogue and structure resemble those in the film . . . this does not necessarily imply that Hines took the majority of creative decisions in adapting the book', and adds of Loach that while 'the subject of *Kes* comes from Hines' imagination and experience, he (and Garnett) chose to film Hines' novel'.[1] Clearly, then, Hill is attributing a kind of hierarchy to the distribution of creative energy in the film, which places Loach at its peak, followed by the film's producer, Tony Garnett. But we wish to argue by examining Hines's writerly contribution that a more balanced picture emerges. Similarly, Stephen Lacey's study of Tony Garnett's career implicitly marginalises Hines in his discussion of *Kes*. In a sentence that is subtly revealing about the status afforded to writers in discussions of film, Lacey notes: '[b]ased on *A Kestrel for a Knave*, a novel by Barry Hines, *Kes* marks a pivotal moment in Garnett's career (the same is true of the careers of its director, Ken Loach, and cinematographer, Chris Menges)'.[2]

More recently, in two separate books, Stephen Glynn has examined *Kes* as a film illustrating elements of British cinema's relationships with education and football, respectively. In the first, Glynn acknowledges Hines's career as a teacher as a formative factor in the novel's genesis, and for the film's locations (it was shot at the school, St Helens in Athersley, where he had worked). But his thoughtful discussion of the film's broader examination of the politics of education finds no space to acknowledge Hines's pivotal role in this area. Glynn rightly suggests that the film 'endorses the pedagogical "Murray method" . . . to find and run with pupil interests', arguing that the film centres on the point that Billy has 'a talent that could – and in a caring society would – be nurtured'.[3] However, not only had Hines been a teacher, but many of his novels and his works for film and television repeatedly position education and the representation of school life as the platform for the examination of class politics. Indeed, in the afterword for the Modern Classics edition of *A Kestrel for a Knave*, Hines himself articulates precisely the point Glynn makes:

> In academic terms Billy Casper is a failure. He is in the bottom form of a rough secondary modern school . . . Yet once he becomes interested in falconry, he acquires a book on the subject which is full of esoteric vocabulary and technical descriptions . . . If there had been GCSEs in Falconry, Billy Casper would have been awarded an A grade, which would have done wonders for his self-confidence and given him a more positive self image.[4]

Similarly, in his football book, Glynn acknowledges Hines's background in the game (he played for England Grammar School boys, and Barnsley reserves), and that his first novel, *The Blinder* (1966), was about a young footballer. But he then locates the discussion of football in *Kes* within a wider discussion of Loach's football films made with other writers, such as *The Golden Vision* (1968), scripted by Neville Smith and Gordon Honeycombe, and *My Name is Joe* (1998) by Paul Laverty, once again connecting thematic content to a singular authorial presence.[5] Our purpose is not to dispute that Loach's own interest in football can be connected to its representation in his work, but to suggest that these sorts of thematic preoccupations should not be understood solely within a filmic auteurist discourse. Indeed, Hines himself would return to football repeatedly in his career across a range of his works for the page and screen, where it is frequently drawn upon in a manner similar to its function in *Kes*: ambivalently as a site of both expression and working-class performance, and as a mechanism of exploitation and toxic masculinity. In more practical terms, Hines himself was a teacher of physical education, and recruited one of his former colleagues, Brian Glover, to play the iconic role in *Kes* of Mr Sugden.

Hines's personal networks and lived experiences were therefore critical to the film. He fell into writing at the age of twenty-one, when his roommate at Loughborough College of Education, Dave Crane, lent him a copy of Orwell's *Animal Farm*. This sparked Hines's creative instincts, and inspired him to write a dissertation entitled 'Flight of the Hawk' as a piece of creative writing about a young man caught between football and academia (it would form the basis of *The Blinder*). By the time he was twenty-five and working as a teacher in Barnsley, Hines was writing in his spare time and had his first play, *Billy's Last Stand* (1965), broadcast by the BBC. The play is a stark, allegorical duologue about the corruption of an innocent coal shoveller, Billy, by a shadowy figure, Darkly, who attempts to commercialise his business. It was well received and was adapted as BBC Play for Today in 1971 (now lost), having been performed on stage at the Royal Court (Upstairs) in 1970, with Ian McKellen playing Darkly. The producer who had originally commissioned *Billy's Last Stand*, Alfred Bradley, nurtured the young writer, and along with another mentor, Stan Barstow (author of *A Kind of Loving*), worked to secure Hines his first and only literary agent, Sheila Lemon (who negotiated Hines's contract for *Kes*). Bradley recognised that Hines needed time away from his day job in order to develop his writing, and so the BBC's Northern Region awarded him a bursary, which Hines used to fund a writing retreat to complete his second novel, *A Kestrel for a Knave*. It was during this period that, as Tony Garnett recalls, Bradley 'tipped me off about a young man who was living just outside Barnsley'.[6] Hines's career up to this pivotal point, therefore, had been the result of collaborative networks offering access to and platforms for his talent, and his meeting with Garnett, and subsequent relationship with Ken Loach, was no different.

The producer, like Hines politically committed and from a working-class background, met the writer and offered him the opportunity to script a Wednesday Play. While Hines was enthusiastic about the proposal, he told Garnett he wanted to finish his second book. A year later, Garnett got back in touch to enquire about the manuscript, read it with enthusiasm and sent it to Loach, and the collaboration was born. Once Garnett had eventually secured finance for the film, thanks to the crucial intervention of Tony Richardson, the trio committed to make *Kes* in the very locations that inspired it. 'Ideologically it was an absolute article of trust and faith on our part to go to the actual place Barry had written about', Garnett recalls, and thus the very communities of Hines's childhood and working life were identified immediately as pivotal elements within the adaptation, authenticating the film through the writer's authorship.

Hines describes the relationship as a 'composite thing . . . I was there all the time on the film', while Loach has remarked that 'the script was a collaboration . . . the film is close to the book anyway'.[7] In recent times, Garnett has suggested that the politics shared by the trio were fundamental to the film's success, describing filmmaking as a 'social project', and *Kes* as a 'collective work'.[8] On the screenplay, Garnett claims that he and Loach should not have had 'the credit' but rather that Hines should have been listed as sole writer. While this perhaps willfully underplays the influence of the producer and director, Garnett had also previously described the adaptation process as a 'cut-and-paste job', because 'Barry Hines had written it so visually', acknowledging the convergence between literary and filmic *mise en scène*.[9] Loach's archive at the BFI attests to this, with the stage directions on early scripts – often describing Billy's lyrical encounters with the landscape, and with Kes – literally copied directly from Hines's novel. The formative influence of the novel is therefore felt not only at the level of the film's narrative content, but through its poetic atmosphere, too.

KES AND THE 1960S

The appeal of both the novel *A Kestrel for a Knave* and its film version *Kes* is frequently ascribed to their 'universal' or 'timeless' quality. Despite the clearly place-specific detail of landscape and voice, and such features of the late-1960s setting as the presence of the mining industry and corporal punishment in schools, this impression is part of the texts' fabular tendencies. In neither novel nor film is there any mention of contemporary figures other than footballers, nor of politics or world events outside the seemingly self-contained community. In this way, the story of Billy Casper and his kestrel seems to answer back to conceptions of the late 1960s as a period of youthful hedonism and consumerism alongside political protest.[10] Equally, *Kes* is a counter-example to the representation, however ambivalent, of youth in such social realist films of the time as *Room at the Top* (1959). As John Hill has argued, *Kes* is a post-New Wave film in its centring on Billy not for the purpose of following his individual efforts to escape his destiny, as Clayton's film follows those of Joe Lampton (Laurence Harvey), but for revealing the workings of '*systemic*' disadvantage.[11] The title of novel and film emphasise this, *A Kestrel for a Knave* citing a formalised instance of class hierarchy, *Kes* titled not for a character but for a creature which embodies the possibility of 'excitement and transcendence',[12] in circumstances such as these where a future workforce is being disciplined.

Only small hints at the era's specificity occur in *Kes*. In visual terms, these include cars and clothes, such as the fact that Billy's older half-brother Jud still wears his army uniform to work, a reminder of the national service which had ended in 1960.[13] Billy's small and 'malnourished' appearance is likened in the film by another schoolboy to that of a 'Biafran', in reference to the famine of that Nigerian region between 1967 and 1970. In the novel the proximity of the Second World War is signalled by the narrator's comment when Billy has undressed after the football match that, 'For an instant, as he hurried into the showers ... he resembled an old print of a child hurrying towards the final solution'.[14] These parallels are not idly drawn. The shock of a teenager in first-world Britain at the end of the 'swinging sixties' living in such a way is central to the critique of industrial capitalism and its human cost, shrinking the difference between events at home and in the wider world.

The various draft screenplays for *Kes* held in Ken Loach's archive at the BFI testify to the collaboration between the director, the producer Tony Garnett and Hines, in the construction of the final film as a work of this kind, as revealed by the mixture of notes and amendments on the different variants in their respective handwriting. However, the centrality of Hines's writerly contribution to the film is revealed by the fact that, although the draft screenplays experiment with different plot-lines or re-order the narrative, the final version of *Kes* often returns to follow *A Kestrel for a Knave*. It is true that some of the novel's significant episodes could not easily be adapted for the screen and had to be omitted. But in other instances, extra episodes designed to augment the narrative's filmic potential, including scenes in which Billy takes part in pranks with fellow pupils, to contrast with his later withdrawing to care for the kestrel, as well as the staging of a school opera, were drafted for the screenplay but then omitted.[15] Some new material does appear in the film's final version, including the scene in the pub where Jud and Mrs Casper spend Friday night listening to a band and a comic singer, none of which was from the novel. The draft screenplay again hints at a division of labour in composing this episode in the pub. While the new scene is sketched out in six pages of script, described as material that Garnett judged ought 'to be re-thought', it was Hines, by evidence of handwriting, who wrote it up.[16] In the released film, the director's vision is evident, since the pub scene is filmed in a documentary style, familiar for instance from Loach's *Cathy Come Home* (1966), with which it shares the form of wild-track utterances and 'observational shots'.[17] The effort to add this significant scene, including the process of its casting, was a shared one, created as it was to show Jud and Mrs Casper away from Billy's viewpoint. However, Hines's is the crucial compositional contribution.

As this example shows, Hines's role in the production of the film alternated between that of author of the original text, and responsive and even impromptu scriptwriter. The novel itself shows evidence of these two tendencies. The narrative sometimes takes the form of a screenplay, for instance Billy's unintended interruption of Mr Crossley's (Trevor Hesketh) attendance register, where the surname 'Fisher' prompts him to blurt out the next marine location from the shipping forecast:

> Casper? Yes Sir! /
> Ellis? Here Sir! /
> Fisher? German Bight. / (p. 54)

Moreover, the screenplay's frequent use of text transferred verbatim from the novel is clear in the moment just before his first sight of the pair of kestrels, when Billy grazes his palms while climbing a tree in the woods: 'the rawness showed through like the dull red of a cooling poker glowing through the soot'.[18] In the version of the screenplay where this line appears, as if the allusion to a 'red hot poker' and 'soot' is a reminder of the pit's existence, there follows a cut, part of a series, to Jud's work as a miner. In this instance, we see Jud at snap time, discussing the relentless nature of the work with his fellow miners, as he puts it:

> If some o' them bloody politicians and professors and whatnots had to work down here for a couple of weeks, tha'd see an increase in leisure then. T'bill'd go through Parliament that bloody fast, the bugger'd be red hot.[19]

There are compelling reasons for the series of cuts between Billy in the countryside and Jud at work at this early point in the screenplay as they create a contrast between the brothers by suggesting the root of the latter's violence and resentment, as well as reminding us of Billy's determination not to go down the pit. The sequence as written gives extra force to Hines's observation that his portrait of Jud should have been more sympathetic, perhaps by showing 'Jud hard at work in the darkness, shovelling coal on a three-foot face': the draft screenplay shows that such detail was indeed contemplated.[20] However, in keeping with *Kes*'s 'alignment of its own narrative with Billy's experience' at this crucial point, the film reverts to the novel's original form and consequently there are no cuts between Billy in the woods and his brother's workplace, and only one scene of this kind showing Jud at the pit appears in the film.[21] The focus here remains instead solely on Billy, who proceeds uninterruptedly to Monastery Farm, the location of the kestrel's nest.

Filming the Novel

Several instances of what Derek Malcolm describes as the 'incidental' scenes set in Billy's school show that even changes to Hines's novel in the process of filming reveal its centrality in the construction of *Kes*.[22] In these scenes, fictionalised details drawn from Hines's experience as a teacher are mingled with stories he heard from colleagues at other secondary modern schools and from his brother Richard. Along with all the other school sequences, the two examples we discuss here were filmed at St Helens in Athersley, near Barnsley, where the author himself had taught PE. In the first example, set in Mr Gryce's office, the changes that take place in the adaptation of novel to film arise from and are the consequences of Hines's fictive vision. In the second example, Billy's interview with the Youth Employment officer, the small alterations due to the change in medium serve to emphasise how much has remained untouched.

One of the anecdotes that Hines encountered during his career as a teacher furnishes the basis of an episode in which a boy (Martin Harley) trying to deliver a message to the headmaster, Mr Gryce (Bob Bowes), is caned by mistake along with the other boys who are awaiting punishment. These boys include Billy, his antagonist MacDowall (Robert Naylor) and three others from what Gryce calls 'the smokers' union'. This episode from the novel is transferred to the screen with setting and dialogue almost intact. However, there are three instances of alteration which take the form of moments of bodily response to events. They arise from the process of filming, but can be seen as visual elaborations of Hines's novelistic vision, rather than divergences from it.

In the novel's version of the scene, the 'messenger', as he is referred to throughout, knocks at Gryce's door, only to be told by the others that the headmaster is not in. The boy tries to resist pressure from the smokers to take their cigarettes as they all wait for Gryce to arrive:

> 'I'm not having them, you're not getting me into trouble as well . . . I don't want 'em'.
> 'Does tha want some fist instead?'
> The smokers surrounded him, all three holding out their smoking equipment. The messenger took it. Billy, looking across the foyer and through the wired glass doors, stood up off the wall.
> 'Hey up, he's here; Gryce pudding.' (p. 66)

CREATIVE COLLABORATIONS

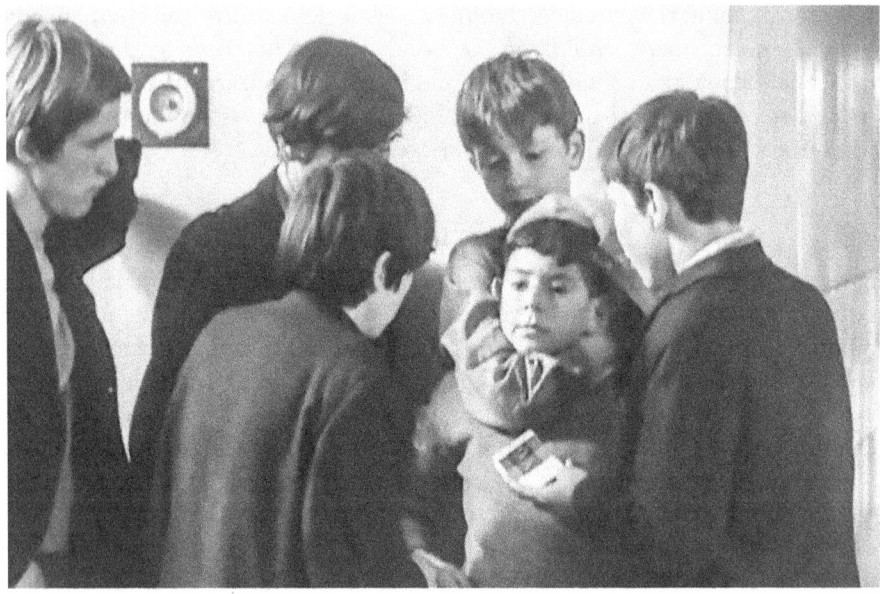

Figure 7.1   The 'smokers' union' scene in *Kes* (1969).

In the film, by contrast, Billy is not just a look-out, he helps to pressure the messenger into accepting the 'smoking equipment' by putting him in a headlock while someone else warns that 'Gryce pudding' is approaching. We see that Billy can be a bully himself, adding to the impression sought by Hines that his protagonist should not simply be 'weak [and] blameless'.[23] Once the boys are inside Mr Gryce's office, we see evidence of improvisation while the shape of Hines's dialogue remains, a process described by Harley, who played the messenger: 'You were just offered what to say and made it up from there . . . although phrases were offered to me'.[24] Thus in the novel Gryce's question to the messenger when emptying the boy's pockets of a pile of smoking paraphernalia – 'You're a regular cigarette factory, aren't you, lad?' (p. 71) – is met with silence, but in the film the boy is frightened into answering, 'Yes, sir', to this leading question.

The boy's attempts in the film to tell Mr Gryce that he has just come with a message rather than to be punished elaborate on those in the novel. In both versions, the messenger tries three times with a timid 'Please sir' to explain, but is interrupted on each occasion by the headmaster. In the film, we also hear him pleading, 'But sir, you don't understand', and witness his desperately preparing to speak before making a final effort, 'But sir, I've brought a message', cut off by Gryce's impatient, 'Quiet, lad!' The scene's realism is clear in its casting of Bowes, who was at the time the headmaster of a secondary modern school in Castleford, in the role of Gryce, along with local schoolboys as pupils and the use of real-life caning, for which the actors were paid 'per stroke'.[25] Such an impression reaches its apotheosis in the highly naturalistic appearance of the messenger's reaction to the assault, an affront even within Gryce's highly unjust system of punishment (and, perhaps, within the film's filming process as well).

The casting of the messenger and his visual presence expands upon the novel's scenario of injustice, by showing him, as played by Harley, to be a solemn and neatly dressed child whose 'angelic' appearance makes him look even younger than the actor's twelve years.[26] The episode in the novel concludes with a stark observation that undercuts the scene's humour: 'The first stroke made him cry. The second made him sick' (p. 71). Rather than showing such an extreme bodily response to the caning on the messenger's part in the film, the camera lingers instead for over fifteen seconds on the boy's face, as his eyes fill with tears and his chin trembles. The novel's image of sickness as a bodily response to institutional cruelty is not reproduced on screen, the film's close-up presenting instead an image of its subjective cost. This functions like the narrator's description in the novel, to conclude the sequence with an image of cruelty's effects rather than its comedy.[27]

This pattern of filmic expansion upon the novelistic base is also clear in relation to the boys' reaction to the long and hectoring speech Gryce delivers before administering corporal punishment, following that in the novel almost 'word for word', as Jacob Leigh acknowledges.[28] The headmaster's violence in both action and discourse is accompanied by the revelation that he, like the PE teacher Mr Sugden, is mocked for it within the action of the film. Gryce uses a rhetoric of nostalgia for a non-existent past, a reactionary way of thinking that is a frequent object of satire in Hines's work. In his later school-set play *Fun City* (1983), the headmaster of a comprehensive school regrets the grammar school boys of the eleven-plus system which had ended six years earlier. This 'ruinously divisive' system, in Hines's phrase, is one of which Billy, as well as the protagonist Ronnie in Hines's Play for Today *Speech Day* (1973), are shown to be the victims.[29] Even more ironically in Gryce's case, it is the elements of the late 1960s which do not feature in *Kes* that he claims to deplore: 'Nobody can tell you anything . . . You know it all, you young people, you think you're so sophisticated with all your *gear* and your music' (p. 68). If Gryce's reference to 'music' is meant to include the chart hits of the era, whether Motown, Beatles or rock, it is conspicuously absent. The film's soundtrack is that of a different late-1960s kind, consisting of almost twenty minutes of extra-diegetic folk music, composed by John Cameron for the outdoor sequences, notably those where Billy is shown with Kes,[30] as well as the intra-diegetic scene in the pub. Gryce's throwaway reference to 'gear', italicised in the novel to show that the headmaster disdains what he considers to be a voguish term, is also undercut by the visual appearance of his pupils, particularly Billy, who attends even his youth employment interview in torn and dirty clothes.

In the novel, the narrator emphasises that Gryce's rhetoric is not only unfair but overblown: the headmaster's claim not to be able to understand why things aren't getting any better is followed by the narrator's satirical observation, 'The boys couldn't understand it either . . .' (p. 67). A second rhetorical declaration of incomprehension on Gryce's part prompts the narrator's comment, 'The boys met him with serious expressions . . . as though they were trying their hardest to solve his problems' (p. 70), yet we understand that, rather, the boys are 'serious' simply in 'trying their hardest' not to provoke him further. In the film, the irony of the headmaster's words is emphasised by the camera. 'The same old faces', Gryce complains as the boys enter his office, but a mid-shot of the messenger's anxious expression reminds us that these are not in fact the 'same old faces'. By this means, and through the framing of Gryce's face by the backs of the boys' heads in an over-the-shoulder shot while he delivers his harangue, we learn that he cannot really see, let alone understand, the 'young people' in his charge as he claims. The reverse shots of the boys' faces show us their responses. At first, only the messenger tries to catch Gryce's eye, while the others look sullenly downwards. Gryce's critique of his pupils in terms of the era's consumerism causes a reaction absent from the book, where we learn simply that 'the boys winked at each other' (p. 69). In the film, they start to laugh uncontrollably.

Such a response arises from Gryce's declaring his regret for the lack of 'respect' from former pupils, an implicit lament for a shifting of social boundaries which, in the world of film, are nonetheless shown to be firmly in place: 'But what do I get from you lot? A honk from a greasy youth behind the wheel of some big second-hand car.'[31] Gryce's stress on the word 'honk' first prompts the boys to start laughing, an effect redoubled by his adding, 'They took it then, but not now . . . No guts, no backbone . . . you've nothing to commend you whatsoever. You're just fodder for the mass media!' (p. 69). This time it is the word 'guts', uttered in Gryce's bombastic style, that causes even the messenger to laugh, while one of the 'smokers' union' boys has to clap both hands over his mouth. These words constitute an irruption of grotesque bodily imagery into Gryce's otherwise abstract polemic, exposing his own culpable confusion of the two realms. Like the messenger's tears, the boys' laughter in the film seems realist to the point of authenticity, making clear the mock-heroic status of Gryce's harangue, not least because he is oblivious to their reactions. Yet these responses also stand in for those novelistic details, including the boys' winking and the messenger's vomiting, which evade translation into cinematic form.

The film's version of Billy's interview at school with the Youth Employment officer (Bernard Atha) is significant in bringing to the narrative's surface the role of the school in sealing Billy's adult destiny. This is redoubled by the interview's effect in the plot, since it delays Billy from checking that Kes is safe from Jud's vengeful wrath and increases his impatience to leave. The scene follows the novel's narrative and dialogue so closely that the small differences loom large. The novel's representation of Billy's first sight of the interviewer uses very short, staccato sentences to convey the surprise of his waiting in solitude being interrupted, and the rapidity of his startled visual perceptions:

> Then the door opened. Billy swung round. Boy. Woman. Man at desk behind, between them . . . He looked up, out at Billy.
> 'Are you next?'
> Billy looked in, not moving . . . at the bald crust of a man writing.
> 'Well, come in, lad, if you're coming, I haven't got all day.' (p. 168)

Although such a description is filmic in style, it does not have a direct cinematic equivalent. In the film, Billy waits in a shabby corridor, sitting beneath a reproduction of the face of Leonardo da Vinci's *Virgin of the Rocks*. The Youth Employment officer is heard before he is seen, shouting 'Get out!' in response to Billy's trying to enter the room without knocking. His next peremptory command, 'Come in, lad, if you're coming', takes almost exactly the form it does in the novel. However, we hear these words before seeing the officer, so that they take an acousmatic form audible over a shot of Billy entering the room. Reversing the priority of sight and sound in this way emphasises the bureaucratic nature

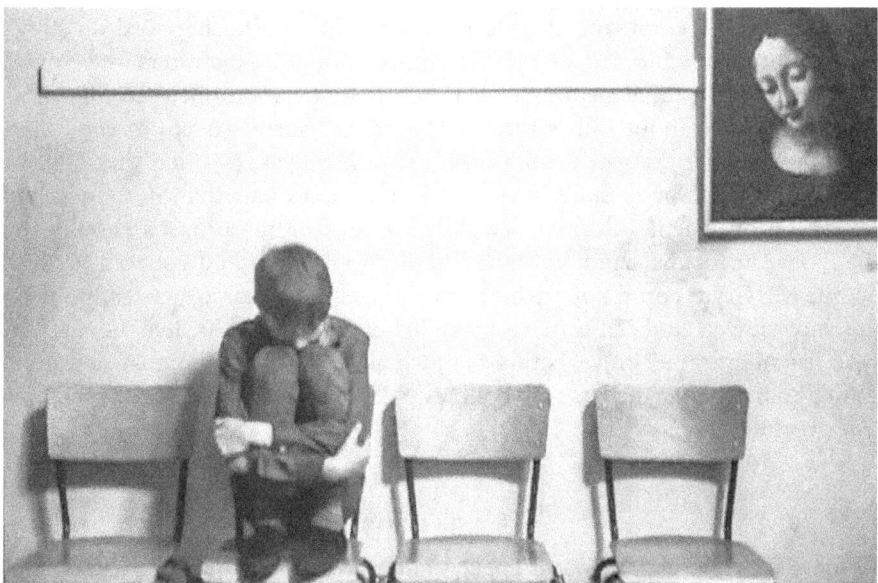

Figure 7.2 Failed by the education system: Billy Casper (David Bradley) in *Kes*.

of the transaction, since the commands are at first impersonal. When Billy does at last see the interviewer, rather than his having a 'bald crust', which in the novel implies a grouchy distance from youthful concerns, in the film he is an equally un-empathetic middle-aged man incongruously sporting a barely-tamed head of curls.

The ensuing exchange between Billy and the interviewer includes another small alteration to the novel which, like the device of the acousmatic voice, reveals in filmic terms the reality of Billy's pre-ordained path. Although the alteration is dictated by the change of medium, it enhances the fictional meaning. In the novel, we read:

> He consulted Billy's record card again.
> 'Offices held . . . Aptitudes and Abilities . . . right then. Would you like to work in an office? Or would you prefer manual work?'
> 'What's that, manual work?'
> 'It means working with your hands, for example, building, farming, engineering. Jobs like that, as opposed to pen-pushing jobs.'
> 'I'd be all right working in an office, wouldn't I? I've a job to read and write'.
> The Employment Officer printed MANUAL on the form, then raised his pen hand as though he were going to print it again on the top of his head. (p. 169)

In the film, the employment officer does not just write the word on Billy's form, but pronounces it aloud: 'Hmm – manual.' This alters the novel's implication of a judgement recorded silently and clandestinely, to that of an explicit verdict about Billy's future. The novel's surreal detail of the officer seeming to write the word again on his own head suggests that this is Billy's viewpoint, since he is more interested in the man's hair than in the topic of conversation. In the film, we see Billy's face over the officer's shoulder as he looks out of the window, signalling both boredom and concern for Kes. While Mr Gryce could not see his pupils, the employment officer cannot hear his interviewee, so keen is he to make his own speech. His demanding, 'Are you listening to me?' reveals this as much as Billy's failure to answer a question about whether he has any hobbies, a silence which is, for the spectator, the greatest irony of all.

Conclusion

While Hines's written text and Loach's cinematic version of *Kes* are often seen to be at odds, our analysis of these small but significant changes from novel to film suggests that there exists instead a continuum between them. For instance, although Leigh claims that the 'dominant tone of comedy' in the scene in Gryce's office arises not from Hines's writing but from the 'casting and performances', it is, rather, that these filmic elements themselves are inspired by and respond to the novel.[32] Making visual the boys' reactions, of laughter or tears, to Gryce's behaviour reinforces the comedy as it already exists. In the interview scene, changes in the process of adaptation bring out the novel's effects in filmic ways, emphasising Billy's withdrawal in the face of authority. Thus his deliberate under-selling of himself, saying he has 'a job to read and write' when we have witnessed his writing the terms of falconry on the blackboard in class, is turned in the film into part of a dialogue, since the interviewer's spoken response is to consign Billy to manual labour.

It is not only the filmic quality of Hines's writing, and the often verbatim retention of his dialogue in the screenplay, that reveals his central role in the film's construction. We can also see in *Kes* the origins of quite specific topics that preoccupied the author in his later, less well-known work, including those that formed the basis of the subsequent three collaborations with Loach. Most strikingly, the figure of the kestrel, despite the insistence on its entirely realist form by both writer and director, shares the same contradictory symbolism as the pheasants which are reared to be shot in Loach's film of Hines's novel *The Gamekeeper* (1980). In the latter, the birds embody the powerlessness of the working-class characters but also constitute the material of their work.[33] Billy's kestrel too has a double signification, that of offering a way out of his circumstances, embodying 'freedom and spiritual affirmation',[34] yet the bird also echoes his own status, as wild and untameable but, if caught, subject to domestication and training. As Frank Collins points out, Kes is killed by Jud, who meant simply to turn her loose, because she 'tries to resist', giving an ominous sense of fatality to the film's ambiguous ending.[35] As well as these narrative continuities, Hines's dramas about young people, including *Speech Day*, *Shooting Stars* (1990) and the never-filmed *Fun City*, include directions for similar cinematic effects to those in *Kes*. These include the punctuation of the action by the jarring sounds of 'time discipline', such as alarm clocks and school or factory bells, as well as the ironic use of non-simultaneous sound in the form of school songs and hymns whose lyrics are heard before we see the action that contradicts them.[36]

This case study of *A Kestrel for a Knave*'s becoming *Kes*, using the evidence of both archival material and the specific detail of how Hines's words make the journey to the screen, does not deny the crucial role of director, producer and cinematographer in the film's genesis. Rather, it allows us to restore an awareness of the animating role of Hines's novel to the film, and equally the already filmic nature of his writing. For these reasons, Derek Malcolm's verdict on Loach, that he is 'a very good film-maker ... when encouraged by good writers such as Barry Hines', accords perfectly with our own.[37]

Notes

1. John Hill, *Ken Loach: The Politics of Film and Television* (London: BFI, 2011), p. 62.
2. Stephen Lacey, *Tony Garnett* (Manchester: Manchester University Press, 2007), p. 82.
3. Stephen Glynn, *The British School Film: From 'Tom Brown' to 'Harry Potter'* (Basingstoke: Palgrave Macmillan, 2016), p. 153.
4. Barry Hines, 'Afterword', in Hines, *A Kestrel for a Knave* (London: Penguin Modern Classics, 2000 [1969]), p. 201.
5. Stephen Glynn, *The British Football Film* (Basingstoke: Palgrave Macmillan, 2018), p. 212.
6. Tony Garnett, 'Working in the field', in Sheila Rowbotham and Huw Beynon (eds), *Looking at Class: Film, Television and the Working Class* (London: Rivers Oram Press, 2001), p. 75.
7. Mo Bhula, 'Mo Bhula Talks to Author Barry Hines and Director Natasha Betteridge About Fairness, Football and Several Vicars . . .', *Kes*: West Yorkshire Playhouse, Leeds [play programme], 10 April – 8 May 1999, p. 7; Graham Fuller, *Loach on Loach* (London: Faber and Faber, 1998), p. 42.
8. Tony Garnett, interview with the authors, 15 October 2015.
9. Garnett, 'Working in the field', p. 75.
10. See Michel Foucault on the fact that the 1968 *événements* in Paris were undertaken by those students whose subjection by the 'educational system', with its 'constraining forms of conservatism and repetition', was followed by 'revolutionary battle'. *Discipline and Punish: The Birth of the Prison*, trans. Alan Sheridan (New York: Pantheon 1977), p. 223.
11. John Hill, 'A working-class hero is something to be? Changing representations of class and masculinity in British cinema', in Phil Powrie and Bruce Babington (eds), *The Trouble with Men: Masculinities in European and Hollywood Cinema* (New York: Wallflower Press, 2004), pp. 100–9, p. 103.
12. Hill, 'A working-class hero', p. 103.
13. Alan Sinfield, 'Boys, class and gender: from Billy Casper to Billy Elliott', *History Workshop Journal* 62: 1, 2006, pp. 166–71, p. 169.
14. Hines, *A Kestrel for a Knave*, p. 130. All further page references are in the text.
15. Script, BFI Ken Loach archive, KCL 6/1/1.
16. Script, BFI Loach archive, KCL 6/1/7, pp. 234–5.
17. Jacob Leigh, *The Cinema of Ken Loach: Art in the Service of the People* (London: Wallflower 2002), p. 75.
18. Script, KCL 6/1/1, p. 32; Hines, *A Kestrel for a Knave*, p. 34.
19. Script, KCL /6/1/1, p. 38.
20. Hines, 'Afterword', *A Kestrel for a Knave*, p. 206.
21. Leigh, *The Cinema of Ken Loach*, p. 65.
22. Derek Malcolm, 'Ken Loach: Kes', from his list of 100 Best Movies, no. 73. Available at <http://derekmalcolm.com/top-100-movies/ken-loach-kes/> (last accessed 1 September 2019).
23. See also Leigh, *The Cinema of Ken Loach*, p. 68; Hines, 'Afterword', p. 203.

24. Simon Golding, *Life After Kes* (Bridgnorth, Shropshire: 2005), p. 201.
25. Alex Godfrey, interview with David Bradley, *The Guardian*, 27 October 2016.
26. Golding, *Life After Kes*, p. 202.
27. Golding describes attempts by the production team actually to film the boy being 'sick as a dog', but the substitute of the close-up succeeds in its own cinematic terms, *Life After Kes*, p. 199.
28. Leigh, *The Cinema of Ken Loach*, p. 82.
29. Hines, 'Afterword', p. 201.
30. Chris Darke ('Sweet Bird of Youth', Film Comment, July/August 2007), describes the soundtrack as 'very late-Sixties', a 'British jazz' soundtrack whose line-up of 'strings and trilling flute' was accompanied by a deliberately chosen penny whistle, as the notes to the 2002 CD release show. Available at <http://www.trunkrecords.com/turntable/nowweareten.shtml> (last accessed 1 September 2019).
31. See Leigh, *The Cinema of Ken Loach*, p. 82.
32. Ibid. p. 71.
33. Loach, quoted in Frank Collins, 'Kes', Frame Rated, 7 November 2016. Available at <https://www.framerated.co.uk/kes-1969/> (last accessed 1 September 2019).
34. Philip French, 'Kes: review', *The Observer*, 11 September 2011.
35. Collins, 'Kes'.
36. See E. P. Thompson, 'Time, Work-Discipline and Industrial Capitalism', *Past and Present*, 38, 1967, pp. 56–97.
37. Malcolm, 'Ken Loach: Kes'.

8. 'I'D LIKE TO REMEMBER YOU AS YOU ARE – AS JUST A GRUMPY OLD MAN': JOSEPH LOSEY AND THE MAKING OF *FIGURES IN A LANDSCAPE* (1970)

Llewella Chapman

Joseph Losey, the blacklisted American film director, relocated to Britain in 1953. He restarted his career with *The Sleeping Tiger* (1954) and continued to make a further twenty films in the United Kingdom until the mid-1970s.[1] Throughout his career, Losey developed a reputation for being a temperamental and intense director, both awkward and accomplished in equal measure. His critical reputation in the early 1960s was mixed. *Sight & Sound* labelled Losey a 'cult' director, and gave *Blind Date* (1959) a one-star rating.[2] *Movie*, however, treated him with reverent adulation, noting that: 'Losey has managed to produce three films which can stand comparison with practically anything that other countries can offer: *Time Without Pity* [1957], *Blind Date*, and *The Criminal* [1960].'[3] He was the highest rated 'British' director in a talent histogram the magazine devised for its inaugural issue in 1962 (rated 'Brilliant') with no apparent irony that he was in fact American.[4] It was after the release of *The Servant* (1963) that *Sight & Sound* began to lionise the director, affording the film a three-star rating, and noting: 'One does not need to subscribe wholeheartedly to the *auteur* theory to be convinced that this quality derives as much from Losey['s . . .] strong personal style and drive.'[5] Beyond an evolving critical reputation, it is also evident that while Losey developed positive working relationships with actors such as Stanley Baker and Dirk Bogarde, he was disliked equally by others, including Glenda Jackson and Malcolm McDowell.[6]

Losey's films and career have been written about extensively by David Caute, Edith de Rham and Colin Gardner among others, with much of the analysis focusing on him as a creative and artistic *auteur*.[7] However, less research has been conducted on his filmmaking practices. In exploring Losey through the lens of production history, this chapter draws upon the director's personal papers held in the British Film Institute's Special Collections and, of particular significance, the production files held in the archive of the completion guarantor Film Finances Limited.

Founded in 1950 by Robert Garrett, a film producer, and Peter Hope, an insurance broker for Lloyds, Film Finances specialises in providing guarantees of completion on film productions to lending banks and distributors. The company employed John Croydon, a highly experienced studio and production manager, as an external consultant to assess the script, budget and schedule and report on the viability of offering a guarantee on a proposed film production. Over the course of the 1950s and 1960s, Film Finances would come to develop close relationships with various independent producers and directors. Of Losey's many films, Film Finances guaranteed the completion of eleven productions: *Time Without Pity*, *Blind Date*, *The Servant*, *King & Country* (1964), *Accident* (1967), *Boom!* (1968), *Figures in a Landscape* (1970), *The Go-Between* (1971), *The Assassination of Trotsky* (1972), *A Doll's House* (1973) and *The Romantic Englishwoman* (1975).

The production histories of these films indicate that Losey was generally an efficient filmmaker, usually completing his films to schedule and on budget, especially when working with regular collaborators, particularly producer Norman 'Spike' Priggen and film editor Reginald Beck. The exception to the rule, however, was *Figures in a Landscape* which proved to be one of Losey's most problematic productions with members of the cast and crew falling out, authorial control issues, delays caused by weather, disputes over Spanish air space, and arguments over the film's credits. This chapter will analyse why and how this production is the anomaly within Losey's otherwise efficient filmmaking practices, providing a snapshot of this most celebrated director at work on the film that would mark his own personal transition between the 1960s and 1970s.

Joseph Losey and Film Finances, 1957–68

The first film directed by Losey which Film Finances guaranteed was the thriller *Time Without Pity*, produced by John Arnold and Anthony Simmons for Harlequin Productions Limited, starring Michael Redgrave. It was budgeted at £104,836 with a production schedule of six weeks. Reporting on the papers Film Finances had received in relation to *Time Without Pity*, Croydon noted that: 'So far as the director is concerned, again I know nothing of his ability, except that his direction of *The Sleeping Tiger* was completely acceptable.'[8] However, Croydon felt that 'assurance' was needed that the distributor, Eros Films Limited, were aware of 'the market limitations that will apply by his employment. His name is quite unacceptable in America', referring to the blacklisting of Losey by the House Un-American Activities Committee (HUAC).[9] While the studio schedule appeared 'to flow along in a manner that any competent director could achieve, is not too onerous and sensibly laid out', Croydon expressed his concern that for the day and night location shooting: 'In neither case do I feel that the director has the remotest chance of achieving the target, and neither is well planned.'[10]

After receiving a new budget, schedule and script, Croydon reported that: 'To a very large extent it must be considered a new project [. . .] It now seems obvious that Mr Losey has rewritten the script', though the schedule remained the same, and: 'To achieve the quantity of material in the given time, the director must apply some very slick methods.'[11] On Losey, Croydon was concerned that: 'I would ask – is this possibly a case of an experienced director taking advantage of immature producers? There is a curious strength and defiance in the writing that makes me wonder if this script has emerged despite the producers!'[12] Croydon therefore recommended that Garrett should 'satisfy' himself and 'seek assurance' from the distributors that 'the producers are not being "ridden" by the American influence [Losey] in this proposition – or, if they are, that the Americans will not run away with the production in defiance of the producers'.[13] Nonetheless, Film Finances agreed to guarantee *Time Without Pity* for a fee of £3,890. In the event, the production did fall slightly behind schedule by three days, and 'it is estimated that the budget will be exceeded by approximately £4,000'.[14] According to Maurice Foster, the co-managing director of Film Finances, the reason for this was 'mainly due to exceptionally bad weather of the last few weeks, together with the effects of the labour disputes which have caused delays in set construction'.[15]

The murder-mystery *Blind Date* was the next Losey film guaranteed by Film Finances. Produced by David Deutsch for Independent Artists (Production) Limited, it starred Stanley Baker, and was distributed by the Rank Organisation. The production schedule was a total of eight weeks, with a budget of £139,841. Croydon was more positive this time in his initial assessment of the project:

> there is no reason why anything at all should go wrong with either schedule or budget [. . .] In fact, it is such a long time since I have studied a schedule giving the director a leisurely eight weeks, and if he is not up to schedule at any time in the allowed period, then he ought to be shot![16]

But Croydon remained wary of the director, writing: 'To the best of my recollection Joseph Losey was associated with a film which went over budget, and where the producers were somewhat weak, and I believe we had the impression that Losey took advantage of that situation.'[17] This was an unfair accusation, due to the evidence of *Time Without Pity* going over budget and schedule due to weather and labour disputes. Nonetheless, Film Finances went on to guarantee *Blind Date* for a fee of £6,354.[18] In the event, the production ran smoothly, and the film was completed within budget and schedule, and delivered on time to the Rank Organisation.[19] Film Finances therefore awarded a No Claim Bonus of £1,589, 25 per cent of the guarantee fee, to Independent Artists (Production) Limited.[20]

The Servant was produced by Norman Priggen for Springbok Films Limited, with a cast including Dirk Bogarde, James Fox, Wendy Craig and Sarah Miles, and distributed by Elstree Distributors. The film was budgeted at £141,725 on a seven-week schedule. Croydon was unimpressed with the script, calling it 'Awful!': 'Some of the scenes I find – even for me – absolutely repulsive – how on earth is Losey going to put them on screen in an acceptable manner?'[21] Finding the story 'baffling', he continued:

> I think that somewhere along the line [Kenneth] Harper, [Robin] Maugham, [Harold] Pinter, [Joseph] Losey and [Dirk] Bogarde must have got together to decide amongst themselves how they can do this to earn an X certificate without incurring a complete ban![22]

Despite this reservation, Croydon noted: 'I can see no reason why this shouldn't be shot in seven weeks [. . .] On the whole I cannot really criticise these papers', and Film Finances guaranteed the film for a fee of £6,391.[23] While production of *The Servant* went over schedule by twelve days, mainly due to Losey contracting pneumonia, the film came in under budget at £138,005.[24]

The following year, Film Finances guaranteed *King & Country*, a First World War drama about a private accused of desertion starring Tom Courtenay and Dirk Bogarde. Produced by Losey and Priggen for BHE Films, the budget for the film was a very modest £82,728, and the schedule was just three weeks in studio, one day on location and two days photographing stills. While unsure of the film's 'entertainment values', Croydon believed it to be 'a subject of some social significance' and 'the sort of film which it is impossible to criticise'. It was also in

> the hands of very capable people [. . .] I find it hard to believe that people of these names in the film industry would set out on a project of this sort without the best intentions, and therefore must state that in my opinion we can enter into this guarantee.[25]

Film Finances guaranteed *King & Country* for £3,707 and, as Croydon predicted, the film proved to be 'in capable hands' and was delivered on time to the distributors. The production did, however, go marginally over budget by £3,107, due to increased costs for cast, film and laboratory charges and studio rentals.[26]

Accident was guaranteed for a fee of £13,452, based on a budget of £299,772 and nine-week schedule. As with *The Servant*, this featured a screenplay by Pinter, starred Bogarde, and was produced by Priggen. The film focuses on the infatuation of two Oxford lecturers with a female student, and the abuse of social and intellectual power. Croydon had little issue with the script, budget and schedule, stating: 'These papers strike me as being very well prepared, and, obviously, a great deal of thought has been given to them.'[27] *Accident* came in on schedule and under budget by £18,217.[28] Consequently, Priggen received a No Claim Bonus of £4,484.[29]

Losey had worked with Elizabeth Taylor on *Secret Ceremony* (1968) for Universal, and subsequently on *Boom!*, produced by John Heyman, in which Taylor co-starred with her husband, Richard Burton. Tennessee Williams's script was adapted from his 1963 play *The Milk Train Doesn't Stop Here Anymore* and focuses on the relationship between a terminally ill and rich older woman and a younger man.[30] *Boom!* had the largest budget for a Losey-directed film to date, at £1,531,224, that Film Finances agreed to guarantee for a fee of £40,000. On the script, schedule, and budget Croydon reported: 'I think this will prove to be an acceptable proposition . . .'[31] Croydon noted that the budget Film Finances guaranteed omitted Taylor's and Burton's fees, which Caute believes were $2,500,000 (£892,857).[32] Film Finances arranged for Alessandro Tasca, Film Finances' Italian representative, to report on the production's progress while the film was shooting on location in Italy, and he regularly wrote to the company to update them. While certain issues arose, including the set not being ready on time, problems with Taylor's costumes and a wind storm causing damage to

Table 8.1 Budgets and estimated final production costs for Joseph Losey's films guaranteed by Film Finances prior to *Figures in a Landscape*

Film	Budget	Estimated final production cost	Over/under budget (%)
Time Without Pity	£104,836	£110,889	+£6,053 (5.77%)
Blind Date	£139,841	£138,438	−£1,403 (1.00%)
The Servant	£141,725	£138,005	−£3,720 (2.62%)
King & Country	£82,728	£85,835	+£3,107 (3.75%)
Accident	£299,772	£281,555	−£18,217 (6.07%)
Boom!	£1,531,224	———	−£10,000 (0.65%)

the set, Tasca reported that the 'estimate to complete is projected to the 10th of November [1967] – I believe this to be a safe estimate.'[33] In a later report, Tasca confirmed in relation to the production cost 'that unless unforeseen circumstances interfere we should finish the film by going into the contingency to the amount of £50,000'.[34] The table is indicative of the budgets and final production costs for Losey's films which were guaranteed by Film Finances and included the percentages to which they individually were over or under budget. This, along with the correspondence in the Film Finances Archive, demonstrates that Losey was generally on efficient film maker.

Film Finances and *Figures in a Landscape*

This brings us to *Figures in a Landscape*, adapted from Barry England's novel of the same name, published in 1968.[35] It focuses on the relationship between two escaped prisoner of war soldiers, Ansell and MacConnachie, who attempt to navigate the hostile terrain of an unnamed country in the tropics in order to cross the border. On their journey, the soldiers continuously battle with an omnipresent police helicopter, which observes and hounds them throughout their journey. England's novel was critically well received and nominated for the Booker Prize.[36] Amidst this success, John Kohn, who had co-written and co-produced *The Collector* (1965), produced *Fathom* (1967) and *The Magus* (1968), and had a multiple picture deal with the production company Cinecrest Films Limited, acquired the film rights. The adaptation was by Stanley Mann (Kohn's co-writer on *The Collector*) and the production was to be directed by Peter Medak. It was also reported in *Variety* in December 1968 that Peter O'Toole had been signed by Cinecrest to 'head the cast'.[37]

In January 1969, Kohn contacted Bernard Smith, co-managing director of Film Finances, to request that the company consider guaranteeing the project and enclosed the film's script, budget and schedule.[38] Kohn noted that while these documents were based on filming the production in Spain, either Africa or South America were more likely destinations.[39] This letter also reveals that Robert Shaw, rather than Peter O' Toole, had been cast in the lead role of MacConnachie, with Malcolm McDowell as Ansell. Moreover, Cinema Center Films, a production/distribution arm of the American television network Columbia Broadcasting System (CBS), was to distribute the film. Croydon's report describes the schedule and budget for *Figures in a Landscape* as 'tentative', with the former set at twelve weeks and the latter an estimated £1,055,316.[40] He also believed that before Film Finances could offer a guarantee, the location needed to be determined and the budget amended to reflect this, yet believed the production to 'be in good hands'.

It is unclear precisely when Medak left the picture, but when Croydon wrote a further report on the film's revised budget and schedule in May 1969, he listed Losey as being its new director.[41] Accounts vary on how Losey came to be involved in the project. According to one, the director 'had read and hated the novel and disliked the film script, but had been persuaded to do it by its leading actor Robert Shaw', who also offered to rewrite the script.[42] Indeed, in interview with Michel Ciment, Losey said of England's novel:

> I was given the book to read and I detested it. I was also given the script written by an American [Mann] . . . and while it was a little better, I didn't like it either. I found the book very amoral – violence for violence's sake.[43]

In a different account, Kohn recalled that it was Losey who had called him stating: 'I heard you lost your director. Can you use me?'[44] As to why Losey accepted the project when he disliked the source material, reports are more consistent, as Gardner puts it: 'By all accounts, Losey's involvement in *Secret Ceremony*, *Boom!* and *Figures in a Landscape* was a case of blatant economic necessity: he was having crippling tax problems and simply needed the money.'[45] The director's fee for the latter film was the considerable sum of $291,667 (£104,167).[46]

In the new budget and schedule documentation, Spain was confirmed as the main shooting location, with one week in Almena, six weeks in Grenada and five weeks in Malaga. However, Croydon warned that 'a considerable amount of uncertainty still applies to this film'.[47] He opined that the direction was crucial to the success of the production, particularly as 'there is very little time before the film starts shooting':

> Kohn tells me that a great deal of Losey's direction will be ad lib and that, in all probability, no final script will be published. On the other hand he assures me that such alteration as Losey makes will tend to modify the hazards in production [. . .] If, for instance, Ken Annakin were directing this film, I would have a shrewd idea of how he would tackle these difficult sequences, but with Losey I have no idea at all [. . .] a successful conclusion will be very largely a matter for Losey and I think we must make it clear to him the extent to which we will be relying on him.[48]

In the event, Film Finances agreed to guarantee *Figures in a Landscape* for a fee of $112,124 (£46,718), based on the budget of $2,576,171 (£1,073,404). Prior to the production commencing, Croydon went to Spain in June where he viewed the locations with Frank Green, production supervisor, and John Peverall, a representative of CBS. Writing to Garrett, Croydon emphasised his concerns that there was a large cost for the 'Cane Field', at 1,900,000 pesetas (£11,309), because 'once the cane field is destroyed it will be too late for replanting a crop in 1970', which had not been budgeted for.[49] Croydon also believed that he 'should return to Grenada as soon as possible and stay with the unit until I am satisfied that the obvious difficulties of shooting this film have been overcome', and he remained on set throughout the film's production period.[50]

Shooting began on 11 June, and problems arose from the start. In the first week, the crew experienced 'abnormally bad weather' which caused the film 'to be two days behind schedule in the first four days of shooting' according to the daily progress reports.[51] In the second week, two further problems occurred. The British helicopter's arrival in Grenada was delayed due to bad weather and problems with the Spanish authorities as reported on 23 June.[52] The second problem was more serious, and was reported by Croydon to Garrett on the same day: 'I came away from Grenada [. . .] unhappy about the personality splits which are going on inside this unit', and explained that meetings had been held the previous day, 'which I hope have cleared the air'.[53] Croydon believed that: 'No-one seems to be happy about the quality of the first few days work', and was concerned that this might lead to 'quality' re-takes being made, which Film Finances would not be in favour of.[54] Furthermore:

> On Friday I heard [David] Tringham, assistant director, and Connie Willis, continuity, declare that as Losey couldn't make up his mind what he wanted or where he wanted to put the camera they were intending to sit back and await instructions and not attempt to participate.[55]

Croydon also believed that there was confusion within the unit as to who was directing the film, Losey or Shaw, and wondered: 'There could be an element of truth in this, as again, to my surprise, I found the script from which they are shooting has been written by Shaw.'[56] These factors had led to 'a fairly violent disagreement between Losey and Kohn. Kohn spoke to Shaw (with Losey's permission) but also involved McDowell, the immediate result in which [sic] Losey accused Kohn of interfering with his actors'.[57] Croydon also shed further light on the issues with the British helicopter:

> I also understand that the Inspector General of Customs in Madrid refused to accept the Minister of Aviation's personal letter that the machine should be cleared until he had personally spoken to that Minister to assure himself that the signature was that of the Minister.[58]

Losey provided his perspective on the rift developing between himself and Kohn in a letter to his agent, Robin Fox, in the third week of shooting:

> Break-in periods are never easy, but this one has been exceptionally difficult, not only because of the physical problems of the locations (which everyone accepts) but because of the unnecessary difficulties which

Figure 8.1 The helicopter as it appears in the final cut of *Figures in a Landscape* (1970).

cannot have any other origin than lack of organisation, lack of production direction, incompetence, lack of communication, under staffing and wrong policy . . .[59]

Offering a lengthy explanation as to who he perceived to have caused these complaints – namely Kohn – Losey threatened that if the following 'basic' conditions were not met then he would request 'to be relieved of my post':

1. Change of Lab (already accomplished?)
2. Courier for handling rushes exclusively.
3. A full-time skilled projectionist concerned only with projection and rushes.
4. Control of rushes attendance to permit serious discussion among technicians concerned as opposed to the present prevailing 'English tea party' atmosphere.
5. Adjustment to [David] Tringham's staff as per discussion.
6. A discontinuance of all 2nd Unit work excepting under my supervision and precise instruction.
7. ~~Changes of all camera personnel as soon as possible.~~
8. Additional make-up man not in Malaga, but immediately.
9. Immediate Associate Producer or equivalent addition to the staff to bring about proper coordination ~~from which almost all of the above complaints stem.~~ [Redacted as per original][60]

For a brief period following the issue of these demands, the relationship between the director and producer settled down. However, this proved to be short-lived, and tensions soon resumed between the pair.

Writing to Garrett on 16 July, Croydon described the situation in Grenada as being 'highly charged'.[61] He explained that two letters shown to him by Kohn revealed that more than half of the current overage on production had been caused by 'artistic re-shooting'. Along with the rising costs, Losey continued to be unhappy with the situation, 'stating in his opinion, his unit is incompetent and that because of their incompetence he has not been able to work as he is accustomed'.[62] He also reported personnel problems on set:

> There seems no doubt that the two people on whom he should be relying, Tringham, the first assistant, and Connie Willis, the continuity girl, have lost interest and certainly as far as Connie Willis is concerned, treat it as more of a joke than a serious operation.[63]

Croydon believed Losey's accusation to be unfair, and that 'the trouble is that apart from [Reginald] Beck, the editor, [Losey] seems to have no confidant upon whom he can lean, as one presumes is the case when he has [Norman] Priggen as his producer'.[64] Certainly, the director was unhappy having to work with Kohn's 'crew' as opposed to his own, as he later recalled:

> [Kohn] said 'Will you accept the crew that I've got because they've already been paid and I have a certain obligation to them?' I went through the lot and I said 'Look, I don't know any of these people but they have perfectly good credentials . . .' So I accepted another man's crew.[65]

It was evident that Film Finances were concerned over the issues arising between Losey and Kohn, and perhaps based upon Croydon's belief that Losey 'had no confidant' to rely on, contacted Norman Priggen to ascertain whether he could be of assistance to Kohn.[66] In a cable from Smith to Croydon on 30 July, he explained that: 'Priggen at moment only possibly available but prepared to talk to Kohn. I feel he could be persuaded to come if only for a short time . . .'[67]

In a letter to Garrett on 3 August, Croydon revealed that he was confused by Losey's methods:

> There is no doubt that he has little idea where he is going to put his camera, or, once it is there, what he is going to do with it. It seems to be a continuous improvisation [. . .] And he simply won't accept the 2nd Unit. I know them, they have done fine work in the past. Kohn makes Losey use them, but he [Losey] won't accept their work in rushes.[68]

On the 'Priggen subject', as Croydon put it, the director 'came the nearest to a stand up fight with Kohn I have yet encountered', explaining:

> Losey wants him [. . .] but now accepts the idea that it might be embarrassing all round, and is, I hope, reconciled to not having him. Kohn puts

it that he doesn't want Losey to have another prop and a shoulder to cry on. I think too, Kohn wouldn't like the idea that with Priggen, he might find himself displaced.[69]

Signing off his report with: 'Best wishes and regards to everyone from this particular version of Dante's *Inferno*', Croydon's letter reveals that the issues between Losey and Kohn remained far from resolved.[70]

Losey later complained of Kohn:

> It is impossible to get anywhere with him. He can be provoked to the point of shouting but not to the point of doing anything or listening. I don't doubt that his intentions are good but the effect is worse than the Hakim's.[71]

Losey is referring here to Raymond and Robert Hakim, producers of *Eve* (1962), who cut the film from 155 to 116 minutes, thus 'butchering' it, in Losey's opinion. Referring to Kohn as a 'marshmallow' and stating that he was: 'exhausted and absolutely fed up', the director's latest grievance against his producer was 'that Kohn would have no picture without me and Robert Shaw and that everything that has been done has accomplished through sheer persistence and nerves':

> [Kohn] tells me he is over budget by which he means he is in to contingency but I doubt everything he says as he never produces the same facts twice [. . .] On no point has he or production been other than a handicap. I cannot attach even goodwill to the flagrant obstruction and inefficiency of the production. You may still have to come down here to deal with the inflexible ice cream Kohn.[72]

The film finally completed shooting around 2 September 1969. However, tensions continued to run high, especially in the film's post-production period.

Having viewed the first and last reels of the edited film, Losey wrote to Kohn in March 1970 that he 'was shocked and appalled', firstly by the optics, 'which are badly out of focus and a completely wrong color', and secondly by the titles which 'are much too black and heavy [and] badly composed and placed'.[73] However, Losey's main issue with the titles was that they were 'full of superfluous words we had agreed to leave out':

> showing cumulative producer credits as follows: John Kohn, producer; [Frank] Green, supervising producer; 'Sir' Somebody-Somebody [Sir William Pigott-Brown], executive producer; Judy Goodman, associate producer. Considering that, in effect, we had no producer on the picture, the above for a picture with a cast of two will be, to say the least, funny.

> This totally defeats the whole title arrangement [. . .] I also strenuously object to the size of the credits [. . .] and I object even more strenuously to the title 'Sir' – not even Carol Reed does that.[74]

Furthermore, the director 'strenuously' objected to:

> Reginald Beck, one of the chief creators, having to share a credit with [Frank] Green, one of the chief destroyers [. . .] Lastly, did Judy Goodman have a contract as an associate producer? I was not aware of it, and she certainly <u>did not</u> function in that capacity.[75]

Losey accusing Green of being the film's 'chief destroyer', while exaggerated, is not without some foundation. During the production, Croydon had also reported: 'I am very much afraid, too, that Frank Green is running very much to form. He seems to have no grasp on the situation.'[76]

In Kohn's reply to Losey, he stated that he found the director's letter 'very offensive': 'In view of our long acquaintanceship I don't think I deserve this kind of ill-tempered outburst, particularly since I have leaned over backwards in every instance to follow your instructions to the letter in every phase of this production.'[77] Explaining that the titles and opticals were completed by himself and Beck, the producer suggested that Losey should blame himself 'for not being here to supervise them personally'.[78] Kohn also believed that if the titles were 'anything but black' then they would have been unreadable. On the inclusion of 'superfluous words' in the credits, Kohn explained that the production company was under contractual obligation to include Pigott-Brown, as with Green's credit. On Goodman, the producer explained: 'I discussed this with you before you left and you had no objections at that time.'[79] Kohn's displeasure at Losey is clear in his concluding remarks:

> Lastly, don't ever write me a letter like this again. I've had a year of your witless sarcasm and I'm sick of it. I don't expect courtesy any longer, but I think even you – with your total lack of grace – could manage civility. On second thought, don't even write to me civilly. I'd like to remember you as you are – as just a grumpy old man.[80]

Although *Figures in a Landscape* was complete, the final cost statement available for the film reveals that it went around 10 per cent over budget, by $278,402 (£116,000), the highest over-cost of a film directed by Losey and guaranteed by Film Finances. However, the production guarantee was not called upon to complete the film and the additional costs were absorbed by the distributor.[81]

Reviews for *Figures in a Landscape* after its release in November 1970 were mixed, often using the term 'curious' to describe the film; however critics were generally positive towards Losey's direction, and it is evident that despite the

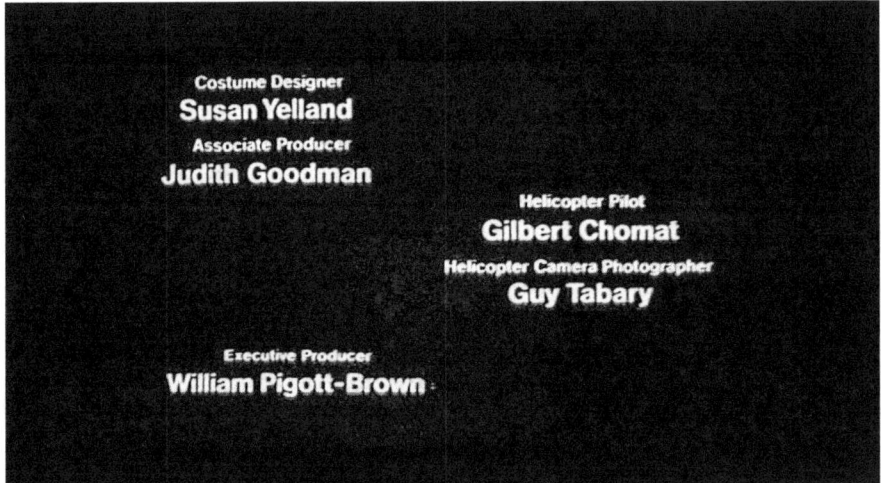

Figure 8.2 End credits for *Figures in a Landscape*: the 'Sir' was removed from William Pigott-Brown's credit at Losey's request.

fraught relationship that developed between the director and producer during the production period it did not directly impact on the released film. Dick Richards enjoyed the film, believing that it was a 'gripping suspense'.[82] Cecil Wilson believed it to be a 'magnificently photographed film', and Michael Walsh went further, exclaiming: 'the title gives no hint of the underlying drama which makes this one of the most thrilling and arresting films in the annals of motion pictures'.[83] Similarly, Margaret Hinxman believed that 'it is a pleasure to hail *Figures in a Landscape* as the best Joseph Losey film since *Accident*'.[84] Others appeared to applaud Losey's direction and yet were confused by the film: 'Scenically it's breathtaking', wrote Madeline Haringworth, but questioned: 'Why then, did I come away with so many reservations? Dare I admit I was slightly bored at times?'[85] Tom Hutchinson wondered: 'The best films by Joseph Losey are usually a considerable shock to the nervous system [. . .] Why is it then that I found *Figures in a Landscape* electric but not electrifying?'[86] Derek Malcolm noted that while it 'looked like a masterpiece', the film 'is scarcely likely to be recalled as one of Joseph Losey's very best movies [. . .] *Figures in a Landscape* was conceived as a *tour-de-force*, and has somehow been degutted.'[87]

Conclusion

This chapter has demonstrated how *Figures in a Landscape* was the anomaly in Joseph Losey's normally efficient filmmaking practice. The available evidence suggests there were three main reasons why this film proved to be more problematic. Firstly, it was not Losey's project originally, and this appears to have caused tensions between the director, producer, and other members of the cast and crew on the set, with Losey noting: 'My problem was how to make a statement that was mine.'[88] This is an example of where archival evidence supports the *auteur* theory: Losey evidently felt uncomfortable as he had not initiated the project, and therefore was unable to find his own 'voice'. The director was also forced to adopt a crew he had not chosen who were not used to the director's working methods. In his letter to Willis after shooting was completed, Losey wrote: 'Many thanks for your forbearance and goodwill. I know this has been an irritating picture for you particularly and I trust we can work together under better circumstances another time.'[89] Secondly, it is arguably the case that Losey was not as aware of the budget as he had been on previous productions where he had been attached as director from the start, as evidenced by his disbelief that the film was going over budget.

Thirdly, it is clear that Losey had little respect for Kohn, whom he referred to as a 'dilettante producer'.[90] When Croydon reported on *Time Without Pity* in 1957, he believed that the project might be 'a case of an experienced director taking advantage of immature producers' and needed confirmation that 'the Americans will not runaway with the production in defiance of the producers'. While this did not come to pass on this occasion, Croydon's prediction came true thirteen years later with *Figures in a Landscape*, where Kohn was certainly out of his depth in attempting to control Losey. While this film did not irreparably damage the director's relationship with Film Finances, who continued to guarantee his films after *Figures in a Landscape*, the next being *The Go-Between*, the same could not be said for the relationship between Losey and Kohn. According to de Rham the pair met once more at a gathering in 1977, with Kohn saying to Losey: 'I think we're both getting a bit too old to bear grudges, don't you?', to which Losey replied 'I guess we are.'[91] The pair never met, nor spoke, again.

Acknowledgements

I would like to express my thanks to staff working in the British Film Institute Special Collections and Reuben Library, particularly Jonny Davies. I would also like to thank Dr Charles Drazin and all at Film Finances for supporting my research and allowing me access to the Film Finances Archive, especially to James Shirras and Thoko Mavolwane.

Notes

1. After which, Losey made films in France until his death in 1984.
2. Penelope Houston and John Gillett, 'Conversations with Nicholas Ray and Joseph Losey', *Sight & Sound*, 30: 4, Autumn 1961, p. 185.

3. V. F. Perkins, 'The British cinema', *Movie*, Issue 1, June 1962, p. 6.
4. For a comparative analysis of *Sight & Sound*'s list of 'British feature directors' and the 'talent histogram' published in *Movie*, see Peter Hutchings, 'The histogram and the list: the director in British film criticism', *Journal of Popular British Cinema*, 4, 2001, pp. 30–9.
5. John Russell Taylor, '*The Servant* and *The Caretaker*', *Sight & Sound*, 33: 1, Winter 1963/4, p. 38; John Gillett, 'State of the Studios', *Sight & Sound*, 33: 2, Spring 1964, p. 56.
6. Edith De Rham, *Joseph Losey* (London: André Deutsch, 1991), pp. 98, 203, 204, 243.
7. David Caute, *Joseph Losey: A Revenge on Life* (London: Faber and Faber Limited, 1994); Colin Gardner, *Joseph Losey* (Manchester: Manchester University Press, 2004).
8. Film Finances Archive (FFA) Realised Film Box 180: John Croydon to Robert Garrett, 15 May 1956.
9. Ibid.
10. Ibid.
11. Ibid.: Croydon to Garrett, 11 June 1956.
12. Ibid.
13. Ibid.
14. Ibid.: Maurice Foster to Tufnell, Satterthwaite & Co. Limited, 2 August 1956.
15. Ibid.
16. FFA Realised Film Box 257: Croydon to Garrett, 14 March 1959.
17. Ibid.
18. Ibid.: 'B. H. L.' to Bernard Smith, 28 April 1959.
19. Ibid.: Julien Wintle to Foster, 4 August 1959.
20. Film Finances would offer a No Claim Bonus, usually to a producer, on the provision that if they had not made a claim on their previous guarantees, another no claim would bring a rebate of part of the guarantee fee. The reason behind offering a No Claim Bonus was to encourage repeat business. The percentage of No Claim Bonus was determined on a case-by-case basis. Ibid.: Foster to Wintle, 10 August 1959.
21. Ibid.: Croydon to Garrett, n.d.
22. Ibid.
23. Ibid.
24. Ibid.: Statement of production cost, 14 June 1963.
25. FFA Realised Film Box 380: Croydon to Garrett, 25 April 1964.
26. Ibid.: Statement of production cost, 22 September 1964.
27. FFA Realised Film Box 416: Croydon to Garrett, 14 June 1966.
28. Ibid.: Statement of production cost, 13 January 1967.
29. Ibid.: Smith to Priggen, 31 January 1967.
30. Elizabeth Taylor was actually younger than Richard Burton by seven years.
31. FFA Realised Film Box 434: Croydon to Garrett, 2 July 1967.
32. Caute, p. 219.
33. Ibid.: Tasca to Garrett, 18 September 1967.

34. Tasca to Bill Hill, 28 September 1967.
35. Barry England, *Figures in a Landscape* (London: Jonathan Cape, 1968).
36. See Roger Baker, 'Steel', *The Times*, 8 June 1968, p. 23.
37. 'O'Toole in to *Landscape*', *Variety*, 11 December 1968, p. 4.
38. FFA Realised Film Box 466: John Kohn to Bernard Smith, 6 January 1969.
39. Ibid.
40. Ibid.: Croydon to Garrett, 10 January 1969.
41. Ibid.: Croydon to Garrett, 22 May 1969.
42. De Rham, *Joseph Losey*, p. 203.
43. Michel Ciment, *Conversations with Losey* (London: Methuen, 1985), p. 296.
44. De Rham, *Joseph Losey*, p. 204.
45. Gardner, *Joseph Losey*, p. 180.
46. FFA Realised Film Box 466: Final production budget, no. 3, 19 May 1969.
47. Ibid.: Croydon to Garrett, 22 May 1969.
48. Ibid.
49. Ibid.: Croydon to Garrett, 9 June 1969.
50. Ibid.
51. Ibid.: Daily progress report, no. 4, 14 June 1969.
52. Ibid.: Daily progress report, no. 11, 23 June 1969.
53. Ibid.: Croydon to Garrett, 23 June 1969.
54. Film Finances were concerned that when retakes were made for the purposes of 'quality' as opposed to necessity, then this would normally mean unnecessary delays to schedule and the rise of film costs.
55. FFA Realised Film Box 466: Croydon to Garrett, 23 June 1969.
56. Ibid.
57. Ibid.
58. Ibid.
59. British Film Institute (BFI): Joseph Losey – JWL/1/17/7: Joseph Losey to Robin Fox, 26 June 1969.
60. Ibid. The redactions were made on the original document by Losey.
61. FFA Realised Film Box 446: Croydon to Garrett, 16 July 1969.
62. Ibid.
63. Ibid.
64. Ibid.
65. Ciment, *Conversations with Losey*, p. 297.
66. FFA Realised Film Box 446: Croydon to Garrett, 21 July 1969.
67. Ibid.: Smith to Croydon, 30 July 1969.
68. Ibid.: Croydon to Garrett, 3 August 1969.
69. Ibid.
70. Ibid.
71. BFI: Joseph Losey – JWL/1/17/7: Losey to Fox, 28 August 1969.
72. Ibid.
73. BFI: Joseph Losey – JWL/1/17/11: Losey to Kohn, 11 March 1970.
74. Ibid.
75. Ibid.

76. FFA Realised Film Box 446: Croydon to Garrett, 23 June 1969.
77. BFI: Joseph Losey – JWL/1/17/11: Kohn to Losey, 17 March 1970.
78. Ibid.
79. Ibid.
80. Ibid.
81. FFA Realised Film Box 446: Statement of production cost, 21 March 1970.
82. Dick Richards, 'Terror chase from the sky', *Daily Mirror*, 19 November 1970.
83. Cecil Wilson, 'Escape – but from what and where?', *Daily Mail*, 19 November 1970; Michael Walsh, 'Behind a mild title – drama full of thrills', *Daily Express*, 18 November 1970.
84. Margaret Hinxman, 'A winner by Losey', *Sunday Telegraph*, 22 November 1970.
85. Madeline Haringworth, 'Thrilling chase . . . But nowhere to go', *Sunday Mirror*, 22 November 1970.
86. Tom Hutchinson, 'Tinkling symbols', *Spectator*, 28 November 1970.
87. Derek Malcolm, 'Losey in a landscape', *Guardian*, 19 November 1970.
88. Ciment, *Conversations with Losey*, p. 297.
89. BFI: JWL/1/17/7 – O-Z: Losey to Connie Willis, n.d.
90. Ciment, *Conversations with Losey*, p. 297.
91. De Rham, *Joseph Losey*, p. 206.

PART THREE

STYLE AND GENRE

9. 'WHOLESOME ROUGH STUFF': HAMMER FILMS AND THE 'A' AND 'U' CERTIFICATE, 1959–65

Paul Frith

The horror films made by Hammer Film Productions in the late 1950s and 1960s have often been discussed in terms of their exploitation of the 'X' certificate (for over-sixteens only at that time), offering violence and sex in full colour in order to counter the effect of dwindling audience numbers in Britain.[1] Following the success of their first colour horror productions, *The Curse of Frankenstein* (1957) and *Dracula* (1958), Hammer and the 'X' certificate embodied an alternative to family-friendly entertainment, represented by the lesser 'A' and 'U' classifications, and also to the rising popularity of television.[2] This reputation would be further augmented as a result of 'X' films often being exhibited in particular cinemas 'with a reputation for art-house or exploitation trade'.[3]

Hammer have been accused of acts of duplicity during this period by going against the wishes of the British Board of Film Censors to ensure that their more explicit scenes of sex and violence were not cut. This encompassed submitting black and white prints to the Board in the hope that the examiners would be less able to detect the more objectionable material; primarily shots of bloody gore and female cast members in various states of undress.[4] However, records suggest that the BBFC were not entirely against this process, and that using black and white film stock during post-production had more to do with cost-cutting than an attempt to outwit the censor.[5] The correspondence between Hammer and the BBFC indicates that the two maintained a professional relationship during this period via a series of negotiations seeking to protect the interests of both parties. As an organisation funded by the film industry, the BBFC understood Hammer's success rested upon the inclusion of sex and violence to satisfy audience expectations of the 'X' certificate. However, they also had a duty to protect the industry from the threat of state censorship, which had dogged the BBFC since its formation, and the power held by the local authorities in Britain to overrule any of the Board's decisions, including the right to ban a film in their region.

Following the backlash faced by the BBFC after their decision to pass Michael Powell's *Peeping Tom* (1960) uncut with an 'X', Hammer found themselves reconsidering their production strategy as a result of the Board's harsher stance on films warranting the 'X' classification. This came at an opportune moment for Hammer who were already looking towards the wider audience offered by the 'A' certificate in response to underwhelming box office performances from their most recent 'X' horrors. Therefore, for a period in the early 1960s, Hammer's colour output largely comprised a series of 'A' and 'U' classified films featuring familiar casts and period locales from the earlier horror productions, but now alongside a more restrained approach to subject matter and treatment.

Through an analysis primarily of BBFC reports and trade reviews of key films, this chapter looks at a significant moment in the history of Hammer during which the company's commitment to box office success took precedence over the production of 'X' certified gothic horrors with which the studio is now most commonly associated. Their willingness to seek out new audiences rather than continuing to pursue a less lucrative production strategy is apparent in their negotiations with the BBFC, which demonstrate how Hammer worked closely with the censors to ensure that, whilst retaining some of the action and violence befitting the Hammer brand, their 'A' and 'U' productions passed as family-friendly entertainment. Looking beyond traditional perceptions of Hammer's relationship with the BBFC, often centred upon the circumvention and restriction of the colour 'X' films, this discussion will demonstrate how their close working relationship sought to preserve the interests of both parties during an uncertain transitional period in British cinema.

Hammer's Colour Films and the BBFC

Hammer Film Productions were early adopters of the monopack Eastmancolor process, introduced in the UK in the mid-1950s, experimenting with the new stock for their first colour productions: *Men of Sherwood Forest* (1954), *Break in the Circle* (1955) and a series of CinemaScope shorts including the *Cyril Stapleton and the Show Band* (1955) and *Dick Turpin – Highwayman* (1956). The greater flexibility and lower cost of Eastmancolor over the previous standard for the industry, three-strip Technicolor, did not result in an immediate increase in the number of colour films being produced in the UK as black and white still dominated until the middle of the next decade. The reasons for this are varied although, perhaps most significantly, colour was recognised as being most effective in fantasy genres which emphasised vivid set designs, costumes, and special effects, while black and white was more closely associated with cinematic 'realism'.[6]

Prior to the release of *The Curse of Frankenstein* and *Dracula*, the horror genre was typically associated with the monochrome expressionistic aesthetics of the Universal films of the 1930s and 1940s. During the subsequent decline of the genre in the late 1940s, science fiction filled the void, becoming the primary source of these horrific thrills during the 1950s; as seen in the success of Hammer's own *Quatermass Xperiment* (1955) and *X – The Unknown* (1956). When the decision was made to move into production on a series of gothic horrors, the company had to offer something which differentiated them both from earlier horror films and the monochrome world of contemporary science fiction.[7] As Peter Hutchings suggests, Hammer's biggest generic transgression within the horror film was not the 'controversial representation of sexuality or violence but was simply the fact that it was in colour'.[8] As depictions of sex and violence became increasingly commonplace in the post-war period, a principal concern for the British censor became how these scenes appeared when filmed in colour. During their negotiations with Hammer during the production of *The Curse of Frankenstein*, the BBFC raised a number of issues at the script stage, focusing primarily on scenes likely to present problems once seen in colour. For example, in reference to page 96 of the script, the BBFC advised: 'This shot of the creature with a bloodstained bandage round its face [. . .] may well be troublesome in the completed film.'[9] While such potentially troublesome scenes concerned the censor, they were clearly essential to Hammer's plans to shoot in colour, as producer Anthony Hinds noted in his response to the BBFC, stating that 'as I am setting out to make a "blood chiller" I must incorporate a certain amount of visual horror as that is what the public will be paying to see'.[10]

Though it has been suggested that Hammer made every effort to circumvent the restrictions of the censors, in order for more vivid depictions of blood and violence to make it onto the screen, the BBFC reports demonstrate that the majority of what appeared in the final version only did so through a process of negotiation.[11] Hammer's acquiescence through sacrificing certain objectionable elements within their scripts, or early versions of the completed film, would be met with the BBFC's approval of similar scenes elsewhere. There is little evidence to suggest that the BBFC showed Hammer leniency in these matters, particularly considering the caution they demonstrated when handling sex and violence in vivid colour. Following the BBFC's first encounters with those early colour horror films made by Hammer, it becomes increasingly evident that both were simply finding their feet in terms of how much blood and gore would be deemed permissible without there being any repercussion from the British press or local authorities. The BBFC, therefore, had a duty to ensure that their decisions served to protect the industry neither through courting unwanted controversy nor by taking an over-zealous approach to censorship resulting in films which failed to deliver on audience expectation.

Though *The Curse of Frankenstein* had been screened on the ABC circuit in Britain, through their distribution agreement with Warner Brothers, the deal struck between Hammer and Universal for *Dracula* meant that the film would appear on Rank's 'family-friendly' Odeon circuit, albeit though their Gaumont subsidiary.[12] The popularity of Hammer's first colour horror meant that Rank were willing to depart from their usual policy of avoiding more exploitative modes of filmmaking, relinquishing this stance to the demands of changing cinema audiences at a time of precarity for the British film industry as a whole.[13] However, following the comparative underperformance of *The Revenge of Frankenstein* at the British box office, Hammer's venture into 'X' certified horror was already in doubt as they looked towards the possibility of catering for the wider family audience.[14]

As *The Revenge of Frankenstein* went on general release in early autumn 1958, filming commenced on Hammer's next two colour projects, *The Hound of the Baskervilles* (1959) and *The Man Who Could Cheat Death* (1959). Released with an 'A' certificate in May 1959, *The Hound of the Baskervilles* opened with a successful first week at the London Pavilion, breaking records held for the previous four years.[15] While the film has been regarded as a commercially unsuccessful venture, this has more to do with its considerable expense compared to their previous colour productions.[16] But conversely, the relatively low-budget 'X' certified film *The Man Who Could Cheat Death* garnered lukewarm reviews and a poor showing at the box office stood in stark contrast to their previous 'X' efforts. As a result of these forays, Hammer became increasingly committed to making horror-inflected productions for audiences excluded by the 'X' certificate.

During the successful run of *The Hound of the Baskervilles*, Hammer's next project, *The Mummy* (1959), was submitted to the BBFC for approval. Coming less than a year before the controversial release of *Peeping Tom*, *The Mummy* went into production at a time when the BBFC were becoming increasingly conversant with (and wary of) full-colour blood, gore and sex. As expected, when it came to the reader's report for the script of *The Mummy*, dated 5 February 1959, the BBFC's primary objections included the more descriptive instances of violence, such as 'maidens weltering in their gore' and 'small piece of mangled, bloody flesh', with a warning that:

> The shots of the Mummy with 'a great gaping hole in the bandages and in what passes for flesh underneath, but which is in fact a dirty grey, mouldlike substance', should not be as unpleasant as these words suggest that it might be.[17]

Despite these concerns, and even though it may not yet have been in colour, the BBFC were prepared to consider the film for an 'A' certificate once the first black and white print had been viewed by the examiner:

> This is to confirm, for the purposes of record, that we will defer the decision on category for 'The Mummy' until we see the film again in colour. In black and white it looks as though it might well be considered for the 'A' category, but it is possible that the colour version, which is certain to have more impact, may make it more suitable for the 'X' category.[18]

Although at this stage the BBFC could not yet guarantee an 'A' for the finished product, Hammer were certainly open to the idea, as evidenced in their memo to John Trevelyan, dated 15 May, in which Michael Carreras responded:

> I have discussed the problem of the certificate on the above film with Jimmy [Carreras], and he is delighted to think there is a possibility of our getting an 'A' for this subject . . . Can you, then, give me a detailed 'do-s' and 'don't-s' before I start dubbing?[19]

Considering that these negotiations were taking place shortly after the successful West End run of the 'A' classified *The Hound of the Baskervilles*, the prospect of securing the same classification for *The Mummy* had clear incentives for Hammer and the circuit on which the film was to be released. Furthermore, as there appears to have been no indication from the BBFC that the company's earlier colour 'X' films might have also been re-worked for 'A', the fact that they were willing to pursue the wider certificate once the opportunity arose is particularly revealing. Subsequently, in a memo dated 16 May, Trevelyan remarked that 'I had a word with Jimmy [Carreras] today and we decided to leave the question of category open until we can see the complete colour version and until he has discussed the question of distribution with Jack Goodlatte.'[20] The Managing Director of the ABC circuit had already been handling Hammer releases in various capacities for over a decade at this point and James Carreras evidently wanted to discuss the pros and cons of the 'A' and 'X' with his long-term associate before settling on a final decision with the BBFC.[21] Whatever discussions went on between Trevelyan, Goodlatte and Carreras, it is uncertain who had the final say over the film's classification as no further files exist at the BBFC. What is clear, however, is that once the final version of *The Mummy* was viewed again, this time in colour, the BBFC passed the film as an 'X' *without* cuts. As Hammer's previous colour horror productions had all been subjected to cuts before even an 'X' certificate could be approved, it would appear the censor saw less to object to in *The Mummy*. But had the company opted to

Figure 9.1 Confirming the Hammer brand: 'X' rated horror in *The Mummy* (1959).

make the necessary cuts to ensure that the colour version remained acceptable for the wider classification of 'A', the resulting film would have contained very little of the 'visual horror' thought to be the main draw of their trademark productions. Therefore, in this instance, Hammer appear to have played it safe by appealing to their established audience through the inclusion of the visuals warranting the higher classification when seen in colour.

However, it is also important to remember the BBFC's general approach to horror and the vigilance they displayed when it came to a film's national release beyond London. Though the film may have been worthy of the 'A' when seen in both black and white and colour, it is likely that the BBFC would have been wary when authorising the certificate for a horror subject given the problematic history of horror in the UK. Released shortly after *The Mummy*, *The Stranglers of Bombay* (1959) received criticism as a result of the BBFC's decision to pass the film with an 'A' as it was deemed to contain 'too much nastiness and gruesomeness'.[22] Following the review of the script for *The Terror of the Tongs* (1961), in some respects a colour remake of *The Stranglers of Bombay*, the BBFC advised Hammer that, although the film 'should be acceptable for the "A" category', they would be 'careful in our judgement of the new film' as a result of their previous decision.[23] While *The Terror of the Tongs* was subsequently passed with an 'X' certificate, the once lucrative appeal of the classification would soon become even more problematic for both Hammer and the censor.

Hammer's *Phantom* and the Family Audience

After the poor performance of their 'X' film *The Curse of the Werewolf* (1961), Hammer's concerns over the higher certificate reached a turning point. In response to a warning from the BBFC during the negotiations for *The Curse of the Werewolf*, the company insisted that films depicting similar themes of sex and explicit violence 'will have been deleted from our programme' for the following year.[24] As evinced by the decisions made in the aftermath of *Peeping Tom*, explicit colour horror production appeared to be off the agenda, bringing to an end the first cycle of Hammer horror films and allowing other production companies, including Amicus, to challenge Hammer's dominance of the market. In response to the script for the planned production of *The Phantom of the Opera* (1962), Trevelyan warned Anthony Hinds that:

> criticism of the 'X' category horror films has increased in the last two years and we have to react to more criticism than we used to get. In the circumstances I must ask you to take special care in the shooting of all shock sequences.[25]

As with previous scripts for Hammer's colour films, the BBFC's main objections were to scenes containing violence and gore, particularly during the scene revealing the Phantom's scars and the copious amounts of blood throughout the film suggested in Hinds's script. In light of the BBFC's concerns regarding colour horror productions in general, it seemed unlikely that much of what was included in their original script would find its way onto the screen, regardless of Hammer's fruitful negotiations with the censors in the past.

Following completion of shooting, *The Phantom of the Opera* was viewed by the BBFC 'with a view to seeing whether we could by cutting make the film suitable for the "A" category'.[26] A decision had been made between Hammer and Rank to place *The Phantom of the Opera* on a double bill with *Captain Clegg* (1962), an interpretation of the Dr Syn story with Peter Cushing as the lead, which had received an 'A' certificate. Considering the initial warning from the BBFC regarding the 'X', had Hammer chosen to pursue this certificate for the film, the censors were unlikely to have permitted many of the 'shock sequences' anyway. The 'A' certificate therefore provided Hammer with an opportunity to rework one of horror's most iconic characters for a more family friendly audience and avoid disappointing expectations of the 'X'.[27]

A number of cuts were required by the BBFC for *The Phantom of the Opera* to be passed with an 'A', specifically those already highlighted at script stage containing the graphic death of the rat-catcher and the scarred face of the Phantom. In a memo to James Carreras, dated 7 May 1962, Trevelyan requested the removal of:

> the shot of the dwarf stabbing the rat-catcher in the face and the shot of his bleeding face immediately afterwards ... [and] all shots of the Professor's face without the mask. The shots immediately following the removal of the mask must be removed, but, if it is impossible to remove all the other shots for reasons of continuity, we will consider retaining one or more of them.[28]

Characteristically, Hammer made the decision to disregard the previous request, resubmitting the film with little or no attempt made to address the primary concerns of the censor. This is illustrated in the subsequent memo from Trevelyan, on 17 May, indicating that 'the shot of the rat-catcher's bleeding face has not been deleted. It must be removed' with a request for 'further reduction of the shots of the Professor's face without the mask. These shots are really rather strong for the "A" category.'[29] While images of the Professor's face were inevitably removed by the time the film reached cinemas in the Britain, Hammer's approach to negotiating the 'A' certificate with the BBFC echoed similar attempts to retain as much graphic details as possible for their 'X' horror productions. Even though the BBFC were unlikely to allow anything particularly explicit to appear in a film to which children would be admitted, the producers knew that, as a horror subject, *The Phantom of the Opera* required some of the blood and gore anticipated by devoted audiences.

Following a response from Rank Film Distributors acknowledging that the cuts would be made in time for the trade show in the following week, the film premiered in London on 7 June 1962 to mixed reviews and an underwhelming UK box office performance.[30] Despite Hammer's efforts to cater for a younger audience, *The Phantom of the Opera* ultimately fell between two stools as suggested in a review of the film in *The Times* which stated that 'it is not altogether clear from the direction [. . .] whether the film is being played "straight" or for laughs'.[31] Coupled with the poor performance of several other recent productions, including *The Two Faces of Dr Jekyll* (1960) and *The Curse of the Werewolf*, the response to Hammer's 'A' certified horror resulted in a significant shift in their colour productions. While they would later return to those original characters and themes which brought them success in the 1950s with *Kiss of the Vampire* (1963), *The Curse of the Mummy's Tomb* (1964) and *The Evil of Frankenstein* (1964), the uncertainty surrounding the 'X' initially led the company to look beyond horror in search of a new audience.

Indeed, between 1960 and 1965, the 'X' classified gothic horror productions now synonymous with Hammer represented only seven of the twenty colour films made by the company during this period. Though they continued to produce a number of black and white contemporary psychological horrors, including *Taste of Fear* (1961) and *Maniac* (1963), colour production focused primarily upon a series of 'A' or 'U' classified adventure films employing many of the same cast and crew drawn from their earlier colour horrors. Released as Hammer's first colour feature in 1954, Robin Hood swashbuckler *The Men of Sherwood Forest* offers a glimpse of the direction the studio might have taken had they not succeeded with their venture into horror. Significantly, the company returned to the Robin Hood character in 1960 with the minor box office hit *Sword of Sherwood Forest*, a film emblematic of the film choices the company were to make in the following decade. Hammer had a long-standing reputation for exploiting already popular stories and characters, and the return to Robin Hood followed the success of TV series *The Adventures of Robin Hood* (1955–9). *Sword of Sherwood Forest* was directed by Terence Fisher, who had helmed every colour production at Hammer since *The Curse of Frankenstein*. Though the film's 'U' classification ensured that the vivid blood and gore would be absent from this production, the association between Fisher and horror, coupled with the appearance of Peter Cushing as the Sheriff of Nottingham, and the company's regular-in-waiting Oliver Reed, maintained some connection with the company's trademark style. Moreover, the *Monthly Film Bulletin* review for the film cited the brutality of the 'needless flogging scene' as part of 'a tradition that remains specifically Hammer's'.[32] *Kine Weekly* announced that the film 'can hardly fail to amuse and thrill the "ninepennies" and youngsters' which is credited to the appearance of 'wholesome rough stuff with appropriate aplomb'.[33] The action and violence with which Hammer came to be associated, combined with the colourful period settings, characters and themes familiar to the younger audience, offered a successful formula for the studio, who subsequently altered their production strategy to reflect this.

Following *Sword of Sherwood Forest*, both *The Pirates of Blood River* (1962) and *Captain Clegg* were added to the production schedule for 1961, intended as a double bill to be released during the school holidays in 1962. During the production of *The Pirates of Blood River*, however, Hammer entered into an agreement with Columbia to release the film alongside *Mysterious Island*, based on the Jules Verne novel, with *Captain Clegg* left as the supporting feature for *The Phantom of the Opera*. While *Captain Clegg* maintained a distance from the trappings and themes typically associated with horror and the 'X' certificate, the film still managed to incorporate more in the way of horror and violence than the lacklustre *Phantom*. Once again, *Monthly Film Bulletin*'s review picked up on familiar ingredients, noting *Clegg's* 'obsession with injury, degradation and death [which is] more dispiriting than ever', while *The Observer* acknowledged 'some of Hammer's most sickening make-up effects, and a vile scene in which a maimed mute is made to try and sing'.[34] Though these reviews take a disparaging tone concerning this particular

Figure 9.2   Cultivating a family audience: Christopher Lee in *The Pirates of Blood River* (1962).

brand of violence, the adventure films along similar lines to *Captain Clegg* were among Hammer's most profitable during this period, leaving little doubt as to the importance of violence to their continued appeal. Given the complexities surrounding the production of 'X' horrors at the turn of the decade, the increasing popularity of sword-and-sandal epics offered a new milieu within which Hammer were able to offer their brand of violence to a wider audience, whilst subsequently avoiding the restrictions imposed on the horror genre. While the reviews of *The Phantom of the Opera* suggest that the film failed to deliver on the shocking visuals associated with Hammer's horror productions (the BBFC even removed the infamous unmasking sequence), *Captain Clegg* demonstrated how these more explicit scenes could be incorporated into a film with the same 'A' classification.

This potential avenue for success was evident in *The Pirates of Blood River*, a swashbuckler intended for release during the summer of 1962, which was trimmed by the censors from an 'X' to a 'U' at the behest of Hammer who clearly wanted to establish the film as family entertainment. Released on a double bill with *Mysterious Island*, the gamble paid off for Hammer, earning $1 million in the UK on its first run during the August holiday season and featuring in the top ten box office hits for that year.[35] *The Pirates of Blood River* stars Hammer regular Christopher Lee as LaRoche, captain of a pirate crew who terrorise and pillage a village of puritans whilst in search of hidden treasure. The film has much in common with the 'Boys Own' adventures typical of children's Saturday matinees, although the company's approach ensures touches of their own brand of macabre violence; notably in the constant and brutal attack upon the villagers and the suicide of the shamed Maggie (Marie Devereux) following accusations of an adulterous affair with protagonist Jonathon Standing (Kerwin Matthews).

Kine Weekly's review pointed towards the 'spectacular fights' and 'action galore' as being key selling points for the film, as was 'the blood [which] flows freely against exotic backgrounds . . . vividly presented on the Hammerscope and Technicolor screen'.[36] Though aimed towards a universal audience through negotiations with the BBFC, this inclusion of vivid depictions of action and violence, coupled with the casting of Christopher Lee, demonstrates both Hammer's willingness to adapt their strategy during a period of uncertainty alongside a commitment to ensuring these films retained trademark elements of the company's horror productions.

This is also apparent in their adaptation of *The Old Dark House* (1963) which remained unseen in Britain until 1966 as a result of the confusion surrounding its status as a horror–comedy hybrid. Given the issues surrounding the classification and release of *The Phantom of the Opera*, Hammer were clearly taking another gamble when it came to deciding upon the appropriate certificate for *The Old Dark House*; a film which they'd hoped would fall into the 'U' category. Finding it impossible to rework the film for a 'U' following recommendations from the BBFC, notably the removal of numerous shots of dead bodies in the film and the particularly gruesome sight of Agatha Femm (Joyce Grenfell) impaled by her own knitting needles, Hammer were forced to make a difficult decision. Though the 'A' certificate could offer little in the way of blood and gore for the horror fans, and also excluded unaccompanied children from screenings, the emphasis upon the comedic elements to the story ensured that there was also a lack of the visually explicit violence audiences would likely anticipate if the film were to be advertised with the 'X'. In the event, Hammer indeed opted for the 'X' and *The Old Dark House* failed to secure a release in Britain.

The commercial triumph of *The Pirates of Blood River* was therefore reason enough for Hammer to actively pursue the 'U' certificate for their subsequent non-horror productions, with *The Scarlet Blade* (1963), *The Devil-Ship Pirates* (1964), and *The Brigand of Kandahar* (1965) released over consecutive summer holiday periods in order to emulate that original success. Set in Cromwell's England of the mid-seventeenth century, *The Scarlet Blade* closely resembles the premise of *The Pirates of Blood River*, with the battle between the Royalists and Roundheads substituting for the pirates and puritans of the earlier film. Another success for Hammer, the film again entwined the exciting 'Boys Own' adventure with similar themes of kidnap and torture. Almost a carbon copy of *The Pirates of Blood River*, *The Devil-Ship Pirates* again features Christopher Lee, this time in the role of Captain Robeles, a Spanish pirate who invades a small Cornish coastal village in the sixteenth century. As *Monthly Film Bulletin* recognised, the film maintains an 'overt sadistic bent' throughout with the more brutal instances of pillage, flogging and hanging.[37] *Kine Weekly* defined the film's appeal as a 'rousing schoolboy adventure in which villainy is blacker than black and virtue always triumphs', noting that 'the Hammer boys have given this one every ingredient of the recipe' aided by Lee's 'saturnine and implacable cruelty'.[38] As with their other non-horror productions released during this period, *The Devil-Ship Pirates* can be seen as an attempt by Hammer to offer younger audiences a somewhat restrained version of the action and violence previously associated with their 'X' films; a lure which became crucial for Hammer during this uncertain period.

Conclusion

The poor box office performance of the last of the swashbucklers from this period, *The Brigand of Kandahar*, starring Oliver Reed as Eli Khan, leader of the brigands on the North West Frontier of India, came at an opportune time for Hammer. The success of *She* (1965), a fantasy adventure released earlier that same year, set a new trend for their schedule of bigger budgets and more family-friendly material emphasising period fantasy, mysticism, exoticism and sex appeal of stars such as Ursula Andress and Raquel Welch, who appeared in *She* and *One Million Years B.C.* (1966) respectively. As the controversy surrounding the 'X' certificate faded, and the popularity of horror was once again on the rise in Britain, Hammer also returned to their popular Dracula, Frankenstein and Mummy franchises with an unrelenting dedication to providing ever-increasing amounts of sex and violence. While the swashbucklers offered an alternative mode of production during this transitional period, these films demonstrated how Hammer were able to adapt their own particular style of full-blooded violence for younger audiences whilst simultaneously offering the tried and tested 'X' horrors for those who demanded more explicit entertainment. Though there would be one last hurrah in the form of *A Challenge for Robin Hood* (1967), released on Christmas Eve 1967 with a 'U' certificate and aimed squarely at the younger holiday audience, the later half of the 1960s at Hammer would be dominated by the likes of *One Million Years B.C.*, *Prehistoric Women* (1967) and *Slave Girls* (1968) which combined some of the diluted brutalism of the swashbucklers with the increased demand for sex appeal on the screen; something which would come to dominate the company's 'X' horrors as they moved beyond the 1960s.

Notes

1. For example see: Peter Hutchings, *Hammer and Beyond: The British Horror Film* (Manchester: Manchester University Press, 1993), pp. 38–9; Howard Manxford, *Hammer, House of Horror: Behind the Screams* (London: B. T. Batsford, 1996), pp. 28–9. There are also numerous fan publications which have discussed the relationship between the BBFC and Hammer at great length, including: *The Dark*

Side; Halls of Horror; House of Hammer; The House that Hammer Built; Little Shoppe of Horrors. The exploitation of the 'X' certificate is most apparent for two of Hammer's earlier black and white science fiction films, *The Quatermass Xperiment* (1955) and *X the Unknown* (1956), for both of which the marketing emphasised the appearance of the letter 'X' in their titles.
2. The 'U' certificate represented a universal audience, open to all, while the 'A' required children under the age of sixteen to be accompanied by an adult.
3. Denis Meikle, *A History of Horrors: The Rise and Fall of the House of Hammer* (London: Scarecrow Press, 1996), p. 46.
4. Paul Frith, '"The curse of the thing is Technicolor blood: why need vampires be messier feeders than anyone else?": the BBFC and Hammer's colour films, 1957–1962', *Historical Journal of Film, Radio and Television*. 39: 2, 2018, pp. 230–50.
5. BBFC, *Frankenstein Must Be Destroyed* File, John Trevelyan to James Carreras, 1 April 1964. Hammer continued to submit their films to the BBFC in black and white as late as 1969 without objection from the censor.
6. Steve Neale, *Cinema Technology: Image, Sound, Colour* (London: Macmillan, 1985), p. 145.
7. Steve Neale, 'Questions of genre', *Screen* 31: 1, 1990, pp. 45–66, p. 46.
8. Peter Hutchings, *Terence Fisher* (Manchester: Manchester University Press, 2001), p. 19.
9. BBFC, *The Curse of Frankenstein* File, Audrey Field to Anthony Hinds, 19 October 1956.
10. BBFC, *The Curse of Frankenstein* File, Anthony Hinds to Arthur Watkins, 24 October 1956.
11. There have been numerous fan publications favouring the idea of black and white prints being used to circumvent the BBFC restrictions, including: *The Dark Side; Halls of Horror; House of Hammer; The House that Hammer Built; Little Shoppe of Horrors*. See also: Steve Chibnall, 'From *The Snake Pit* to *The Garden of Eden*: a time of temptation for the Board', in Edward Lamberti (ed.), *Behind the Scenes at the BBFC: Film Classification from the Silver Screen to the Digital Age* (London: Palgrave Macmillan, 2012), pp. 29–52, p. 48.
12. Meikle, *A History of Horrors*, p. 74.
13. For more on the relationship between British film distributors and the 'X' certificate see: John Hill, *Sex, Class and Realism: British Cinema 1956–1963* (London: BFI, 1986) and Geoffrey Macnab, *Delivering Dreams: A Century of Film Distribution* (London: I. B. Tauris, 2016).
14. David Pirie, *A New Heritage of Horror* (London: I. B. Tauris, 2008), p. 85.
15. Marcus Hearn and Alan Barnes, *The Hammer Story: The Authorised History of Hammer Films* (London: Titan, 2007), p. 39.
16. Winston Wheeler Dixon, *The Charm of Evil: The Life and Films of Terence Fisher* (London: Scarecrow Press, 1991), p. 368; David Pirie, *A New Heritage of Horror*, p. 72. Sir Arthur Conan Doyle's son Adrian was brought on as technical consultant, adding a considerable amount to the budget.
17. BBFC, *The Mummy* File, John Trevelyan to Michael Carreras, 5 February 1959.
18. BBFC, *The Mummy* File, John Trevelyan to Michael Carreras, 14 May 1959.

19. BBFC, *The Mummy* File, Michael Carreras to John Trevelyan, 15 May 1959.
20. BBFC, *The Mummy* File, John Trevelyan to Michael Carreras, 16 May 1959.
21. For further reading on the relationship between Jack Goodlatte and Hammer see: Dixon, *The Charm of Evil*, p. 126.
22. BBFC, *The Terror of the Tongs* File, John Trevelyan to Kenneth Hyman, 30 March 1960.
23. Ibid.
24. BBFC, *The Curse of the Werewolf* File, James Carreras to John Trevelyan, 22 August 1960.
25. BBFC, *The Phantom of the Opera* File, John Trevelyan to Anthony Hinds, 19 July 1961.
26. BBFC, *The Phantom of the Opera* File, John Trevelyan to James Carreras, 7 May 1962.
27. Universal's 1942 colour version of *The Phantom of the Opera* had also been passed by the BBFC with an 'A' certificate at a time when similar concerns regarding horror led to the removal of 'H' classified films from British screens.
28. BBFC, *The Phantom of the Opera* File, John Trevelyan to James Carreras, 7 May 1962.
29. BBFC, *The Phantom of the Opera* File, John Trevelyan to James Carreras, 17 May 1962.
30. BBFC, *The Phantom of the Opera* File, Rank Film Distributors to John Trevelyan, 25 May 1962.
31. Anon., 'A disappointing miscellany of new films', *The Times*, 8 June 1962, p. 6.
32. Anon., 'Swords of Sherwood Forest', *Monthly Film Bulletin* 28: 325, February 1960, p. 25.
33. Anon., 'Swords of Sherwood Forest', *Kine Weekly*, 24 November 1960, p. 12.
34. Anon., 'Captain Clegg', *Monthly Film Bulletin* 29: 342, July 1962, p. 92; Penelope Gilliatt, 'The Gospels into grand guignol', *The Observer*, 10 June 1962, p. 23.
35. Anon., 'ABC campaign honors 154 theatre managers', *Variety* 228: 11, 7 November 1962, p. 18.
36. Anon., 'Pirates of Blood River', *Monthly Film Bulletin* 29: 341, June 1962, p. 83.
37. Anon., 'Devil-Ship Pirates', *Monthly Film Bulletin* 31: 366, July 1964, pp. 105–6.
38. Anon., 'Devil-Ship Pirates', *Kine Weekly*, 4 June 1964, p. 9.

10. WIDESCREEN PYROTECHNICS: SHOT COMPOSITION AND STAGING IN THE COLD WAR FILMS OF JOSEPH LOSEY AND SIDNEY J. FURIE

Steven Roberts

Widescreen film technology was gradually adopted in Britain after 1953, the year which saw the introduction of CinemaScope by Twentieth Century-Fox. In a strategy that would incite the Free Cinema movement to state that 'size is irrelevant' to British documentary film, global marketing frequently emphasised the visual and budgetary scale of widescreen films.[1] By the end of the 1960s, a number of significant widescreen epics such as *The Guns of Navarone* (1961), *Lawrence of Arabia* (1962), *Zulu* (1964), *Those Magnificent Men in their Flying Machines* (1965) and *2001: A Space Odyssey* (1968) had been made in Britain. Unfolding over more than two hours while showcasing widescreen colour cinematography and large-scale production design, such titles fit comfortably within or adjacent to the Hollywood tradition of film epics and spectaculars outlined by Steve Neale and Sheldon Hall.[2] Lavish spectaculars have helped to ensure that British cinema features in historical surveys of the widescreen era. But despite providing one of its most significant formal trends, these types of film do not capture the diverse widescreen output of the 1960s. Indeed, with the increasingly extravagant James Bond series aside, of which *Thunderball* (1965) would be the first entry in Panavision, major widescreen productions such as *Lawrence of Arabia* were marketed in prestigious terms largely because of their rare occurrence.

There have been few attempts to broaden the analysis of authorship, genre and style in British widescreen films of the 1960s since Charles Barr's 1963 essay on CinemaScope, and Duncan Petrie's *The British Cinematographer*, published in 1996.[3] In response, the widescreen films examined in this chapter do not align with the familiar canon of film epics outlined above, though they contain stylistic experiments that might be considered visually spectacular in other, more challenging ways. By the 1960s, European widescreen films spanning a range of genres and budgets became more common thanks to commercially ambitious studios including Hammer Films in Britain, and the diffusion of affordable widescreen formats such as Techniscope in Italy and Dyaliscope in France. In this expanded context, film directors were allowed to trial idiosyncratic widescreen compositions and staging with the help of relatively small crews, modifying their approach to camera movement, montage, and other storytelling devices. Consequently, my two case studies, Joseph Losey's *The Damned* (1963) and Sidney J. Furie's *The Ipcress File* (1965), can be broadly described as low-to-medium budget Cold War thrillers, filmed entirely in British studios and locations in the widescreen aspect ratio of 2.35:1.

Joseph Losey and Sidney J. Furie

These two directors might initially seem an odd choice for comparative textual analysis. Losey's modernist tendencies and interest in European art cinema can contrast with Furie's flexibility in his choice of genre subjects. The two directors reportedly met at a screening in 1964 and neither enjoyed the other's company due to a clashing of competitive egos.[4] Yet a number of techniques, themes and career choices link them. Both were émigrés who still had something to prove to the film industry in the early 1960s, for example.

Displaced to Britain by the McCarthyite Hollywood blacklist and resuming his career by directing *The Sleeping Tiger* (1954) under the pseudonym of 'Victor Hanbury', Losey languished in obscurity and financial insecurity through much of the 1950s, requiring him to work more flexibly than we might recall given the overwhelming reputation of his 1960s films.[5] Losey's first use of widescreen technology, and his first directorial credit in Britain, was *A Man on the Beach* (1956), a CinemaScope short produced by Anthony Hinds at Hammer to supplement the growing programme of widescreen features in cinemas and which the director dismissed as a 'half-hour divertissement'.[6] He would finally gain mainstream British film establishment acceptance with *The Servant* (1963) and *King & Country* (1964), though only after completing another Hammer assignment to film *The Damned* in Dorset, a lesser known feature again produced by Hinds, at a budget of £170,000 for distribution via Columbia.[7] But like many of his 1960s films, *The Damned* showcases Losey's penchant for virtuoso long takes and elaborate camera movement, which are encouraged and shaped by the widescreen aspect ratio. The two widescreen films at Hammer, marketed as 'Hammerscope' titles, also established Losey's predilection for widescreen cinematography in outdoor settings, including the private island in *Boom!* (1968) and the Spanish locations in *Figures in a Landscape* (1970), both of which employed the improved Panavision anamorphic format.

Sidney J. Furie began his directing career in television, at the Canadian Broadcasting Corporation (CBC). He was able to independently produce and direct two low-budget features in Canada, though the post-war industry remained geared towards television and shorts, as the flawed Canadian Co-operation Project prolonged Hollywood's domination of feature film distribution between 1948 and 1958. Fortunately, Furie's former assistant director at CBC, the British filmmaker Fred Slark, secured him a contract to direct *Doctor Blood's Coffin* (1961) for independent producers George Fowler and David E. Rose in London. Having relocated to Britain in 1960, Furie's commercial prospects were boosted by the popularity of the Cinema-Scope musical, *The Young Ones* (1961), beaten only by *The Guns of Navarone* in the annual domestic box office takings for its year of release. The director's artistic breakthrough came with his ninth British film, *The Ipcress File* (1965), produced by Harry Saltzman for distribution via Universal, and selected for the Cannes Film Festival. The film's budget of £309,000 was almost twice that of Losey's *The Damned*, though intentionally much lower than Saltzman's multi-million Bond thriller, *Thunderball* (1965), co-produced with Albert R. Broccoli and shot simultaneously at Pinewood. As with the fleeting references to atomic mutation and brainwashing in *The Damned*, *The Ipcress File* foregrounds its characters and setting over the action set pieces and Cold War technologies described in the Len Deighton spy novel from which it is adapted. Furie lends a psychological intensity to humdrum London locations with elaborate Techniscope shots and a moody Eastmancolor palette. Similar to Losey's notoriously baroque film style, and contrary to Saltzman's economical vision for the film, Furie's bold camera angles, staging and latticed compositions in *The Ipcress File* have proven aesthetically divisive.[8] It remains an innovative example of Furie's widescreen filmmaking, which varied in tone and style from colourful Cliff Richard musicals to the social realist biker film *The Leather Boys* (1964).[9]

Losey and Furie both evolved signature techniques within the constraints of funding, genre conventions, locations and widescreen technology. As such, their careers exemplify the 'dearly bought concessions either to art or to commerce' that Robert Murphy ascribes to 1960s British cinema.[10] But production constraints had transfigurative potential for these two directors in that their distinctive styles are enhanced by the widescreen formats and the bareness of the *mise en scène*, which captures the differing moods of Cold War unease, working-class culture and British locales.

THE DAMNED (JOSEPH LOSEY, 1963)

The Damned is adapted from the H. L. Lawrence science fiction novel *The Children of Light*, though the source text is barely evident in the film. Instead, the prospect of filming in 'Thomas Hardy and John Cowper Powys territory' would provide the literary touchstone that initially attracted Losey and his usual production design consultant, Richard MacDonald, to south-west England.[11] An American yachter and his companion, the sister of a hoodlum, are pursued by the latter's motorbike gang from Weymouth harbour to the military 'Edgecliff Establishment', where radiation-resistant children are being prepared to inherit a post-nuclear earth. The mysterious isle of Portland Bill, where the laboratory is located, recalls the brutal magnitude of the early sequences of Michelangelo Antonioni's *L'Avventura* (1960). In conversation with Michel Ciment, Losey explained that making *The Damned* in a widescreen format supplemented his long-take style with the spatial latitude demanded by coastal locations:

> I wouldn't want to make every picture that way. On the other hand, there are certain ones like *The Damned* and *Figures in a Landscape* that would have suffered greatly from not being that shape. In *The Damned* I could do long sustained shots, not so much between actors because there was very little chance for that, but movements across landscapes and across rocks and with boats and with helicopters, partly because of the shape of the screen. [. . .] Sometimes the compositions that can be achieved are much more interesting.[12]

The opening shots of Portland Bill capture Losey's sustained camera movement and horizontal compositions in action. The title credits are presented over a rolling sea extending to the horizon, the slight curvature of which is captured by the wide frame. The camera pans slowly left before the movement is 'cushioned' by the appearance of cliffs and begins to trace them, bending right into the foreground. The camera angles down as it pans toward the half-way point on its circular route. We peer over the brink directly beneath, the title of the film appears, and brass instruments overwhelm the flute melody dominating the soundtrack. The title and the brass horns fade away and the camera passes quietly over fragmented sculptures littering the ground. An elevated workbench drifts into the centre of the frame as the soundtrack and camera rise, again in concert. We linger on a mysterious headless sculpture laid across the bench beneath the director credit, the horizontality of the artwork echoing that of the opening seascape. Losey's approach to the visual construction of the sequence is probing, confrontational even. As in his earlier film *The Prowler* (1951), he uses 'sustained takes where the camera virtually becomes a character', the slow pan over fragmented sculptures comparable to the procedural investigation of a crime scene.[13]

Caressing in turn the line of the horizon, cliffs and sculpture, the lateral camera movement during the title credits of *The Damned* may remind us of Losey's previous film, *Eve* (1962), which opens with a geometric pan along the riverbank and ornate rooftop before resting on a Venetian statue. Since the director was wary that shooting in widescreen 'affects camera movement because if you don't move quite slowly you get a bad judder', he foregoes the lithe 180-degree turn of *Eve* to introduce troubling elements into the tranquil vista.[14] Crucially, it is unclear whether the title sequence of *The Damned* depicts a time before or after the film's main narrative events. In *Eve*, a voice-over positions the Venetian statue within the romantic narrative. But in *The Damned*, we are forced to dwell on the alien form of the Elisabeth Frink sculpture as if it were one of the voiceless artefacts of nuclear disaster which opens Alain Resnais's *Hiroshima Mon Amour* (1959). Moreover, the framing of the sculpture is isomorphic, so that the aspect ratio and subject parallel one another. Self-conscious framing provides pause for critical reflection, unlike the anticipation built by the preceding lateral movement. Similarly, at the end of the film the camera pans across the subterranean 'prison' on the Isle of Portland to Weymouth's symmetrically framed seafront, as the children cry out to distant leisure-seekers. The ambiguous tone is set purely through the formalistic directing, location and soundtrack.

The real interest in Losey's widescreen filmmaking, lies in the overall rhythm of his sequences. I have elsewhere suggested that the cumulative flow of compositions is of academic interest, particularly as average cutting rates in widescreen films sped up from the late 1950s.[15] The introduction of the main characters well conveys Losey's rhythmic style. An abrupt match-cut from the Portland sculpture to the horizontal Weymouth seafront, accompanied by driving rock music, establishes the restless world of the biker gang. The camera moves slowly down a historic clocktower, before Joan (Shirley Anne Field) strolls into shot to ask Simon (Macdonald Carey) – and us – 'never seen a clocktower before?' Due to the slow movement and limited height imposed by widescreen technology, the old clocktower is steadily unveiled from top to bottom: a gesture matched precisely by Simon's perverse glance at Joan. As in the title sequence, Losey's camera movement interlaces divergent figures in a game of gradual disclosure.

Losey would subsequently open *King & Country* by slowly panning along the stone surface of war memorials in close-up. Through a similar technique, the monumentality of the Weymouth landmarks contrasts with youthful irreverence in *The Damned*, creating what Colin Gardener calls a 'bricolage of upper-class style and working-class aggression'.[16] Losey explained that the 'Victorian-Edwardian seaside resort was absolutely ideal for contrast because it was obviously a kind of place for the Teddy boys, whose name is diminutive for Edward because they affected Edwardian dress', showing 'the children of the working class trying to recapture some kind of power out of past elegance'.[17] The discordant combination of rock music, dynamic staging and royal statues captures the pomposity of gang leader King, played by Oliver Reed. Following the exchange between Joan and Simon around the clocktower, there is a close-up on a unicorn belonging to a statue of George III and royal heraldry. King has presumptuously hung his umbrella on the unicorn's horn, which extends across the shot as if it were a clothes peg. Losey's camera obligingly traces the umbrella's vertical length to find the gang arranged along the screen at the base of the statue. Like so many widescreen shots in the film, King's entourage are staged in imperious lateral formation. The camera re-centres to track one of King's number catcalling a passer-by, before following the architectural line of the plinth up to the figure of George III – King's counterpart – who gazes regally towards the horizon. Again, Losey's camera deliberately and open-endedly traverses curved and straight lines to elide otherwise incongruous figures in close and full body shots.

While differing in terms of narrative and genre, all Losey's widescreen films share an emphasis on outdoor settings and political themes. In *The Damned*, we have the theme of the hunt, and fight or flight, which the director would return to with the 'Angel of Death' character in *Boom!* and the anthropomorphised helicopter in *Figures in a Landscape*. Joan lures Simon towards her brother's gang and both are, in turn, pursued by the sociopathic, incestuous King. Simon asks Joan to sail to France with him, but his advances seem to confirm her brother's view that Simon is a sexual predator. As Simon, Joan, King and the sculptress, Freya (Viveca Lindfors), learn of the experiments on children undertaken by the scientist Bernard (Alexander Knox), everyone's freedom is in turn threatened by the state. Tense static compositions frequently establish and then transgress the wide space between hunter and prey. For example, after Joan lures Simon towards a confectionery stand, and following a conspiratorial glance with her brother King, they are framed separately within two shop windows on opposite sides of the screen before Joan looks over and approaches Simon. Losey first experimented with tense polarised staging in *A Man on the Beach* (1956). In it, a murderer hides out in a beach house and watches around a corner – and from one side of the partitioned screen – as its owner arrives home. A similar example of spatial suspense comes as two helicopters land either side of King's car, and the screen, during the concluding chase sequence in *The Damned*.

Losey's widescreen features were released at a time when the director claimed to have graduated from making 'message pictures' with a single moral to 'pictures of provocation' which engage the viewer with conflicting 'situations and attitudes'.[18] The conflict between predator and prey is almost always a microcosm of broader social attitudes toward personal liberties and the widescreen allows Losey to contextualise his characters accordingly. In *The*

THE COLD WAR FILMS OF JOSEPH LOSEY AND SIDNEY J. FURIE

Figure 10.1   Staging working-class unrest in widescreen: Joseph Losey's
The Damned (1963).

Damned, Losey tracks King's cohort winding through a busy Weymouth street, dispensing with the traditional rank and file of military marches and strongly recalling *The 400 Blows* (François Truffaut, 1959), filmed in Dyaliscope, in which a gym teacher and his unruly schoolchildren snake through Paris. King is followed by an aggravated policeman, Joan and an unwitting Simon – all in the same take. Similar to the motorbikers' high-speed invasion of picturesque landscape shots, Losey exploits the screen width to stage working-class unrest at odds with polite society.

In describing Losey's political themes and mobilisation of widescreen space, the phrase 'line of flight' strongly suggests itself. Cars, motorbikes, boats and helicopters of predators and victims traverse the director's widescreen compositions. There is also an interest in movements across landscapes and the linear horizontal flightpath of the camera. The Portland Bill and Weymouth sequences from *The Damned* show in detail how the moving camera problematises the relationship between figures and their physical environment. Finally, there are Losey's motifs of the wide-open sea and, in *The Damned*, wingless bird sculptures which pertain to flight, if only to suggest the implausibility of escape.[19] Losey noted that, 'while the close-ups are much bigger, there is a lot of extra screen' in anamorphic 2.35:1.[20] This allowed the primordial line of the ocean's horizon to feature prominently and emblematically in one dialogue scene, where Bernard lectures Freya on the coming apocalypse and divulges his plan to assassinate her. We should also recall that the director's preferred title for the film – 'The Brink' – was meant to foreshadow the act of falling from an ocean cliff and the end of the world.[21] In all cases, physical and symbolic lines of flight evidence Losey's fascination with the rectilinear aspect ratio and its rhetorical potential.

It is also possible to speak of the overall flow and texture of Losey's widescreen sequences. Despite the director's concerns about widescreen judder, the smoothness of the long takes is punctuated with divergent lines, static frontal compositions and abrasive brief takes. The aerial assassination of King and Freya both involve disorienting helicopter shots, and the match-cut from Freya's sculpture to the Weymouth seafront is similarly jolting. During one extended point of view shot, the camera slides over the straight lines of mid-century modern décor as one of Bernard's minions approaches the laboratory bedroom. At the point where a child is about to be abducted, Losey suddenly cuts to a vertical view over the brink, using the full length of the widescreen to depict waves crashing over rocks. Aided by the rapid efficiency of cinematographer Arthur Grant and camera operator Anthony Heller on location, rhythmic alternations of camera movement and shot composition helps to distinguish Losey's provocative widescreen style from that of his contemporaries.[22]

The Ipcress File (Sidney J. Furie, 1965)

The 'deviant' style of *The Ipcress File* would partly stem from Furie's desire to reinvent himself as a director. His insecurities in this regard were fuelled by producer Saltzman, who regarded Furie as nothing more than a journeyman assigned to direct in an efficient manner. According to Furie, the combination of artistic differences with Saltzman and the need to improvise on a feeble screenplay strained his process and wellbeing:

> I was very depressed always when we started shooting, thinking that it was going to be really lousy and I didn't know what to do, so I told myself I would come up with a style of shooting that is different. I put shoulders across the screen, I shot up at things, I shot down, just to make it different, to give it ambiance. It was done out of insecurity, with a little cognac spiked in my morning coffee to give me courage.[23]

Furie uses his setting resourcefully to find steep camera angles and block widescreen shots with actors and objects of décor including keyholes, lampshades, office in-trays and telephone booths. His version of the production process is shaded with desperation and artistic risk, and a somewhat romantic account of the auteur finding inspiration in difficult circumstances. It can also give the impression that the approach to shot composition was purely instinctive, whereas 'shooting through key holes and so on gave a certain style to the film [which] fitted well into the overall concept', according to production designer Ken Adam, who proved his adaptability by simultaneously designing in widescreen for *The Ipcress File* and *Thunderball*.[24] In contrast to Losey's penchant for long takes, Furie's widescreen style more often resembles a constant barrage of static shots; the resulting confusion in point of view might then be seen to complement the film's themes of surveillance and conspiracy.

The Techniscope format, introduced by Technicolor Italia in 1961, fulfilled the different commercial and artistic priorities of Furie and Saltzman. Techniscope used a two-perforation frame negative, instead of the standard four, requiring only half the normal amount of stock. The completed film was subsequently enlarged through an optical printer to produce an exhibition print with a 2.35:1 aspect ratio. Techniscope granted economic savings and visual depth. Each half-sized frame required less illumination, allowing cinematographer Otto Heller to capture dimly lit scenes even when using colour stock. As the image was expanded during the printing stage, a spherical lens could be placed on the Techniscope camera instead of the anamorphic lens used for other widescreen formats, the latter of which restricted deep focus cinematography. Heller's expressionist techniques effectively explode the quotidian sets of Adam, supplying what Petrie describes as some of 'the most accomplished British Techniscope cinematography'.[25] A drawback of Techniscope was the enlargement of grain in the blow-up print, which arguably cheapened the look of 1960s genre films. As Daniel Kremer states, the gritty 'Techniscope luster' gives *The Ipcress File* 'a depressed, washed-out edge as a complement to its overcast cityscapes'.[26] Kremer also credits Furie's 'prowess with creative framing, composition, and shot fluidity'.[27] Others have dismissed the director's Techniscope shots as self-indulgent. *Monthly Film Bulletin* reported that 'Sidney Furie's direction is unremittingly mannered, and almost passionately concerned with the finding of odd camera angles'.[28] More recently, Christopher Bray affirms that 'viewers have rarely been won over by the pyrotechnics of his style' in *The Ipcress File*.[29]

One counterargument to the labelling of Furie's approach as meretricious would be that stylistic excess has value for his film's spy story, in which the defiant agent Harry Palmer (Michael Caine) is tasked with investigating the disappearance of prominent British scientists during the Cold War. For example, in one scene, Palmer enters the Science Museum Library to find his prime target. It is made clear through several shots that Palmer is being tailed by an intimidating figure: the target's bodyguard. When Palmer reaches the library ground floor, an inconspicuous man is revealed in long shot as the bodyguard withdraws. A close-up shifts our interest to the same individual, who later turns out be an American CIA agent following the British investigation, though his face is obscured by heavy glasses and Furie's composing the shot with a horizontal reading lamp in the foreground. The obscured shot visually conveys the epistemic suspense driving espionage thrillers, in which agents or objects can unexpectedly shift meaning and allegiance during an assignment.

David Bordwell has likewise argued that the 'stylistic gymnastics' of British widescreen films *The Ipcress File* and *The Italian Job* (1969) were encouraged by 'genres that emphasize narrational gambits'.[30] According to Bordwell, Furie's filming 'through telephone booths and hanging lampshades', alongside 'other 1960s tendencies, such as split-screen imagery, slow-motion, and even the spiralling shot and the handheld camera, can be seen as signs of a willingness to make narration more obtrusive'.[31] The argument seems logical, so long as we are not overly taxonomic about genre conventions, and that by making the narration 'more obtrusive', we do not in turn presume that 'stylistic gymnastics' can be explained away by reference to conventional plotlines or character motivations. An examination of the telephone booth sequence referred to by Bordwell shows that what he calls 'self-conscious narration' can make the act of storytelling obtrusive without necessarily laying bare narrative causation; in fact, a strict adherence to widescreen experimentation unhinges the film from familiar storytelling cues like analytic editing and eyeline matching.[32]

Surveillance is a central activity in the film, though it is not always made clear who is observing who. Harry Palmer observes his assigned target from a telephone booth as he passes by the Royal Albert Hall. Four shots detail: the prime suspect and his bodyguard passing within the frame of the booth, Palmer looking through the window, a deep-focus shot of the men framed by the window, and a final shot of Palmer calling over to the two men. As in all his latticed compositions, Furie uses the widescreen format not for open vistas but as negative space. The camera remains in the booth as we see Palmer approach and fight the bodyguard in long shot, after which an American agent enters the scene. Two shots show the American spectating from outside the booth as the combat continues to be shot through its metal window frames, only this is now magnified so that we see the two combatants in medium shot behind the giant 'crosshair' shape of the metalwork. The sequence presents different possible narrative perspectives: Palmer's point of view, as well as omniscient narration, which seems the most apt way to describe shots where Furie provides vantage points or chinks in décor to allow the audience to 'spy' on his protagonist. We spot Palmer suspiciously approaching his flat, which has been broken into, through a steeply angled shot on the stairs above. We also watch Palmer meet the bodyguard in a prison cell through small perforations in the closed door; a more elaborate version of a shot in which Palmer is filmed at his desk through the latticework of an office in-tray. In this case, it is tempting to speak of *The Ipcress File* only in very general terms of concept and ambience, as Furie and Adam do.

Omniscient shots imply the watchful presence of another character, but they do not pertain to any particular individual, as when Furie distorts the entire widescreen after Palmer removes his glasses. Nor are they examples of the kind of paranoid psychological realism found in Orson Welles's *The Trial* (1962). Unlike Josef K., Palmer is cool, collected and bored by

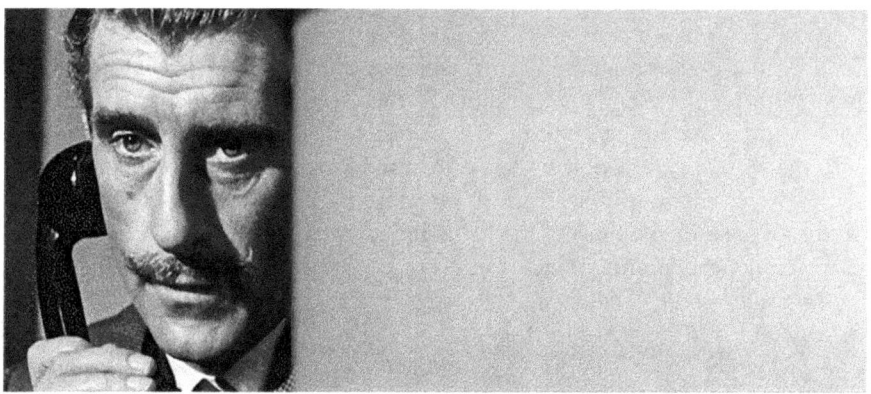

Figure 10.2   Major Dalby (Nigel Green) marginalised by Sidney J. Furie's expressionistic *mise en scène* in *The Ipcress File* (1965).

bureaucracy. It is only when Palmer has undergone brainwashing and torture that his sober character traits begin to fade and psychological realism comes to the fore. At this point, Furie frames Major Dalby (Nigel Green) in close-up, intoning command words over the phone to Palmer. The lurid *mise en scène* matches the dialogue by distorting reality. A red lampshade takes up two thirds of the screen, to the extent that it resembles a flat rectangle, and 'spills over' into the red framework of the phone box in which Palmer receives the call.

Furie's bravura widescreen shots dominate the film in such a way that our identification with particular characters and spaces becomes difficult to negotiate. By charting the narrative disruptions that widescreen technology introduces, and the different possibilities for storytelling therein, I do not mean to suggest that behind Furie's elaborate style there lies an equally elaborate system of storytelling. One achievement of the film may be its widescreen pyrotechnics, through which a relatively straightforward and improvised story has been made to seem more complex because of elaborate narration. Frequently, the style seems to exceed the quotidian nature of Palmer's investigation.[33] In one sequence, we see a prime target meeting Dalby and Palmer in the park in a deep focus shot, and as he approaches, the miniature figure is framed between the closing cymbals of a hi-hat. Another response to the criticism that the film is a florid experiment in film style, then, would be to point out that its tone is often humorous and irreverent. Furie's social themes share some resonance with Losey's here. Like the public-school caricature of Major Dalby, the taut compositions are sometimes pulled so tight that the film's self-conscious style verges on self-parody, or at least playful excess.

Conclusion

Hollywood auteurs such as Otto Preminger, Nicholas Ray and Douglas Sirk have traditionally dominated studies of widescreen style rather than any directors working extensively within the British industry, and historical research into the widescreen revolution has prioritised the dominant Hollywood industry.[34] However, the publication of new textual analyses and industrial case studies is steadily globalising the field, including Steve Chibnall's research into British independents and widescreen formats in the 1950s, in the landmark collection *Widescreen Worldwide*.[35] Ripe for further investigation are the diverse styles employed by film directors Joseph Losey, Sidney J. Furie, Jack Cardiff and Jack Clayton in Britain during the 1960s. All created arresting, modestly budgeted widescreen films in the claustrophobic vein of the thriller and melodrama genres, just as Peter Collinson, Anthony Harvey and David Lean did in internationally produced films with multi-million budgets.

Comparing shot composition and staging in the Cold War thrillers of Losey and Furie highlights spatial and narrational experimentation with widescreen technology. Losey tends to use elaborate long takes whereas Furie prefers static compositions, though both would make some use of frantic camera movement and polarised staging along the horizontal frame at times. Both directors also expressed self-consciousness in their use of widescreen technology in interviews and several of their widescreen films have proven to be lastingly influential. Cinematographers John Mathieson (*The Man From U.N.C.L.E.*, 2015) and Phil Mehéux (*Casino Royale*, 2006) both found inspiration from the visual style of *The Ipcress File*.[36] At Bradford's Widescreen Weekend festival in 2015, Pasquale Iannone selected *The Damned* alongside European art films such as Alain Resnais's *Last Year in Marienbad* (1961), Federico Fellini's *La Dolce Vita* (1960) and Jean-Luc Godard's *Le Mépris* (1963) to showcase radical widescreen styles of the early 1960s. There is also evidence that European auteurs appreciated one another's widescreen films. A year after *The Ipcress File* was nominated for the Palme d'Or, Furie was personally congratulated by François Truffaut on his artistic success.[37]

The idea of an innovative new wave of widescreen auteurs is appealing; however, it is important not to wrest Losey and Furie from the localised conditions that influenced their craft. Cinematographers and production designers also demonstrated their versatility in widescreen film productions in Britain. While these production teams experimented with visual techniques in the 1960s, access to widescreen technology was itself dictated by commercial rather than artistic preference. Widescreen pyrotechnics are also evident in earlier British films but it would take time for the technology to be developed and more widely utilised. If stylistic analysis can begin to trace continuity and change from a diverse sample of widescreen films, studies of industrial structure are also needed to explain the rate and nature of aesthetic change. A combined stylistic and production history to complement existing research on widescreen cinema might comprehensively show how filmmakers in Britain used these technologies to broaden their creative horizons.

NOTES

1. From an original Free Cinema manifesto, re-published in a booklet released with the BFI (2006) DVD.
2. Steve Neale and Sheldon Hall, *Epics, Spectacles and Blockbusters: A Hollywood History* (Detroit: Wayne State University Press, 2010), pp. 159–212.
3. Charles Barr, 'CinemaScope: before and after', *Film Quarterly* 16: 4, 1963, p. 5; Duncan Petrie, *The British Cinematographer* (London: BFI, 1996), pp. 48–52.
4. Daniel Kremer, *Sidney J. Furie: Life and Films* (Lexington: University Press of Kentucky), p. 74.
5. Michel Ciment, *Conversations with Losey* (London: Methuen, 1985), p. 154.
6. Ibid. p. 139. My thanks to the British Film Institute for allowing me to view *A Man on the Beach* on 35mm film.
7. David Caute, *Joseph Losey: A Revenge on Life* (New York: Oxford University Press, 1994), p. 143.
8. On *Time Without Pity* (1957), Losey felt that 'English critics didn't receive it terribly well: it was larger than life, they said pejoratively – my customary "baroque" and exaggeration label which had already begun before *Eve* [1962]': Ciment, *Conversations*, p. 143.
9. Losey and Furie both directed biker characters with a degree of sensitivity and attention to sociocultural factors: J. J. Ward, 'Outlaw motorcyclists they're not: a contrarian reading of Joseph Losey's *These Are the Damned* (1961) and Sidney Furie's *The Leather Boys* (1964)', *Journal of Popular Culture* 43: 2, 2010, pp. 381–407.
10. Robert Murphy, *Sixties British Cinema* (London: BFI, 1992), p. 101.
11. Ciment, *Conversations*, p. 198.
12. Ibid. p. 206.
13. Ibid. p. 104.
14. Ibid. p. 206.
15. Steven F. Roberts, 'Visual composition in widescreen and colour film', BAFTSS Colour and Film SIG Notes, 7 July 2018. Available at <https://colourandfilm.com/2018/07/07/visual-composition-in-widescreen-and-colour-film-by-steven-f-roberts/> (last accessed 1 September 2019).
16. Colin Gardener, *Joseph Losey* (Manchester: Manchester University Press, 2004), p. 104.
17. Ciment, *Conversations*, p. 200.
18. Ibid. p. 97.
19. Colin Gardener has also described how Losey's 'use of widescreen brings out the contrast between the wide-open spaces of the terrain and the characters' inescapable entrapment' in *Figures in a Landscape*: Gardener, *Joseph Losey*, p. 205. For

example, in one abstract composition, a rural expanse is shown with each tree and shadow symmetrically aligned. Like Losey's isomorphic shots of Weymouth, the location is simultaneously real and unnaturally forbidding, providing no cover under which to hide from the helicopter.

20. Ciment, *Conversations*, p. 206.
21. Ibid. p. 204.
22. As Petrie states, 'Grant had a reputation for speed and economy, which made him a valuable asset' to an economical studio like Hammer Films: Duncan Petrie, 'A changing visual landscape: British cinematography in the 1960s', *Journal of British Cinema and Television* 15: 2, 2018, pp. 204–27. Prior to *The Damned*, Arthur Grant was cinematographer on *Jigsaw* (1962) and *Hell is a City* (1960), while Anthony Heller worked as second unit cinematographer on *The Guns of Navarone* (1961), all of which were in CinemaScope.
23. Kremer, *Sidney J. Furie*, p. 81.
24. Ken Adam, speaking in a 2014 interview released with the Network Blu-ray (2014) of *The Ipcress File*.
25. Petrie, *The British Cinematographer*, p. 50. See also, Petrie, 'British cinematography in the 1960s', p. 218.
26. Kremer, *Sidney J. Furie*, p. 76.
27. Ibid. p. 90.
28. Penelope Houston, *Monthly Film Bulletin*, 32: 376, 1965, p. 70.
29. Christopher Bray, 'A different class – Michael Caine and *The Ipcress File*' (2005), published in a booklet released with the Network Blu-ray (2014) of *The Ipcress File*.
30. David Bordwell, *The Way Hollywood Tells It: Story and Style in Modern Movies* (Berkeley: University of California Press, 2006), p. 182.
31. Ibid. p. 182.
32. Ibid. p. 182.
33. As highlighted in a negative review by Penelope Houston, *Monthly Film Bulletin*, pp. 70–1: 'Nor does the film really get very far in its effort to show intelligence men monotonously labouring among files and forms, when the office scenes are shot and recorded with such aggressive emphasis as to suggest that a gunman is concealed behind every filing cabinet.'
34. For example, the discussion of Preminger's *River of No Return* (1954) spans decades. See: Barr, 'CinemaScope', p. 11; David Bordwell, 'Widescreen aesthetics and mise en scene criticism', *The Velvet Light Trap* 21: Summer, 1985, pp. 22–3; Harper Cossar, *Letterboxed: The Evolution of Widescreen Cinema* (Lexington: University Press of Kentucky, 2011), pp. 101–19.
35. Steve Chibnall, 'The scope of their ambition: British independent film production and widescreen formats in the 1950s', in John Belton, Sheldon Hall and Steve Neale (eds), *Widescreen Worldwide* (New Barnet: John Libbey, 2010), pp. 149–62.
36. Phil Rhodes, 'Superspy alliance', *American Cinematographer* 96: 9, 2015, p. 58; Jon Silberg, 'High stakes for 007', *American Cinematographer* 87: 12, 2006, pp. 44–5.
37. Kremer, *Sidney J. Furie*, p. 90.

11. THE RISE AND FALL OF THE COLOURFUL CORPORATE FANTASY IN 1960s BRITISH CINEMA

Carolyn Rickards

In an opening internal monologue, performed direct to camera and set against a striking, deep blue twilight, protagonist Jimmy Brewster (Alan Bates) announces: 'let's face it, it's a filthy, stinking world. But there are some smashing things in it – and I want them.' The title sequence that follows features a series of opulent images from champagne glasses to fancy sports cars; all bleached in vibrant tones. The 'smashing things' Brewster refers to are not merely the most expensive or glamourous but also, crucially, the most colourful.

The film in which this scenes features, *Nothing but the Best* (1964), was released at the moment when colour was beginning to enliven the British cultural scene during the early 1960s and would go on to eventually dominate in cinema by the end of the decade. In this prologue, the pursuit of wealth and status is seen as desirable, presenting the prospect of a more exciting and colourful existence. Moreover, in an era characterised by increased social mobility, British cinema of the 1960s showcased a succession of films featuring male protagonists determined to succeed in the world of big business and entrepreneurialism. This chapter focuses on the figure of the aspirational climber, tracking his progression and development in films throughout this period. It explores how the aesthetic features of such films engaged with the masculine narratives they played out on screen. Specifically, it considers how the full-scale conversion to colour during this time impacted on the corporate fantasises presented in such films, focusing on two movies that epitomised these tropes and trends. *Nothing but the Best*, written by Frederic Raphael and directed by Clive

Donner, provides an early sixties example of a young man on the make, determined to succeed at any cost, and is presented in the mode of black comedy. It will be compared with *The Man Who Haunted Himself* (1970), directed by Basil Dearden and written by Dearden and Michael Relph (with uncredited help from Bryan Forbes); a film that includes similar themes of corporate ascendency but with much darker overtones of self-destruction.

This shift highlights changes in the filmic identity of the aspirational climber throughout the decade, as each film portrays the differing psychological effects on its male protagonists. While both films have received some critical attention in the intervening years since their release, this work has largely centred on narrative features, production contexts and star appeal (particularly the rising profiles of Alan Bates and Roger Moore). This chapter contends that the employment of colour in each film demands equal investigation, revealing expressive and symbolic visual statements that explicitly capture broader thematic concerns. By focusing analysis on *Nothing but the Best* and *The Man Who Haunted Himself*, this chapter traces how the colourful corporate fantasy emerged and then departed from British cinema screens, with the latter film providing a despondent cinematic coda to the decade.

Men on the Make

Issues of masculinity and professional male identity constitute a consistent theme in the history of British cinema.[1] However, the 1960s was a particularly productive time for this trope, which resonated through some of the most popular and well-known films produced during this era. *Room at the Top* (1959) presents a notable example of this trend, released at the beginning of a period that witnessed significant cultural and social change. The film embodied the concerns of a new generation of educated young men, typically from working-class backgrounds, with ambition to overcome the traditional class barriers engendered by previous generations. In *Room at the Top*, Joe Lampton (Laurence Harvey) covets success and schemes his way up the corporate and social ladder, leaving a bitter trail of broken relationships and heartache along the way. Lampton's ambitious and self-determined protagonist resonated with the times, particularly growing resentment from younger people towards the hierarchical social and corporate structures still considered firmly in place, exemplified by the 'Angry Young Man'. Yet, although Lampton is conniving and occasionally brutal in his treatment of friends, colleagues and most especially Susan Brown (Heather Sears), naïve daughter of a wealthy local businessman and his prospective love interest, he suffers personal torment through his extramarital affair with Alice Aisgill (Simone Signoret), the older woman he loves and eventually loses under the most tragic of circumstances. *Room at the Top* presented class boundaries and socio-economic hierarchies as barriers that could certainly be challenged and overcome, but not without emotional cost or moral sacrifice. The film appeared to define the anxieties and frustrations experienced by some young men at this time and formed a repeated theme in British cinema of the 'New Wave' throughout the early 1960s.

However, as the decade continued, new trends began to emerge which would throw into conflict the moral questions posed by such films. Growing affluence and prosperity transformed the workplace and certain sectors such as building societies, insurance companies, solicitors and property investment companies were experiencing rapid growth.[2] This new accessibility to prospective job opportunities and socio-economic horizons was imbued with the sense that anyone (or more specifically any man) could achieve their goals, dreams and desires; whatever background they came from. This growing sense of optimism was reflected in British cinema by way of a distinct shift of tonal and aesthetic emphasis. As Jeffrey Richards argues:

> Sober realism and earnest social comment gave way to fantasy, extravaganza, escapism; black and white photography to colour; the grim north to the glittering metropolis; puritanical self-discipline to hedonistic self-indulgence [British cinema] switched to the bright side, to self-assertion, personal fulfilment and the good life.[3]

It is perhaps surprising to note how quickly this change took place. The male anxieties that featured in films released only a few years earlier, such as *Room at the Top*, were replaced by productions that actively promoted the individualistic benefits of making it to the 'top' with far less 'earnest' consideration towards the potential negative outcomes.[4]

Nothing but the Best

Described by Robert Murphy as 'one of the seminal swinging London films of the decade', *Nothing but the Best* is set in an exclusive London estate agent and auctioneer company.[5] As a new junior executive, Alan Bates's Jimmy Brewster embodies ruthless ambition. In his calculated pursuit to achieve 'personal fulfilment and the good life' he negotiates dubious business deals, pursues the wealthy daughter of his boss at the same time as conducting an affair with his landlady, all the while disguising and resenting his upbringing, at one point sending his respectable and decent working-class parents off for a long-stay vacation to Australia. This behaviour is fuelled after a chance encounter with a roguish gentleman called Charlie Prince (Denholm Elliot) who appears to embody everything Brewster covets: upper-class arrogance and impeccable tailoring. In exchange for a cheap place to stay, Prince agrees to school the young pretender in appropriate dress, manners and etiquette. What begins as a light, observational comedy of class disparities and personal ambition diverges into murkier territory when Brewster eventually completes his training by murdering Prince, rather appropriately, with his old school tie. *Nothing but the Best* delivers its amoral message with sparkling effect.

Contemporary critics were quick to comment on the close similarities with *Room at the Top*, with Brewster and Lampton sharing equal disdain at their positions in life, and actively seeking opportunities for personal advancement. However, the acerbic script by Frederic Raphael, who would later go on to pen award-winning screenplays for *Darling* (1965) and *Two for the Road* (1967), gave *Nothing but the Best* extra edginess. There was 'no *Room at the Top* remorse'[6] with the earlier film's premise 'reconstructed for laughs'.[7] The emotional upheaval faced by Lampton's ambitious yet ultimately repentant character was replaced by an attitude that ambitious goals could be achieved via any means for those who craved success. As Murphy outlines, the film was 'almost a metaphor' for the wider socio-political changes taking place in Britain during the early 1960s.[8] In addition to relative affluence and economic prosperity, recent scandals such as the Profumo Affair had led to growing public disenchantment with the political elite. Labour's win at the general election in October 1964 was led by the image-conscious Harold Wilson: a man who appeared to represent the majority and not the few. In *Nothing but the Best*, Prince's upper-class rogue represents a (rather literally) dying breed, and his depravity and contempt towards others marks him out for attack. Brewster was a new man for a new generation, dressed in the latest Savile Row fashions, and charming and scheming himself from relatively humble beginnings up the socio-economic ladder. Although the final denouement for his mentor is provocatively violent, Brewster's motives are clearly addressed and foregrounded by the satirical statements on class and social inequity embedded in the film's narrative. This is underscored by Prince, who remarks during a scene whilst the pair are out shooting rabbits as gentlemanly sport: 'always learn to kill with a smile, James'.

Nothing but the Best embodied the message that ambition and success was a matter of style over substance. As Charles C. Gregory argues, the emphatic black and white moralising of earlier films such as *Room at the Top* appeared obsolete in comparison:

> All the serious social statements of the 'kitchen sink' school were in a grim greyish black and white. Yet they were often so sentimental and obvious. Perhaps we need to know just how lush and 'best' things can be at the top [. . .] the richly coloured *Nothing but the Best* illustrates the ambiguities confronting the social climber.[9]

In this context, the presence of colour in *Nothing but the Best* also connotes broader cultural meanings for a decade witnessing significant socio-political

Figure 11.1   Ruthless ambition: Alan Bates as Jimmy Brewster in *Nothing but the Best* (1964).

change. This was particularly evident in the fields of fashion, advertising and media with colour defining new styles and trends, especially for younger people.[10] However, in terms of British filmmaking at this time, the application of colour was still viewed with some apprehension. There remained a general, occasionally explicit, consensus that colour was imbued with escapist, romanticised connotations, and deemed inappropriate for dramatic settings and circumstances. As Sarah Street notes, the continued 'equation of realism with black and white' meant directors remained 'wary of taking risks' and 'caution over colour continued to prevail'.[11] *Nothing but the Best* was therefore considered somewhat exceptional by contemporary standards.

A few years before, director Clive Donner (who had a background working in commercials for the J. Walter Thomson advertising agency) had made *Some People* (1962), a vibrant colour film about the Bristol youth scene, produced in co-operation with the Duke of Edinburgh award scheme.[12] It was championed by V. F Perkins as a 'triumph in the context of British film-making' for its 'natural and un-emphatic' camera style, and was distinct from other films of the New Wave by being shot in colour.[13] Colour was incorporated to similar effect in *Nothing but the Best*, which benefitted from a creative team that included *Some People* collaborators cinematographer Nicolas Roeg and production designer Reece Pemberton.[14] Donner embraced the possibilities of colour film, asserting that 'the common belief that black and white is somehow more realistic than colour is rubbish'.[15] This certainly applies when comparing the colourful Nouvelle Vague realism of *Some People* with the highly stylised, Brechtian monochrome of Donner's next film, *The Caretaker* (1963). However, despite various developments and improvements in colour stock such as Kodak Eastmancolor (an industry standard by this time for 35mm feature film), the correct and appropriate application of colour presented the production team with various challenges. As Donner described in a 1964 interview: 'one of the difficulties with colour, technically, is to control it: it runs away with you, it becomes too violent'.[16] This description of colour as being uncontrollably violent refers partly to the definition and clarity of colour reproduction which was often lost by the final product. But technical innovation could overcome such challenges and in *Nothing but the Best* a combination of careful production design, costume, lighting and camera techniques was used to create its look of heightened naturalism.

Donner conceived *Nothing but the Best* as a psychological journey, as Brewster climbs up through the social scene, and the colour scheme reflects the changing moods of the film. We are introduced to Brewster as a charismatic young man dressed for an evening out with his girlfriend, Nadine (Lucinda Curtis). The colour in the opening outdoor scenes is saturated in striking electric blues and neon reds, colour coming from the illuminated advertising boards of local bars and restaurants. Once Brewster meets Prince, and their uneasy relationship of convenience develops, the dramatic tone shifts to a darker, subversive narrative that is underscored by subtle changes in colour towards a murky palette of browns, beiges and sepias. Brewster emulates his mentor by dressing in similar brown tweed suits and jackets, which is most notable in the sequence where the men travel to the University of Cambridge and appear to merge into the elegant sandstone architecture. The intention of this visit is to educate the working-class Brewster in the correct etiquette of a classical education as experienced by Prince, and there follows a humorous montage exchange on the importance of exclaiming 'bloody' as an adjective describing political, literary and historical figures. In contrast to Cambridge's opulence, Brewster's dwellings are cramped and drab, with low level lighting accentuating the stained, brown coloured walls. His parents' house is in equivalent shades of brown and beige in the living room, a pink wafer providing the only bright colour, glimpsed briefly inside a novelty biscuit tin. This scene tells us more about Brewster's lower income background, his father left recovering after an industrial accident, and presumably unable to provide for the family, and his mother dreaming of more prosperous opportunities for her son. While the ambience in his parents' house is muted and despondent, hinting at stoic acceptance, the same gloomy brown shades found in Brewster's apartment function as exactly the environment from which he wants to escape.

The intention was to maintain a sense of colour unity throughout *Nothing but the Best* through a combination of production design and technical effects. Clive Donner explained how this was achieved by using a series of gauzes on the camera lens:

> the gauze was a black one [and] it gave a sort of tinge to it which somehow and when Nicko, Nick Roeg, the director of photography suggested it, it seemed to give a sort of feeling of black depths, of murky depths.[17]

By applying a black gauze, this provides the film with a dark quality that muffles even the brighter scenes. Indeed, there are a couple of moments where the whole screen turns sepia and funnels down into an 'iris shot' before an edit into the next scene.[18] As we are consistently made aware of Brewster's thoughts and feelings through voice-over, this particular effect appears to be designed to provide a humorous visual representation of his malicious intentions. The 'murky depths' of the film are most evident once Brewster dispatches Prince's dead body in a locked trunk and hides the evidence in his landlady's cellar, which looks like a dungeon straight from a Hammer horror. After this point in the film, the colour and aesthetic tone shifts once more as Brewster begins to achieve his aspirational goals. With no apparent moral qualms or remorse, he forges Prince's identity before embarking on a relationship with his boss's daughter, Ann Horton (Millicent Martin).

This latter section of the film is bathed in regency shades and elegant tones. In one scene, the couple visit a stately home which is due for auction and Brewster wears a mid-length, beige suede coat that 'matches his personality, tells of his circumstances, and fits in with the mahogany, brocade and old stone glow' of his regal surroundings.[19] The coat was specifically chosen for symbolic effect, designed to depict a man who is embracing the traditional while still being thoroughly modern. The cut, fabric and colour of the garment not only had to fit with the grandiose location but also had to be 'in' with contemporary fashions so costume designer Sally Jacobs selected the suits and dresses from high-end fashion chains, and hats from the prestigious Woollands department store in Knightsbridge.[20] Pauline Delaney, who plays Brewster's lusty landlady, Mrs March, wears a host of colourful attire from pink dressing robes to a lime green dress with added purple flower for brassy adornment. Millicent Martin's character appears in a range of elegant outfits including a low-cut, pink chiffon dress which serves to emphasise her pale skin and coiffured red hair. Rather than innocent victims, both women match Brewster in terms of cunning and tenacity, exuding confidence in their striking and colourful costumes. This unified style, captured in smart production design, costume and colour photography was praised by critics who described the film as 'handsome' which was 'decidedly rare in British cinema'.[21] *Nothing but the Best* embraced a new colour consciousness that mirrored the changing times, and the film looked bright and vibrant, complementing the sharp satirical humour running throughout. Its aspirational message that anyone could make it to the top captured the zeitgeist: a colourful exemplar of the 'swinging London' movement on screen.

The Man Who Haunted Himself

The aspirational climber re-appeared in several films throughout the 1960s.[22] Andrew Spicer has identified the 'heartless professional on the make' character in films such as the Boulting brothers' *Rotten to The Core* (1965) with Anton Rodgers's criminal entrepreneur, Laurence Harvey's slimy advertising executive in *Darling* (1965), and Ian Hendry's seedy journalist in *The Beauty Jungle* (1964).[23] However, towards the end of the decade this archetype was beginning to evolve into a much more destructive anti-hero. *I'll Never Forget What's'isname* (1967), *Charlie Bubbles* (1967) and *The Reckoning* (1970) all featured disillusioned and detached men who had achieved financial success at the cost of personal fulfilment. In these films, the character's journey was often a gloomily retrospective one, typically escaping the present by returning to the past. Perhaps one of the most subversive films that utilised this trope was *The Rise and Rise of Michael Rimmer* (1970) which starred an impassive Peter Cook who appears out of nowhere on his path to political glory. Although pitched as a fantastical satire, the eventual denouement of democracy suggests one man's narcissism can have disastrous consequences for everyone. The aspirational climber was evolving at a time when British economic, political and social certainties were starting to break down.

If *Nothing but the Best* explored the entrepreneurial male psyche with bellicose humour, *The Man Who Haunted Himself* presented a more despairing appraisal of the consequences of desiring rampant wealth and success. The film was the work of the director/producer team of Basil Dearden and Michael Relph, both graduates of Ealing who had collaborated on later 'social problem' films such as *Violent Playground* (1958), *Sapphire* (1959) and *Victim* (1961). By the mid-sixties, Dearden and Relph were working on films aimed at the wider world market and for Hollywood companies based in the UK. *The Man Who Haunted Himself* was commissioned as part of Bryan Forbes's ambitious production programme designed to revitalise the flagging EMI/ABP organisation. The film stars Roger Moore as respectable businessman Harold Pelham, who suffers from an acute case of stolen identity, and Hildegard Neil as Eve, his bored and frustrated middle-class wife. This was Moore's next big screen role after appearing in the television series *The Saint* (ITV, 1962–9) and before his iconic stint as James Bond. Pelham presented viewers with a very different protagonist, as the Warner Pathe pressbook announced at the time: 'gone the slick smoothness. Gone the cunning, the scheming, the sleuthing. Roger Moore, so help us, has gone respectable'.[24] Despite more recent interest in the careers of Dearden and Relph, the film has largely been absent from historical accounts of British cinema. This might be because the film received a negative reception at the time of release with critics bemoaning the 'simple dialogue', 'absurd plot' and 'abominable special effects'.[25] In a later account, Ian Conrich admits that 'the visual effects are indeed weak' when discussing the back projection used in the establishing shots of London.[26] Yet, *The Man Who Haunted Himself* remains an interesting curio, 'existing at a junction between creativity and decline'[27] in the British film industry and provides an emphatic rebuttal to the excesses of sixties Britain.

The film portrays what can potentially happen once personal aspirations have been achieved. Pelham leads a comfortable existence as the employee of a major trading firm whose life changes abruptly during the opening moments when he suffers a near-fatal car crash. Following this event, he begins to experience strange occurrences such as conversations and business deals made unbeknownst to him which would appear to suggest identity sabotage. There are shades of the television series *The Prisoner* (ITV, 1967–8) as he chases his own shadow around London and, as the tension slowly escalates, it gradually transpires that the car accident initiated a doppelganger who is more assertive and aggressive than the original Pelham. The film climaxes in a bizarre confrontation between the two men which is then followed by a night-time car chase through the rain as the 'real' Pelham struggles with his own identity, sanity and soul.

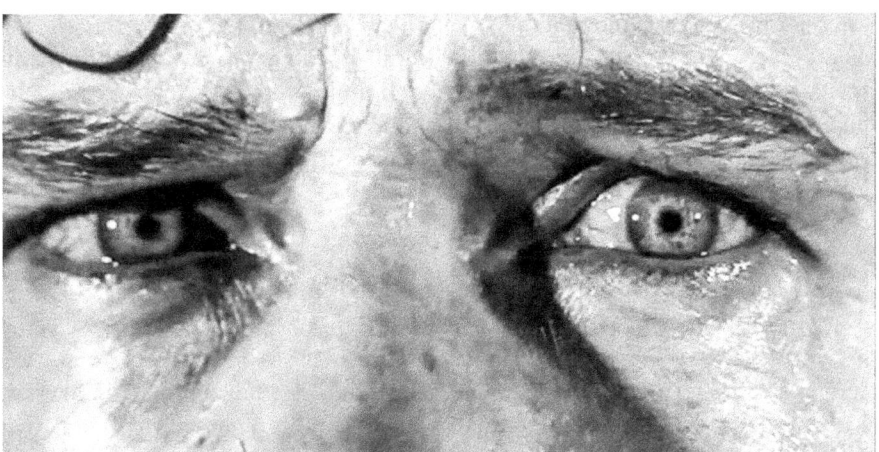

Figure 11.2   Losing a grip on reality: Roger Moore as Harold Pelham in *The Man Who Haunted Himself* (1970).

The production and costume designs (by Albert Witherwick and Beatrice Dawson) throughout most of the film are staid and orderly, designed to reflect Pelham's character, and the colour scheme ranges from elegant white for the family home to mahogany brown for the company boardrooms and offices. However, colour becomes more obvious and intrusive as the film progresses, with negative connotations. This can be seen in the contrast between Pelham's functional, brown Rover P5 with leather upholstery compared with the ostentatious blue silver Maserati Mistrale as driven by his malevolent alter ego. The apartment of Pelham's possible mistress, Julie (Olga Georges-Picot), also invites an exotic colour scheme, with leopard skin prints and oriental decor. Yet it is during the final chase sequence that the 'otherness' of colour becomes most striking as Pelham suffers a complete mental breakdown. The action shifts from 'reality' to fantasy as Pelham witnesses a host of images from his past and present flash in quick succession in front of his viewfinder including a moment where his other, mocking self is literally smashed into a multitude of fractured images. The scene becomes suffused with blue, yellow, green and red light effects that wash across the windscreen. In the final moments before his denouement, the camera closes on Pelham's face as the sound builds and the colour red bleaches out the entire screen.

This saturated use of colour has been described by Laure Brost as a form of visual 'hyperbole', articulating what could otherwise be difficult to convey through other stylistic choices 'in order to express the full depth of a heightened and extreme circumstance'.[28] An example of this can be seen in Michael Powell's and Emeric Pressburger's *Black Narcissus* (1947) where Sister Ruth's (Kathleen Byron) rejection by Mr Dean (David Farrar) is registered through a literal red mist that descends and colours 'everything in the frame with the association of anger and jealousy'.[29] In *The Man Who Haunted Himself*, the colour red envelops the screen, providing a shocking 'hyperbole' which contrasts vastly from the restrained palette employed throughout the rest of the film, and is 'layered through figuration with emphasis and significance, creating a chromatic sheath that is thick, striking and conspicuous'.[30] We are essentially watching a man lose his grip on reality. And the ending offers no satisfactory conclusion to these dramatic events. The imposter is not destroyed and instead the film comes full circle as the two men appear reunited as one; signified by the double heartbeat sound. This circular narrative is prefigured at earlier moments in the film: Pelham's fastidious attention to repeated actions (always placing his umbrella on the car seat and arranging his suits in the correct order), the spinning car tyres and hospital trolley wheels witnessed during the initial crash sequence, and the rotating camerawork when he visits an eccentric psychiatrist (Freddie Jones). Such repetition evokes the Ealing classic *Dead of Night* (1945), a portmanteau film with a supernatural twist featuring work by Dearden and Relph. The same foreboding sense of doom that closes in on Walter Craig

(Mervyn Johns) in *Dead of Night* is replicated in *The Man Who Haunted Himself* by the cyclical narrative and absence of closure. It provides a bleak finale whereby 'the domesticated model of manhood' appears to be 'crushed and destroyed by its nemesis, the "Playboy" ideal'.[31] Such narrative underscores a sentiment of masculinity in crisis, with uncertainties regarding traditional gender roles emerging at a time of significant social change. Of course, this would also have later significance for Moore who would go on to embody the ultimate 'Playboy' as Bond, a character that would define his future career.

Despite the star presence of Moore, the film ultimately failed to garner media interest or box office success. By the late 1960s, the films produced by Dearden and Relph were considered safe and unimaginative; maintaining values and ideologies from an earlier era of British society, while the production values appeared archaic for contemporary tastes. As Stanley Price remarked in *The Observer*: 'it is an unmitigated piece of hokum that looks and sounds more like Pinewood 1948 than Elstree 1970'.[32] This comment alludes to various meanings associated with aesthetic style and production design. The restrained, psychological horror of *The Man Who Haunted Himself* was considered tame compared with the gruesome spectacle offered by a new generation of horror films while the explosive colour effects used in the final chase scene also appeared to hark back to the high contrast, expressive Technicolor films of the 1940s. Such criticism may point to broader concerns about the appropriate application of colour at a time when this was now ubiquitous in film production. But the main point of contention was that British cinema had moved on and Elstree studios should be producing more ambitious films for the approaching new decade.

However, it should be acknowledged that the underwhelming critical and box office response to *The Man Who Haunted Himself* was also influenced by wider problems faced by the British film industry, which was beginning to flounder after a period of sustained creativity and increased investment by American studios ceased during the late 1960s. Other failed projects and financial difficulties led to the resignation of Forbes from Head of Production at EMI/ABP in 1971. The frantic chase sequence that ends the film could therefore be interpreted allegorically: the respectable and restrained ethos of British studio production overwhelmed by the unconstrained and ultra-competitive demands of corporate enterprise. In retrospect, the critiques of the film offered by reviewers like Stanley Price present the film in a positive light, aligning it with the Pinewood productions of Powell and Pressburger which encountered similar critical derision but now rank as some of the most impressive and visually exciting examples of British cinema. While *The Man Who Haunted Himself* may not reach the same esoteric heights as *Black Narcissus*, it deserves reappraisal not only for the performance of Moore, firmly playing against self-confident macho stereotype, but also for its critique of fractured masculine identity and sixties culture. Criticism of the film's clichéd narrative, excessive colour and 'abominable' special effects can be contextualised by revisionist accounts of British cinema history. The film also has added poignancy as this was to be the last collaboration between the director and producer duo. Dearden was tragically killed in a road accident on the M4 near Heathrow airport and close to the location of the initial car crash featured in the film; uncanny similarities which were not lost in press reports. The film remains intriguing for what Dearden and Relph could have potentially gone on to achieve given different circumstances.

No More Room at the Top

By the early 1970s, the aspirational climber archetype no longer resonated with British audiences due to a significant decline in economic prosperity and changing national mood. However, in tracing the development of this figure over time, it is clearly not a straightforward case of ascension and decline. In *Nothing but the Best*, the dark satirical emphasis encourages viewers to question the motives of Brewster, despite his obvious charm, energy and ambition. *The Man Who Haunted Himself* raises similar questions in its summation that the pursuit of wealth and success comes with the sacrifice of morality. Furthermore, each film includes the death of the doppelganger or other 'self' which is shown as outright murder in both examples, neither film offering a satisfactory or conclusive outcome to deal with the obvious repercussions. The main difference lies in the formal execution of these films, particularly the aesthetic style which received so much attention in the respective critical responses. In *Nothing but the Best*, the design, costume and cinematography combined to create a stylish and glamorous look that projected the upward mobility of its protagonist. The sophisticated colour schemes were employed with careful consideration, providing insight into Brewster's shifting mental state throughout the film. In contrast, the excessive colour found in *The Man Who Haunted Himself* offered a wholly expressionistic approach in dealing with similar themes. The colour used in both films engenders the same psychological meanings; however, the delivery is strikingly different. This perhaps demonstrates a development of broader colour awareness, with the earlier film released when realist dramas were still predominantly filmed in black and white. This would not only have garnered critical interest but also locates the film at a time when colour was beginning to influence the British cultural scene. The later film clearly suffered due to unfortunate timing, employing a more traditional approach at the precise moment when the national film industry was trying to innovate and stay afloat.

What this comparative analysis demonstrates is that sixties British films which employed colour for psychological effect were influenced not only by developments in colour processing capabilities but also by broader production and reception contexts. It also shows that colour was utilised to evoke a moral response to the masculine narratives played out in each film. A new kind of aspirational climber arrived at the beginning of the 1960s, capturing a moment of significant change in the national mood. Later films from this decade remorsefully lamented the individualistic pursuit of wealth and status by evoking the past as opposed to the future. For the British film industry, the storm clouds were already on the horizon, and although creativity and experimentation continued into the 1970s and beyond, the feeling that anyone could succeed at whatever cost had faded into a fantastic memory.

Notes

1. For examples of work on the topic of masculine identity and British Cinema see: John Hill, *Sex, Class and Realism: British Cinema 1956–1963* (London: British Film Institute, 1986); Christine Geraghty, *British Cinema in the Fifties Gender, Genre and the 'New Look'* (London: Routledge, 2000); Andrew Spicer, *Typical Men: The Representation of Masculinity in Popular British Cinema* (London: I. B. Tauris, 2001); Andrew Spicer, 'Male stars, masculinity and British cinema 1945–60', in Robert Murphy (ed.), *The British Cinema Book*, 3rd edn (London: British Film Institute, 2010), pp. 296–303, amongst others.
2. Robert J. Bennett, *Local Business Voice: The History of Chambers of Commerce in Britain, Ireland, and Revolutionary America, 1760–2011* (Oxford: Oxford University Press, 2011), p. 705.
3. Jeffrey Richards, 'New Waves and old myths: British cinema in the 1960s', in Bart Moore-Gilbert and John Seed (eds), *Cultural Revolution? The Challenge of the Arts in the 1960s* (London: Routledge, 1992), pp. 218–35, p. 228.
4. The sequel to *Room at the Top* entitled *Life at the Top* (1965) progressed the story of its protagonist Joe Lampton by showing the disillusionment and entrapment that can happen once ambitious goals have been achieved.
5. Robert Murphy, *Sixties British Cinema* (London: British Film Institute, 1992), p. 122.
6. William Johnson, *Film Quarterly* 18: 1, 1964, p. 62.
7. P. H., *Monthly Film Bulletin* 31: 363, April 1964, p. 53.
8. Murphy, *Sixties British Cinema*, p. 122.
9. Charles T. Gregory, 'There'll always be *Room at the Top* for *Nothing but the Best*', *Journal of Popular Film* 2: 1, 1973, pp. 59–73, p. 70.
10. Eric P. Danger, *Using Colour to Sell* (London: Gower Press, 1968), p. 27.
11. Sarah Street, 'The colour of social realism', *Journal of British Cinema and Television* 15: 4, 2018, pp. 469–90, p. 471, p. 474.
12. Street discusses the colour used for *Some People* in 'The colour of social realism', pp. 478–82.
13. Victor Perkins, 'Clive Donner and *Some People*', *Movie* 3, October 1962, pp. 22–5.
14. Nicholas Roeg worked as an assistant editor on *Some People* with principal cinematography by John Wilcox.

15. Clive Donner quoted in M. G. McNay, 'Clive Donner – director', *The Guardian*, 18 March 1964, p. 9.
16. Jonathan Gili, 'Interview with Clive Donner', *ISIS* 9 May 1964, p. 16.
17. Ibid.
18. The 'iris shot' is a fade in or out in which the image appears or disappears as an opening or closing circle.
19. McNay, 'Clive Donner – director'.
20. Ibid.
21. Richard Roud, *The Guardian*, 28 February 1964. Dilys Powell, *Sunday Times*, 1 March 1964.
22. This character trope was also a common figure on British television throughout the 1960s and 70s with programmes such as *The Plane Makers* (ITV, 1963–5), *Man at the Top* (ITV, 1970–2) and *The Man From Haven* (ITV, 1972).
23. Andrew Spicer, *Typical Men: The Representation of Masculinity in Popular British Cinema* (London: I. B. Tauris, 2001), p. 117.
24. Warner Pathe News Pressbook, 'The Man Who Haunted Himself'. Accessed BFI library, 2 August 2017.
25. Cecil Wilson, *Daily Mail*, 24 July 1970; David Robinson, *The Times*, 24 July 1970; Anon., *Monthly Film Bulletin* 37: 439, August 1970.
26. Ian Conrich, 'The Man Who Haunted Himself' (1970), in Alan Burton, Tim O'Sullivan and Paul Wells (eds), *Liberal Directions: Basil Dearden and Postwar British Film Culture* (London: Flicks Books, 1997), pp. 222–30, p. 222.
27. Ibid.
28. Laure Brost, 'On seeing red: the figurative movement of film colour', in Wendy Everett (ed.), *Questions of Colour in Cinema: From Paintbrush to Pixel* (Bern: Peter Lang AG, International Academic Publishers, 2007), p. 131.
29. Sarah Street, *Colour Films in Britain: The Negotiation of Innovation 1900–55* (London: Palgrave Macmillan, 2012), p. 181.
30. Ibid. p. 132.
31. Alan Burton and Tim O'Sullivan, *The Cinema of Basil Dearden and Michael Relph* (Edinburgh: Edinburgh University Press, 2009), p. 156.
32. Stanley Price, *The Observer*, 26 July 1970.

12. WITCHFINDERS AND SORCERERS: SORCERY AND COUNTERCULTURE IN THE WORK OF MICHAEL REEVES

Virginie Sélavy

Although Michael Reeves directed only three feature films in his short life, he is an influential figure and a strikingly singular voice in the countercultural context of the 1960s–70s. Yet, as Benjamin Halligan has pointed out in his biography, Reeves remains 'marginalised', 'excluded' from British history, often mentioned only in the context of horror cinema, a footnote to mainstream British film history.[1] But while working primarily in the horror genre, Reeves deployed its codes and motifs to construct complex and ambitious works that challenged the clichés of the counterculture. More specifically, in all three of his films, he used the theme of sorcery to frame a unique and contrary take on the polarities that structured the period.

In connecting witchcraft and counterculture in the second half of the 1960s, Reeves appeared in tune with the spirit of his time. During those years, the counterculture's rejection of social, political and religious forms of authority increasingly tied in with an interest in alternative forms of spirituality, from Eastern religions to witchcraft and the occult. As a female-focused, nature-based religion, witchcraft offered a symbolic alternative to the dominant male-led, capitalist, imperialist, technocratic order of Western societies. For anti-establishment figures generally, including feminists, the witch was a potent symbol of resistance against the system, embodying a cluster of elements that were central to countercultural movements: non-conformity, sexual freedom, female empowerment and environmentalism.[2] Correspondingly, witchcraft became a popular motif in cinema from the late 1950s to the late 1970s, channelling countercultural concerns as well as contemporary anxieties.

Making sorcery films revolving around ideas of freedom, rebellion and permissiveness between 1966 and 1968, Michael Reeves thus seems to be firmly located within current trends, but his take fundamentally differs from that of many other filmmakers of the period, and is radically at odds with the views of his own generation. Aged twenty-three to twenty-five when he made his three feature films, he was part of the juvenile wave that was driving the countercultural revolution and rejecting the values of the previous generation. And yet, Reeves, who was not only young, but also in close contact with the underground youth culture of the time, did not feel part of it. Instead, what he saw in the hedonistic, liberated, anti-authoritarian surface of the 1960s youth rebellion was the eternal propensity of mankind for violence. The recurring central story in his films, from *Revenge of the Blood Beast* (1966) and *The Sorcerers* (1967) to *Witchfinder General* (1968), is that of an ordinary man confronted with the savagery inherent to humanity. As Ian Sinclair has put it, 'the stock Reevesian preoccupation' is 'the apparently decent, "normal" citizen pushed to locate the evil within himself, to absorb and reciprocate all the venom of his oppressor'.[3] For Reeves, underneath the apparent radical changes of the 1960s, the violent tendencies of human beings remain the same. As a result, although his work is dominated by countercultural motifs, it sets out a darkly discordant vision of mankind that jars with the spirit of the time.

Revenge of the Blood Beast: Witchcraft and Women's Liberation

After an assistant director job on *The Castle of the Living Dead* (*Il castello dei morti vivi*) in 1964, Reeves made his professional directorial debut with the British-Italian co-production *Revenge of the Blood Beast* (*La sorella di Satana/Il lago di Satana/The She-Beast*). With a script co-written by Reeves and American scriptwriter Chuck Griffith, the film opens with the execution of the witch Vardella by a mob of villagers in eighteenth-century Transylvania, an effectively horrifying scene that prefigures the opening of *Witchfinder General*.[4] Two centuries later, newlyweds Philip and Veronica come to the same village, where they meet a sleazy innkeeper and the eccentric Count Von Helsing, the descendant of Dracula's killer, who has been made destitute by the Communist state. As the honeymooners drive away from the village, they crash into the lake where Vardella was drowned. Philip manages to get out of the car, but Veronica never surfaces. In her place, Vardella is fished out of the lake. Von Helsing, who has studied the old legends, helps Philip in his attempt to send Vardella back and retrieve Veronica.

Revenge of the Blood Beast is clearly indebted to Mario Bava's seminal gothic tale *Black Sunday* (*La maschera del demonio/The Mask of Satan*, 1960). For a start, it borrows its star, Barbara Steele, who brings the connotations of her previous role to the part of Veronica. Like *Black Sunday*, *Revenge of the*

Blood Beast begins with the spectacular execution of the witch. Although Bava was not the first to use this kind of sensational opening, he cranked up the visceral horror of the scene and accentuated its moral ambivalence.[5] Reeves assimilated both of those lessons: as in *Black Sunday*, the opening scene of *Revenge of the Blood Beast* is horrifically brutal and disturbingly ambiguous: the repellent witch may be a demonic creature, but her persecutors are just as murderously bloodthirsty.

Starting the film with the witch's execution establishes a strong contrast between the barbaric nature of the past and the civilised modernity of the present. Philip and Veronica are sassy, urbane, chic Londoners. In their initial appearance, Veronica wears oversized sunglasses, a fashionable and rather daring pink trouser ensemble and a smart tweed porkpie hat. Philip, played by Ian Ogilvy (a school friend of Reeves's who stars in all three of his features), is dressed in a sharp black suit, accessorised with stylish designer sunglasses. As the insouciant modern young couple arrives in strange, unfamiliar, archaic Communist Transylvania, swinging London comes face to face with the dark forces of the past.

Superficially the film may therefore appear to contrast modern and ancient times, civilised Britain and barbarous foreign lands, Western democracy and Eastern Communism. But as is the case throughout Reeves's work, such facile oppositions are subverted. The continuity between past and present quickly appears in the replacement of Veronica with Vardella after the car crash, and Veronica's chilling final words, loaded with menace, suggest that the attractive young fashionista and the vile old witch are one and the same. Under the veneer of 1960s rational urban sophistication lies the same hideous wildness as in the eighteenth-century satanical creature.

Figure 12.1   Tourists in Transylvania: Veronica (Barbara Steele) and Philip (Ian Ogilvy) in *The Revenge of the Blood Beast* (1966).

The replacement of the beautiful bride with the monstrous witch chimes with a common theme of 1960s and 1970s horror cinema. The uncertainty about the nature of the loved woman and the danger she may pose to the man who desires her is a major motif of the period, echoing uneasiness about growing female assertiveness and rapidly changing social roles. It is at that time that the witch as a seductive, lustful, potent and lethal woman became a recurrent presence on cinema screens. Cinematic witches before the 1950s generally tended to appear in romantic comedies, historical films or fairy tales.[6] From 1960 the witch became a full-blown figure of terror, and the two decades that followed saw an influx of these ambiguous monsters, which associated unfettered female desire with evil power.[7]

Bava played a key part in initiating this new type of character with Asa in *Black Sunday*. The opening scene makes clear that Asa is punished not simply for her purported Satanic allegiance, but also for her sexual transgression, and throughout the film she is presented as both alluring and monstrous, seductive and repulsive.[8] This ambivalence is compounded by the doubling up of Asa and her descendant Katia: both played by Barbara Steele, the evil witch and the innocent maid look exactly the same. Through this duplicated character, Bava spells out the ambiguity about female sexual freedom that lies at the heart of many witch films of the period.

As in *Black Sunday*, those films are built around a series of oppositions: good and evil, beautiful and ugly, chaste and promiscuous. This is sometimes embodied in a contrast or conflation between witch and wife, as in *Revenge of the Blood Beast*. This is the case in *The Night of the Eagle* (1962), where the good witch/wife has to fight the bad witch/wife. In *The Eye of the Devil* (1966), the older wife has to fight the younger witch in order to save her husband. *Daughters of Satan* (1972) pits a conflicted wife/reincarnated witch who seeks revenge against her husband, whose ancestor burned her at the stake. In *Season of the Witch* (1973), witchcraft appears as a way out of the domestic sphere for the frustrated housewife.

Although *Revenge of the Blood Beast* seems to convey the same kind of preoccupation with female liberation as contemporary witch films, Reeves's concern is quite different. Unlike Asa, Vardella is anything but attractive, and her punishment is not connected to sexuality. With her crooked teeth, tangled hair and inarticulate grunts, Vardella is more beast than woman. Her oddness and monstrosity are accentuated by the fact that she is played by a male performer.[9] This contributes to position Vardella beyond conventional boundaries. In *Revenge of the Blood Beast*, the witch is not simply ugly and repulsive, she is a creature of uncertain nature, neither male nor female, neither truly human nor fully feral. By making her uncategorisable, Reeves places Vardella beyond gender and its implications.

This is confirmed by the fact that it is not just women who harbour a dark side, but all humans, as shown in a very Reevesian scene where Philip beats up the innkeeper who was peeping at the young couple making love. The violence of the scene is startling, the impact of the blows heightened by images of blood seeping from the man's head as Philip bashes it against the wall. The force he uses seems disproportionate to the offence, and there is the suggestion that he could kill him. Doubt hovers over the true nature of both the female and male character equally, and evil is not associated with female liberation, which sets Reeves's film apart from many of the witch films of the period. The barely human, ambiguously gendered Vardella is the personification of the dark archaic forces that run through both men and women, a 'symbol of eternal and indestructible evil', in the words of Robin Wood.[10] In this manner, *Revenge of the Blood Beast* undermines the polarity between ancient and modern, male and female, British and foreign, to demonstrate the continuity of violence in the whole of mankind.

The Sorcerers: Psychedelia and Generational Conflict

The witchcraft theme continues into Reeves's next film, *The Sorcerers*, but this time it is used metaphorically to reflect on 1960s culture from a different angle. It is the only one of Reeves's features that is set in contemporary London, and its take on witchcraft is modern and science fictional. The film is based on the novel *Terror for Kicks*, written by John Burke, who penned the first version of the script, later revised by Reeves and his school friend Tom Baker. The story revolves around an elderly professor of hypnotism, Marcus Monserrat, and his wife and assistant Estelle (Catherine Lacey). Marcus, played by an elderly, dignified Boris Karloff, has invented a machine that can control people's minds. Walking the streets at night in search of a suitable subject on whom to test the machine, Marcus meets Mike (Ian Ogilvy), a young man bored with the hedonistic thrills enjoyed by his generation. After using the machine on Mike, the Monserrats are able to control him and to experience everything he experiences. Soon, Estelle yearns for stronger sensations and she manipulates Mike to commit theft and later murder, despite Marcus's attempts to stop her.

The film opens with a parallel montage alternating between the Monserrats' drab, tawdry, old-fashioned flat and the bright colours and dynamic sounds of the nightclub where Mike and his girlfriend are drinking, surrounded by hip young people in mini-skirts and polo shirts, dancing to a live pop band. As in *Revenge of the Blood Beast*, the film initially appears to be constructed around the opposition between present and past, young and old. But as in the earlier film, this apparently clear contrast is blurred in a way that directly challenges the era's dominant themes of youthful freedom and generational conflict.

Key to this, and a central preoccupation of the film, is the obsession with new thrills. Monserrat lures Mike back to his flat by promising him exactly that, because as he says, reflecting 1960s clichés, it is what young people want. But soon, it is his elderly wife Estelle who yearns to vicariously experience thrills without danger, who wants exactly what she had guaranteed Mike, 'intoxication without a hangover, ecstasy without consequence'. She takes control of Mike's mind as he goes on a motorcycle ride with his girlfriend, pushing him to drive recklessly fast at the risk of crashing. The motorcycle encapsulates youth, danger, excitement, freedom and individualism, and it would become a key countercultural motif in the biker films that proliferated in the late 1960s and early 1970s, culminating with *Easy Rider* (Dennis Hopper, 1969). The biker film cycle was only just starting when *The Sorcerers* was made, kickstarted by Roger Corman's *The Wild Angels*, released the previous year.[11] But here, the image of young people dangerously speeding along on a motorcycle, which would become a countercultural commonplace, has a much darker meaning: it does not represent individual freedom and carefree hedonism, but mind control; it is not about young people doing what they want, but about elderly people enjoying pleasures by proxy.

A similar displacement takes place in the innovative psychedelic sequence, which represents the workings of the machine used by the Monserrats on Mike. According to Halligan, the later versions of the script that were authored by Reeves and Baker in 1966–7 departed in major ways from Burke's initial script because they incorporated the momentous changes that were taking place on the London underground scene.[12] Reeves and Baker decided to use the psychedelic light show as metaphor for brainwashing, an idea that Burke disliked. Reeves was aware of the nascent psychedelic scene emerging in London at that time. Halligan explains that he 'had stumbled across the Pink Floyd and the Spontaneous Underground, that occurred in the Marquee Club in Soho on dates throughout 1966'.[13] Reeves was so in the know that he asked Joe Gannon, who had been involved in the early Pink Floyd light shows, to create the visuals for the psychedelic scene in the film.[14]

On the hippy underground scene, psychedelic light shows were meant to replicate the hallucinogenic experience of taking LSD, and both were construed as spiritual experiences that would open up the mind to new perceptions, to a new consciousness. Countercultural interest in alternatives to institutional religion included drugs and the trance-inducing combination of psychedelic music and light shows. *The Psychedelic Experience: A Manual Based on the Tibetan Book of the Dead*, in which Timothy Leary, Ralph Metzner and Richard Alpert connected the use of psychoactive drugs to mystical experience, had been published in 1964, two years before *The Sorcerers* was written.

Reeves's linking of sorcery and psychedelia thus shows how attuned he was to his time, but his approach is very different from the pervading countercultural vision. In *The Sorcerers*, the psychedelic light show is not associated with the young characters, or the nightclub scenes, as you would expect in a film of the period, but produced by the elderly scientists in their lab. Reeves dismisses as a total delusion the idea that psychedelic experiences may expand consciousness and help achieve a freer, more enlightened state. For him, drugs were not an instrument of liberation, rather the opposite, and he was very sensitive to the sinister side of the psychedelic underground.[15] Instead of consciousness expansion, pleasure and freedom, the light show in *The Sorcerers* represents the loss of agency and the giving in to the darkest impulses of the mind: it is 'a trap, not a trip', as Halligan quips.[16]

Through his unusual take on the conflict between young and old, Reeves demonstrates that his generation is no different from the previous one, or any other. He sees the same obscure forces, the same violent drives and desire for gratification running through the successive generations. Both the jaded young man and the frustrated old woman want to experience excitement and danger, and both bear some responsibility for their joint acts. Indeed, although Estelle outwardly controls Mike, the film carefully maintains a great deal of ambiguity as to Mike's responsibility in the objectionable acts he commits. Although he perpetrates these transgressions under Estelle's control, Mike comes across from the start as an unpleasant man who may be capable of violence. As Marcus says, they need a 'willing' subject to test their machine, and if Mike was not willing, Estelle would not be able to control him. During these scenes, Mike and Estelle share the same mental space and the same urges towards pleasure and violence. With this unusual representation of the universal impulses governing human behaviour, Reeves fundamentally undermines the structuring of the 1960s around an era-defining generational conflict. He draws from his knowledge of underground youth culture to construct a story that exposes the more disturbing implications of its key concepts and manifestations, displaying a great detachment from his own generation and its easy enthusiasm for the fads of the time.

Witchfinder General: Witch Hunting and Anti-authoritarianism

Reeves's most famous film, *Witchfinder General*, his third and final feature, continues the theme of sorcery, returning to a historical setting and a literal interpretation of 'witch'. Yet, it is a witch film where there are no witches. Even though, like *Revenge of the Blood Beast*, *Witchfinder General* refers back to a murky past, the witches here are not supernatural creatures, but ordinary people victimised in the name of religion. And although *Witchfinder General* starts with the execution of a witch, like *Black Sunday* and *Revenge of the Blood Beast*, the grim realism of the scene immediately sets the film apart. Taking place in East Anglia during the Civil War, the story is based on Ronald Bassett's novel about the historical figure of Matthew Hopkins, a witch hunter who goes from village to village to rid them of supposed servants of the devil, accompanied by his assistant John Stearne. When Hopkins's attention falls on the pretty young Sara and her uncle, the village priest, she and her fiancé, Richard Marshall, a soldier in Oliver Cromwell's army, are forced into a confrontation with Hopkins.

As in Reeves's previous films, *Witchfinder General* is again structured around an opposition between young and old, pitting Sara (Hilary Dwyer) and Marshall (Ian Ogilvy) against Hopkins (Vincent Price) and his vicious henchman (Robert Russell). In all three of Reeves's films, the young characters are unobtrusively presented as sexually free and unencumbered by social or religious conventions, and this is the case here too, despite the seventeenth-century setting. If anything, the love between Marshall and Sara is more warmly depicted than the relationships in the two previous films. Initially, the conflict between the natural desires of the young lovers and the tyrannical repression of older authority figures seems to chime with the period's central themes. The setting of the English Civil War seems particularly conducive to reflecting these ideas: young Marshall is a soldier in Cromwell's reforming, idealistic, democratically inclined Parliamentarians, fighting against the King's despotic rule, while the older Hopkins brutalises innocent people in the name of the overbearingly dogmatic Christian religion.

This generational clash corresponds to a shift in the witch films of the period: in *Witchfinder General* and its followers, including *The Bloody Judge* (*Il trono di fuoco*, 1970), *Mark of the Devil* (1970) and *The Devils* (1971), the monster is no longer the witch, but the witch hunter or inquisitor.[17] This new take on witchcraft resonated with the anti-authority mood of the period, which came to a peak around the time of *Witchfinder General*'s release: 1968 was marked by an escalation of civil rights and anti-Vietnam protests in the USA, a general strike that paralysed France, and brutally repressed student protests in Eastern Europe, Japan and Mexico among others. Ostensibly looking back at a barbarous past of superstition and violence, these witch-hunting films used their historical framework to explore the central conflict of the era. *The Bloody Judge* and *The Devils* set liberated, hopeful young people who simply want to live and love as they please against the persecutions of an abusive monarchy supported by a powerful, oppressive Christian Church.

But whereas these later films are squarely aligned with youthful revolt and countercultural positions, Reeves adopts a far more nuanced position, once more complicating simple binaries. In *Witchfinder General*, the religious torturer is a self-appointed expert who takes advantage of the breakdown of order to indulge his penchant for abusing others and to make money. Although Marshall initially appears to be a dashing young hero fighting the cruel, venal, self-righteous Hopkins, the film gradually undermines the distinction between them. The conflict is not between the iron-handed older generation and the

Figure 12.2 'A soldier with a talent for killing': Richard Marshall (Ian Ogilvy) in *Witchfinder General* (1968).

freespirited youth as in *The Devils* or *The Bloody Judge*, but between a rogue bully and a soldier with a talent for killing.

Both Marshall and Hopkins have a complex relationship to law and lawlessness, as Brian Baker observes.[18] As a soldier on the side of Cromwell and the Parliamentarians, Marshall challenges royal rule, in keeping with the revolutionary spirit of the 1960s. But as Cromwell himself later became a despotic leader, the idea of rebellion represented by Marshall is muddled and fraught with contradictions. Once he leaves his post to pursue his vengeful quest against Hopkins, Marshall effectively becomes a deserter and thus occupies an even greyer area in relation to the law. In parallel, Hopkins neither represents legitimate authority, nor is he completely outside of the law; like Marshall, he is on the fringes of it. Although Hopkins uses the language of religion, he is not a religious figure, but rather a lawyer. His insistence on 'the foul ungodliness of women kind' resonates with the Puritanism that defined Cromwell. Thus while his activities are not fully sanctioned, they are also not completely at odds with the beliefs of the Parliamentarian forces.[19] Consequently, in contrast to *The Bloody Judge* and *The Devils*, in *Witchfinder General* Marshall and Hopkins are not on opposite sides: although his allegiances are not made clear, Hopkins is not a Royalist, and his activities are not incompatible with the side for which Marshall is fighting.

While Hopkins is ostensibly the villain of the piece, Marshall is 'willing': like Philip in *Revenge of the Blood Beast* and Mike in *The Sorcerers*, he promptly engages on the bloody path opened by his ill-intentioned antagonist. This is hinted at in an early scene where Marshall kills for the first time, saving his captain from an enemy soldier. Although this first act of violence is presented in a light-hearted manner, it prefigures the shockingly brutal ending. What this scene suggests is that the capacity for violence was always in Marshall. It is not simply the case that Marshall is contaminated by Hopkins's ferocity, it is latent in him from the very beginning. In *Witchfinder General*, there is no reassuringly clear-cut divide between young and old, individual revolt and oppressive system: both idealistic young hero and abusive authority figure are capable of the same savagery.

In fact, the film suggests that Marshall's very idealism is as destructive as Hopkins's cynical exploitation of religion. This idealism motivates his fighting for the Parliamentarian cause, but also shows through in his behaviour towards Sara. On discovering the rape of his fiancée he becomes cold and distant, and his love for her is displaced by an all-consuming thirst for revenge. Although Marshall appears open and liberated in an early lovemaking scene, his response to the assault hints at a puritanical obsession with Sara's virginal integrity and an inability to deal with her desecration. Disturbingly, Marshall and Hopkins have similar reactions to Sara's rape: both reject her as though she were degraded or spoiled. Ultimately, it is Marshall's fanatical attempt to avenge Sara's violation that will destroy her.[20]

In muddying the line between Marshall and Hopkins in such a troubling and intricate manner, *Witchfinder General* goes completely against the countercultural grain. It suggests that the problem is not authorities or institutions, but rather the violence that is in all humans, whether it is expressed individually or collectively, whether as part of an organised system, a power vacuum, or a revolutionary movement. Reeves was weary of the system, but also of the anti-system; of the culture and of the counterculture. For him, the very same urges and forces run through all of these apparently opposed human constructions.

This reflection is framed by the glorious East Anglian landscapes that are so poetically and expansively filmed by Reeves. *Witchfinder General* was born from a trip to Suffolk, and Reeves and Baker wrote the script around the places they found.[21] Such use of landscape was not entirely new in horror films of the time (*The Witches* had already connected witchcraft with the English countryside in 1966). But it was not common, as production companies like Hammer and Amicus predominantly shot in studios. For Reeves, it was crucial to film in exterior locations in order to achieve an unprecedented level of realism. Just as Reeves had grounded *The Sorcerers* in the reality of contemporary London, he similarly strove to anchor the story of *Witchfinder General* in a realistic representation of the period.[22]

The central place of landscape in *Witchfinder General* had a distinctive influence on the British occult and folk horror films that followed in the late 1960s and early 1970s, most notably *Blood on Satan's Claw* (1971), which was made by Tigon, the company that produced *The Sorcerers* and *Witchfinder General*. There is also a connection between the rural setting and the occult, witchcraft or paganism in *The Wicker Man* (1973), *Curse of the Crimson Altar* (1968) and *Virgin Witch* (1972). Those films map out the relationship between witchcraft and the landscape along the key dividing lines that define the 1960s and 1970s: female–male, young–old, permissive–repressive. *The Witches*, *Blood on Satan's Claw* and *The Wicker Man* feature ancient, nature-based, orgiastic (and in the first two cases, female-led) cults evoking the hedonistic youth culture of the 1960s, which are confronted with puritanical (and in the last two cases, male) authority figures. Although those films are deeply ambivalent about the permissiveness of the pagan cults they depict, witchcraft is unmistakably presented as a counter-discourse, a rejection of the prevailing social order.

In contrast, the landscape in *Witchfinder General* is not associated with ancient worship, and witchcraft is not presented as a form of resistance to authority; it is not used to reflect anxieties about the growing power of women, or the Dionysian excesses of modern youth. Instead, the idyllic beauty of the land indifferently frames the barbarity of man. This conception of the landscape is strongly connected to the fact that Reeves conceived *Witchfinder General* as an English Western, a revenge Western set among the verdant hills of England.[23] As in the American Western, *Witchfinder General* stages a battle between civilisation and savagery among a grandiose landscape. But in contrast to its classic model, the nature is harmonious and pleasant, rather than monumental and hostile, and the battle takes place within the human heart, rather than between man and wilderness. Like the American genre, Reeves's English Western is connected to national identity. To choose the English Civil War as setting for the story is not incidental: in that key moment of historical turbulence, the relationship between the land, the individual and the ruling order was radically questioned, and it was a foundational moment for national identity. In Reeves's film as in the American Western, national identity is built on the violent relationship between man and nature. But whereas in the American Western, that violence is exteriorised and projected on to the surrounding wildness, in *Witchfinder General*, it is squarely attributed to the human, and contrasted with the peacefulness of nature. The landscape in *Witchfinder General* is thus the realistic setting that grounds the film's tale of man's perpetual ferocity. The loveliness and serenity of the rolling hills provides a poignant foil to the terrible deeds of the humans, suggesting that both the beauty of nature and the savagery of mankind are as enduring and unchanging as each other.

Conclusion

Although they are set in divergent political and geographical environments, all three of Michael Reeves's films, taken together, demonstrate that the violence of the human is an eternal constant, unaffected by changes in socio-political organisation: whether it is the Communist state of Transylvania, the liberal democracy of 1960s Britain or the Civil War chaos of seventeenth-century England, the same urges propel mankind along. For Reeves, the key issues that so concerned his time and his generation are simply surface variations that mask the dark immutability of human nature, his detached pessimism offering a sobering commentary on some of the commonplace tenets of the 1960s. In his films, the theme of witchcraft that so fascinated his peers refers not so much to the binary oppositions that defined the era, but rather serves as a potent image for the primal forces that lie dormant in the human heart, always there, more or less obscured and controlled, but always ready to burst through and furiously erupt back to the surface.

Notes

1. Benjamin Halligan, *Michael Reeves* (Manchester: Manchester University Press, 2003), pp. 3–4.
2. Most evidently the fringe feminist group W.I.T.C.H. (Women's International Terrorist Conspiracy from Hell), which appeared in the late 1960s.
3. Iain Sinclair, *Lights Out for the Territory* (London: Penguin, 2003), p. 296.
4. Also known as Charles B. Griffith.
5. *I Married a Witch* (1942) starts with the execution of a witch, and so does *The City of the Dead* (1960), released the same year as *Black Sunday*.
6. For more on the evolution of witch characters in cinema, see Sharon Russell, 'The witch in film: myth and reality', in Barry Keith Grant and Christopher Sharrett (eds), *Planks of Reason: Essays on the Horror Film* (Lanham, MD: Scarecrow Press, 2004), pp. 63–71.
7. The same period was also marked by a multiplication of films featuring female vampires with similar characteristics to witches. It is worth noting that Asa in *Black Sunday* is alternately described as a witch and a vampire.
8. For more on this, see Lindsay Hallam, 'A beautiful life of evil and hate; the vampire-witch in Mario Bava's *Black Sunday*', in Douglas Brode and Leah Deyneka (eds), *Dracula's Daughters: The Female Vampire on Film* (New York: Scarecrow Press, 2014), pp. 69–82, p. 70.
9. The retired black ballet dancer Jay Flash Riley. For more on Riley, see John B. Murray, *The Remarkable Michael Reeves: His Short and Tragic Life* (Baltimore, MD: Luminary Press, 2004), p. 77. Reeves may have been inspired by *The Castle of the Living Dead*, where the witch was played by Donald Sutherland in a very early role.
10. Robin Wood, 'In Memoriam Michael Reeves', p. 4.
11. Pun intended.
12. Halligan, *Michael Reeves*, p. 73.
13. Ibid. p. 73.
14. Ibid. p. 74.
15. Ibid. p. 76.

16. Ibid. p. 76.
17. See Leon Hunt, 'Necromancy in the UK: witchcraft and the occult in British horror', in Steve Chibnall and Julian Petlay (eds), *British Horror Cinema* (London: Routledge, 2002), pp. 82–98, p. 83, and Kim Newman, *Nightmare Movies: Horror on Screen Since the 1960s*, 2nd edn (London: Bloomsbury, 2011), p. 60.
18. Brian Baker, 'The occult and film', in Christopher Partridge (ed.), *The Occult World* (Oxford/New York: Routledge, 2015), pp. 446–58, p. 455.
19. Ibid. p. 455. For Baker, 'it is clear that Hopkins' activities are really an extension both of mid-17th century Puritanism and of Parliamentarian rule: Hopkins and his helpers would have required passes of parliamentarian forces to travel around East Anglia'.
20. Like *Revenge of the Blood Beast* (and Reeves's 1961 amateur film *Intrusion*), *Witchfinder General* is about a young couple confronted with violence, where aggression against the woman triggers murderous impulses for revenge in the man.
21. Murray, *The Remarkable Michael Reeves*, p. 132. For identification of some of the locations of *Witchfinder General* see pp. 132 and 170.
22. See Murray, *The Remarkable Michael Reeves*, pp. 107 and 110, for a list of some of the locations, including for the club scenes. Ibid. p. 155.
23. Ibid. p. 131.

PART FOUR

CULTURAL TRANSFORMATIONS

13. 'AN IMPULSE OF ANGER, INSTANTLY REGRETTED': REBELLION AND REACTION IN THE EARLY-1960s NAVAL FILM

Mark Fryers

On the 17 September 1961, a crowd gathered in London to demonstrate against the continued development of nuclear weapons. Earlier in January of the same year, prison mutinies broke out at Maidstone and Shrewsbury.[1] Whilst far from encapsulating a mood of rebellion, such events did foreshadow huge societal shifts that would typify the so-called 'countercultural rebellion' of the 1960s. A nascent youth culture was also developing, typified by the fights between 'Mods' and 'Rockers' at Clacton, Margate and Brighton, leading to fears and 'moral panics' surrounding Britain's youth.[2] In film, literature and theatre, the youth movement was exemplified by the work of the 'Angry Young Men', meanwhile, with East Enders once again fighting with Oswald Mosley's fascists, it is easy to look back at this era as being one of violent rebellion.[3] Allied to this, the old certainties of empire were changing rapidly. The Suez and Cuban Missile crises had shown how isolated and insignificant Britain now was on the world stage. The former imperial power had become, in the words of Schyler and Auschul, a 'strange island anchored off the continent'.[4] It is within this context that a short cycle of British films emerged in 1962–3 that dealt with themes of mutiny, rebellion and resistance in Britain's most revered institution: the Royal Navy. This chapter will explore how *HMS Defiant* (1962), *Billy Budd* (1962) and *Carry on Jack* (1963), alongside the US production *Mutiny on the Bounty* (1962), served to open a fleeting window of enquiry into Britain's naval past and established notions of national identity.

The British Naval Film

The naval film had long been emblematic of all that was held sacred to British hearts and minds. The introduction of cinema coincided with the age in which Britain's Royal and Merchant navies patrolled and protected its vast empire. The 'cult of the navy' was such that the traditional 'wooden walls' that protected Britain were culturally revered as the apotheosis of British national identity, while the men who sailed in them – 'jacks' and 'tars' – represented the solid oaken heart of the nation, almost beyond ridicule or reproach.[5] This was reflected in naval films from the earliest days of moving pictures, with films of ship launches and fleet reviews weaving the cult of the navy into a new audio-visual tapestry and thus providing powerful new propaganda opportunities to the institution. This was galvanised during the First World War with fictional films such as *Nelson* (1918) reminding the British public of the nation's finest naval hero during a time of national crisis. The phenomenon was repeated in the Second World War with *In Which We Serve* (1942) a prime example, offering the naval destroyer as nation in miniature, sitting alongside a number of other films which re-affirmed the Royal Navy as upholder of freedom and liberty. The pattern continued after the war and into the 1950s as naval films celebrated the heroism and sacrifice of the recent conflict, reaffirming naval victory as an integral part of the defining British national myth of the twentieth century.

By the early 1960s, however, these myths were being interrogated. The biopic, in particular, was serving a particular function to re-assess the 'black and white' rendering of history, with films such as *Lawrence of Arabia* (1962) and *Khartoum* (1966) challenging uncomplicated narratives of British imperial history and often positioning national heroes (particularly the officer class) as vain, individualistic, dangerous and flawed. However, alongside these new developments there was also a certain continuity of tradition which served to buffer society from instant and violent upheaval. Depictions of the Second World War as the defining British myth of the twentieth century continued in naval films which valorised the heroism of (often) small homo-social units in defence of Britain and her empire. Films like *Sink the Bismarck!* (1960), *The Valiant* (1961), and later *Submarine X-1* (1968) and *Hell Boats* (1969) returned to a recent naval past where victory against the forces of evil were a largely foregone conclusion – emotion was subsumed for duty and there was a clear sense of what the British were fighting for. As Kenneth More's character declares in *Sink the Bismarck!*, 'getting emotional about things is a peace-time luxury'. Andrew Spicer describes this film as 'offering a consolatory reassertion of national self-esteem through celebrating the heroics of the officer class in winning the war'.[6]

The early 1960s saw a brief burgeoning of historical naval films which directly questioned the conduct of the navy, war and the hierarchy of naval servitude. In 1962, MGM produced an updated version of *Mutiny on the Bounty*, tapping into the vein of contemporary youth culture by casting Hollywood rebel Marlon Brando as the mutinous Fletcher Christian. Although an American film on a British subject, there was substantial British involvement (Carol Reed had been the original director before being fired, Eric Ambler contributed un-credited to the screenplay and the crew was mostly made up actors from the British Isles). Significantly, Trevor Howard took the role of the power-crazed and sadistic Captain Bligh. Synonymous with *Brief Encounter* (1945), Howard represented an old England of emotional restraint and duty to protocol against the anti-authoritarian rock and roll spirit of Marlon Brando. By contrast, Brando had appeared in *The Wild One* (1953), as a juvenile delinquent, thus becoming identified with a particular strain of 'youth rebellion' during the 1950s, before becoming known as a radical and activist in his own right, being outspoken on civil rights and emancipation issues (particularly black and Native American movements). The casting of Brando and Howard therefore bought an extra-textual relevance to this historic tale of naval defiance that pitted the youth movements against a symbolic member of the glorious Second World War generation. But 1962 also saw two British films which presented the same scenario: *HMS Defiant* and *Billy Budd*.

Mutiny! *HMS Defiant* (1962)

HMS Defiant was released in February 1962 and featured Alec Guinness as Captain Crawford of the eponymous *Defiant* in 1797 at the time of the Spithead mutinies, and Dirk Bogarde as his sadistic second-in-command, Lieutenant Scott-Padget. The film was based upon Frank Tilsley's novel *Mutiny*, which was the working title of the production.[7] *HMS Defiant* opens with Scott-Padget leading a violent press gang through the streets on an unseemly spree contrasted with the domestic tranquillity of Crawford's home as he prepares for duty aboard the *Defiant* and the initiation of his young son into navy life. It becomes clear that the Lieutenant's excessive and sadistic methods such as drilling the men until they are unable to stand and meting out harsh punishments such as flogging begins to inculcate mutiny amongst the crew. Moreover, Scott-Padget and Crawford clash so violently over these issues that this initiates a battle of wills for control of the ship and the men. Mutiny is agitated below decks by division in the ranks between those wanting swift and violent overthrow – Evans (Tom Bell) – and those wanting to do things with due legal recourse – Vizard (Anthony Quayle). After a seaman is admonished for raising his hands instinctively to Scott-Padget, he offers the legal phrase 'an instance of anger, instantly regretted'. Meanwhile, Scott-Padget realises he can attack the Captain by proxy by terrorising his son and beating him every day, realising that intervention would be seen as favouritism/nepotism. Crawford puts a stop to this by transferring his son to a captured French warship. After a surprise attack by a French frigate, in which the *Defiant* is victorious, Scott-Padget stretches the crew to breaking point by issuing another flogging which leads to mutiny. The injured Captain, realising that the men have been wronged, promises to support the crew's legal claim as there has been no bloodshed and the news filters out of the mutiny at Spithead and the Admiralty's concessions. However, Evans kills Scott-Padget, leaving the crew in an invidious position. These events are interrupted by another engagement with French warships and this galvanises the crew into a fighting unit again as old hierarchies are restored. The film ends on this triumphant note accompanied by an equally stirring, romantic and bombastic soundtrack.

HMS Defiant, at times, certainly does engage with established audio-visual tropes of naval bombast and romance. The opening sequence includes a shot of the rear of the ship accompanied by romantic music, echoed elsewhere throughout the narrative alongside sailing shots and montages of naval work and camaraderie. It also allows for the male rite-of-passage paradigm particular to nautical drama as, like Nelson and the fictional Hornblower, Crawford's young son joins the *Defiant* as midshipman. This was reflected in the film's critical reception, which deployed naval language to describe a standard sea adventure. The *Kinematograph Weekly* in particular relished its patriotic virtues: 'it stoutly supports the lofty contention that neither privation nor ill-treatment can destroy the Britisher's patriotism'.[8]

Ultimately, the status quo of naval order is restored in the film, as it is not the benign and paternally minded Captain who is the target of the crew's anger, but the sadistic Scott-Padget, who turns the men against the strict authority and discipline of service and who sets himself against the Captain as well. Once he is removed, order can be restored. Similarly, it is one rotten apple (or malcontented youth) amongst the crew that threatens the unity and legality of the mutiny, who once removed also allows for parity to be restored. It is therefore dangerous individualism that threatens the security of the group, and by extension the nation. Much is made in the film of the difference between French and English revolution, as Captain Crawford declares, 'The only enemy is the Frenchman.' When the captured French, upon seeing the mutinous actions of the crew declare 'we are all revolutionaries now', the crew sneer and see their actions in a new way, as though resistance to protocol is a form of debasement that is un-British. It is significant that it is warfare, and unity against the French enemy, that helps to restore the equilibrium aboard the *Defiant*, exemplifying a continuity of British attitude towards revolution.

There is a discourse of responsibility in the film which positions negative individuality against positive group and national identity. Warfare and a common enemy subsume the needs of the individual as the threat to communal identity is greater, as continually iterated by the officers: 'If you care for the safety of your country. If you don't want to see her humiliated and overrun by the Frenchman' then conformity is a necessity. The film therefore shows the utility of (justified) rebellion, but there is a stress on legality and due process, a focus on collective unity both against internal grievances and common enemies, a suggestion that order is only upset by the actions of rare and isolated malcontents and that rebellion must return to the natural order and hierarchies of established institution. In short, it suggests a very 'English' sense of revolution, whereby decency prevails over barbarity and violent upheaval – dangerous individuals are removed and patriotism and institutional deference restored through potent acts of warfare.

'Ever seen so much ignorance all in one place?'
Billy Budd (1962)

In America, *HMS Defiant* was occasionally shown on a double bill with Peter Ustinov's adaptation of Henry Melville's *Billy Budd*, under the title *Damn the Defiant!*, and a review in the journal *Show* in October 1962 pointed to the 'peculiar' similarities between the two films.⁹ Ustinov's production, although closer to the themes of rebellion in *HMS Defiant*, sits somewhere between the *Bounty* and *Defiant* in its history, provenance and production context. A British film made with Hollywood money of an American novella which deals with a very British subject, the material has a curiously transatlantic flavour, perhaps apt for a text about the sea. The plot, set in 1797, sees young Billy Budd (Terence Stamp) drafted into military service from the British merchant ship *The Rights of Man*, into the naval frigate *Avenger*. Sociable and adored by all sections of the crew, Budd's popularity and simple innocence infuriates Claggart (Robert Ryan), the sadistic Master-at-arms (echoing Dirk Bogarde in *Defiant*), who makes it his business to destroy Billy by framing him for mutinous behaviour. In a terse exchange in which Claggart accuses Billy of mutiny in front of the Captain (Peter Ustinov), Billy, unable to defend himself verbally due to a stammer that manifests at times of great emotion and confusion, lashes out and punches Claggart who falls and accidently dies from the impact. Despite knowing Billy to be innocent, a court martial takes place during which Captain Vere and his three subordinate officers debate doing what is 'right' (acquitting Billy) or following naval protocol and hanging him for striking a superior officer, especially pertinent at a time of war. After much debate, and to the dismay of the court, they realise that the only way they can continue is to condemn Billy to be hanged. As the execution is carried out Billy's only words – 'God Bless Captain Vere' – seem to incite the men to mutiny. Just as this occurs, however, a French ship is spotted and the vicissitudes of war jolt the company out of their existential angst and back into the mundanities of warfare. Like *Defiant*, the film ends at this point.

Figure 13.1   The destruction of innocence: the crew's reaction to the execution of *Billy Budd* (1962).

Shot in black and white CinemaScope, *Billy Budd* is striking in its formal qualities. The visual and aural configurations of the text create a space for an examination, and interrogation, of the myths of British naval and national identity, one that in many ways denies the patriotic pleasures of *Defiant*. The film begins with a close-up of a relatively calm sea, whilst the camera slowly tracks forward from a high angle to reveal the stern of the *Avenger*. Already, the formal elements of composition begin to subvert the established visual language of maritime film, whereby, if a ship is slowly revealed in an establishing shot, it is traditionally the prow of a boat – normally from left to right, not overhead from south to north as here. The soundtrack, which features the non-diegetic voices of the crew of the *Avenger* introducing themselves and their position on ship, followed by the crew of *The Rights of Man* doing the same, exacerbates such subversions (again, compare with the romance of *Defiant*). The last voice we hear is Billy Budd whose broad Bristolian accent contrasts jarringly with the clipped voices of the senior naval officers. A sense of subtle unease is thus established over the opening titles by the flouting of traditional conventions of maritime films.

The first scene then follows the *Avenger* as it attempts to flag down *The Rights of Man* to impress members of its crew into naval engagement (echoing *Defiant*'s 'press-ganging' opening). Here the differences between the British Merchant Navy and the Royal Navy are underlined in dramatic fashion. The Captain of *The Rights* knows that he is likely to lose some of his best crew and proclaims 'It's worse than any enemy – if she's British, I'll not heave to.' Captain Vere has to resort to firing across her bows before she relents and heaves to. Penny Summerfield suggests that the 'liminal presence' of the Merchant Navy on screen 'hint[s] at the fragility of imperial masculinity' and represents a disruptive presence which 'undermined the secure portrayal of national unity'.[10] Here, certainly, there is a clear dichotomy between the merchant and naval crews. On relenting and heaving to, the Captain orders Billy to sing to keep spirits up, at which the crew join in. Melville was perhaps not attempting subtlety by naming the merchant vessel *The Rights of Man*, and as the narrative unravels, it is clear that the Royal Navy is a menace which threatens the natural order of things (Billy says 'goodbye Rights of Man' as he leaves the craft at which the naval commander snaps 'what do you mean by that?'). When Claggart asks Billy what he did on his previous ship, his reply suggests an equal and collective community; 'we took it in turns to do everything', to which he is told 'here you'll have a station'. An inversion of Summerfield's notion of the disruptive presence of the Merchant Navy is therefore enacted with the navy representing the threat to communal unity.

There is a formalism to the film's composition as scenes of the men on deck are ordered and arranged in distinct clusters (much like the strict hierarchy of the navy) and below decks as mainly cluttered and claustrophobic. The eerie austerity of this formally ordered geometry provides a subtle and brooding sense of impending menace which mirrors the narrative drama, as the disordered mass ranks below rise up to threaten the ordered symmetry above, yet that symmetry, in its unrelenting sense of order, restores everything to its rightful place. Similarly, the contrast between ordered scenes and disarray suggests the injustice and iniquity that lies beneath the ordered structure of the naval universe. This can be seen distinctly in the scene in which the crew witness Billy's execution. The contrast between the vindictiveness of the middle-man, the compassionate, but anchored-by-duty Captain, and the innocent everyman paradigm established in *HMS Defiant* is also in evidence here. The ship, both in its geographical and bureaucratic organisation, can roughly exemplify the divisions and stratifications of British society.

Comparing the two films, it is interesting to note that both Captains, Vere and Crawford, as commanding officers, are not presented as evil but rather as benevolent and institutionally bound to the old order and protocol. It is the middle men, Scott-Padget and Claggart, who represent the danger in both films, perhaps suggesting that the rebellious spirit of the time was more inclined to vent its true anger not at the old establishment, but the aspirant middle classes who more directly exercise power and punishment.

On a more philosophical level, the spirit of the times is represented both textually and extra-textually by Terence Stamp as Billy Budd. In his film debut, the angelic-looking and noticeably white Stamp perfectly embodies the innocence of youth that so irks Claggart, and whose jealousy of his popularity among all classes ferments a vendetta and will to destroy him. Stamp went on to become a defining cultural icon of the era who David Boxwell describes as 'symbolis[ing] the free-wheeling counter-cultural impulses energising culture in the 1960s', and therefore in retrospect it is difficult to analyse the film, as with Brando in *Bounty*, without considering this extra-textual detail.[11] Although *Billy Budd* has its provenance as a story written seventy years before the film was produced, and is based on historical events from the late seventeenth century, it is clear that the themes are timeless. Moreover, this iteration in its particular time and context of production, has resonance with both emergent working-class anger and the rise of youth culture at this particular historical moment.

Casey Harrison connects the original novel, its time of writing (not publication, as this was not until the 1920s) and the revolutionary spirit of the British rock band The Who.[12] Specifically, he links the use of Billy's stammer, a physical defect that hinders the verbal articulation of his anger at injustice, with the use of the stammer in The Who's song *My Generation*, which symbolises generational conflict. Harrison suggests the stammer in both texts as exemplifying an 'inarticulacy among the working classes that finds an outlet in violence'.[13] Harrison describes 'certain acts of violence as natural . . . even redemptive' in this context, a view which squarely places the film within the contexts of the acts of (largely) working-class violence and rebellion occurring in Britain at the time. Billy does not even know his age or where he comes from, yet still has a humane and rational view on corporal punishment: 'it's wrong to flog a man; it's against him being a man'. There is an obvious link here to the fists raised towards Claggart in *Defiant* but also to the notion of 'two wars' that Spicer discusses in relation to the class divisions in the Second World War and specifically the case of Pete Grafton, a young officer who struck an officer after being falsely accused of an indiscretion.[14]

Billy Budd offers an endless cycle of inhumanity leading to more anger and violence which finally is ended, as in *HMS Defiant*, by the state sanctioned intervention of naval warfare. There is an important link here with the American myth of 'manifest destiny' and the mythology of the old West. Slotkin describes the process of violence and expansionism on the frontier as 'regeneration through violence', in which national progress is only contingent on warfare and conflict, a concept he argues has continued to inform American foreign policy.[15] With both *HMS Defiant* and *Billy Budd* ending on an implicit (if not critiqued in the former) necessary conflict, the same act of violent national regeneration is evident.

Significantly, as well as being borne of the vindictiveness and jealousy of the human condition, the inhumanity and degradation presented in *Billy Budd* are borne out of naval culture, masculine culture in general and the manner in which these two cultures intersect. Boxwell describes this as a 'rendition of the destructive (and self-destructive) consequences of all-male institutions'.[16] Before he sees the hopelessness that his condition as ship's Captain, upholder of navy propriety and judge of a man's life at Billy's court martial, he offers a speech to the crew designed specifically to quell any suggestion of mutiny:

> May I remind you that this ship is at war . . . A crew that I shall mould into a weapon. One lawless act, one spurt of rebel temper from any of you, high or low, I shall pay you out in coin you know of. You have only two duties here – to fight, and to obey.

Here, the conflation between rebellion and capital punishment is also bound to the crushing of the spirit and the de-humanisation of individuals into a single 'weapon', clearly suggesting that both naval servitude and the articles of war degrade all who become involved, either by choice or by force. Vere later concedes that 'battle makes a mockery of justice'. It is the common man, Billy, who is eventually cut down, perhaps prefiguring the abolition of the death penalty in Britain, as the last men to be hanged, Peter Allen and John Walby, were cut down two years later in August 1964.[17]

It is interesting to compare this projection of Britain's naval past with earlier representations in literature. John R. Reed, assessing the representation of the navy in nineteenth-century literature, identifies a strain of dissatisfaction with what he describes as the 'degrading features of service'.[18] Reed suggests that 'naval service constitutes an assault upon, rather than a refinement of, one's manhood', suggesting that naval service represents an inhuman masculine space of debasement.[19] He also notes that even in that time period there was a vast range of depictions of the navy in literature, so rather than a simple 'continuity of tradition', the navy then, as here, represents an impermanent symbol: a 'tabula rasa' in which to explore the present.[20] In Ustinov's version of *Billy Budd*, as with *HMS Defiant*, the open questioning of Britain's triumphant naval and mythic military past of unity is contextualised by the uncertainty of the early 1960s. It is perhaps more difficult to conceive of this in a pre-1960 context in British naval films.

This notion of an assault on masculinity also engages with the Manichean central themes of good and evil in Melville's novella, which some critics suggest embodies an overt homosexual discourse.[21] *Billy Budd* has been the source of several adaptations, including Claire Denis's later highly regarded *Beau Travail* (1999) which relocates the service to the French foreign legion and the setting to Djibouti. Undoubtedly the most famous adaptation is Benjamin Britten's opera of 1951, with a libretto by E. M. Forster (*Beau Travail* also references this). Perhaps due to the fact that both Britten and Forster were homosexual, it is the opera that is positioned at the forefront of interpretations of the text as an exploration of latent homosexual desires. It is perhaps inevitable that the notion of men alone at sea together in cramped quarters and engaging in close physical work in half-naked attire would lead to this question arising, as well as its antonymic trope – the virile heterosexual sailor with a girl in every port and a voracious sexual proclivity for prostitutes. As Roy and Lesley Adkins point out, 'The idea that sexual frustration would lead the men of the lower decks to "unclean acts" of homosexuality was one reason why prostitutes were permitted on board when the ships were in port.'[22] It is Budd in the novella as 'Handsome Sailor' who embodies delicate feminine features as well as masculinity: 'feminine in purity of natural expression'.[23] The prominence of Terence Stamp in habitual close-up foregrounds the conflict within Claggart and helps to explain his cruelty, as it engenders a confusion within that he cannot resolve (again, the use of violence and sadism is a masculine form of expression that elides language). Eve Sedgwick also interprets the threat of mutiny with homophobia and as Dana Silva suggests, 'Claggart's fear of society's reaction to homoerotic relations creates within him a dichotomist state, pinning his true desires, homosexuality, against his societal expectations, heterosexuality.'[24] So not only does *Billy Budd* utilise this era to question the value of strict institutional law, it also allows for an examination of a specific nation's suppression of desire and the brutality that characterises it (significantly, homosexuality was not legalised in Britain until 1967). This is also evidenced extra-textually in *HMS Defiant* by the presence of actors Alec Guinness, Dirk Bogarde and Murray Melvin. As Griffiths suggests:

> Britain's queer audiences have had to activate their own very unique form of cultural identification, that are either mobilised around particularly significant themes and scenarios (from public school sublimation to war-time homosociality), or coloured by the tacit extra-textual nuances that surround the directors, writers and stars involved (from the loaded linguistic inflections of Noel Coward and Kenneth Williams to the 'cottaging' scandals of Alec Guinness and John Gielgud).[25]

A similar sadism as that discussed in relation to *Billy Budd* is also at work in the sadism of Scott-Padget in *HMS Defiant*, portrayed by Bogarde, who was synonymous in many ways with the homosexual lawyer in *Victim* (1961), alongside his own repressed sexuality. Andy Medhurst persuasively argues that Bogarde's star persona and performances act as a form of subversion in 1950s and early 1960s British cinema.[26] Murray Melvin (who had previously appeared as the young homosexual Geoffrey in *A Taste of Honey* [1961]) as Wagstaffe in *HMS Defiant* is particularly positioned as a metropolitan 'effete' form of masculinity which is shown as being at odds with the rough physicality of press-ganged naval servitude, as he attempts to talk his way out of service and is then shown struggling with the tasks alongside the more 'physical' recruits. Melvin's performance emphasises this, with his soft voice, intonations, gestures and slight physical frame providing a 'disruption' to 'traditional' naval masculinity. Melvin's and Bogarde's performances adhere to what Griffiths describes as the 'sad young man', linking these films to the New Wave and to the repression of homosexuality both within the texts and within the social context of the time.[27]

CARRY ON JACK (1963): QUEERING THE NAVAL/NATIONAL NARRATIVE

The following year, 1963, *Carry On Jack*, in the honoured budget-paring style of the popular comedy series, utilised some of the same sets and props from *HMS Defiant*, while Percy Herbert was cast as Mr Angel, Bosun, following his appearance as seaman Matthew Quintal in *Mutiny on the Bounty*. Set in the same Napoleonic era, it was the first *Carry On* film to take place in the historical past. Its comedic orientation meant that its take on the navy differed from the high drama of *Mutiny*, HMS *Defiant* and *Billy Budd*, yet it provided its own manner of subversive undertow. It is perhaps significant that *Carry on Jack* marked the first foray into lampooning popular genres as it appeared at a time when the traditional contemporary 'service comedy' that itself had provided comic material for the early *Carry On* series, was in decline. These had been in rude health within British cinema since the 1930s and in evidence in recent films such as *Carry on Sergeant* (1958) and *The Bulldog Breed* (1960). One of the main reasons for the sudden disappearance of these films after 1961 is likely to have been agitated by the abolition of National Service, first initiated in 1957 and ending in 1963 (when the last recruits completed training).

Carry On Jack signals its intentions from the outset by spoofing the mythical Nelson deathbed scene. As the press-book points out, the film sought to

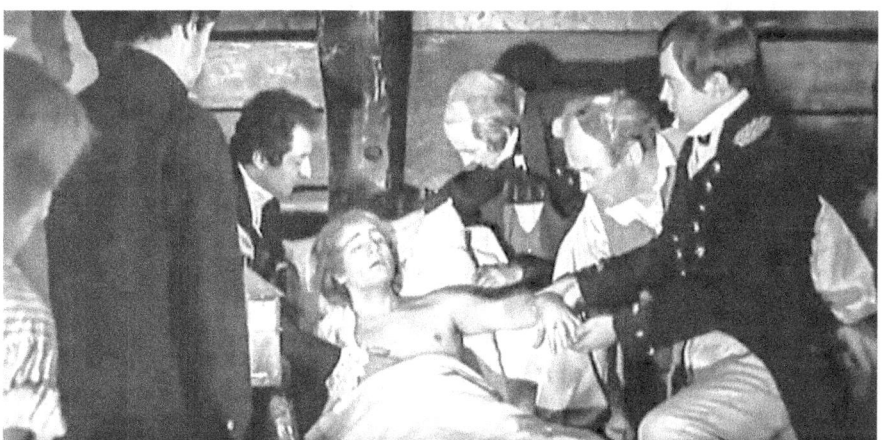

Figure 13.2   The death of Horatio Nelson, Carry On style: *Carry On Jack* (1964).

lovingly re-create the details of Arthur William Devis's famous painting of this scene.[28] No such reverence is afforded the event though, which is given the full *Carry On* treatment: Nelson implores a reluctant Hardy to plant a kiss on him, after which he expires – 'told you so' is Hardy's response. The film then follows the exploits of Albert Poop-Decker (Bernard Cribbins), a midshipman (in naval tradition) assigned to the frigate *HMS Venus*. Visiting the bar/brothel 'Dirty Tricks' (which bears comparison to the tavern in *HMS Defiant*) on the eve of sailing, he is lured upstairs by Sally (Juliet Mills), a barmaid seeking to follow her beloved to sea. In order to do this, she knocks Albert unconscious and steals his clothes, leaving him to be press-ganged aboard as an ordinary seaman, wearing Sally's dress, and forced to do the job of a rating with the equally inept and press-ganged Walter Sweetly (Charles Hawtrey). Echoing both *Billy Budd* and *HMS Defiant*, they incur the wrath of belligerent First Officer Howett (Donald Huston) and Bosun Angel who are also frustrated by Captain Fearless's (Kenneth Williams) reluctance to punish their insubordination and incompetence. In response, Howett fakes an enemy attack forcing Albert, Walter and the Captain to escape to Spain, where more cross-dressing high-jinks take place as they attempt to pass themselves off as Spaniards. Eventually the crew inadvertently fend off pirate attacks and those of the Spanish to be greeted back in England as heroes as Fearless is made Admiral.

In line with the subversive potential of comedy, as well as what Medhurst describes as 'us' comedy, *Carry On Jack* allows for much masquerade, cross-dressing, role reversal and the disruptive presence of a female aboard an all-male vessel.[29] Distinctions of class, status and gender are temporarily elided. Much is made, then subverted, of accepted naval standards of masculinity and virility. The flogging scene, whereby the implementation of naval servitude is enacted upon the body of the common seaman, is interrupted by comic discourse, as Poop-Decker's vest gets caught up in the cat-o'-nine-tails. Echoing the discomfort of Alec Guinness's Captain towards corporal punishment in *Defiant*, and Vere's to capital punishment in *Billy Budd*, Williams's Fearless is equally averse to flogging, fainting at the prospect of Poop-Decker's punishment, and causing his officers, in a reversal of *Bounty* and *Defiant*, to plot against him. He does, however, admire the masculine body of Juliet Mills: 'very fine manly chest'. This follows what Landy describes as the undercurrent of defiance in British comedy in which 'the complacency of the status quo and the rigidity of social structures is threatened by eruptions of physical and psychic energy'.[30]

Sacred British naval history is therefore presented in *Cary On Jack* with transgressive irreverence, replacing heroism with incompetence and 'queering' the strictly homo-social space of the ship with gender performativity of various kinds, from the cross-dressing women on board to the camp performances of Hawtrey and Williams, as well as the displaced and perpetually deferred corporal punishment. Again, with homosexuality still several years away from decriminalisation, these films open up a space for rebellion and subversion, which again, are eventually closed when the business of naval warfare is reasserted.

Conclusion

Billy Budd and *HMS Defiant*, alongside *The Mutiny on the Bounty* and *Carry On Jack*, appear at a particular flashpoint in British social history that was both in the process of and on the precipice of major social changes. Violence, rebellion and male working-class anger are in evidence in these productions, which choose to highlight a period in British naval history offering a slightly different narrative of group unity to the 'glorious' victory at Trafalgar which followed, by focusing on mutinies at Spithead and on the *Bounty*. Meanwhile, *Carry On Jack* lampoons naval traditions at a time when the institution it represented was becoming increasingly irrelevant to modern British identity. Although *HMS Defiant* ultimately couches its rebellion in English and anti-French sentiment, it does demonstrate the brutality inherent in naval life. *Billy Budd* is clearly more of an expansive and philosophical work and offers no easy answers to the existential questions it raises except that life continues in any circumstances, especially when warfare necessitates it. Many of these films also display impulses of anger which do not always seem to be regretted at all, whilst undercurrents of homosexuality threaten to subvert hetero-normativity. But despite creating a space or subversion and rebellion, these examples of 1960s naval films ultimately and summarily close this down, either by the vicissitudes of warfare, the necessity for patriotism and protocol, the proper performance of masculinity, a necessity to return to a status quo or, put more simply, the requirement for 'playtime' to end.

Notes

1. Rodney Castleden, *British History: A Chronological Dictionary of Dates* (London: Parragon, 1994), p. 359.
2. '40 youths arrested at Margate', *The Times*, 18 May 1964, p. 8. '1,000 youths fight at Brighton', *The Times*, 19 May 1964, p. 12.
3. 'Thirty fined after Mosley rally', *The Times*, 31 July 1962, p. 4; Castleden, *British History*, pp. 358–72.
4. In Paul Johnson, *The Offshore Islanders: A History of the British People* (London: Phoenix Giant, 1995), p. 392.
5. Cynthia Behrman, *Victorian Myths of the Sea* (Athens, OH: Ohio University Press, 1977).
6. Andrew Spicer, 'The "other war": images of the Second World War in service comedies', in Stephen Caunce, Ewa Mazierska, Susan Sydney-Smith and John K. Walton (eds), *Relocating Britishness* (Manchester: Manchester University Press, 2004), p. 1. Available at <https://westengland.academia.edu/AndrewSpicer> (last accessed 14 September 2018).

7. *Kinematograph Weekly*, 'Brabourne is to make "Mutiny" for Columbia', 7 July, 1960, p. 8.
8. Josh Billings, *Kinematograph Weekly*, 'Reviews for Showmen', 13 September 1962, pp. 10, 19.
9. 'Billy Budd; Damn the Defiant', *Show*, October 1962, p. 31.
10. Penny Summerfield, 'Divisions at sea: class, gender, race and nation in maritime films of the Second World War, 1939–60', *Twentieth Century British History* 22: 3, 2011, pp. 330–53.
11. David Boxwell, Review of *Billy Budd*, *Senses of Cinema* 17, 2001. [online]. Available at <http://sensesofcinema.com/2001/cteq/billy-2/> (last accessed 14 November 2013).
12. Casey Harrison, 'Redemptive violence and stuttering across the Atlantic: The Who's "My Generation" and Herman Melville's Billy Budd in historical perspective', in *Atlantic Studies: Cultural and Historical Perspectives* 8: 1, 2011, pp. 49–68.
13. Ibid. p. 50.
14. Spicer, *Service Comedy*, p. 4.
15. Richard Slotkin, *Gunfighter Nation: The Myth of the Frontier in the 20th Century* (Norman: University of Oklahoma Press, 1998), p. 1.
16. Boxwell, *Billy Budd*.
17. Castleden, *British History*, p. 364.
18. J. R. Reed, *The Army and Navy in Nineteenth-Century British Literature* (New York: AMS, 2011), p. 72.
19. Ibid. p. 72.
20. Ibid. p. 72.
21. For example, Dana Silva, 'Exploring homo-eroticism in Herman Melville's novella Billy Budd', *Agora Journal*, 2006. Available at <http://mseffie.com/assignments/billy_budd/criticism/Sliva.pdf> (last accessed 28 March 2014).
22. R. and L. Adkins, *Jack Tar: Life in Nelson's Navy* (London: Little, Brown: 2008), p. 154.
23. Henry Melville, *The Confidence-Man and Billy Budd, Sailor* (London: Penguin, 2012), pp. 306, 313.
24. Eve K. Sedgewick, *Epistemology of the Closet* (Berkeley: University of California Press, 1990), pp. 91–130; Silva, 'Exploring homo-eroticism'.
25. In Robin Griffiths (ed.), *British Queer Cinema* (Oxford: Routledge, 2006), p. 6.
26. Andy Medhurst, 'Dirk Bogarde', in Charles Barr (ed.), *All Our Yesterdays: 90 Years of British Cinema* (London: BFI, 1986), pp. 346–54.
27. Robin Griffiths, 'Sad and angry: queers in 1960s British cinema', in Griffiths (ed.), *British Queer Cinema* (Oxford: Routledge, 2006), pp. 71–91, p. 79.
28. *Carry On Jack* Pressbook, BFI Holdings.
29. Andy Medhurst, 'The music hall and British cinema', in Barr (ed.), *All Our Yesterdays*, pp. 168–88.
30. In I. Q. Hunter and Laraine Porter (eds), *British Comedy Cinema* (Abingdon: Routledge, 2012), p. 2.

14. NARRATIVES OF RACE AND IDENTITY IN SIXTIES BRITISH CINEMA

Phillip Drummond

Among the many 'liberations' of the 1960s were the changing racial and interracial identities of the UK population as a new multiculturalism began to emerge. As Britain's ethnic composition became increasingly complex, new intercultural relations were forged in the shadow of Civil Rights struggles in the United States, where during the course of a divisive decade some of the fundamentals of racial equality remained unachieved. The older world of Britain was itself undergoing rapid change, with the diminution of the former British Empire as many of its former colonies in Africa and the Caribbean moved into independence and thus into a new relationship with the former 'mother country' under the umbrella of the fast-expanding Commonwealth. At home change was powered by the Windrush generation and subsequent migrations, while successive stages of race legislation attempted to regulate Britain's new multicultural mix, with a focus on vexed questions of post-imperial nationhood and citizenship.[1]

In turn, new forms of black cultural organisation and expression emerged and fought against predictable forms of resistance to change. British cinema provided a variety of responses to the new situation. These included a range of films appealing, nostalgically and/or critically, to the long years of empire; features dealing with contemporary themes which sought to dramatise the new multiculturalism from both optimistic and less positive perspectives; and the fragile beginnings, through the vehicle of the independent short film, towards an authentically 'black' cinema in Britain. The latter development would eventually culminate in the first British feature film to be centrally concerned with the lives of black Britons and made by a black director, Horace Ové's *Pressure* (1976), following his documentaries *Baldwin's Nigger* (1969) and *Reggae* (1970). This chapter offers a survey of those different kinds of films, culminating in analysis of one film from the period which, despite its evident interest, has languished in critical obscurity, Ted Kotcheff's *Two Gentlemen Sharing* (1969).

The 1960s produced films as different as *Till Death Us Do Part* (1968) and *Lawrence of Arabia* (1962), both focusing on male outsiders, but one looking back nostalgically to an older dispensation, the other looking forward to new intercultural formations. If *Lawrence* marked a new post-imperial understanding of the global struggles of the First World War, then other sixties films looked still further back, typically to mourn the loss of empire through dramas involving great defeats by earlier foes in Africa. Cy Endfield's *Zulu* (1964) recalls the horrors of Rorke's Drift, while Basil Dearden's *Khartoum* (1966) remembers General Gordon and the Mahdi – the latter hammed up by Laurence Olivier, not long before he brought his blacked-up Othello to the screen. Evoking fearful fantasies of invasion and defeat at home, these were intensely *racial* dramas with white British minorities overcome by hordes of colour. A more light-hearted solution was offered in Ralph Thomas's *Carry On* films, which chose to mock both sides of a racially divided empire in *Follow that Camel* (1967), *Carry On Up the Khyber* (1968), and *Carry On Up the Jungle* (1970).

Africa functioned variously as a backdrop for white interactions with threatened wildlife in James Hill's *Born Free* (1966), and journeys of escape in Alexander Mackendrick's *Sammy Going South* (1963) and Nathan Juran's *East of Sudan* (1964). It also provided the setting for Sidney Lumet's *The Hill* (1965), a searing exposé of the brutality of a British military prison during the Second World War which offered an important insight on race and racism through the character of black inmate Jacko King (Ossie Davis) and his interactions with white officers. John Guillermin's *Guns at Batasi* (1964), the backdrop for which is the recent liberation of Kenya, dramatises the tensions between two officers of colour on opposing sides, Captain Abraham (Earl Cameron) and Lieutenant Boniface (Errol John). Both films, however, ultimately focus on the traditional values represented by the white British protagonists played by Sean Connery and Richard Attenborough respectively. More diverse representations of Africa are provided by intimate and passionate short films associated with the Anti-Apartheid Movement such as John Krish's *Let My People Go* (1961) and Lionel Ngakane's *Vukani/Awake* (1962). In this context Philip Mottram's harrowing experimental short *Contact* (1965) is a symbolic and expressionistic tribute to white-and-black solidarity under dire if abstract conditions of imprisonment and torture.

Where the Caribbean is concerned, the first James Bond picture, Terence Young's *Dr No* (1962) may have launched a cinematic legend but the film is also highly symptomatic in its engagement with ideas of race. It opens in Jamaica with the brutal murders of a male and then a female British intelligence official by a gang of black assassins first seen posing as blind beggars. We then move on to the introduction of James Bond in a London nightclub, suavely at his leisure and engaged in sexual flirtation. Such images of black duplicity, barbarism, and gendered violence, pitched against the calm sophistication of the white metropole, strike curious chords in 1962, the year in which Jamaica gained its independence from Britain.[2]

Displacements of Blackness

Back in UK settings, films of the British New Wave and their contemporaries and successors engaged with an increasingly visible ethnic minority presence. Intercultural relationships were to become an accepted dramatic theme, but characters of colour were still typically subsidiary to overarching concerns with white identity and values. This is the case in Roy Ward Baker's *Flame in the Streets* (1961), a film which foregrounds issues of race, transposing Ted Willis's TV drama *Hot Summer Night* (directed by Ted Kotcheff in 1959, and featuring British television's first interracial kiss) to Camden Town locations on Bonfire Night. The plot centres on the controversial promotion of a black worker, Gabriel Gomez (Earl Cameron), to the position of foreman at a furniture factory, a decision fiercely defended by Trades Union Branch Chair Jacko Palmer (John Mills) in the face of some resistance by fellow workers. But Palmer is then confronted with the news that his schoolteacher daughter Kathie (Sylvia Syms) wishes to marry a colleague of Jamaican origin, Peter Lincoln (Johnny Sekka). The film dramatises racial divisions and conflict amongst workers and the challenges of a racist housing market where Gomez and his white wife Judy (Ann Lynn) are concerned. At this broad social level, *Flame in the Streets* makes a bold statement about employment practices, inequity in 1960s housing provision, interracial relationships, and youth violence.

With its ethnically diverse factory floor and school classrooms, the film also encompasses an unusually large population of black characters, including minor roles for Harry Baird, Thomas Baptiste, Dan Jackson, Lionel Ngakane, Pearl Prescod, and Corinne Skinner-Carter. But once again the main narrative focus is on white characters, with powerful roles allocated to women. These include Jacko's socially aspirational wife, Nell (Brenda De Banzie), whose profoundly dramatised racism dominates the later stages of the film; his daughter Kathie, who is committed to an interracial relationship against the wishes of her family; and Judy Gomez, who is all too well aware of the social costs of her own marriage with Gabriel. A double resolution is required: between the

Palmers as a couple, and then between them and Kathie and Peter; the final shot, depicting the two couples facing each other across a room in the Palmer home, indicates the distance still to be traversed.

Similar displacements of blackness from the narrative focus occur in Tony Richardson's *A Taste of Honey* (1961) where Jimmy (Paul Danquah) leaves Jo (Rita Tushingham) pregnant when his ship sails from Salford early in the film, and in Bryan Forbes's *The L-Shaped Room* (1962) where Johnny, a lonely jazz trumpeter, finds himself on the margins of the central romantic relationship. In a film concerned with the proxemics of domestic space, Johnny – played by Brock Peters, shortly to star as the tragic Tom Robinson in Robert Mulligan's *To Kill a Mockingbird* (1962) – lives in the Notting Hill boarding house that confines and conditions the lives of its struggling characters. When Peters returns in the social parable of Christian Socialism that is the Boultings's *Heavens Above* (1963), he enjoys a meteoric rise from dustman to churchwarden thanks to a progressive vicar played by Peter Sellers until, in a moment redolent with real-world racial violence, he is hounded out by townsfolk hurling stones and racial abuse.

Following *The L-Shaped Room*, Michael Winner's *West 11* (1963) and Vernon Sewell's *The Wind of Change* (1961) – the latter's title invoking Macmillan's famous speech endorsing African independence – position London's Notting Hill as a key focus for the new multiculturalism. In the former, a study of white male alienation, the area is presented as broadly free from racial strife, with a white nationalist resisted by local people when he tries to address a meeting. The latter focuses on the murder of a nameless young black man, played by Ken McGregor but known only in the credits as 'Coloured Boy', which is the way he is addressed by a desirous white woman whose arrival saved him earlier from a white gang. He is at the apparent centre of the drama, but even prior to his murder he is largely occluded, with the bulk of the narrative centring on white family relations, notably the tensions between the young racist murderer Frank (Johnny Briggs), his sister Jose (Ann Lynn), who is the girlfriend of the victim, and his more tolerant father, 'Pop' Marley (Donald Pleasence).

New Generations

The first fiction film written and directed by a black filmmaker in the UK was Jamaica-born Lloyd Reckord's twelve-minute short *Ten Bob in Winter* (1963). It is a wry tale of black Caribbean masculinity and socio-economic identity in early multicultural London, with a small sum of money (the 'ten bob' of the title) its central symbol as it travels between various hands. Three young students – two black, one white – run through the City of London, having heard that Christmas vacation work is available in the cold storage depot of Hudson's Bay Company. One of the black students (played by Winston Stona) loses out, borrowing a ten shilling note from his white friend to help him on his way. A different London emerges; an unsuccessful visit to an employment exchange features a montage of haunting stills of jobless men, many of them black. The unnamed student reluctantly loans the money to a musician (Bari Jonson) whom he does not know, but who is desperate to pay for dry cleaning so that he can then pawn his suit and in turn retrieve his guitar from pawn in order to play a gig that evening.

While waiting outside the pawnshop for the return of his money, the student cannot avoid recognition by a smarter-looking middle-aged black man, Andrew (Andrew Salkey), who is amused to find the young man in such a spot, and whose perceived snobbery the student finds himself imitating. In his embarrassment, the student ignores the musician when the latter attempts to pay back the loan, but eventually accepts the money once the businessman has gone. Made with the support of the BFI's Experimental Film Fund, *Ten Bob in Winter* features a lightly jazzy score by the Joe Harriott Quintet, together with Reckord's own voice-over narrating events and exploring the student's self-conscious subjectivity in this otherwise speechless film.

South Africa-born Lionel Ngakane's bittersweet short *Jemima and Johnny* (1966) links together issues of race and gender. It tells the story of a young black girl (Nicolette Robinson), a new immigrant from Jamaica, and a young white boy (Patrick Hatfield) who strike up an acquaintance on the streets of West London when she is overlooked in the excitement of a family celebration. 'Welcome to Two More Jamaicans' reads the banner at their doorway as Jemima begins her discovery of a white world in which her relatives (led by Thomas Baptiste) and the boy's father, an organiser for the local 'White Tenants' Association' (Brian Phelan), symbolise tense polarities. This twenty-nine-minute short is not without its own bleak humour, displaying *graffiti* announcing 'We shall overcome', to which a local racist has added 'the blacks'.

Jemima's and Johnny's journey across the neighbourhood, exploring spaces and making acquaintances, follows the familiar trope of childhood's unique amalgam of innocence and ingenuity in the negotiation of an adult world, played out in the physical environment of the bleak post-war cityscape. After various encounters, the young friends repair to a den in the basement of an abandoned terraced villa. The police arrive, with both families in tow, and the children are rescued as part of the building caves in. Johnny's father carries out Jemima and, deep in thought, hands her over; Johnny says goodbye to Jemima with a kiss on the cheek. Despite this moment of connection and the fact they live close together, the two families go off in different directions.

Films centring on children, and the wisdom of their innocence, are thus able to project a greater ease with the emerging multiculturalism. This is true of Jim O'Connolly's featurette, *The Little Ones* (1965), this time by means of a partial reversal of the migration trope. A young white Londoner, Ted Turner

(Kim Smith), and his somewhat older, bigger and smarter bi-racial friend Jackie Matthews (Carl Gonzales), stow away in a removals van heading to Liverpool, which they hope will be the point of departure for their eventual journey by sea to Jamaica. Ted is escaping a cruelly indifferent and racist family life in London, while Matthew has been left behind with his white mother and her black 'bloke' by a father who for his own reasons chose to return to Jamaica for 'a visit' a couple of years previously and has not returned. The boys are inspired by postcards from the Caribbean, Ted's memories of his father's evocations of the Jamaican seaboard idyll, and publicity at a local cinema for Robert Rossen's drama set in the colonial Caribbean, *Island in the Sun* (1957). In Liverpool they steal a case from a Rolls Royce to get money for food, and are arrested. But in an ending implying that there may be more adventures to come, the boys roar with laughter when they learn, on their way to the train station in the back of a police car, that London, too, is a major seaport.

The American Connection

Given the increasing American involvement in British cinema during the 1960s, it is unsurprising that Hollywood was to bring its own intercultural interests to Europe with films such as Paul Henreid's *Ballad in Blue* (1965), starring Ray Charles, or Richard Donner's *Salt and Pepper* (1968) and Jerry Lewis's *One More Time* (1970), both featuring Sammy Davis Jr and Peter Lawford. It is significant that the representation of blackness in British films of the period thus not only involved actors and actresses from the British Commonwealth, but also drew upon African American stars such as Ossie Davis (*The Hill*), Al Freeman Jr (*Dutchman*), Hal Frederick (*Two Gentlemen Sharing*), Calvin Lockhart (*Leo the Last, Joanna*), and Brock Peters (*Heavens Above*).

The even more famous black star Sidney Poitier played the central role in James Clavell's celebrated and highly lucrative *To Sir, with Love* (1967), an adaptation of the autobiographical 1959 novel by Guyanese/American author E. R. Braithwaite. Born to Oxford-educated parents, Braithwaite served as an RAF pilot in the Second World War and went on to a Cambridge PhD in Physics, aspiring to work as an engineer but eventually becoming a schoolteacher and later a social worker involved in the foster placement of non-white and mixed-race children. This experience is recounted in his 1962 book *Paid Servant: A Report About Welfare Work in London*. The film version follows Poitier – the key figure in the racial liberalisation of American cinema in the post-war years – as a charismatic teacher negotiating the chaos of a working class secondary school in London's East End.

The film is a humane and sentimental account of the eventual rapprochement between teacher and initially resistant pupils as they mature and respond to his dignified authority in what is as much an exploration of adult–child power relations and the British class system as it is about race and race relations. Seen in terms of its vision of the schooling system, the film is also a milder reprise of Richard Brooks's *The Blackboard Jungle* (1955), in which Poitier had played an unruly pupil up against teacher Glenn Ford, and which fuelled controversy as the era of teenage rebellion exploded. The difference between the two films is enshrined in the cultural and musical contrast between Bill Haley's insistent 'Rock Around the Clock' theme song for *Blackboard Jungle* and the equally successful but less hectic and more romantic 'To Sir with Love' by Lulu.

A much less sanguine intersection between British and American cinematic meditations on race (and gender) is to be found in Anthony Harvey's debut mini-feature *Dutchman* (1966), a fifty-five-minute adaptation of the celebrated and highly controversial play by the African American Black Arts pioneer Leroi Jones (later to become Amiri Baraka), created amidst the great upheavals of early sixties America. The story deals with the murderous encounter, in a New York subway car, between an apparently mild-mannered young black man, Clay (Al Freeman Jr), and Lula, a mockingly vampish older white woman (Shirley Knight). A distinguished British film editor, Harvey saw the play in New York, met Jones, and bought the rights. He took time off from editing Bryan Forbes's production *The Whisperers* at Pinewood, mocked up a subway car at Twickenham Studios, and shot the film in a week on a budget of £20,000 raised piecemeal by producer Gene Persson, Knight's then husband. Harvey worked faithfully with Jones's richly demotic dialogue, rendering highly cinematic its complex investment in the often violent and contradictory sixties rhetoric of race and sexuality, as well as his fluid and often anti-real play with fictional identity and backstory. The result is a tortured invocation of urban *anomie*, interracial desire and the sacrifice of black masculinity in one of sixties cinema's most desperate invocations of the 'monstrous feminine'.

BLACK AND WHITE MASCULINITIES

The historically controversial theme of miscegenation offers a further key focus for representations of race in British cinema of the period. David Andrews's twenty-eight-minute short *Top Deck* (1962), written by John Arden, dramatises intercultural relations through the suburban love affair between white suburban bus conductor Marlene (Ruth D'Arcy) and a black US sergeant, Johnny (James Anderson). Supported by Norman Cave's happy-go-lucky score, which provides essential sonic information in the absence of a dialogue track, the film follows the couple's growing intimacy as they stroll, flirt, cuddle, embrace and sneak upstairs in the terraced house where she lives. The affair starts well, and appears to move towards sexual consummation, but then turns sour and falls apart as Johnny becomes an obsessive, ominous and threatening figure. A film which began by celebrating inter-racial romance, thus culminates in a gloomy evocation of black male chauvinism and menace.

A similar dynamic characterises Mike Sarne's *Joanna* (1968), the story of an emblematic 'swinging sixties' carefree heroine (Geneviève Waite) who arrives in London from the country to become an art student and is soon confronted by the freewheeling *mores* of a capital which is notably multicultural and ethnically diverse. Joanna develops a close friendship with Beryl (Glenna Forster-Jones), and following a string of failed affairs, becomes romantically involved with Beryl's charismatic brother Gordon (Calvin Lockhart). As in *Top Deck*, however, the narrative grows darker, culminating in Gordon's imprisonment for manslaughter as Joanna leaves behind the urban whirl and heads back to her rural parental home.

Lockhart and Forster-Jones would also take supporting roles as a significant, if somewhat subsidiary, black couple in John Boorman's *Leo the Last* (1970) alongside the Italian star Marcello Mastroianni. It is a film which takes us back once more to Notting Hill, where Leo (Mastroianni), the scion of an aristocratic family, returns to inherit his father's mansion after birdwatching in the Galapagos, a pastime he brings back to London. Searching for a new, more active identity, he is repelled by the social rituals of the indulgent world associated with the house, and is entranced instead by the different kinds of vision enabled by his telescope.

Leo emerges out of isolation, drawn to the domestic dramas unfolding across the way in a troubled multicultural environment featuring a variety of black characters including the lovers Roscoe and Salambo, but also darker elements of white rapacity and black gangsterism. He discovers that he himself is central to these problems, being the principal landlord of this deprived area. He is unable to protect Salambo from sexual assault, but he rescues her from prostitution, and, joining forces with local people, he helps bring the lovers back together, and with Roscoe leads the crowd in burning down the family mansion, expunging his old life. This extraordinary film is both an experimental masterpiece, counting amongst its influences Beckett, Berio and Brecht, but also, for all its evident fascination with the multicultural environment, a confirmation (albeit of a quite fantastical kind) of the symptomatic role of the 'white saviour'.

A different kind of anti-realism informs *Death May Be Your Santa Claus* (1969) by St Lucia-born Frankie Dymon Jr. A riddling thirty-six-minute drama of black male subjectivity and desire, it is on the one hand reminiscent of the tradition of the experimental psychodramas associated with the US avant-garde. The film is at the same time preoccupied with racially inflected philosophical and political theories inspired by the director's role in Michael X's Racial Adjustment Action Society, and charged with a version of the European modernism with which Dymon had identified himself when he appeared as a Black Power militant in Godard's *One Plus One* (1968).

The central concern here is with the social and sexual politics of protagonist Raymond (Ken Gajadhar), especially in terms of his real/fantastical relationships with white and black women, a schema linked to a chain of opaque messages which provide bewildering hermeneutic connectivity. While this highly eclectic film incorporates straightforwardly 'realistic' material, overall it is an extremely mysterious episodic compendium, a hybrid text studded with quotations from social and political theory, as well as emblematic figures and allegorical scenes extraneous to the main narrative. Progressing via the subjectivity of multi-vocal voice-over, *Death May Be Your Santa Claus* culminates in a series of freeze-frames which suspend the main characters in motion in the street, trapped in close proximity and yet in terminal apartness.[3]

INTERSECTIONS: *TWO GENTLEMEN SHARING*

Intersections between race, social class and gender were however not the sole preserve of independent filmmakers. As the 1960s drew to a close, these themes were explored in more naturalistic style in the social tragicomedy *Two Gentlemen Sharing* (1969), a film largely lost in the interstices of British film history. Directed by émigré Canadian director Ted Kotcheff, who had already made a name for himself in British television, *Two Gentlemen Sharing* is adapted from David Stuart Leslie's 1963 novel by Jamaican writer Evan Jones, most famous in this period for his regular work with Joseph Losey. The film brings together the established English actors Robin Phillips and Judy Geeson with the emerging talents of African-American Hal Frederick and Jamaican Esther Anderson.

Andrew Mackenzie (Frederick) is a trainee black solicitor from Jamaica working in Brixton. He finds himself sharing a flat in a smart house in Knightsbridge with Roddy Pater (Phillips), a young white Englishman who is a director of TV commercials. The two men differ in confidence about their sexuality: Andrew has a steady girlfriend, Caroline Harcourt (Anderson), while Roddy struggles and fails as he moves from frustrations with Ethne Burrows (Hilary Heath) to a new relationship with Jane Archer (Geeson). The plot follows the ups and downs of the relationship between the two men, their differing connections with women, and their difficult connections to a racially diverse metropolis, before reaching a gloomy conclusion about the doubtful prospects for the integration of troubled masculinity – of any skin-colour – into the fabric of late 1960s British society.

Two Gentlemen Sharing opens with a scene (invented for the film and playing upon the screenwriter's own British ancestry) centring on a telephone box alongside Westminster Bridge, with the iconography of the Houses of Parliament looming large in the background. Andrew is making a call, in his cut-glass English accent, in search of rented accommodation. He confirms that his surname is Scottish, but when he feels obliged to point out that he

Figure 14.1 Early in *Two Gentlemen Sharing* (1969), Andrew (Hal Frederick) visits Roddy's (Robin Philips) flat as a potential co-tenant.

is 'black', he is asked 'how black?' Giving the answer 'hopelessly' – the dismissive sarcasm of which also implies less tractable issues to come – he puts the phone down and walks off. Roddy is the child of what he calls 'sort of decayed gentlefolk . . . a relic left over from the Ice Age', living in a country house in Oxfordshire – or rather in just part of an empty and decaying mansion; a visit with friends in a key episode in the film illustrates the emotional aridity of Roddy's upper class family background, and a younger generation's very different sense of social style. Roddy attended 'a minor public school – homosexuality at reduced prices', a comment which leads Andrew to question Roddy's sexual inclinations – 'Are you . . . Queer?' – and which heralds a later, negative representation of race and homosexuality in the person of the flamboyantly camp Marcus (Ram John Holder). Tensely confirming their heterosexuality, the two men agree to try out a flat share.

Roddy is initially fascinated by Andrew's girlfriend Caroline. But this is based on a more fundamental social *naïveté* about the new intercultural environment. At their first meeting, Roddy promptly asks her 'Have you been over here long?', to which her response is 'Do I look like a dammed immigrant?' Her claim to come from Beckenham leads Roddy to regard her as the first person of colour he has met to have been born in England, until Andrew reveals that she has only been in the country a couple of years, and is in fact 'Kingston [i.e. Kingston, Jamaica] middle class'. Caroline's aspirational duplicity is revealing, and she also embodies an important discourse on race and sexuality, explaining to Roddy that Englishmen make her feel 'frigid', where with Andrew she can be 'a woman'. She also confronts what she sees as limited and negative English stereotypes of black women, claiming that if she were white, Roddy wouldn't be enquiring into her sex life.

The turning point in the narrative for Roddy comes at a 'jump-up' dance, a lengthy scene in which raced and gendered identities criss-cross in telling but confused ways. Our unlikely guide into the scene is Roddy's cynical advertising sidekick Phil Carter (Norman Rossington), dancing over-enthusiastically with a tolerant Caroline, with the camera moving to Ethne and Roddy as they move in a somewhat disengaged manner. The camera follows Phil as he runs into the queenly Marcus and his companion, Amanda (Daisy Mae Williams), a black woman wearing a pink wig. But when Amanda accepts Phil's invitation to dance, a new and unlikely relationship is set in train, which in its carefree way will complicate the film's equations between masculinity, femininity and race. The dance scene also confirms Andrew's sense of difference from fellow black Londoners, and brings Roddy into contact with Jane Archer, her opposition to fascism, and, later, her bi-racial family.

Differentiations: Andrew and Roddy

The film contrasts the *ingénu* Roddy with two other versions of masculinity represented by Andrew and Phil. With Andrew he shares an Oxford background, but their trajectories are very different: unlike Roddy, Andrew may lack a backstory but his impeccably stylish dress, behaviour and cut-glass accent mark out a degree of *savoir faire* not enjoyed by the hapless Roddy. This appears to endow him with a sense of power and control, complicating the film's central concerns with race, masculinity and social power. Phil, on the other hand, is forthrightly racist and sexist. When at the jump-up he claims that he can find Amanda work as a model, we know from his previous comments that he is simply lying. And yet they become in turn one of the film's more unexpected pairings, with Amanda even granted the power to laugh off Phil's eventual suggestion of marriage.

Andrew, for his part, is distinguished by a degree of professional expertise, in marked contrast to the shallow world of advertising within which Roddy moves, as well as by his more advanced physical prowess in the domains of sexuality and sport. He has been a distinguished university cricketer, which stands him in good stead when a firm of City lawyers expresses an interest in employing him. Andrew's relationship with Caroline is already sexually advanced, and the film contains scenes of their intimacy, celebrating the beauty of black bodies, male and female. This is indeed the reason for their eventual exclusion from the flat: they are thrown out by the landlady when she becomes disturbed by the noise of their love-making. Andrew leaves Roddy a note informing him that they have 'Gone back to the ghetto', their destination a single room in a run-down terraced house which Andrew dubs 'Notting Hall'.

From this point on, the two main characters diverge. Roddy is drawn into the world of Jane, her mother Helen (Shelagh Fraser), and her stepfather Charles (Earl Cameron). Andrew goes for a job interview in the City but walks out when confronted by endless images of white power, announcing to Roddy in a walk through Hyde Park that he intends to stop being 'the British Uncle Tom' and to return to Jamaica 'when the black man's king'. Visiting Phil and Amanda, Roddy on the other hand wants to talk about 'integration', but quickly dismisses Phil's version of it with the judgement 'it's corrupt', before promptly leaving. At a closing party at Roddy's, Andrew continues to define himself against the buzzwords of 'black power', 'negritude', 'black pride', and

Figure 14.2 At the final party, Marcus (Ram John Holder) enters Roddy's bedroom with a different understanding of the phrase 'two gentlemen sharing'.

even simply 'love', claiming that all this amounts to nothing more than 'heroin and dark glasses'. Roddy becomes increasingly drunk, but in the process he also announces his intention to marry Jane, whom he claims to love. Quashing his aspirations for a new form of identity, however, she flatly states: 'You're always going to be exactly what you are.'

Roddy is pursued by the now highly predatory Marcus, who frankly expresses his plan to move in with Roddy, assuring him that 'There's nothing wrong with two gentlemen sharing', giving the title of the film a new meaning, and one which threatens Roddy's fragile sense of sexual self-definition. Roddy punches him. When neighbours call the police, Roddy agrees to close down the party, but his words – the last in the film – now also take on a wider meaning in relation to his previous concern with integration, and in the context of real-world late sixties white British anxieties over immigration: 'Throw them all out, officer . . . THROW THEM ALL OUT!' The film which began with the challenges faced by Andrew, now closes on the darkness of Roddy's troubled face.

The screenwriter's intercultural legacy and his experience as a bi-racial figure of Welsh heritage inform the welcome elimination of the obsessive racism of the novel's characters and of its narrative voice. The film also rearranges the exterior and domestic topography of the original and upgrades the status of the central black character to create a clearer parallel with his white counterpart, whilst reducing the variety of supporting characters and their interrelationships. The bleak parallel conclusion, for both central characters, marks a disenchanted openness beyond the breezy finale of the novel. The film's producer, Barry Kulick, wished to avoid 'impeccably liberal answers', as he explained to Alexander Walker at the time: 'We tried to show that there were liberal myths which approximate as little to reality as racial prejudices. It's this new frame of reference which was received with intense dislike.' But a film of such provocative ambition is understandably not without its own problems. Issues are often treated in somewhat telegrammatic form; in closing on Roddy, the film inevitably favours the psychodrama of white masculinity; the fate of Andrew is left unclear, while in the case of Marcus, who eventually assumes the interracial contact with Roddy, the elision between blackness and predatory gayness marks a controversial negativity.

Conclusion: Contemporary Connections

As Britain has become a more complexly hybrid society, questions of identity are no longer binary but manifold. Blackness – a concept used in a quite simplified way in this essay – is no longer largely an issue to do exclusively with Afro-Caribbean identities. Given the larger context of British Asian and Eastern European migration, questions of race and ethnicity now need to be addressed within a broader sense of difference and sameness, and within the intersectionalities of social class and gender. A Britain still beginning to forge a new multicultural identity in the era of globalisation currently seeks to create a new version of itself amidst complex articulations between Europe, the Commonwealth, and a former empire. Membership of the European Union has forced Britain to negotiate anew the perennial question of migration and citizenship, with all its national and racial subtexts, while a deeper xenophobia is signalled by the 'little England' mentality so desperate for Brexit to be delivered. In Britain, as across Europe, deep-seated racism maintains its virulence.

We thus return to these sixties films for a number of reasons – to honour the work of pioneers, and to trace trajectories towards the present.[4] The films I have been discussing, and the issues which they depict, thus sometimes feel entirely familiar, and yet sometimes also quite remote. A *locus* for multiculturalism such as London's Notting Hill, for example – an iconic focus for the dramas of *West 11*, *The L-Shaped Room*, *Jemima and Johnny*, and *Leo the Last* – no longer exists in the ways we see in these films, and yet the shadow of Grenfell reminds us of still pressing current stories of otherness, disenfranchisement, and betrayal. The Windrush scandal of recent times also brings the postwar decades back into focus as a triumphal and yet partly tragic episode where the politics of national identity are concerned. We therefore excavate these early works not to set them at a nostalgic or reverential distance, but precisely to recognise the permanence of many of their concerns and wider implications.

Notes

1. For standard histories of black Britain, see Pete Fryer, *Staying Power: The History of Black People in Britain*, 2nd edn (London: Pluto Press, 2010 [1984]); Ron Ramdin, *The Making of the Black Working Class in Britain* (London: Gower Press, 1987); *Reimaging Britain: 500 Years of Black and Asian History* (London: Pluto Press, 1999). See also Paul Gilroy, *Black Britain: A Photographic History* (London: Saqui Books, 2007); David Olusoga, *Black and British: A Forgotten History* (London: Macmillan, 2016). Olusoga's *The World's War* (London: Head of Zeus, 2014) powerfully reminds us of the huge contributions made by people of colour during the First World War, while Stephen Bourne turns his attention to both World Wars in *Mother Country: Britain's Black Community on the Home Front 1939–45* and *Black Poppies: Britain's Black Community and the Great War* (Stroud: History Press, 2010 and 2014), and *War to Windrush: Black Women in Britain 1939 to 1948* (Plymouth: Jacaranda Press, 2018). Sheila Patterson, *Immigration and Race Relations in Britain* (Oxford: Oxford University Press, 1969), offers a highly informed contemporary study of the 1960s on behalf of the Institute of Race Relations. See also Clair Wills, *Lovers and Strangers: An Immigrant History of Post-War Britain* (London: Allen Lane, 2017), and Rob Waters, *Thinking Black: Britain, 1964–1988* (Oakland, CA: University of California Press, 2019). The significance of the 'Windrush' era is the subject of Mike and Trevor

Phillips, *Windrush: The Irresistible Rise of Multi-Racial Britain* (London: HarperCollins, 1998). For the autobiography of a colossus emerging in the 1960s, see Stuart Hall, *Familiar Stranger: A Life between Two Islands* (London: Allen Lane, 2017).
2. Essential accounts of British cinema in the 1960s range from Alexander Walker, *Hollywood England: The British Film Industry in the Sixties* (London: Michael Joseph, 1974) to Robert Murphy, *Sixties British Cinema* (London: BFI, 1992) and Richard Farmer, Laura Mayne, Duncan Petrie and Melanie Williams, *Transformation and Tradition in 1960s British Cinema* (Edinburgh: Edinburgh University Press, 2019). John Hill, *Sex, Class and Realism: British Cinema 1956–1963* (London: BFI, 1986) offers an illuminating account of the 'New Wave', while Lola Young re-orients discussion of key films of the period in '"Miscegenation" and the perils of "passing"', in *Fear of the Dark: 'Race', Gender and Sexuality in the Cinema* (London: Routledge, 1996), pp. 84–114. Stephen Bourne offers wider biographical and contextual studies in *Black in the British Frame: The Black Experience in British Film and Television* (London: Continuum, 2001). On British cinema and empire, see Young, *Fear of the Dark*, especially ch. 3, 'Imperial cultures: the primitive and the savage, and white civilization', pp. 55–83; Jeffrey Richards, *Films and British National Identity: From Dickens to Dad's Army* (Manchester: Manchester University Press, 1997); James Chapman and Nicholas J. Cull (eds), *Projecting Empire: Imperialism and Popular Cinema* (London and New York: I. B. Tauris, 2009); Lee Grieveson and Colin MacCabe (eds), *Empire and Film* (London: BFI, 2011) and *Film and the End of Empire* (London: Palgrave Macmillan, 2011); and Jon Cowans, *Film and Colonialism in the Sixties: The Anti-Colonialist Turn in the US, Britain, and France* (Abingdon: Routledge, 2018). For pioneering studies of Bond, see Jeremy Black, *The Politics of James Bond from Fleming's Novels to the Big Screen* (Westport, CT: Praeger, 2001) and James Chapman, *Licence to Thrill: A Cultural History of the James Bond Films*, revised edn (London: I. B. Tauris, 2007). For fuller accounts of key films discussed here, see Sheldon Hall, *'Zulu': With Some Guts Behind It – The Making of the Epic Movie*, revised edn (Sheffield: Tomahawk Press, 2014). On Lawrence, see Kevin Jackson, *Lawrence of Arabia* (London: BFI, 2007) and Chapman and Cull, *Projecting Empire*, ch. 6, 'The watershed: *Lawrence of Arabia*', pp. 87–112; on the *Carry On* films, see also ch. 8, 'Camping up the Empire', pp. 137–52.
3. On some of the key post-New Wave feature films mentioned here: on *Leo the Last*, see Brian Hoyle, *The Cinema of John Boorman* (Lanham, MD: Scarecrow Press, 2012), ch. 3, 'Man versus . . . ', especially pp. 57–71, and Young, *Fear of the Dark*, ch. 5, 'Family life', pp. 115–32. On *To Sir with Love*, see Aram Goudsouzian's biography, *Sidney Poitier: Man, Actor, Icon* (Chapel Hill: University of North Carolina Press, 2004), especially ch. 13, 'Useful negroes (1966–1967)', pp. 253–76, and for an interesting comparison between novel and film see <http://www.british60scinema.net/book-to-film-adaptations-in-the-1960s/to-sir-with-love/>. For background on *Joanna*, see the booklet accompanying the Blu-ray release (London: BFI, 2012), especially Chris Campion's essay, '*Joanna*', pp. 1–5.

On the origins of *Dutchman*, see Amiri Baraka, *The Autobiography of Leroi Jones* (New York: Freundlich Books, 1984), pp. 187–90; for the play script, followed faithfully by Harvey's film, see *'Dutchman' and 'The Slave'* (New York:

HarperCollins, 1971). On the film, see Lindsey Campbell, 'Shirley Knight and the performance of gendered race in *Dutchman*', *Offscreen* 19: 1, January 2015. Available at <https://offscreen.com/view/shirley-knight-and-the-performance-of-gendered-race-in-_dutchman_>. On *Two Gentlemen Sharing*, Walker explains the film's production context in *Hollywood, England*, pp. 405–8; Bourne focuses on the negative portrayal of the black predatory queen, Marcus (played by Ram John Holder), in *Black in the British Frame*, pp. 154–6; Samira Ahmed reflects on the film's confused ambitions in 'Two Gentlemen Sharing: swinging London's "race" picture'. Available at <http://www.samiraahmed.co.uk/two-gentlemen-sharing-swinging-londons-race-picture/>.

On key short films mentioned here: for background on *Ten Bob in Winter* and *Jemima and Johnny*, see Bourne, *Black in the British Frame*, ch. 13, pp. 125–31; see also Inge Blackman, 'Our forefathers – the pioneers of black British filmmaking', *Black Filmmaker* 5: 20, July 2003, pp. 42–3. On *Death May Be Your Santa Claus*, see the essay by Kodwo Eshun on pages 17–20 of the booklet accompanying the Blu-ray release of the film as an extra supporting Sarne's *Joanna*. For an ambitious theoretical discussion, see Adrian Rifkin and David Dibosa (London: Institute for Visual Arts, 2012). Available at <https://www.artrabbit.com/events/death-may-be-your-santa-claus-1>.

4. The 1960s provided the nursery for future talent in the field of black British cinema. Born in Trinidad in 1939, Horace Ové arrived in London in 1960 at the age of twenty-one, but this is the decade in which other major contemporary black filmmakers were being born or were still children. Along with Ové, figures such as John Akomfrah, Isaac Julien, Steve McQueen and Amma Asante have gone on, with Ové, to major recognition by the industry, the academy, and even by the State. In the case of the latter, the clutch of MBEs and CBEs shared by this eminent group of course also marks a powerful reorientation of the symbolism of 'empire'.

15. PANIC AT THE DISCO: BRAINWASHING, ALIENATION AND THE DISCOTHEQUE IN SWINGING LONDON FILMS

Sophia Satchell-Baeza

To stand in a pop club in any of the world's larger cities in these days is to experience a sensation rather like that of being suspended over a vat of boiling oil.

Jeff Nuttall, Bomb Culture (1968)

[W]hat is certainly a major art form of the future could emerge just as well as a brain-washing nightmare.

Robert E. L. Masters and Jean Houston,
Psychedelic Art (1968)

British post-war youth culture flourished amid jazz bars, basement clubs and coffee bars, social spaces catering to a new group of young people with small yet expendable incomes. Progenitors of the discotheques that came to define the cultural mythology of Swinging London in the 1960s, these were more than just venues for dancing and live music. Rather, they functioned as meeting places where young people could define and explore their countercultural affiliation. A number of post-war British films about youth culture portray the beat club or expresso bar as an integral feature in advancing subcultural practices. In *The Tommy Steele Story* (1957), *Expresso Bongo* (1959), *Beat Girl* (1959), *Sapphire* (1959) and *The Party's Over* (1965), the beat club or coffee bar provides the setting for energetic musical sequences and group expressions of generational disaffiliation, such as jiving, smoking, and intense encounters with rock 'n' roll music. Cinematic representations of this early youth culture often use such environments to stress the social problems of juvenile delinquency.[1]

By the mid-1960s, jazz clubs and coffee bars were replaced by discotheques as prominent locations in films about youth culture. Preceding and then briefly overlapping with the emergence of psychedelia as a musical and aesthetic phenomenon, discotheques had, in this period, become increasingly intermedial, merging live and moving image performances such as experimental theatre and dance, light shows, and film and moving slide projections. Although many of these spaces played a tangible role in establishing and developing underground social networks closely connected to mod, rocker, beat and hippy subcultures, they also became part of the popular cultural mythology surrounding Swinging London.

'Swinging London' is often mobilised as a critical framework to describe the commercial explosion of youth scenes and fashion and music cultures in mid-1960s London, marking a transitional moment in which interconnected subcultures became a part of the dominant culture, at least in terms of their media exposure. In a now famous 1966 cover feature in *Time* magazine, in which American journalist Piri Halasz heralded London as a 'Swinging City', high-society nightclubs such as Dolly's, Annabel's and The Scotch of St James featured prominently in her rhapsodic tour of the capital's hotspots. Furthermore, Geoffrey Dickinson's cover image for the *Time* story also included a discotheque in its Pop-influenced collage of key swinging London icons. As a glamorous and image-saturated environment attracting the so-called 'new aristocracy' of musicians, socialites and media producers, the discotheque soon became a symbol of swinging London's shallowness and the crass commercialisation of counterculture.

Although critics have since noted that Halasz was not the first to alert readers to the explosion of youthful creative experimentation in the city, it was the first time the term 'swinging' was used to describe a phenomenon that quickly became 'a form of currency where its promissory sensations could be turned into hard cash, and particularly at the cinema box-office'.[2] The term has retrospectively been used to refer to a short-lived film cycle, and has acted primarily as a marketing category. Some of the cinema of this period was thus actively implicated in, and inextricably bound up with, producing an idea of swinging London and its youth scenes.

Several Swinging London films rely on the discotheque (and the associated intermedial practices of the liquid light show) to highlight and exploit their permissive social setting. In a variety of productions including Michael Reeves's horror film *The Sorcerers* (1967), Jack Bond's art film *Separation* (1968) and the comedies *Smashing Time* (1967) and *Wonderwall* (1969), colourful or amniotic light projections and their attendant rock and electronic soundtracks provide the backdrop to kinetic dance sequences or visually spectacular set pieces. These sequences lend the film a modish psychedelic atmosphere, as well as flagging up creative practices from both the counterculture and 'new art world'.[3]

These films at once revel in the dynamism afforded by frenetic dance sequences or psychedelic aesthetics, even as they variously foreground societal anxieties related to young people.[4] This chapter will argue that cinematic representations of 1960s club culture also foreground a wider and more pervasive set of anxieties related to the mind's fundamental vulnerability to environments of extreme sensory overload. Swinging London films portray the discotheque as a space that facilitates states of social alienation or group trance, outbursts of repressed violence, and even brainwashing; this dynamic is particularly apparent in *The Sorcerers*, *Wonderwall* and Michelangelo Antonioni's existential art film *Blow-Up* (1966). Discotheques and light show environments, here, become sites for anxieties about the dehumanising potential of multimedia spectacle within 1960s youth culture.

Discotheques and the Problems of Counterculture

In his study of post-war British cultural life, *The Neophiliacs*, Christopher Booker singles out the discotheque as the 'ultimate dream environment', an imaginal space of 'peculiar importance' to the decade's obsession with novelty.[5] Booker saw this fixation on continual sensation and restless innovation as evidence of a form of 'mass hysteria', a collective hallucination involving the mass projection of numerous individual neuroses.[6] A key agent driving this feverish vitality fantasy, Booker suggested, was the decade's explosion in mass media; specifically, the increasing importance of advertising, fashion photography, 'with-it' cinema, and the new colour supplements that launched in this period. Booker saw the mass media as generating 'auto-suggestive illusions' that were propelling individuals to act unthinkingly.[7] For Booker, the discotheque was a by-product of the decade's vitality fantasy, whose increasing demands for novelty and sensationalism were invariably spiralling towards burnout.

Booker's schema informs Alexander Walker's later study of the British film industry in the 1960s, *Hollywood, England*. Walker distinguishes between cinematic representations of the 'swinging' phenomenon and those of earlier youth groups, noting that Swinging London is not portrayed as a source of threat in these films, but rather provides a sense of 'continuous vitality', as contemporary events on the social scene are fed back and reworked into new films.[8] This reading invariably reflects what Robert Murphy has described as the critical tendency to ascribe to swinging London films a sense of unremitting optimism, when in fact most of them exhibit 'disturbing undertones'.[9] Even those productions that are purportedly comedies, like *Wonderwall*, touch on themes of addiction, alienation, depression, and suicide. The tone throughout many of them is unstable. As Moya Luckett has noted, swinging London films:

> do not simply celebrate freedom, superficiality, popular culture and affluence, but instead fuse optimism with a keen and often self-reflexive social criticism [. . .] Swinging London's intersections with youth culture facilitate a range of social critiques and formal innovations that express a very *un*-Hollywood self-reflexivity.[10]

In several examples, this strand of critique extends to condemning, or at best containing, the influence of mass or popular culture on young people. The increased visibility of youth culture in the mid-to-late-1960s provided mainstream narrative cinema with a wealth of material to appeal to an emergent youth market. Yet Swinging London films engage with psychedelic aesthetics, pop and club cultures in ambiguous and often contradictory ways, both celebrating and containing their liberatory potential. In this regard, these films share qualities with the British 'social problem' film, a post-war cycle of films produced between 1947 and 1963 that are united by an unsympathetic treatment of subcultural rebellion. As John Hill identifies in his formative essay on the cycle, the social problem film reflects a reactionary desire to maintain 'social order by either assimilation or containment'.[11] Correspondingly, expressions of youthful idealism, hedonism, experimentation and activism are similarly assimilated or delimited by the corrective narratives of many Swinging London films, where young people are portrayed as being easily coerced – and even brainwashed – by the promises of new media, drugs and sexual liberation.

Psychedelic Brainwashing: *The Sorcerers*

Scholarship on cinematic representations of brainwashing in British 1960s cinema has largely concentrated on the spy drama, while its relationship to youth and counterculture practices has received notably less attention.[12] Recently, Marcia Holmes has suggested that the depiction of brainwashing in the British Cold War spy thriller *The Ipcress File* (1965) reveals a 'consciously cinematic, almost psychedelic, composition of flashing images and pulsating noises' to posit that sensory bombardment had the power to 're-programme a spectator's consciousness'.[13] Holmes argues that the film reflects the view that 'the mind was inherently vulnerable to sensory perception, to conditioning from the environment'; and yet, that 'these mental processes could be consciously intervened in, even guided, by the spectator as a means to resist coercion or gain enlightenment'.[14] Whereas Holmes presents the brainwashing sequence in *The Ipcress File* as exhibiting an 'accidental' resemblance to psychedelic art, *The Sorcerers* explicitly locates the dangers of mass and unthinking behaviour within the psychedelic multimedia practices of mid-1960s London youth culture.

The Sorcerers was Michael Reeves's second feature after the 1966 British-Italian horror co-production *La Sorella di Satana (Revenge of the Blood Beast)*, and one of only three features the young director made before dying of a barbiturates overdose at twenty-five. It was also the first film produced by Tony Tenser's recently established Tigon British Film Productions Ltd.[15] Tigon would go on to specialise in low-budget horror and exploitation cinema, subsequently producing Reeves's celebrated final film, *Witchfinder General* (1968). Following on from the success of Roman Polanski's *Repulsion* (1965), which Tenser had co-produced with Michael Klinger, *The Sorcerers* similarly blurs the distinction between art and exploitation, adopting a conspicuously bleak swinging London setting to explore states of psychological displacement, alienation and violence.

The film follows a restless young antiques dealer named Mike Roscoe, played by Reeves's regular collaborator and friend, Ian Ogilvy. Visibly disillusioned by the transience of the swinging London scene and its endless array of nightclubs and pop singers, Mike is enticed by a medical hypnotist to become the subject of a brainwashing-telepathy machine. After walking out on his friends, Mike encounters Professor Marcus Monserrat (Boris Karloff), the inventor of a powerful light machine capable of hypnotising its subjects through an overload of sensory stimuli. The professor and his wife Estelle (Catherine Lacey) are on the lookout for a youthful stranger whose alert and 'pliable' mind might be conducive to hypnotic experiments with the machine.

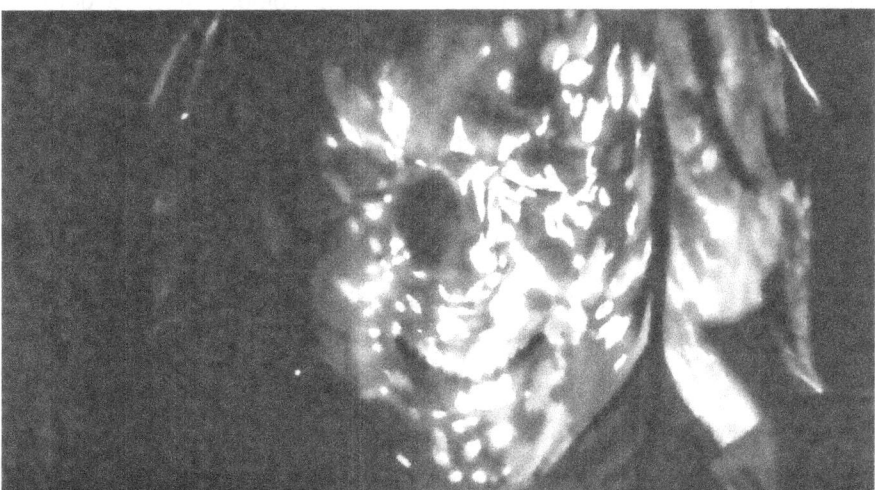

Figure 15.1   Psychedelic brainwashing in *The Sorcerers* (1967).

The brainwashing that Mike undergoes is both a psychedelic and cinematic experience. Although Monserrat's original intention for the machine was to help the elderly relive their experiences of youth, he is driven by Estelle's increasingly sadistic intentions to use it to control people's minds. After luring Mike back to their house, they lead him into the brainwashing room, whose minimalist interior evokes a sensory deprivation chamber. By contrast, the experience Mike is submitted to is clearly one of sensory overload. Invited to sit in a chair wired up to a headset and switchboard, Professor Monserrat instructs him to 'relax, empty your mind, clear your mind of all thought.' As the room goes dark, the couple appear in a two-shot illuminated by bright pink light, before colourful liquid projections are forced onto Mike's face.

Attention is repeatedly drawn in the sequence to the hypnotic powers of technology. The walls of the room are lined with equipment including slide projectors, switchboards, speakers, and reel-to-reel tape recorders. Extreme close-ups and rhythmic camera push-ins on the various technologies of projection, especially the Aldis slide projector and Truvox reel-to-reel tape recorder, emphasise the mesmerising potential of media technologies. The inclusion of reversed footage showing smoke in the projector invokes contemporaneous concerns around the subliminal potential of rock music; specifically, how backward messages on records (a process referred to as 'backmasking') could either encode satanic messages or allegedly invoke listeners to act out violently.[16] As the pitch of the electronically manipulated music rises, the camera repeatedly pulses in and out on extreme close-ups of Mike's face, awash with psychedelic projections.

Under the guidance of cinematographer Stanley A. Long, artist Joe Gannon produced a liquid light show involving swirling and colourful inks. He describes the set-up as follows: 'he's sitting in his chair and the camera moves in on him very tight. And the liquid chemical slide effects are all over his face and in his eyes.'[17] Gannon was working at the time as a lighting technician for psychedelic rock band Pink Floyd, and was part of the countercultural scene that the film was referencing.[18] As with the light show projections of artist Mark Boyle in Bond's *Separation*, Dutch collective The Fool's psychedelic designs in *Wonderwall* (which also features a light show party sequence) or Bruce Lacey's performances with automata in *Smashing Time*, the inclusion of work by countercultural artists brings a sense of authenticity to the depiction of underground London and its creative practices.

Liquid light shows were an integral element of many countercultural environments in this period. Often referred to as a 'wet show' or 'ink-slide projection',[19] analogue light shows incorporate translucent liquids of different densities and viscosities (such as ink, glycerine, oil and water), which are then heated on glass slides, and often projected in tandem with other forms of live performance. Colour inks, acetates, ripple wheels and kaleidoscopic lenses further distort and interfere with the images, while the heightened colour palettes of the projections would increasingly become identified as psychedelic. Several artists in the period explicitly sought to translate the sensory experiences of hallucinogenic drugs, rock music and new technologies into various forms of graphic and projective media.

Placed in the context of mainstream narrative cinema, light shows are often plundered as sources of countercultural contemporaneity and visually spectacular special effects, yet also critiqued for their mesmeric impact on young people. As David E. James aptly observes, light shows act as 'productive' resources in Hollywood cinema, increasing a film's value through its appeal to young audiences, and thereby participating in the renewal of the industry. However, as an expanded cinematic practice in competition with mainstream cinema for young people's money and time, light shows also represent a 'cultural threat that must be denigrated and policed'.[20] The 'cultural threat' that the counterculture represents is similarly monitored in *The Sorcerers*, where psychedelic effects are briefly mobilised to appeal to young people, who represent the residual audiences of a rapidly declining cinema-going culture. However, rather than offering a transformative or "mind-expanding" group experience, the light show acts as a potent source of mesmerism that unleashes repressed and murderous impulses. Over the course of the film, Mike's brainwashing leads him to murder two young women on the London pop scene: the pop singer Laura (Dani Sheridan) and his ex-girlfriend, Audrey Woods (Susan George). Violence is here understood as the ultimate outcome of young people's seemingly fruitless search for new experiences and immediate sensory gratification.

Anxieties concerning young people's susceptibility to mental coercion actually bridged both mainstream and more underground discourses on psychedelic art and countercultural production. Although American critics Robert E. L. Masters and Jean Houston cast the psychedelic discotheque in a fairly positive light in *Psychedelic Art*, the first book-length study of psychedelia as an artistic phenomenon, they still express concerns about the risk of overstimulating participants. Multimedia environments, they suggest, have the potential to liberate individuals by deconditioning the mind and encouraging them to break through old categories of thought and moribund 'constancies of perception'.[21] Nevertheless, as 'techniques are perfected, what is certainly a major art form of the future could emerge just as well as a brain-washing nightmare'.[22] Correspondingly, in an early article on psychedelic art, American multimedia artist Jud Yalkut goes as far as warning readers that the 'brainwashing cubicle' of *The Ipcress File* is 'now a reality, and that a consideration of who is programming what should be of vital concern to the general public if brainwashing and so called "bad trips" are to be avoided'.[23] In both texts, psychedelic art – which here encompasses light shows and underground intermedia discotheques – is understood as offering a potentially liberating sensory and cognitive experience, yet also risks the danger of descending into mental coercion, with violent and unpredictable outcomes.

Light Shows as Analogues for Mental Dislocation and Mesmerism

Given that light shows were also widely understood by several commentators in the period as having both aesthetic features and affective qualities that overlapped with the psychedelic drug experience,[24] light show special effects sequences were often brought in as stand-ins for drug-taking in mainstream films about the counterculture. This is apparent from American 'head' films such as Richard Rush's *Psych-Out* (1968) and Roger Corman's *The Trip* (1967), and psychedelia-informed art films like *Separation* (1968) and Richard Lester's British-American co-production *Petulia* (1968). In these films, light show effects signal a character's mental transition into states of fantasy or madness, as well as indexing the visceral and internalised pleasures of hallucinogenic mind expansion.

Special effects have historically been used in narrative cinema to visualise interior states such as those relating to dreams, hallucinations or states of mental dislocation. As Gregory Zinman argues, the artisanal nature of analogue special effects often sets them 'apart from' or at a 'heightened' remove to the film's diegesis; the fundamental 'strangeness' of this imagery suggesting 'an opening up of perceptual experience' that cannot be captured by language.[25] As well as implying an expansion in perceptual experience through heightened colour schemes and tensile, ever-shifting imagery, light show effects also helped to circumnavigate censorship, given that representations of drug use were explicitly forbidden by the film censors.[26]

In *Petulia*, psychedelic light show inserts evoke the titular character Petulia Danner's (Julie Christie) increasing psychic dislocation, as well as referencing the communal forms of hallucinogenic mind expansion taking place within the West Coast hippy scene that acts as a backdrop to her breakdown. Correspondingly, Mark Boyle's projections for *Separation* similarly mark the mental transition between real and fantasy states experienced by its dislocated central character, played by the Welsh actor and playwright Jane Arden, who also wrote the film's screenplay and original story. *Separation* explores the fragmented inner life of an unnamed woman, as she attempts to negotiate a number of challenging emotional situations. The film is concerned with visualising and exploring states of mental alterity, including fantasy, madness and schizophrenia. Boyle's projections blur the already fragile boundaries between the past, present and future actions of its central protagonist. Alongside colourful liquid projections, Boyle also incorporates photographic slides from earlier moments in the film, which burn and bubble in the projector, thereby disturbing illusions of narrative linearity while also suggesting that the character's hold on reality is unstable. Boyle's psychedelic lights gesture towards those experiments in consciousness expansion that were taking place within the London counterculture of the period, not least in the sequence where Arden dances to psychedelic music, nude and awash in a bath of swirling liquid projections.

By contrast, in *The Sorcerers*, the light show brainwashing sequence functions as a comment on the youth culture's insatiable quest for new experiences, a craving that Booker compares to the ever-destructive pursuit of a drugs high.[27] The visual pleasure of cinematic spectatorship is here transposed onto the embodied pleasures of sensory gratification enabled by multimedia environments and hallucinogenic drugs. When discussing their ideal 'transmitter', Monserrat couches this search for new experience in terms of drug-taking, describing the abundance of 'children out on the streets taking pills to keep themselves awake'. Meanwhile, the psychedelic brainwashing is explicitly framed as a surrogate drug experience, as the couple promise Mike 'intoxication with no consequences'.

Benjamin Halligan observes that critics who reviewed *The Sorcerers* in the 1960s drew comparisons between the brainwashing sequence and the mesmerising potential of popular entertainment.[28] David Austen, for instance, wrote that the 'real weight' in *The Sorcerers* derives from the analogy between brainwashing and 'cinematic sublimation',[29] understanding Estelle's promise of intoxication as coinciding with the pleasures of vicarious experience provided by the cinema. The 'questions that the film triggers off about vicarious experiences soon trap one', Austen notes, 'in a mirror maze of identification'.[30] These reviews provide evidence of Andreas Killen's hypothesis that cinematic depictions of mind control often exhibit elements of self-reflexivity about the historical role of moving-image media in coercing or conditioning audiences.[31] Halligan concludes that in *The Sorcerers*, 'LSD and film are both reduced to their common denominator: false experience for those hungry for experience.'[32]

Like other Swinging London films, *The Sorcerers* incorporates a self-reflexive critique of the role of youth cinema in providing vicarious experiences for 'straight' mainstream culture. The new world of sensation, which the young have committed themselves to, is out of reach of an older generation, who instead have to experience it second-hand through telepathy. Dramatic action often unfolds along generational lines, with older people portrayed as passé, voyeuristic, manipulative or criminal. In *Wonderwall*, reclusive academic Professor Collins (Jack McGowran) resorts to spying on his hippy neighbours through a peephole in the eponymous wall that separates them, in a visual elaboration of the so-called 'generation gap'. In the same year, the British sex comedy *What's Good for the Goose* (1969) shows how assistant bank manager Timothy Bartlett (Norman Wisdom) revitalises his humdrum life and ailing marriage by actually immersing himself in the local club scene, throwing himself (most unconvincingly) into the psychedelic club scene of the Screaming Apple discotheque. Although these films represent the older generation as a pseudo-vampiric force preying on the vital energies of the young, it also contains the utopian energies of the youth culture by revealing its shallowness and hypocrisy.

Bomb Culture: Violence, Alienation and Public Trance in the Discotheque

Rather than the 'Dionysian cultural space' that James identifies as typical of countercultural nightclubs and hippy gatherings,[33] the discotheque sequences in *The Sorcerers* are notably flat: young people drink Coke, dance clumsily with each other, and listlessly smoke cigarettes. These scenes were shot at Blaise's, a club in London's West End that was closely associated with swinging London (but not the underground), and often name-checked in guidebooks and articles on the 'swinging' phenomenon.[34] Perhaps inadvertently, the awkwardness of these sequences foregrounds the alienation that many perceived at the heart of the youth culture at the time. Bored of 'wandering around from club to club', Mike comments that the group spend at least four nights a week in this 'den of iniquity'. Mike's ennui at the temporality of this cultural scene is made visible in his refusal to dance; gesturing to the dancers, he asks rhetorically: 'How long do you think all this can last?'

A similar representation of countercultural alienation in the midst of London's swinging club scene is apparent in *Blow-Up*. Fashion photographer Thomas (David Hemmings) chases a woman (Vanessa Redgrave) into the Ricky Tick Club in London's West End.[35] Walking through the darkened club trying to find her, he is forced to shove past an entranced and immoveable crowd of young people. Staring apathetically as The Yardbirds perform an energetic rendition of 'Stroll On', the audience seem to be frozen – with few exceptions – in a series of static poses. A buzzing sound in musician Jeff Beck's amplifier forces him to smash his guitar into the speakers, before throwing its neck into the crowd. The stunned and passive crowd immediately breaks into violence, and a riot soon follows as the audience throw themselves over each other in an attempt to snatch the guitar neck.

Although Beck's destruction of the guitar was 'much criticized for its unlikelihood',[36] it echoes many of the destructive on-stage performances of The Who's Pete Townshend, who, unlike Beck, regularly smashed his guitars on stage.[37] In an interview with Townshend published in the underground newspaper *International Times*, Barry Miles describes the band as the most popular of the many 'auto-destructive groups' on the music scene at that time.[38] Townshend observes that the demolition of the band's musical instruments on stage was inspired by the theories of the Polish-German artist Gustav Metzger, who

Figure 15.2 The 'entranced and immoveable group of young people' watching The Yardbirds perform in *Blow-Up* (1966).

occasionally lectured at Townshend's art school, Ealing College of Art. Metzger worked across different media, including light projection, and was partly responsible, Townshend observes in this interview, for the college's experiments with light projection. Artistic explorations into social violence and destruction were an active part of Metzger's practice, an interest clearly signalled by the events and discussion that took place amid the Destruction in Art Symposium (DIAS). DIAS was a series of events held in London during September 1966, which Metzger conceived of and organised with the assistance of the poet and filmmaker John J. Sharkey. As Kristine Stiles has noted, DIAS aimed to explore the 'use of destruction as a mode of resistance to psychological, social, and political violence'.[39]

Artist, musician and cultural commentator Jeff Nuttall identified the discotheque or 'pop club' as one of several new art forms reflecting the profound alienation of modern life in the wake of the threat of nuclear war. Nuttall famously described the creative output of this period as entailing a *bomb culture*, a moment in which 'art itself has never been closer to its violent and orgiastic roots'.[40] Although more sympathetic than Booker to the attitudes and practices of the counterculture – Nuttall was, after all, an artist and active participant in many Happenings and events in this period – he nevertheless critiques the discotheque for its ability to facilitate trance. Using explicitly militarised language, he describes a 'battery of curdling colours projected round the room', 'brutal stroboscopes', the 'aggressive gobbling of the guitar' and refers to the 'stunned trance of the crowd'; all of which he sees as reflecting the violence threatening the world outside.[41] Elsewhere in *Bomb Culture*, Nuttall notes that the use of electronic music and stroboscopic lighting are driving pop 'music further and further towards public trance'.[42]

Fundamentally, Nuttall appears to interpret the destructive gestures of various Happenings, intermedia environments and underground discotheques as enacting modes of resistance to societal violence. By contrast, in both the public trance state of *Blow-Up*'s partygoers (which eventually culminates in an upsurge of violence) and Mike's psychedelic brainwashing in *The Sorcerers* (which enables him to commit extreme acts of violence on members of the local club scene), violence is depicted as the symptom of an alienated youth culture rather than an active form of resistance to alienation. This is also the case in British filmmaker John Boorman's first Hollywood feature *Point Blank* (1967), in which he makes a psychedelic discotheque, aptly named The Movie House, the site of an unbridled explosion of violence. During an increasingly vicious rampage through the streets of Los Angeles, a gangster named Walker (Lee Marvin) ends up at a psychedelic club. The sequence opens with a wildly gesticulating nightclub singer performing in the centre of a slide projection of a gaping mouth, as psychedelic projections bathe the walls of The Movie House. A fight ensues and several of the men fall to the floor. A series of graphic matches between the wailing singer, slides of screaming women and the real-life screams of the go-go dancer draw together the violent cacophony of the scene into a rapidly edited montage. Finally, red-spattered and moving liquid projections bathe Walker's face as he silently surveys the eruption of violence. Boorman's representation of the discotheque as a high-society environment detached from the pacifist ideology of the West Coast counterculture reveals how the era's politics of sexual liberation have become a marketable commodity.

The more utopian, liberatory and participatory elements of countercultural club networks are largely regulated in mainstream film, with discotheques coming to represent, at best, the faddish commodification of the counterculture, and at worst, a source of distraction, mesmerism and violence. This is in contrast to the concrete material functions that discotheques played within local underground networks. London clubs such as UFO, Middle Earth, The Marquee, or Happening 44, among many others, functioned as spaces in which to explore new models of participation with artistic production and social interaction, rethinking art's capacity to fundamentally transform individual and social consciousness. Film projection and exhibition also underwent a process of radical interrogation in this period, offering a means of resistance to mainstream society's coercion of subjectivity, and offering an alternative to conventional aesthetic forms.

Peter Whitehead's impressionistic documentary on swinging London, *Tonite Let's All Make Love in London* (1967), comes closer to capturing the transformative potential of the London club scene in this period. Although the film has largely been read as a critique of swinging London, there is little evidence for this in the final film. Whitehead confirms his critical stance in an interview with Paul Cronin, when he notes that that the film was 'trying to examine the mythology that everybody in London was having fun'.[43] *Tonite Let's All Make Love in London* is a largely jubilant portrayal of the fashion and music cultures that cohered around swinging London, even if it implicitly suggests that the phenomenon was one promoted by American interests. The film features three short but intensive sequences of discotheques, and opens to a dynamic montage of London's nightlife as the rhythmic discordancy of Pink Floyd's 'Interstellar Overdrive' is introduced on the track. Both here and elsewhere in the film, Whitehead evokes the hyper-affective qualities of underground discotheques through recourse to quasi-abstraction. Animated single frames and long exposures animate the dancers, conveying a sense of audio-visual indeterminacy, kinaesthetic experience, and spatial and temporal disorientation. The film's final sequence, which was shot at 14 Hour Technicolor Dream Happening in Alexandra Palace, captures a countercultural network of artists, dancers, performers, and participants moving freely around the cavernous space, revealing the potential for underground art to alter individual and social consciousness, and generate a sense of belonging to a community.

Conclusion

Although swinging London films often incorporate a self-reflexive critique of the role of popular cinema in providing vicarious experiences for 'straight' mainstream culture, they nevertheless contain the promises of youth and club cultures within the narrative framework of the 'social problem' film. In *The Sorcerers*, the light show operates as a surrogate for the mesmeric qualities of popular culture and psychedelic art, mapping the dangers of mass and unthinking behaviour onto the psychedelic multimedia practices of the 1960s London underground. The youthful quest for sensation and novelty is fundamentally portrayed as an escape from social issues, something we see in the hermetic goings-on of the hippy tribes in *Wonderwall*, or young people's complicity in the co-optation of activist imagery in *Smashing Time*. With few exceptions, these films fail to show how psychedelic multimedia environments and underground discotheques might actively encourage participants to break free from social conventions and rational forms of perception, and thereby repeal the very forms of mental coercion systematically engendered by the commercial media industries.

Many swinging London films would therefore appear to reflect mainstream critiques of psychedelic or underground culture, while simultaneously appropriating the aesthetics of psychedelia to appeal to young audiences, and allowing for greater levels of formal ingenuity and playfulness. In *Expanded Cinema*,

American media theorist Gene Youngblood argues that 'the so-called psychedelic discotheque' was to the cinema of the 1960s 'what the Busby Berkeley ballroom was to the thirties', an imaginative space that generated its own 'ethos' and 'aesthetic' by conveying a sense of the movement, freneticism and posturing of the pop culture. 'Like all commercial entertainment', Youngblood decrees, 'these films were *about* something rather than *being* something, and so were the discotheques they imitated.'[44] Although Youngblood is writing about 'hip' Hollywood cinema, we see a similar dynamic in Swinging London films, where discotheques and psychedelic light environments are ultimately used to foreground young people's ineffective (and even dangerous) search for hedonism, sensation, and 'authentic' experience. The psychedelic discotheque or light show environment, here, simply apes the mesmeric potential of mainstream popular culture, rather than offering up important alternatives to it.

Acknowledgements

This chapter incorporates research from my PhD, titled *Projecting Psychedelia: Psychedelic Aesthetics and the Counterculture in British Films and Light Shows of the Long 1960s*. I'd like to thank my supervisor, Dr Michele Pierson, Professor Steve Chibnall, and the editors of this collection, for their insightful suggestions on this chapter.

Notes

1. For an interesting discussion on the gendered dimensions of moral panics surrounding beat clubs in the post-war period, see Carol Dyhouse, *Girl Trouble: Panic and Progress in the History of Young Women* (London: Zed Books, 2013), pp. 137–75.
2. Alexander Walker, *Hollywood England: The British Film Industry in the Sixties* (London: Harrap, 1986), p. 289. See also Christopher Booker, *The Neophiliacs: A Study of the Revolution in English Life in the Fifties and Sixties* (London: Harper Collins, 1969), and Robert Murphy, *Sixties British Cinema* (London: British Film Institute, 1992).
3. See Pamela Church Gibson, 'From up North to up West? London on screen 1965-1967', *The London Journal* 31: 1, 2006, pp. 85–107, p. 91.
4. The term 'club culture' tends to be used to refer to the rave phenomenon of the late 1980s and early 1990s, marking this period off from prior forms of clubbing in the 1960s and 1970s. In this chapter, I use it to refer to an earlier period of youth dance spaces, delineating a social and cultural practice that relies on the discotheque as a regular meeting-place for dancing, encountering live music and performance and the consumption of alcohol or drugs.
5. Booker, *The Neophiliacs*, p. 27.
6. Ibid. p. 22.
7. Ibid. p. 60.
8. Walker, *Hollywood England*, p. 291.

9. Murphy, *Sixties British Cinema*, p. 4.
10. Moya Luckett, 'Travel and mobility: femininity and national identity in swinging London films', in J. Ashby and A. Higson (eds), *British Cinema, Past and Present* (London: Routledge, 2000), pp. 233–4.
11. John Hill, 'The British "social problem" film: "Violent Playground" and "Sapphire"', *Screen* 26: 1, 1985, pp. 34–9, p. 34.
12. Alan Burton argues that by the mid-1960s, brainwashing had become a firmly established element of the spy drama genre, to the extent that it was conspicuously parodied in films like *Carry On Spying* (1964). See Alan Burton, 'Mind bending, mental seduction and menticide', *Journal of British Cinema and Television* 10: 1, 2013, pp. 27–48, p. 32.
13. Marcia Holmes, 'Brainwashing the cybernetic spectator: *The Ipcress File*, 1960s cinematic spectacle and the sciences of mind', *History of the Human Sciences* 30: 3, 2017, pp. 3–24, p. 5.
14. Ibid. p. 4.
15. The film was released through Tigon Pictures as a Tigon-Curtwel Global Productions.
16. The process of incorporating messages when played backwards was popular on many psychedelic rock tracks. Famously, when American cult leader Charles Manson was arrested for the murder of Sharon Tate, he claimed to have heard subliminal messages urging him to murder on The Beatles' track 'Helter Skelter'.
17. Skype interview with the author, 31 March 2017.
18. Gannon produced some of the earliest light shows for Pink Floyd. At their most rudimentary, these shows involved colourful flashing floodlights, but Gannon's practice increasingly shifted towards liquid light projections, finding particular inspiration in a liquid slide demonstration produced by American light show artists Joel and Toni Brown. Gannon was not, however, a part of Hornsey's Light/Sound Workshop, as several accounts have since claimed. Soon after the making of *The Sorcerers*, Gannon moved to San Francisco, after being introduced to music promoter Chet Helms through John 'Hoppy' Hopkins. Gannon produced light shows for San Francisco's Avalon Ballroom. When he returned to Britain in the 1970s, he reprised his collaboration with Stanley A. Long, and worked as an editor on Long's *Adventures* series of films (1976–8), as well as the sex education documentary *It Could Happen to You* (1976).
19. Sheldon Renan, *An Introduction to the American Underground Film* (New York: E. P. Dutton, 1967), p. 252.
20. David E. James, 'Expanded cinema in Los Angeles: the single wing turquoise bird', *Millennium Film Journal* 43/44, 2003, p. 31.
21. Robert E. L. Masters and Jean Houston (eds), *Psychedelic Art* (London: Weidenfeld and Nicolson, 1968), p. 84.
22. Ibid. p. 85.
23. Jud Yalkut, 'Critique: the psychedelic revolution. Turning on the art trip', *Arts Magazine* 41, 1966, p. 22.
24. See Gene Youngblood, *Expanded Cinema* (London: Studio Vista, 1970).

25. Gregory Zinman, 'The right stuff? Handmade special effects in commercial and industrial film', in D. North, B. Rehak and M. Duffy (eds), *Special Effects: New Histories, Theories, Contexts* (London: BFI/Palgrave Macmillan, 2015), p. 228.
26. See Harry M. Benshoff, 'The short-lived life of the Hollywood LSD film', *Velvet Light Trap* 47, 22 March 2001, pp. 29–45.
27. Booker, *The Neophiliacs*, p. 71.
28. Benjamin Halligan, *Michael Reeves* (Manchester: Manchester University Press, 2003).
29. David Austen, 'The Sorcerers', *Films and Filming* 14: 1, October 1967, p. 25.
30. Ibid. p. 25.
31. Andreas Killen, 'Homo Pavlovius: cinema, conditioning, and the Cold War subject', *Grey Room* 45, 2011, pp. 42–59, p. 54.
32. Halligan, *Michael Reeves*, p. 78.
33. James, 'Expanded Cinema in Los Angeles', p. 31.
34. Blaise's nightclub is mentioned in several swinging London 'guide books' published to capitalise on the phenomenon of swinging London. See, for instance, Karl F. Dallas, *Swinging London: A Guide to Where the Action Is* (London: Stanmore Press, 1967), pp. 14–15. Unlike UFO Club, Blaise's was not a psychedelic discotheque, although it did host numerous psychedelic musicians such as Pink Floyd and Jimi Hendrix.
35. The nightclub was modelled on the Ricky Tick Club at Clewer Mead in Windsor. Although exterior shots of the club were filmed on location in London's West End, where many of London's nightclubs were located, the club's interiors were actually recreated on a film set.
36. Walker, *Hollywood England*, p. 322.
37. Alexander Walker refers to reports of Antonioni and Tonino Guerra researching the 'swinging' scene at dance halls and discotheques in South London and the West End, noting that the guitar smashing scene was one that Antonioni witnessed (see Walker, *Hollywood England*, p. 322). The Who were originally meant to perform in the nightclub scene but allegedly turned down the part.
38. Barry Miles, 'Miles Interviews Pete Townshend', *International Times* 8, 13 February 1967, p. 5.
39. Kristine Stiles, 'The story of the Destruction in Art Symposium and the "DIAS affect"', in Sabina Breitwieser (ed.), *Gustav Metzger. Geschichte* (Vienna/Ostfildern-Ruit: Generali Foundation and Hatje Cantz Verlag, 2005), p. 41.
40. Jeff Nuttall, *Bomb Culture* (London: Paladin, 1968), p. 9.
41. Ibid. p. 9.
42. Ibid. p. 22.
43. Paul Cronin, 'The ceremony of innocence', *Sight & Sound* 17: 3, 2007, p. 23.
44. Youngblood, *Expanded Cinema*, p. 102.

INDEX

2001: A Space Odyssey (1968), 165
400 Blows, The (1959), 171

ABC cinemas, 154, 155
ABC TV, 16
Abortion Act (1967), 51
Accident (1967), 1, 132, 135
Adam, Ken, 172, 173, 174
Adkins, Lesley, 218
Adkins, Roy, 218
Adventures of Robin Hood, The (1955–9), 159
Alcala, Roberto del Valle, 52
Alfie (1966), 1
Allen, Angela, 92
Allen, Peter, 217
Allied Artists, 20
Alpert, Richard, 198
Amicus, 157, 202
Anderson, Esther, 231
Anderson, Lindsay, 5, 18, 82, 83, 99–112
Andress, Ursula, 162
Andrews, David, 229
Antonioni, Michelangelo, 6, 23, 241
Angry Silence, The (1960), 31

Angry Young Man, Angry Young Men, 11, 12, 30, 34, 36, 66, 71, 180, 209
Antrobus, John, 94, 95
Arden, Jane, 246
Arden, John, 104
Armchair Theatre, 16
Arnold, John, 132
Ashby, Justine, 40
Asquith, Anthony, 65, 67, 69–70, 71
Asquith, Herbert, 69
Assassination of Trotsky, The (1972), 132
Associated British Picture Corporation (ABPC), 2, 17
Atha, Bernard, 124
Attenborough, Richard, 224
Austen, David, 247
L'Avventura (1960), 168

Baddeley, Hermione, 64
BAFTA Awards, 82
Bagnold, Edith, 73
Bailey, David, 12
Baird, Harry, 225
Baker, Roy Ward, 225
Baker, Stanley, 29, 32, 131, 133

255

Baker, Tom, 197, 198, 202
Baldwin's Nigger (1969), 224
Ballad in Blue (1965), 228
Baptiste, Thomas, 225, 227
Barnes, Clive, 11
Barr, Charles, 165
Bassett, Ronald, 199
Bates, Alan, 4, 11, 16, 19, 22, 55, 179, 180, 181
Bava, Mario, 194–5, 196
Beat Girl (1959), 31, 239
Beatles, The, 1, 48, 83, 87–8, 123
Beau Travail (1999), 217
Beauty Jungle, The (1964), 186
Beck, Jeff, 248
Beck, Reginald, 132, 140, 142
BECTU, 3
Bed Sitting Room, The (1969), 94, 95
Behm, Marc, 87
Bell, Tom, 211
Belles of St Trinians, The (1954), 47
Bennett, Alan, 87
Berkeley, Busby, 252
Berlin Film Festival, 1
BFI Experimental Film Fund, 227
Biba, 54
Bill Douglas Cinema Museum, 3
Billy Budd (1962), 6, 20, 209, 211, 213–19, 220, 221
Billy's Last Stand (1965), 117
Bitch, The (1979), 58
Black Narcissus (1947), 188, 189
Black Sunday (1960), 194, 196, 199
Blackboard Jungle, The (1955), 229
Blind Date (1959), 131, 132, 133
Blinder, The (novel), 117
Blithe Spirit (1945), 68
Blood on Satan's Claw (1971), 202
Bloody Judge, The (1970), 200, 201
Bloomfield (1971), p. 24
Blow Up (1966), 1, 6, 23, 241, 248, 250
Bogarde, Dirk, 16, 131, 134, 135, 211, 213, 218, 219
Bond, Jack, 240, 244
Booker, Christopher, 6, 241, 247, 249
Boom! (1968), 132, 135, 170
Boorman, John, 250

Bordwell, David, 173–4
Born Free (1966), 224
Boulting Brothers, 2, 186, 226
Bowes, Bob, 121
Boxwell, David, 215, 216
Boyle, Mark, 244, 246–7
Bradley, David, 115, 125
Bradshaw, Peter, 71
Braithwaite, E. R., 228
Brando, Marlon, 17, 21, 38, 39, 211, 216
Bray, Christopher, 173
Break in the Circle (1955), 152
Brecht, Bertolt, 100, 211
Brenda De Banzie, 225
Brief Encounter (1945), 211
Brigand of Kandahar, The (1965), 33, 161, 162
Briggs, Johnny, 226
British Board of Film Censors (BBFC), 5, 151–62
British Film Institute, 3
British Lion, 2
British New Wave, 11, 12, 14, 17, 19, 67, 70, 82, 119, 181, 183, 219, 225
Britten, Benjamin, 217
Broccoli, Albert, 19, 23, 167
Brooks, Ray, 84
Brooks, Richard, 229
Brost, Laure, 188
Browne, Geoff, 100
Bulldog Breed, The (1960), 31, 219
Burke, John, 197, 198
Burke, Paul, 56
Burroughs, William, S. 87
Burton, Richard, 30, 42, 67, 70, 71, 135
Byron, Kathleen, 188

Caine, Michael, 4, 11, 14, 16, 20, 21, 23, 37, 48, 173
Camelot (musical), 24
Cameron, Earl, 224, 225, 234
Cameron, John, 123
Canadian Broadcasting Corporation (CBC), 167
Cannes Film Festival, 1
Caprice (1967), 24

Captain Clegg (1962), 32, 33, 157, 159–60
Cardiff, Jack, 176
Caretaker, The (1963), 184
Carey, Macdonald, 169
Carreras, James, 155, 158
Carreras, Michael, 155
Carry On films, 2, 219, 224
Carry On Jack (1963), 6, 209, 219–21
Carry On Sergeant (1958), 219
Carry On Teacher (1959), 47
Carry On Up the Jungle (1970), 224
Carry On Up the Khyber (1968), 224
Castle of the Living Dead, The (1964), 194
Cathy Come Home (1966), 4, 48, 54, 120
Caute, David, 131
Cave, Norman, 229
Censorship, 151–62
Chalk Garden, The (1964), 73
Challenge for Robin Hood, A (1967), 162
Chaplin, Charles, 68
Charge of the Light Brigade, The (1968), 5, 82, 91–3
Charlie Bubbles (1967), 24, 186
Chibnall, Steve, 176
Chimes at Midnight (1965), 75
Chinese Man from China, The (novel), 87
Christie, Julie, 4, 54, 64, 246
Ciment, Michel, 137, 168
CinemaScope, 165
Cinematography, 166–72
Clavell, James, 228
Clayton, Jack, 176
Clift, Montgomery, 21
Collector, The (1965), 136
Collins, Frank, 127
Collins, Joan, 58
Collinson, Peter, 4, 91, 176
colour, 107–8, 111, 152–3, 183–6
Columbia, 159, 166
Connery, Sean, 4, 11, 14, 16, 19, 23, 24, 30, 37, 42, 224
Conrich, Ian, 187
Contact (1965), 224
Cook, Pam, 29

Cook, Peter, 186
Cooper, Gladys, 64
Corman, Roger, 198, 246
Corona Stage Academy, 47
counterculture, 193–204
Countess from Hong Kong, A (1967), 68
Courtenay, Tom, 4, 11, 22, 17–18, 48
Courtney, Cathy, 102, 105
Cowie, Peter, 69
Craig, Wendy, 36, 54, 134
Crawford, Michael, 83, 88
Cribbins, Bernard, 220
Criminal, The (1960), 131
Croydon, John, 132–42, 144
Cuban Missile Crisis, 209
Cul-de-Sac (1966), 1
Curse of Frankenstein, The (1957), 151, 153, 154
Curse of the Crimson Altar (1968), 203
Curse of the Mummy's Tomb, The (1964), 159
Curse of the Werewolf, The (1961), 32, 37, 157, 158
Curtis, Lucinda, 184
Cushing, Peter, 157, 159
Czech New Wave, 101

Daddy's Gone A Hunting (1969), 56–7
Damn the Defiant! (1962), 213
Damned, The (1963), 5, 7, 33, 36, 82, 166, 167, 168–72
Danquah, Paul, 226
D'Arcy, Ruth, 229, 230
Darling (1965), 182, 186
Darlow, Michael, 67
Daughters of Satan (1972), 196
Davis, Ossie, 224, 228
Davis Jr, Sammy, 228
Dawson, Beatrice, 188
De Rham, Edith, 131, 144
Dead of Night (1945), 188–9
Dearden, Basil, 6, 180, 186, 187, 188, 190, 224
Death May Be Your Santa Claus (1969), 230–1
Deceivers, The (novel), 87

257

Deighton, Len, 167
Delaney, Pauline, 185
Denis, Claire, 217
Deutsch, David, 133
Devereux, Marie, 160
Devil Ship Pirates, The (1964), 161–2
Devils, The (1971), 31, 39, 40, 41, 200, 201
Devine, George, 104
Dexter, John, 109
Diamonds are Forever (1971), 24
Dick Turpin – Highwayman (1956), 152
Dickinson, Geoffrey, 240
Dickinson, Thorold, 71
Dingo (play), 88
Doctor Blood's Coffin (1961), 167
Doctor in the House (1954), 47
Dolce Vita, La (1960), 176
Doll's House, A (1973), 132
Donaldson, Lucy, 109
Donner, Clive, 6, 179–80, 183–4, 185
Donner, Richard, 228
Donovan, 49
Dr No (1962), 1, 225
Dracula (1958), 32, 151, 153, 154
Drake, Philip, 39
Draper, Peter, 35
Drazin, Charles, 101, 108
Dulcima (1971), 57
Dunn, Nell, 49, 50, 58
Durgnat, Raymond, 63
Dutchman (1966), 228, 229
Dwyer, Hilary, 200
Dyaliscope, 166, 171
Dymon Jr., Frankie, 230
Dynasty (1981–9), 58

Ealing, 186, 188
East of Sudan (1964), 224
Eastmancolor, 152, 184
Easy Rider (1969), 198
Ede, Laurie, 103
Elliot, Denholm, 181
EMI/Associated British Pathe (ABP), 186, 189
Endfield, Cy, 224
England, Barry, 136

English Stage Company (ESC), 16
Eno, Brian, 101
Eon Films, 19
Equity, 15
Eros Films, 133
Eurovision Song Contest, 51
Eva (1962), 82
Evans, Edith, 4, 63, 64, 70–4
Eve (1962), 141, 169
Evil of Frankenstein, The (1964), 158
Expresso Bongo (1959), 239
Eye of the Devil, The (1966), 196

Faith, Adam, 31
Faithfull, Marianne, 54
Far from the Madding Crowd (1967), 19
Farrar, David, 31, 33, 188
Fassbinder, Reiner Werner, 108
Fathom (1967), 136
Fear Eats the Soul (1973), 108
Feldman, Marty, 95
Field, Shirley Anne, 31, 169
Figures in a Landscape (1970), 5, 132, 136–44, 167, 168, 170
film certification, 151–62
film finances, 3, 5, 132, 133, 134, 135, 136, 137
Finney, Albert, 4, 11, 15, 17, 22, 29, 30, 40, 42, 73
Fisher, Terence, 32, 159
Fixer, The (1968), 55–6
Flame in the Streets (1961), 225–6
Fleming, Ian, 19
Flynn, Errol, 30
Follow that Camel (1967), 224
Fool, The (Dutch Art Collective), 244
Forbes, Bryan, 73, 180, 186, 189, 226, 229
Ford, Glen, 229
Forster, E. M. 217
Forster-Jones, Glenna, 230
Foster, Maurice, 133
Four Musketeers, The (1974), 82
Fox, James, 134
Fox, Robin, 138
Frankenheimer, John, 55
Fraser, Shelagh, 234

Frederick, Hal, 228, 231
Free Cinema, 165
Freeman Jr, Al, 229
Fu Manchu (novel), 87
Fun City (1983), 123, 127
Funny Thing Happened on the Way to the Forum, A (1966), 88
Furie, Sidney J., 5, 166–7, 172–7

Gainsborough, 37
Gajadhar, Ken, 231
Gambit (1966), 23
Gamekeeper, The (1980), 127
Gannon, Joe, 198, 244
Gardner, Colin, 131, 137, 169
Garnett, Tony, 49, 56, 58, 59, 115, 116, 117–18, 119
Garrett, Robert, 132, 133, 138, 139
Geeson, Judy, 231
George, Susan, 245
Georges-Picot, Olga, 188
Geraghty, Christine, 39
Gielgud, John, 81–2
Gilliat, Penelope, 55
Glancy, Mark, 70
Gledhill, Christine, 102, 112
Glover, Brian, 117
Glynn, Stephen, 31, 116
Go-Between, The (1971), 132, 144
Godard, Jean Luc, 5, 176, 230
Golden Spur, The (1959), 31
Golden Vision, The (1968), 117
Gonzales, Carl, 228
Goodlatte, Jack, 155
Goodman, Judy, 142
Goodwin, Cliff, 32
Grand Hotel (1932), 67
Granger, Stewart, 33
Grant, Arthur, 172
Grant, Cary, 31
Green, Frank, 142
Green, Nigel, 31, 175
Gregory, Charles C. 182
Grenfell, Joyce, 161
Griffith, Chuck, 194
Grunwald, Anatole de, 67, 70
Guillermin, John, 224

Guinness, Alec, 211, 218, 220
Guns at Batasi (1964), 224
Guns of Navarone, The (1961), 165, 167

H, Being Monologues in Front of Burning Cities (play), 88
Hakim, Raymond, 141
Hakim, Robert, 141
Halasz, Piri, 240
Hall, Sheldon, 165
Halligan Benjamin, 193, 198, 199, 247
Hamilton, Guy, 31
Hammer Film Productions, Hammer, Hammer Films, 5, 32, 33, 34, 87, 151–62, 166, 167, 170, 185, 202
Hannibal Brooks (1969), 32, 34
Happiest Days of Your Life, The (1950), 68
Hard Day's Night, A (1964), 48, 82, 83
Harper, Roy, 57
Harper, Sue, 36, 37
Harley, Martin, 121
Harris, Percy, 104
Harris, Richard, 4, 11, 14, 16, 18, 29, 38, 42
Harris, Sophie, 104
Harris, Trevor, 36
Harrison, Casey, 216
Harvey, Anthony, 176, 229
Harvey, Laurence, 92, 119, 186
Hatfield, Patrick, 227
Hawkins, Jack, 17
Hawtrey, Charles, 220
Hayworth, Rita, 65
Heath, Hilary, 231
Heaven's Above (1963), 226, 228
Hell Boats (1969), 210
Heller, Anthony, 172
Heller, Otto, 173
Help! (1965), 82, 87–8
Hemmings, David, 23, 248
Hendry, Ian, 186
Henried, Paul, 228
Hepburn, Audrey, 71
Herbert, Jocelyn, 5, 99–112

259

Herbert, Percy, 219
Hesketh, Trevor, 120
Hill, James, 224
Hill, John, 116, 119, 242
Hill, The (1965), 224, 228
Hiller, Wendy, 4, 63, 64, 65–7
Hills, Gillian, 31
Hinds, Anthony, 153, 157, 166
Hines, Barry, 5, 115–21, 122, 126–7
Hines, Claire, 29
Hinxman, Margaret, 51
Hiroshima Mon Amour (1959), 169
History of Advertising Trust, 3
HMS Defiant (1962), 6, 209, 211–13, 214, 215, 217, 218, 219, 220–1
Hoggart, Richard, 53
Holder, Ram John, 232
Hollywood blacklist, 166
Holmes, Marcia, 242
Honeycombe, Gordon, 117
Hope, Peter, 132
Hopkins, Matthew, 199–200
Hopper, Dennis, 198
Hordern, Michael, 89, 95
Hot Summer Night (1959), 225
Hound of the Baskervilles, The (1959), 154, 155
House Un-American Activities Committee (HUAC), 133
Houston, Jean, 239, 245
Houston, Penelope, 54
How I Won the War (1967), 88, 89–91
Howard, Trevor, 211
Hunter, Ross, 73
Hunting Party, The (1971), 33
Huston, Donald, 220
Hutchings, Peter, 37, 153
Hylands, Scott, 57

Iannone, Pasquale, 176
If . . . (1968), 1, 5, 7, 99–112
I'll Never Forget What's'isname (1967), 4, 31, 34, 35, 36, 37, 54–5, 186
Importance of Being Earnest, The (1952), 71

In Which We Serve (1942), 210
Independent Artists, 133, 134
Ipcress File, The (1966), 5, 20, 166, 167, 172–6, 242, 245
Isadora (1968), 105, 106
Island in the Sun (1957), 228
Italian Job, The (1969), 173–4

Jackson, Dan, 225
Jackson, Glenda, 48, 56, 131
Jacobs, Sally, 185
James Bond, 1, 19, 23, 165, 186
James, David E. 245
Janni, Joseph, 19
Jellicoe, Ann, 82, 83, 88
Jemima and Johnny (1966), 227, 236
Jingo (1975), 88
Joanna (1968), 228, 230
Jocelyn Herbert Archive, 102
Joe Harriot Quintet, 227
John, Errol, 224
Johns, Mervyn, 189
Jokers, The (1967), 31, 34
Jones, Brian, 56
Jones, Evan, 82, 231
Jones, Freddie, 188
Jones, Leroi, 229
Jonson, Bari, 227
Jump, Sophie, 111
Juran, Nathan, 224

Karloff, Boris, 7, 197, 243
Keep Films, 24
Kerr, Deborah, 66, 74
Kes (1969), 5, 115–27
Kestrel for a Knave, A (novel), 115–27
Khartoum (1966), 210, 224
Kind Hearts and Coronets (1949), 47
Kind of Loving, A (1962), 1, 19
Kinematograph Weekly, 212
King, Barry, 39
King & Country (1964), 82, 132, 134, 166, 169
Kiss of the Vampire (1963), 158
Kitchen, The (1961), 108–9
Klinger, Michael, 243

Knack . . . and How to Get It, The (1965), 1, 4, 81, 82–6, 92
Knight, Julia, 102
Knight, Shirley, 229
Knox, Alexander, 170
Kohn, John, 136, 137, 139, 141, 142, 144
Kotcheff, Ted, 6, 224, 225
Kremer, Daniel, 173
Krish, John, 224
Kulick, Barry, 231, 235

Labour Party, 182
Lacey, Catherine, 197, 243
Lacey, Stephen, 116
Lacy, Bruce, 244
LAMDA (London Academy of Music and Dramatic Arts), 15
Lancaster, Burt, 65
Last Year in Marienbad (1961), 176
Launder and Gilliat, 2
Laverty, Paul, 116
Lawford, Peter, 228
Lawrence, D. H., 40
Lawrence, H. L., 168
Lawrence of Arabia (1962), 1, 21, 22, 165, 210, 224
Le Mepris (1963), 176
Lean, David, 2, 21, 176
Leary, Timothy, 198
Leather Boys, The (1964), 167
Lee, Christopher, 31, 32, 160, 161–2
Leigh, Jacob, 116, 123, 126
Lennon, John, 56, 88, 89
Leo the Last (1970), 228, 230, 236
Leone, Sergio, 5
Lester, Richard, 4, 82–5, 86, 88–9, 93, 94, 246
Let My People Go (1961), 224
Lewis, Jerry, 228
Linda (1960), 47
Lindfors, Viveca, 170
Lindsay Anderson Archive, 102
Lion in Winter, The (1968), 24–5
Little Ones, The (1965), 227–8
Littlewood, Joan, 15, 23

Loach, Ken, 48, 49, 53, 56, 58, 59, 75, 115–16, 118, 119–20, 126–7
Lockhart, Calvin, 228, 230
Logue, Christopher, 49
Lombard, Carole, 47
Loneliness of the Long-Distance Runner, The (1962), 18
Long, Stanley A. 244
Long Day's Dying, The (1968), 91
Look Back in Anger (play), 15
Look Back in Anger (1959), 66, 71, 73, 103
Lord Byron, 41
Losey, Joseph, 5, 82, 131–44, 166–72, 175, 176, 231
Lovin' Spoonful, 52
Lowe, Arthur, 95
L-Shaped Room, The (1962), 226, 236
Luckett, Moya, 242
Lulu, 229
Lumet, Sidney, 224
Lynn, Ann, 225, 226

McCartney, Paul, 88
McDayter, Ghislaine, 41
McDonald, Paul, 12, 39
MacDonald, Richard, 168
McDowell, Malcolm, 106, 107, 131, 136, 138
McGowran, Jack, 247
McGregor, Ken, 226
McKellen, Ian, 117
Mackendrick, Alexander, 224
Macnab, Geoffrey, 34
Made (1972), 57
Magus, The (1968), 136
Malcolm, Derek, 121, 127, 143
Malmgren, Yat, 16, 19
Man, Delbert, 65
Man for all Seasons, A (1966), 1, 65
Man in Grey, The (1943), 33
Man on the Beach, A (1956), 166, 170
Man Who Could Cheat Death, The (1959), 154
Man Who Haunted Himself, The (1970), 6, 180, 186–90
Maniac (1963), 159

261

Mann, Stanley, 136
Marcus, Lawrence B., 94
Mark of the Devil (1970), 200
Marquee Club, 198
Martin, Millicent, 185
Marvin, Lee, 250
Marwick, Arthur, 36
masculinity, 29–43
Mason, James, 31, 33, 37, 38
Masters, John, 87
Masters, Robert E. L. 239, 245
Mastroianni, Marcello, 230
Mathieson, John, 176
Matrimonial Homes Act 1967, 51
Matthews, Kerwin, 160–1
Medak, Peter, 136
Medhurst, Andy, 218
Meheux, Phil, 176
Melville, Herman, 213, 217
Melvin, Murray, 218, 219
Memorial Enterprises, 24
Men of Sherwood Forest, The (1954), 152, 159
Menges, Chris, 116
Merrow, Jane, 35
Metzger, Gustav, 248–9
Metzner, Ralph, 198
MGM, 211
MGM British, 70
Mick Travis trilogy, 82
Miles, Sarah, 134
Milk Train Doesn't Stop Here Anymore, The (play), 135
Miller, Jonathan, 31
Milligan, Spike, 94
Mills, John, 225
Mills, Juliet, 220
Miranda (1948), 68
Miss Marple, 68
Moby Dick (1956), 47
Modesty Blaise (1966), 82
Molly Maguires The (1970), 24
Montague, Lee, 89
Montgomery, Elizabeth, 104
Moon, Keith, 41
Moonstone, The (novel), 87
Moore, Roger, 180, 187–9

More, Kenneth, 17, 210
Mortimer, Penelope, 54
Mosley, Oswald, 209
Mottram, Philip, 224
Mouse on the Moon, The (1963), 68
Mummy, The (1959), 154–6
Murphy, Robert, 1, 2, 69, 70, 74, 167, 181, 181
Musser, Charles, 100
Mutiny on the Bounty (1962), 209, 211, 219, 221
My Name is Joe (1998), 117
Mysterious Island (1961), 159, 160

Naremore, James, 38, 39
National Archives, 3
National Film and Television Archive, 3
National Service, 219
Naylor, Robert, 121
Neale, Steve, 165
Neil, Hildegard, 186
Nelson (1918), 210
Never Let Go (1960), 47
Newman, Sydney, 16
Ngakane, Lionel, 224, 225
Night of the Eagle (1962), 196
Niven, David, 66, 74
Nothing but the Best (1964), 6, 19, 179–80, 181–6, 190
Nun's Story, The (1959), 71, 74
Nutcracker (1982), 57, 58, 59
Nuttall, Jeff, 239, 249–50

O Lucky Man (1973), 104
O'Brien Castro, Moira, 36
O'Connolly, Jim, 227
Odeon cinemas, 154
Offence, The (1972), 24
Ogilvy, Ian, 195, 197, 200, 243
Old Dark House, The (1963), 161
Oliver! (1968), 1, 32, 40, 41
Olivier, Laurence, 224
On the Double (1961), 68
Ondricek, Miroslav, 101, 107
One Million Years B.C. (1966), 162
One More Time (1970), 228
One Plus One (1969), 230

Osborne, John, 15, 17, 67, 71, 92, 102, 103, 104
O'Toole, Peter, 4, 11, 14, 21, 22, 24, 48, 136
Ove, Horace, 224

Palme d'Or, 1, 176
Paramount, 68
Paranoiac (1963), 33
Party's Over, The (1965), 31, 35–6, 37, 239
Passport to Pimlico (1949), 68
Peacock, Steven, 107
Peake, Maxine, 58
Pearson, Roberta E., 34
Peeping Tom (1960), 152, 154, 157
Pemberton, Reece, 183
Peters, Brock, 226, 228
Petrie, Duncan, 166, 173
Petulia (1968), 82, 93, 246
Phantom of the Opera, The (1962), 157–8, 159, 160, 161
Phelan, Brian, 227
Phillips, Robin, 231
Pigott-Brown, William, 142, 143
Pink Floyd, 198, 244, 251
Pinter, Harold, 82, 87, 135
Pirates of Blood River, The (1962), 5, 159, 160, 161
Pleasence, Donald, 226
Point Blank (1967), 250
Poitier, Sidney, 228–9
Polanski, Roman, 243
Poor Cow (1967), 4, 48, 49–51, 56
Portman, Eric, 33
Powell, Michael, 152, 189
Prehistoric Women (1967), 162
Preminger, Otto, 176
Prescod, Paul, 225
Pressburger, Emeric, 188
Pressure (1976), 224
Price, Vincent, 200
Priggen, Norman, 132, 134, 135, 140
Prisoner, The (1967–8), 187
Profumo Affair, 182
Prowler, The (1951), 168
Prudence and the Pill (1968), 74

Psych-Out (1968), 246
Pulp (1972), 24
Pygmalion (1938), 65

Quatermass Xperiment (1955), 153
Quayle, Anthony, 211
Queen of Spades, The (1949), 71
Quiet Wedding (1941), 67

Race Relations Act 1965, 51
Rank Film Distributors, 158
Rank Organisation, 2, 17, 22, 133, 154
Raphael, Frederick, 179–80, 182
Rattigan, Terence, 65, 66–7, 70
Ray, Nicholas, 176
Reason, Matthew, 103
Reckoning, The (1970), 186
Reckord, Lloyd, 226
Redgrave, Vanessa, 40, 248
Redman, Joyce, 64, 74
Reed, Carol, 2, 211
Reed, John R., 217
Reed, Oliver, 4, 29–42, 56, 159, 162, 170
Reeves, Michael, 6, 193–200, 202–4, 240, 243
Reggae (1976), 224
Reisz, Karel, 18, 105 106
Relph, Michael, 180, 186, 187, 188
Repulsion (1965), 1, 243
Resnais, Alain, 169
Revenge of Frankenstein, The (1958), 154
Revenge of the Blood Beast (1966), 6, 193, 194–7, 199, 243
Richard, Cliff, 167
Richards, Jeffrey, 7, 181
Richardson, Ralph, 95
Richardson, Tony, 4, 17, 71, 73, 82, 93, 102, 103, 118, 226
Rise and Rise of Michael Rimmer, The (1970), 186
Robin and Marian (1976), 94
Robinson, Nicolette, 227
Robson, Mark, 56
Rodgers, Anton, 186
Roeg, Nicolas, 88, 183, 185

Romantic Englishwoman, The (1975), 132
Room at the Top (1959), 66, 103, 119, 180–1, 182
Roots (1959), 103
Rossen, Robert, 228
Rossington, Norman, 91, 233
Rotten to the Core (1965), 196
Royal Academy of Dramatic Arts (RADA), 15
Royal Court, 16, 17, 18, 82, 104, 111
Royal Navy, 209–10
Rush, Richard, 246
Russell, Ken, 29, 42, 56
Russell, Robert, 200
Rutherford, Margaret, 4, 63, 64, 67–70, 74, 75
Ryan, Robert, 21, 213

Saint, The (1962–9), 186
Saint-Denis, Michael, 103
Salkey, Andrew, 227
Salt and Pepper (1968), 228
Saltzman, Harry, 19, 20, 23, 167, 172, 173
Sammy Going South (1963), 224
Sanderson, Michael, 15
Sandford, Jeremy, 49
Sapphire (1959), 186, 239
Sarne, Mike, 230
Saturday Night and Sunday Morning (1960), 17
Scarlet Blade, The (1963), 33, 161
Schlesinger, John, 19
Sears, Heather, 180
Season of the Witch (1973), 196
Secret Ceremony (1968), 135
Sedgwick, Eve, 218
Sekka, Johnny, 225
Selinger, Denis, 23
Sellers, Peter, 47, 226
Sellers, Robert, 12, 41
Separate Tables (1958), 65–6, 67, 71
Separation (1968), 240, 244, 246
Sergeant Musgrave's Dance (play), 104
Servant, The (1963), 131, 132, 134, 135, 166
Sexual Offences Act, 51

Sharkey, John J. 249
Shaw, Robert, 136, 138, 141
Shaw, Sandie, 51
She (1965), 162
Sheridan, Dani, 245
Sherwin, David, 82, 101, 108
Shooting Stars (1990), 127
Signoret, Simone, 180
Silva, Dana, 218
Simmons, Anthony, 132
Sinclair, Ian, 194
Sink the Bismark! (1960), 210
Sinyard, Neil, 84
Sirk, Douglas, 176
Sitting Target (1972), 32
Skinner-Carter, Corinne, 225
Slark, Fred, 167
Slave Girls (1968), 162
Sleeping Tiger, The (1954), 131, 132, 166
Smart, Billy, 100
Smashing Time (1967), 240, 244, 251
Smith, Ali, 50
Smith, Bernard, 136
Smith, Justin, 37
Smith, Kim, 228
Smith, Neville, 117
Some Call It Loving (1973), 57
Some People (1962), 183
Sons and Lovers (1960), 65
Sontag, Susan, 100
Sorcerers, The (1967), 6, 7, 193, 194, 197–9, 203, 240, 241, 242–5, 247, 248, 250, 251
Speech Day (1973), 127
Spicer, Andrew, 34, 35, 38, 186, 210, 216
Spiegel, Sam, 21
Spinetti, Victor, 87
Squeeze, The (1977), 57
Stamp, Terence, 4, 11, 14, 20, 23, 48, 52, 53, 213, 215, 218
Star Studies, 48
Starr, Ringo, 88
Steaming (play), 58, 59
Steedman, Carolyn, 48, 53
Steele, Barbara, 194, 196
Stollery, Martin, 100

Stona, Winston, 226
Storey, David, 104
Stranglers of Bombay, The (1959), 156
Street, Sarah, 52, 72, 74, 183
Stuart Leslie, David, 231
Stud, The (1978), 58
Submarine X-1 (1968), 210
Suez Missile Crisis, 209
Summerfield, Penny, 214
Swinging London, 6, 11, 12, 19, 34, 68, 74, 86, 181, 240, 241–2, 247, 248
Sword of Sherwood Forest, The (1960), 5, 159
Sylbert, Richard, 109
Syms, Sylvia, 225
System, The (1964), 31, 34, 35, 36, 42

Take a Girl Like You (1970), 31
Tantallon Films, 24
Tasca, Alessandro, 135–6
Taste of Fear (1961), 159
Taste of Honey, A (1961), 49, 218, 226, 228
Taylor, Diana, 103
Taylor, Elizabeth, 67, 70, 135
Technicolor, 152, 189
Technicolor Italia, 173
Techniscope, 166, 173
Ten Bob in Winter (1963), 226, 227
Tenser, Tony, 243
Terror for Kicks (novel), 197
Terror of the Tongs, The (1961), 156
Terry, Nigel, 25
Theatre Royal Stratford East, 18
Thirty Nine Steps, The (1959), 47
This Sporting Life (1963), 18, 108
Thomas, Ralph, 224
Thornton, Frank, 94
Those Magnificent Men in their Flying Machines (1965), 165
Three Michaels (production company), 24
Three Musketeers, The (1973), 82
Thunderball (1965), 165, 167, 172
Tigon British Film Productions Ltd, 203, 243
Till Death Us Do Part (1968), 224

Tilsley, Frank, 211
Time (magazine), 240
Time Without Pity (1957), 131, 132–3
To Sir, with Love (1967), 228–9
Tom Jones (1963), 1, 22, 71–3, 74, 105
Tommy (1975), 42
Tommy Steele Story, The (1957), 239
Tonite Let's All Make Love in London (1967), 6, 250–1
Top Deck (1962), 229
Townshend, Pete, 248
Toys in the Attic (1963), 65
Trap, The (1966), 32
Tree, Sir Herbert Beerbohm, 30
Trevelyan, John, 155, 157, 158
Trial, The (1962), 174
Trip, The (1967), 246
Truffaut, Francois, 171, 176
Tushingham, Rita, 39, 83, 85, 95, 226
Twentieth Century Fox, 74, 165
Two Faces of Dr Jekyll, The (1960), 158
Two for the Road (1967), 182
Two Gentlemen Sharing (1969), 6, 224, 228, 231–5
Tynan, Kenneth, 15, 66

United Artists, 1, 65, 72, 73
Universal, 154
Up the Junction (1965), 4, 48, 49, 54
Upton, Julian, 56, 57
Ustinov, Peter, 20, 213, 217

Valiant, The (1961), 210
Verne, Jules, 87
Veterans, or, Hair in the Gates of the Hellespont (play), 81–2
Victim (1961), 186, 218
Vigo, Jean, 108
Violent Playground (1958), 186
V.I.P.s, The (1963), 64, 67–8, 69–70
Virgin Witch (1972), 203
Vukani/Awake (1962), 224

Waite, Genevieve, 230
Walby, John, 217
Walker, Alexander, 21, 22, 72, 73, 107, 235, 241

Warner Bros., 71, 154
Warwick, Richard, 95
Washbourne, Mona, 95
Watkin, David, 93
Watts, Queenie, 52
Webber Douglas Academy of Dramatic Arts, 15
Wednesday Play, 48
Welch, Raquel, 162
Welles, Orson, 36, 54, 68, 75, 174
Wesker, Arnold, 104, 108
West 11 (1963), 226, 236
Whales of August, The (1987), 104
What's Good for the Goose (1969), 247
Whisperers, The (1967), 64, 73, 74, 75, 229
White, Alan, 91
White, Carol, 4, 36, 47–9
White Bus, The (1967), 101
Whitehead, Peter, 6, 250–1
Who, The, 216, 248
Wicked Lady, The (1945), 33
Wicker Man, The (1973), 203
Wild Angels, The (1966), 198
Wild One, The (1953), 36, 211
Williams, Daisy Mae, 233
Williams, Kenneth, 220
Williams, Melanie, 63, 85
Williams, Tennessee, 135
Wilson, Harold, 182

Winner, Michael, 4, 29, 34, 38, 42, 226
Wisdom, Norman, 31, 247
Witches, The (1966), 202
Witchfinder General (1968), 6, 193, 194, 199–204, 243
Witherwick, Albert, 188
Women in Love (1969), 31, 40, 56
Wonderwall (1969), 240, 241, 244, 247, 251
Wood, Charles, 4, 81–95
Wood, David, 107
Wood, Robin, 197
Woodfall Films, 17, 92
Woodham-Smith, Cecil, 92
Woolf, James, 23

X – The Unknown (1956), 153

Yalkut, Jud, 245
Yardbirds, The, 248
Yellow Rolls Royce, The (1965), 70
York, Susannah, 64, 72
Young, Terence, 225
Young Ones, The (1961), 167
Youngblood, Gene, 252

Zero de Conduite (1933), 108
Zinman, Gregory, 246
Zinnemann, Fred, 71
Zorba the Greek (1964), 19
Zulu (1964), 20, 165, 224

EU representative:
Easy Access System Europe
Mustamäe tee 50, 10621 Tallinn, Estonia
Gpsr.requests@easproject.com

www.ingramcontent.com/pod-product-compliance
Lightning Source LLC
Chambersburg PA
CBHW071830230426
43672CB00013B/2801